PRAISE FOR *THE AGE OF RESILIENCE*

"*The Age of Resilience* calls for the great turnaround from adapting nature to our species to adapting our species back to nature. This requires, as Jeremy Rifkin suggests, 'a wholesale rethinking of our worldview.' Among the most significant challenges will be our educational system that will need to be reimagined and reinvented to proffer new pedagogical approaches to learning, if we are to make the transformation from the Age of Progress to the Age of Resilience. Given Rifkin's amazing track record of envisioning the future, no one can ignore the message of this new book. *The Age of Resilience* is truly an awe-inspiring treatise that must be read, comprehended, and most important, acted upon."

—Jerry Wind, Professor Emeritus,
The Wharton School, and Founder of the Wharton Executive MBA Program

"The most striking feature of our multifaceted economic, social, and ecological global crisis is that none of our major problems can be understood in isolation. They are interconnected and interdependent and require corresponding systemic solutions. Jeremy Rifkin has designed effective systemic solutions to economic and technological problems at the request of governments and business organizations around the world for more than forty years. In this book he uses his rich experience to address the crisis of perception that threatens our species' future survival on Earth. This is a challenging, thought-provoking, yet deeply hopeful book. I recommend it warmly to anyone concerned about the future of humanity."

—Fritjof Capra, theoretical physicist and coauthor *The Systems View of Life*

"Jeremy Rifkin's *The Age of Resilience* takes us through the long history of illusions, culminating in the Age of Progress, by which we came to think of ourselves as both separate from nature and masters of the earth. He asks us to reconsider how our obsession with unlimited growth and hyperefficiency—by which we measure progress—has ruptured the web of life and taken us and our fellow creatures to the very brink of a mass extinction. Rifkin helps us remember that we are an intimate part of an animate nature with the hope that we will rejoin our evolutionary family on an indivisible Earth. In these times of despair and hopelessness, Rifkin points to regenerativity, flourishing, resilience, and hope for the future."

—Dr. Vandana Shiva, feminist, ecologist, and activist in the developing world

"At a moment when humanity's obsession with 'efficiency' has led us to the doorstep of cascading biodiversity loss and a catastrophic climate crisis, Jeremy Rifkin guides us toward an alternate future sparked by a prophetic vision of the Age of Resilience. Humanity's window of opportunity to act on climate change is rapidly narrowing. With this in mind, Rifkin calls on humanity to engage in a deep self-examination of its relationship to nature in order to strengthen our bonds with our earthly home. This is the only path toward building a resilient world prepared to take on this century's challenges."

—Ani Dasgupta, president & CEO, World Resources Institute

"Jeremy Rifkin has given us a vision of the future that can inspire all those who want to be agents of change. He invites us to go beyond the idea of progress, and embrace a holistic and ecological conception of our existence on Earth. In the new era, empathy and biophilia take center stage for our re-affiliation with nature."

—Carlo Petrini, founder and president of Slow Food International

THE AGE OF RESILIENCE

ALSO BY JEREMY RIFKIN

The Green New Deal

The Zero Marginal Cost Society

The Third Industrial Revolution

The Empathic Civilization

The Hydrogen Economy

The European Dream

The Biotech Century

The End of Work

THE AGE OF RESILIENCE

REIMAGINING EXISTENCE ON A REWILDING EARTH

Jeremy Rifkin

ST. MARTIN'S PRESS
NEW YORK

First published in the United States by St. Martin's Press,
an imprint of St. Martin's Publishing Group

www.stmartins.com

Library of Congress Cataloging-in-Publication Data

Names: Rifkin, Jeremy, author.
Title: The age of resilience : reimagining existence on a rewilding earth /
    Jeremy Rifkin.
Description: First edition. | New York : St. Martin's Press, [2022] |
    Includes bibliographical references and index.
Identifiers: LCCN 2022021247 | ISBN 9781250093547 (hardcover) |
    ISBN 9781250093554 (ebook)
Subjects: LCSH: Resilience (Personality trait) | Industrial efficiency.
Classification: LCC BF698.35.R47 R55 2022 | DDC 155.2/4—dc23/eng/20220624
LC record available at https://lccn.loc.gov/2022021247

Our books may be purchased in bulk for promotional, educational, or business use.
Please contact your local bookseller or the Macmillan Corporate
and Premium Sales Department at 1-800-221-7945, extension 5442,
or by email at MacmillanSpecialMarkets@macmillan.com.

First Edition: 2022

10   9   8   7   6   5   4   3   2   1

To Carol L. Grunewald
for giving our fellow creatures a voice

CONTENTS

Part Four
THE AGE OF RESILIENCE:
THE PASSING OF THE INDUSTRIAL ERA

THE AGE OF
RESILIENCE

INTRODUCTION

The viruses keep coming. The climate keeps warming. And the earth is rewilding in real time. We long thought that we could force the natural world to adapt to our species. We now face the ignominious fate of being forced to adapt to an unpredictable natural world. Our species has no playbook for the mayhem that is unfolding around us.

We are, by all accounts, the youngest mammalian species on Earth, with only a two-hundred-thousand-year-long history. For most of that time—95 percent or more—we lived pretty much like our fellow primates and mammals as foragers and hunters living off the land and adapting to the seasons, leaving just a skim of our imprint on the body of the earth.[1] What changed? How did we become the despoilers who brought nature almost to its knees but which now has come roaring back to cast us out?

Let's step back for a moment and look at the now worn narrative regarding our species' special destiny. During the dark days of the French Revolution in 1794, the philosopher Nicolas de Condorcet laid out a grand vision of the future while waiting to be taken to the guillotine for high treason. He wrote:

"No bounds have been fixed to the improvement of the human faculties . . . the perfectibility of man is absolutely indefinite . . . [the] progress of this perfectibility, henceforth above the control of every power that would impede it, has no other limit than the duration of the globe upon which nature has placed us."[2]

Condorcet's promissory note provided the ontological foundation for what would subsequently be called the Age of Progress. Today, Condorcet's vision of humanity's future appears naïve, even laughable. Still, progress is just the most recent incarnation of the ancient belief that our species was cut from a different cloth from that of other creatures with whom we share the earth. While grudgingly admitting that *Homo sapiens* evolved from an ancestral pool dating back to the first glimmer of microbial life, we like to think that we are different.

During the modern era we tossed much of the theological world aside, but managed to keep hold of the Lord's promise to Adam and Eve that they and their heirs would have "dominion over the fish of the sea, and over the fowl of the air, and over the cattle, and over all the earth, and over every creeping thing that creepeth upon the earth."[3] That promise, still taken seriously, but without the religious overtones, has led to the collapse of our planetary ecosystems.

If there is a change to be reckoned with, it's that we are beginning to realize that we never did have dominion and that the agencies of nature are far more powerful than we thought. Our species now seems much smaller and less consequential in the bigger picture of life on Earth.

People everywhere are scared. We are waking up to the hard reality that our species is to blame for the horrific carnage spreading across the earth— the floods, droughts, wildfires, and hurricanes that are wreaking havoc and undermining economies and ecosystems around the world. We sense that planetary forces bigger than us and not easily subdued by the means we have relied on in the past are here to stay, with ominous repercussions. We are beginning to realize that our species and our fellow creatures are edging ever closer to an environmental abyss from which there is no return.

And now, the warnings that human-induced climate change is taking us into the sixth mass extinction of life on Earth have moved from the fringes to the mainstream. The alarm bells are ringing everywhere. Government leaders, the business and financial community, academia, and the public at large are beginning to question, whole cloth, the shibboleths by which we have lived our lives, interpreted the meaning of our existence, and understood the simple realities of staying alive and secure.

Although the Age of Progress is, for all intents and purposes, over and only awaiting a proper postmortem, what's new and being heard from every quarter and getting louder and more determined is that we—the human race—need to rethink everything: our worldview, our understanding of the economy, our forms of governance, our concepts of time and space, our most basic human drives, and our relationship to the planet.

But the talk thus far is at best inchoate and at worst undefined. What does it really mean to rethink every aspect of our lives? We have a clue. The question being asked in so many different ways is how do we "adapt" to the havoc that is coming? We hear it around the kitchen table and in our local neighborhoods where we work and play and live out our lives.

"Resilience," in turn, has become the new defining refrain heard in countless venues. It is how we are coming to define ourselves in a perilous future that is now at the front gates. The Age of Progress has given way to the Age of

Resilience. Rethinking the essence of our species and its place on Earth marks the beginning of a new journey where nature is now the classroom.

The great transformation from the Age of Progress to the Age of Resilience is already triggering a vast philosophical and psychological readjustment in the way our species perceives the world around us. At the root of the transition is a wholesale shift of our temporal and spatial orientation.

The underlying temporal orientation that directed the entirety of the Age of Progress is "efficiency"—the quest to optimize the expropriation, consumption, and discarding of natural resources and, by so doing, increase the material opulence of society at ever-greater speeds and in ever-shrinking time frames, but at the expense of the depletion of nature itself. Our personal temporal orientation and the temporal beat of our society folds around the efficiency imperative. It's what has taken us to the commanding heights as the dominant species on Earth and now to the ruin of the natural world.

Of late, voices are being raised for the very first time from the academic community and even corporate boardrooms and government, challenging this once-sacred value of efficiency, suggesting that its ironclad hold over society's temporal bandwidth is literally killing us. How, then, do we rethink our future?

If the Age of Progress marched in lockstep with efficiency, the temporal choreography of the Age of Resilience strides with adaptivity. The temporal crossover from efficiency to adaptivity is the reentry card that takes our species from separation and exploitation of the natural world to repatriation with the multitude of environmental forces that animate the earth—marking a repositioning of human agency on an increasingly unpredictable planet.

This realignment is already affecting other deep-rooted assumptions about how our economic and social life ought to be conducted, measured, and assessed. The handover from efficiency to adaptivity comes with sweeping changes in the economy and society including the shift from productivity to regenerativity, growth to flourishing, ownership to access, seller-buyer markets to provider-user networks, linear processes to cybernetic processes, vertically integrated economies of scale to laterally integrated economies of scale, centralized value chains to distributed value chains, corporate conglomerates to agile, high-tech small- and medium-sized cooperatives blockchained in fluid commons, intellectual property rights to open-source sharing of knowledge, zero-sum games to network effects, globalization to glocalization, consumerism to eco-stewardship, gross domestic product (GDP) to quality-of-life indicators (QLI), negative externalities to circularity, and geopolitics to biosphere politics.

The emerging third iteration of the industrial revolution that is taking the world from analog bureaucracies to digital platforms enveloping the whole of the earth is re-embedding our species back into the planet's indigenous infrastructures—the hydrosphere, the lithosphere, the atmosphere, and the biosphere. This new infrastructure takes our collective humanity beyond the industrial era. In the emerging economic paradigm, it's likely that "finance capital," the heart of the Industrial Age, will be surpassed by a new economic order primed by "ecological capital" as we move further into the Age of Resilience in the second half of the 21st century and beyond.

Not surprisingly, the new temporality rides alongside a fundamental spatial reorientation. In the Age of Progress, space became synonymous with passive natural resources and governance with managing nature as property. In the Age of Resilience, space is made up of the planetary spheres that interact to establish the processes, patterns, and flows of an evolving Earth.

We are also just beginning to understand that our own lives, and those of our fellow creatures, exist as processes, patterns, and flows. The idea that we are autonomous beings acting on one another and the natural world is being rethought by a new generation of physicists, chemists, and biologists on the cutting edge of scientific inquiry. They are beginning to unearth a different story about the nature of human nature and, in the process, challenging the belief in our autonomous selfhood.

All living creatures are extensions of the earth's spheres. The elements, minerals, and nutrients of the lithosphere, the water of the hydrosphere, and the oxygen of the atmosphere are continually coursing through us in the form of atoms and molecules, taking up residence in our cells, tissues, and organs as prescribed by our DNA, only to be continuously replaced at various intervals during our life. Although it may come as a surprise, most of the tissues and organs that make up our bodies continuously turn over in our lifetime. For example, one's near entire skeleton is replaced every ten years or so. A human liver turns over approximately every three hundred to five hundred days; the cells that line the stomach turn over in five days; and intestinal Paneth cells are replaced every twenty days.[4] A mature adult, from a strictly physical point of view, may be ten years old or younger.[5]

And even then, our body does not belong to us alone but is shared by many other forms of life—bacteria, viruses, protists, archaea, and fungi. Indeed, more than half the cells in the human body and the majority of DNA that make us up are not human but belong to the rest of the creatures that reside in every nook and cranny of our being. The point is, the earth's species and ecosystems do not stop at the edge of our bodies but, rather, continuously flow in and out of our bodies. Each of us is a semipermeable membrane. We are of the planet literally and figuratively—which ought to shatter the cherished notion that our species is somehow separate from nature.

Our inseparability from nature's flows is even more nuanced and intimate. Like every other species, we are made up of a multitude of biological clocks that continually adapt our internal bodily rhythms to the circadian day and the lunar, seasonal, and circannual rhythms that mark the daily rotation of the earth and its annual passage around the sun. Of late, we are also learning that endogenous and exogenous electromagnetic fields that crisscross every cell, tissue, and organ and permeate the planet also play a critical role in establishing the patterns by which our genes and cells line up and take form and assist in maintaining bodily functions.

We are of the earth, to the very sinew of our being. Like the rethinking of our temporality, our emerging understanding of our extended spatiality as a species is also forcing a reevaluation of our relationship to our fellow creatures, and our place on the earth.

With this comes fresh thinking about the nature of governance and how we see ourselves as a social organism. In the Age of Resilience, governance transitions from sovereignty over natural resources to stewardship of regional ecosystems. Bioregional governance, for its part, becomes far more distributed, with local communities taking on the responsibility of adapting to and stewarding their nineteen kilometers of the earth's biosphere that encompass the lithosphere, hydrosphere, and atmosphere—the region of Earth where life unfolds.

In this very different world where we break down the walls between civilization and naturalization, representative democracy, long held in high regard as the fairest and most inclusive governing model, is perceived as increasingly removed from the hands-on engagement with nature required of every member of our species. Already, "representative democracy" is beginning to make way, in bits and pieces, for "distributed peerocracy," as a younger generation becomes active players in the governance of their bioregions.

In the emerging era, the industrious and efficient citizen bystanders to governance—whose only responsibility is to vote for a small coterie of elected officials to represent their interests—gives over, in part, to active peer-led citizen assemblies dedicated to stewarding their bioregions. There is already precedent for this as nation-states have traditionally established citizen juries who are called upon to assess the guilt or innocence of their peers in criminal and civil court cases.

These are just a smattering of developments that are only now rearing their head as our species makes a historic pivot from the Age of Progress to the Age of Resilience. Other developments will emerge as we rethink our sense of agency in a highly animated planet that is evolving in unfathomable ways to which we will need to adapt if we are to survive and flourish.

The pages that follow are a walk-through of where we've come since our first Adam and Eve stood upright and ventured out from the Rift Valley of Africa onto the open savannas and from there trekked across the continents.

Our species is the great wayfarer of the world, in search of more than our daily subsistence. Something deeper and more restless churns inside us—a feeling no other creature possesses. We are in a relentless search, whether acknowledged or not, for the meaning of our existence. It's what moves us.

But somewhere along the journey, we lost our way. For most of our time on Earth, our species—like all others—found means to continually adapt to the larger forces of nature unfolding around us. Then, ten thousand years ago, with the ending of the last Ice Age and the beginning of a temperate climate—christened the Holocene—we steered a promethean new course, forcing nature to adapt to our species. With the rise of the hydraulic agricultural empires five thousand years ago and, more recently, the protoindustrial and industrial revolutions of the late medieval and modern age—what we have come to call civilization—our journey has been marked by increasing domination over the natural world. And now our success—if we can call it that—is measured by a startling statistic. Although *Homo sapiens* makes up less than one percent of the earth's total biomass, by 2005 we were using 24 percent of the net primary production from photosynthesis, and current trends project that we might use as much as 44 percent by 2050, leaving only 56 percent of the net primary production for the rest of the life on the planet.[6] This is obviously untenable. Our collective humanity has become the outlier of life and is now taking our fellow creatures along with us to a mass geological graveyard in the emerging Anthropocene.[7]

Ironically, our species, unlike our fellow creatures, is of a Janus face. If we are the spoiler species, we are also potentially the healers. We have been blessed with a special quality wired into our neurocircuitry—the empathic impulse—that has shown itself to be elastic and capable of infinite expansion. It's this rare and precious attribute that has evolved, only to fall back and resurface again and again, each time reaching new plateaus before another slippage. In recent years, a younger generation has begun to extend the empathic impulse beyond our own species to include our fellow creatures, all of whom are part of our evolutionary family. This is what biologists call biophilia consciousness—a hopeful sign of a new path forward.

Anthropologists tell us we are among the most adaptive species. The question is whether we will use this defining attribute to assimilate back into nature's fold wherever it takes us with a sense of humility, mindfulness, and critical thinking that will allow our species and our extended biological family to flourish once again. The great turnaround from adapting nature to our species to adapting our species back to nature will require abandoning the traditional Baconian approach to scientific inquiry with its emphasis on wresting nature's secrets and seeing the earth as a resource and commodity for our species' exclusive consumption. In its stead, we will need to take hold of a radically new scientific paradigm—what a new generation of scientists call complex adaptive social/ecological systems modeling, or CASES. This new approach to science views nature as a "life source" rather than a "resource" and perceives the earth as a complex self-organizing and self-evolving system whose trajectory is ultimately unknowable in advance, and therefore requires a science of anticipation and vigilant adaptation rather than forced preemption.

A rewilding planet will test our collective mettle. Hopefully, the journey we are now embarked on in the Age of Resilience will steer us to a new Garden of Eden, but this time not as master but as kindred spirit with our fellow creatures with whom we share our earthly home.

Part One

EFFICIENCY VS. ENTROPY

THE DIALECTIC OF MODERNITY

1

MASKS, VENTILATORS, AND TOILET PAPER

HOW ADAPTIVITY TRUMPS EFFICIENCY

There is a quote known by virtually everyone in the business community that captures the spirit of how we have come to define ourselves during the Age of Progress. Adam Smith, the first modern economist and founding father of the discipline, in his opus, *The Wealth of Nations*, wrote the following words—now immortalized—which capture what has been considered the essence of human nature adhered to by successive generations for the past two centuries.

> Every individual is continually exerting himself to find out the most advantageous employment for whatever capital he can command. It is his own advantage, indeed, and not that of the society, which he has in view. But the study of his own advantage naturally, or rather necessarily, leads him to prefer that employment which is most advantageous to the society. . . . He intends only his own gain, and he is in this, as in many other cases, led by an invisible hand to promote an end which was no part of his intention. . . . By pursuing his own interest he frequently promotes that of the society more **effectually** than when he really intends to promote it.[1]

Smith viewed "effectually" as virtually synonymous with "efficiently," and the very goal to which "Homo economicus" strives, and to which society bends.

On May 14, 2021, *The New York Times* published a guest essay with the wonkish headline "Your Car, Toaster, Even Washing Machine, Can't Work

Without Them. And There's a Global Shortage."[2] The article was written by the economist Alex T. Williams.

The story it tells foreshadows an economic disruption and eruption at the very heart of the capitalist system of sufficient magnitude to implode and take down the economic order by which we've structured commercial life for the past two centuries. Buried in the article are faint hints of the kind of system that is likely to replace it.

The article starts blandly enough, pointing to "a global shortage in the supply chain of semiconductors." These are the tiny microchips embedded in the numerous processes and manufactured products that constitute the digitalized smart world. Semiconductors are a half-trillion-dollar industry. To get a handle on how serious the problem is, let's zero in on just one Fortune 500 company, Ford Motor Company. The company announced that the current shortage of semiconductors used in the manufacturing and workings of its vehicles has forced it to forecast a $2.5 billion drop in profits over the coming year.[3] Magnify these losses across the entire global economy dependent on semiconductors— from medical equipment to electricity transmission lines—and we begin to understand the gravity of the crisis.

Behind the scenes, President Joe Biden quietly held a high-level meeting with executives from Ford Motor Company and Google to assess the economic fallout and national security risk of a shortfall of semiconductors, most of which are manufactured overseas. Executives from Verizon, Qualcomm, Intel, and Nvidia, among other corporate giants, have formed an industry coalition to push for urgent federal government funding of semiconductor research and development (R&D) and the underwriting of funds to establish semiconductor manufacturing facilities in the United States. The coalition wants a massive $50 billion set aside in the proposed federal government infrastructure plan—at the get-go—citing the shortages around semiconductors and the security risk that could shut down the U.S. economy.

The problem extends beyond just a short-term lapse in the global supply chain. Further along in the article, readers will find reference to two words that define the very nature of the crisis, and deeper still, foretell a fundamental contradiction in capitalism itself—that is, the unavoidable trade-off between "efficiency" and "resilience."

The enormous expense that goes into erecting giant manufacturing facilities to produce complex semiconductors leads to lower profit margins. Only a handful of the most efficient companies have risen to the top by investing in what is called "lean logistics and supply chains" and "lean manufacturing processes" that eliminate costly buffers and other redundancies in the system that might be necessary to operationalize in case of an emergency. For example, storing surplus inventories; provisioning additional backup manufacturing facilities that can be booted up at a moment's notice; retaining an auxiliary workforce that could be quickly deployed were there a disruption anywhere along the line; and having available alternative supply chain options that can be operationalized to avoid disruptions and a slowdown in the logistics system.

These extra expenses take away from operational efficiency and reduce the revenue stream, eating into the bottom line. For these reasons, such backups are eschewed by management and shareholders because they shrink margins and profit. What the world is left with is a handful of giant corporate heavyweights in the semiconductor market that command the industry. These market leaders have survived the competition by cutting costs across their operations with lean logistics and manufacturing processes, making them increasingly "efficient" but at the expense of being less "resilient" and vulnerable to unexpected events. Williams points out the obvious pitfall, asking, "What good is such a hyper-efficient, super-lean factory if, say, a natural disaster knocks it out of commission and there's no backup supply of the chip it makes?"[4] The bottom line is that efficiency rules, but at the expense of resilience.

The semiconductor shortage is not the first event to cast public doubt on the resilience of the economy in the wake of escalating natural and manmade disruptions. The first inkling of fissures in the capitalist system came unexpectedly in the spring of 2020. Stunned by the fast spread of the deadly COVID-19 virus, countries were caught off guard as their medical facilities were unprepared for the pandemic and their populations found themselves exposed, unprotected, and without recourse in providing the necessities for their families.

The economic firestorm ignited unexpectedly in March 2020 with an opinion piece written by William Galston of *The Wall Street Journal*, who formerly served as deputy assistant to President Bill Clinton. The lead-in to his article read: "Efficiency Isn't the Only Economic Virtue." Galston said he had been reflecting on the economic consequences of the COVID-19 pandemic. While the fallout from the pandemic was worrying, it was accompanied by an especially eye-opening surprise. America was totally unprepared to meet the need. Night after night on the news, governors, medical professionals, and the public at large were asking, where were the N95 masks, personal protective equipment, ventilators, et cetera? Why are there shortages of antibacterial soap and even toilet paper and other basic necessities?

A PUBLIC REPUDIATION
OF EFFICIENCY

It struck Galston that something was askew with a global economic system that could not meet the most basic needs of the American public during a once-in-a-century health crisis. He dared to ask the question that had lain hidden behind the commercial screen—the dirty little secret that underwrites modern capitalism—"What if the relentless pursuit of efficiency, which has dominated American business thinking for decades, has made the global economic system more vulnerable to shocks?"[5] Galston noted that the very success of globalization depends on dispersing the production of goods and services that make up daily necessities to those regions of the world best able to create efficient economies of scale by cutting labor costs and forgoing environmental protection protocols. These products are then transported by container ships and air freight to America and the far ends of the earth.

While Galston said he understood that the efficiencies brought on by globalization were a "trade-off" and "unavoidable," the inevitable result is that "as efficiency increased, resilience declined." He concluded by warning his business audience that "in the relentless quest for increased efficiency, which remains a key source of competitive advantage, the decisions made by individual market actors will produce, in the aggregate, a less-than-optimal supply of resiliency, a public good."[6] It was difficult for the business community to hear such a message. After all, by drawing attention to this unassailable downside of efficiency in a global capitalist system long touted as the best of all possible worlds, Galston stepped on the Achilles' heel of the entire system by which modern society operates.

Had the Galston piece been a single shot across the bow, it might have passed unnoticed. But just weeks later, on April 20, Senator Marco Rubio, a political conservative and a leader of the Republican party, chimed in with a second frontal attack aimed at the heart of the capitalist system, in an opinion piece published in *The New York Times* entitled "We Need a More Resilient American Economy." Rubio took an even more aggressive stance, warning that "over the past several decades, our nation's political and economic leaders, Democratic and Republican, made choices about how to structure our society—choosing to prize economic efficiency over resiliency, financial gains over Main Street investment, individual enrichment over the common good."[7]

Rubio faulted the American business community for offshoring its manufacturing base to developing countries while putting its experience to building up a financial and service-based economy. He writes that it "produced one of the most efficient economic engines of all time," but it "lacks resiliency," which, he pointed out, "can be devastating in a crisis." Rubio struck a deeper, more philosophical note, suggesting that the country needed to come to grips with the consequences that flow from a "hyperindividualistic ethos" by pursuing a renewal of the American spirit of resilience that made the country a beacon to the world.[8]

Galston and Rubio's critique of America's love affair with efficiency at the expense of its earlier resilient roots was already beginning to bubble up to the surface. The difference is that the toll it had been taking on the American economy and society didn't become real to most Americans until they came up against empty shelves in supermarkets and pharmacies during the early months of the COVID-19 pandemic.

Even before COVID-19, voices were being raised from deep within the capitalist establishment. In January 2019, *Harvard Business Review* ran a lengthy essay with the controversial title, "The High Price of Efficiency." Its author was Roger Martin, the former dean of the Rotman School of Management at the University of Toronto. The article was part of a series that was introduced with the following conundrum: "Beginning with Adam Smith, business thinkers have steadfastly regarded the elimination of waste as management's holy grail. But what if the negative effects from the pursuit of efficiency eclipse the rewards?"[9] Martin, like others in the rarefied world of business management, is stepping forward for the very first time in the 250-year history of the profession to challenge the ruling truisms of their discipline. Lest doubters fail to recognize the overriding importance of efficiency as a centerpiece of neoclassical and, more recently, neoliberal economics, Martin sets the record straight:

> The unalloyed virtue of efficiency has never dimmed. It is embodied in multilateral organizations such as the World Trade Organization, aimed at making trade more efficient. It is ensconced in the Washington Consensus via trade and foreign direct-investment liberalization, efficient forms of taxation, deregulation, privatization, transparent capital markets, balanced budgets, and waste-fighting governments. And it is promoted in the classrooms of every business school on the planet.[10]

Martin takes another route in critiquing capitalism's obsession with efficiency. He argues that at the onset of new technological breakthroughs that spur accompanying entrepreneurial opportunities, the early pacesetters quickly consolidate their control over the emerging market potential by increasing their efficiencies across all of their potential value chains and vertically integrating them into their operations to create economies of scale. But becoming a first mover and market leader comes with a negative externality not anticipated in the rush to the top.

Martin uses the example of the few companies that control virtually the entire global almond market. At the time the industry was ratcheting up, the Central Valley of California was considered "perfect for almond growing" and currently more than 80 percent of the almonds produced in the world come from that region.[11]

Unfortunately, centralizing almond production in one spot because of ideal weather patterns ran up against unanticipated environmental triggers. California's almond blossoms require a very narrow seasonal window for pollination and necessitate the transporting of beehives to the region from all across America. In recent years, however, the bee population has been dying in droves. More than one-third of America's commercial bee colonies were wiped out in just the winter of 2018–19—a record.[12] There are many theories about the environmental cause of the bee die-off, but it is enough to say that the monoculture of the almond industry, while initially efficient, has proven to be more vulnerable to externalities and less resilient.

What Martin failed to mention is that almond trees are also voracious consumers of water. Every almond produced requires a gallon of water. Add it all up and almost 10 percent of all the water consumed by agriculture in California annually goes to quenching the thirst of the almond trees in the Central Valley—that's more water than is consumed by the entire populations of Los Angeles and San Francisco in a year.[13]

To make matters worse, climate change has turned the once fertile Central Valley into a drought-stricken region, threatening the future viability of what was a highly efficient place to locate almond orchards. The short-term efficiencies of locating 80 percent of the almond trees that make up world trade in one region came up against the unexpected environmental threats that the industry did not consider . . . what was regarded as a highly commercial business proved not to be resilient.[14] The lesson is monoculture in any commercial enterprise—putting all of one's almonds in one basket—while efficient, lacks sufficient resilience against unknown future events.

THE UNRAVELING OF INDUSTRIAL CAPITALISM

While efficiency is a temporal value, resilience is a condition. It is true that increasing efficiency often undermines resilience, but the temporal value that serves as an antidote is not more efficiency, but rather adaptivity. We've come to realize over the past half century or so that the earth acts like a self-organizing system in which all forms of life are continually adapting moment to moment to the energy fluxes and flows of the planet and to the evolution of the earth's spheres. Adaptivity bears a close resemblance to the concept of "harmonizing" in nature that is a unique characteristic of Eastern religions and philosophies.

Efficiency is about eliminating the friction, a code word for getting rid of redundancies that might slow the speed and optimization of economic activity. Resilience, however, at least in nature, is all about redundancy and diversity. For example, the monoculture of a specific crop variety might be more efficient in terms of speed of growth to maturity, but were that particular monoculture to be subject to blight, the losses can be irreparable.

The discovery in the business community and business schools that efficiency, which has long been heralded as the operating arm of capitalist theory and practice, is largely at fault in increasing the risk and accompanying vulnerability of the economy and society—all of which undermine our collective resilience—seemed to jump out of nowhere. But now, with this realization, comes a heady reassessment of how we should proceed.

If our attachment to efficiency has begun to sour, what then do we do about productivity, its twin, and the other critical agency by which our economy lives and breathes? While efficiency is a temporal value, productivity is a simple ratio of outputs produced by the inputs used, especially those associated with technology and accompanying innovative business practices. Both efficiency and productivity are strictly linear processes and limited in time to the production chain and market exchange, with little attention to or accounting of the negative side effects that may extend beyond the moment the good is exchanged and the service delivered. But of course, it's denying these very negative externalities, created by the increased efficiencies and productivity, that allows companies to increase their profit.

Biological systems are organized around a very different operating regime. While adaptivity, rather than efficiency, is the temporal signature of biological systems, regenerativity, rather than productivity, is the measure of performance. Adaptivity and regenerativity are inseparable in all biological organisms and ecosystems. Consider, for example, the process of autophagy in biology.

Yoshinori Ohsumi is a seventy-six-year-old Japanese cell biologist who has spent a lifetime studying autophagy. The term comes from the Greek words meaning "self-eating." Autophagy is the cell's waste disposal system. It's the process by which "cellular junk is captured and sealed in sack-like membranes, called autophagosomes . . . [and] transported to another structure called the lysosome." Biologists long considered the lysosome as just a "cellular rubbish bin" and of little consequence, just as human society has come to think of garbage dumps and landfills.[15] But what Ohsumi eventually discovered is that autophagy is the recycling mechanism of an organism. Scrap cell components are gathered up and the parts that are still useful are stripped to generate energy and/or build new cells. Ohsumi was awarded the Nobel Prize in Physiology or Medicine in 2016 for his work.[16]

Autophagy is just one of many examples of the processes and patterns deeply embedded in living organisms that are helping reshape our own understanding of economic life. It's become fashionable in recent years across virtually every sector of the economy to mimic the regenerative practices in biological systems by embedding the process of "circularity"—the business term for recycling—into every stage of the economic process, from extraction to production, storage, logistics, and consumption, ensuring a relatively closed loop in which little waste is lost, but rather, reused over and over again in a regenerative way, minimizing the environmental bill for current and future generations.

Is all of this talk about efficiency versus adaptivity and productivity versus regenerativity little more than a momentary acting-out in the wake of a breakdown in supply chains, logistics, and buffer stock inventories that caught the world by surprise in the unfolding of the COVID-19 pandemic? Or is there something of a deeper nature taking root? In the 1960s, when I was a student at the Wharton School and later, between 1995 and 2010, when I taught in the Wharton Executive Education program and particularly the Advanced Management Program, I don't recall a single instance when the discussion ever turned to the question of the shortcomings of efficiency and progress, much less a spirited conversation around a countereconomic narrative focused on adaptivity and resilience.

What has changed is an escalating series of crises. In just the past couple of decades, we have witnessed the September 11, 2001, terrorist attack on the World Trade Center and the meteoric rise of terrorist cells and movements around the world; the collapse of the global economy in 2008 and with it the

Great Recession; the growing disparity in income with the rise of a global elite of financial and business interests and the increasing pauperization of the workforce worldwide; the rise of ultra-right, populist, and fascist political movements and parties, along with strongman rule and the loss of faith in democratic governance. But all these crises, which are threatening to destabilize human civilization, pale in comparison to the two great existential crises of increasing global pandemics in ever-shorter time intervals and the exponential warming of the planet's climate that's taking our species and our fellow creatures into the sixth extinction of life on Earth.

The last time our species faced a crisis even remotely comparable in magnitude and scope occurred seven centuries ago in late medieval Europe, with the spread of the bubonic plague—the Black Death—which ravaged the continent and parts of Asia, beginning in 1348 and continuing to flare up for the next several hundred years, leading to the deaths of an estimated seventy-five to two hundred million people in Eurasia.[17] The social mayhem and political fallout led to a mass disenchantment with the Catholic Church's governance and its accompanying worldview. The church's narrative had long provided solace to the faithful and had steered the course of Western civilization for more than a millennium. The story of Christ and the church's promise of redemption and everlasting life was a powerful narrative that was embraced across the Western world but in the end proved a weak adversary to a tiny bacteria, *Yersinia pestis*, which was invisible to the naked eye.

From the shambles rose a new and overarching worldview and accompanying narrative along with new forms of governance and ways of organizing economic and social life. This new ordering of civilization would take Europe, America, and eventually the rest of the world into the modern era under the loosely defined motif of the Age of Progress.

The Age of Progress has meant many things to many people, including the rise of democratic governance, greater personal freedoms, longer life spans, and the extension of human rights. But, at the core of this new narrative is the improvement of humanity's material well-being by harnessing science and technology to a market-based capitalist economy.

At the very heart of the paradigm shift from the medieval to the modern age lies the promise of perfecting the human condition. But this time the responsibility for its realization would depend on: the wonders of science and the exactitude of mathematics; the new practical technologies to ease life; and the lure of the capitalist marketplace in advancing the economic well-being of society. These three metrics are the foundational cornerstones of the Age of Progress. The binding element is a uniquely modern method for organizing the temporal and spatial orientation of every individual, the community, and the economy and society at large. It's a term so omnipresent that it is little talked about, rarely questioned, but, nonetheless, universally upheld as the ticket to saving time and expropriating space in hopes of creating an earthly paradise.

Efficiency is the temporal dynamic of modernity. Efficiency reorders the use of time and, by extension, space. Implicit in its use is the premise that being efficient saves, accumulates, buys, and extends time and, by so doing, gives the individual, and even society, an extended lease on time. The more efficient an individual, institution, or community becomes, the more convinced they are that they have extended their future horizon, edging ever closer to "a measure" of immortality. With the rise of modern science, ever more sophisticated technologies, and market capitalism, a powerful new trinity came to replace the Father, the Son, and the Holy Spirit. Efficiency, in turn, would come to replace God, long regarded as the universal prime mover, as the new divinity of the Age of Progress.

each coordinated to work in tandem to speed the efficiency of the production process.

After narrowing each worker's contribution to the process down to a single, simple, repeatable task with instructions described in minute detail, supervisors were trained to use stopwatches to analyze the elapsed time of every motion and movement of the worker in order to eliminate unnecessary gestures that might slow his or her response time. They then tweaked each worker's movements to quicken their response time and accuracy. The objective was to determine the best time under the optimal conditions for completing a task and making it the standard for increased efficiency. Often, the slightest changes in gestures that might slow performance were corrected, sometimes eliminating precious seconds from the task.

The workers' performance was standardized, eliminating any individual behavioral idiosyncrasies to secure a work environment in which workers are indistinguishable from the machines they are attending. All factors on the factory floor were viewed as components of a scientifically managed megamachine whose performance was continually measured in improved efficiencies and whose worth would be calculated by way of cost-benefit analysis.

THE GOSPEL OF EFFICIENCY

As it turns out, the factory floor was just the foothold for advancing Taylor's efficiency crusade across the social landscape in the early decades of the 20th century. The brilliance of Taylor's narrative is that it was attached to science, giving it the legitimacy that would make it palpable to an educated middle class while using the term *efficiency*, which was originally an engineering term attached to the performance of machines, to suggest its applicability to every aspect of life. It was the Age of the Machine. New inventions were being introduced into the market at breakneck speed: the telephone, the electric dynamo, electricity, electric lighting, the automobile, airplanes, skyscrapers, radio, film, automated assembly lines, electric appliances, et cetera.

Millions of families attended great world expos and fairs in the first half of the 20th century in the United States and elsewhere, beginning with the Columbian Exposition in Chicago in 1893 and culminating in the New York World's Fair in 1939, to experience a utopian world within reach, made possible by modern science and the new efficiencies of commerce. All of the exhibits were designed to draw the public into the future that they would be making and living in.

2

TAYLORISM AND THE LAWS OF THERMODYNAMICS

Movie buffs are familiar with the great 20th-century comedian Charlie Chaplin's two most iconic films, *The Great Dictator* and *Modern Times*. While film devotees are aware that in the first film Chaplin was parodying Adolf Hitler, they may not know that the second film was also a parody of a famous individual who had a momentous impact on the 20th century. In the film, Chaplin—the Little Tramp—is a factory worker on an assembly line where he screws nuts into pieces of machinery at an ever-faster rate, trying desperately to keep up with the accelerating pace set by management, only to get caught in the gears, plunging the entire factory into chaos.[1] The other parodied man was Frederick W. Taylor, the founding father of the Gospel of Efficiency.

Frederick Taylor was born in 1856 into a well-off Quaker family in Philadelphia. He attended the prestigious Phillips Exeter Academy in Exeter, New Hampshire. After receiving a degree in mechanical engineering, he held several management positions in companies, the most notable being Bethlehem Steel Corporation. He later accepted a teaching position at the Tuck School of Business at Dartmouth College and in 1906 became the president of the American Society of Mechanical Engineers. In 1911, Taylor published *The Principles of Scientific Management*, the book that would become the bible for embedding efficiency into the very heart of modern civilization.

Taylor devised a system of division of labor that would ensure that management controlled virtually every movement of every worker at every stage of the production process. Taylor's system, later known as Taylorism, was based on a single overriding principle—the separation of management and planning from the execution of tasks on the factory floor and, further, dividing those tasks into ever-simpler subdivisions of the overall operation

Where better to start inculcating the public into this new worldview than the home? An avalanche of articles appeared in popular magazines, imploring women to "be progressive and join the efficiency movement." While appealing to their better nature, the articles where not shy to scold. Middle-class mothers were admonished to stop "soldiering" on the job, reminding them that the household was "part of a great factory for the production of citizens."[2] Christine Frederick, an American home economist, published an article in the popular *Ladies' Home Journal* urging housewives to be more scientifically minded and efficient in operating the home economy.

She confessed, "For years I never realized that I actually made eighty wrong motions in the washing alone, not counting others in the sorting, wiping, and laying away."[3] Frederick made an appeal to American housewives to adopt a standard practice of dishwashing to "find what motions are efficient motions, and what motions are unnecessary and inefficient."[4]

"Housekeeping experiment stations" were established to surveil household activities. Time and motion studies were conducted to ascertain the optimum motion and time segments for performing each household chore, providing a database by which to train homemakers in "the principles of domestic engineering."[5] The efficiency crusade was off and running. "The home . . . was to be mechanized, systemized," and optimized to the rhythms of efficiency.[6]

Although the home was the starting gate for introducing Taylorism across society, it was the school system that became the teacher, guide, arbiter, and enforcer of the efficiency agenda. The principles of scientific management were used to remake the schools in the image of factories and mold children into little Taylorites, readying them for the opportunities and challenges that awaited them in "the world of tomorrow."

The popular media played a role in whipping up hysteria over an outmoded approach to education that was not keeping pace with the vocational requirements needed to prepare students for an emerging industrial system whose primary task was to use the principles of scientific management to upgrade efficiency, increase productivity, and create economic abundance. *The Saturday Evening Post* published a seething attack called "Our Medieval High Schools—Shall We Educate Children for the Twelfth or Twentieth Century?" The author ridiculed what laymen regarded as a "gentleman's education" that "should be of no use in the world—particularly in the business world."[7] Another Taylorite scolded that "there is inefficiency in the business management of many schools such as would not be tolerated in the world of offices and shops."[8]

Educators across the country took up the challenge. School superintendents began by urging a wholesale reorganization of responsibilities in public school systems along the lines of scientific management. The first priority would be disempowering teachers from establishing their own individualized approach to learning in the classroom. Taylorites argued that curriculum, classroom presentation, and testing needed to be placed in the hands of school super-intendents and their boards to standardize content and provide instructions on how each teacher was to deliver the product.

In the new schema, school superintendents were akin to the management of industrial companies, and the teachers were akin to the workers on the factory floor who were spoon-fed specific assignments along with detailed instructions on how to deliver the content to students. Knowledge was to be broken up into small bits of easily digestible facts to be memorized and spit back on standardized tests.

Standardized tests and numerical grading became the norm. An older intellectual tradition pondering on the "why" of things was shunted aside to make room for an almost evangelical embrace of optimizing the "how" of things. Efficiency became the chief criterion for determining performance. Assignments were to be completed under strict deadlines. Knowledge was segmented into siloed disciplines—a division of education designed to sim-plify learning into discrete academic tasks. The performance of school sys-tems was judged by the number of students achieving threshold numerical test scores on standardized state-administered exams, allowing them to pass on to the next grade—and later on judged by the students' scores on national SAT and ACT tests.

While there have been some minor modifications to the Tayloresque ap-proach to education over the past hundred years, they have been few and far between. Twentieth-century education has been almost exclusively dedicated to molding students to a Taylorist mindset, readying them to be efficient in the world of industry and commerce.

The U.S. federal government's No Child Left Behind Act of 2001 is right out of the Taylor toolbox. Its core features included high-stakes standardized testing of students and detailed instructions on how teachers were to present their classroom assignments. Curriculum that is not easily reducible to stan-dardized grading was eased out of the classroom.

Wayne Au, a professor in the education program at the University of Wash-ington, in an article in the *Journal of Curriculum Studies* titled "Teaching Under the New Taylorism: High-Stakes Testing and the Standardization of the 21st Century Curriculum," describes the impact of continuing to follow a Taylorist creed in American schools today:

Knowledge learned for U.S. high-stakes tests is thus transformed into a collection of disconnected facts, operations, procedures, or data mainly needed for rote memorization in preparation for the tests . . . consequentially, students are increasingly learning knowledge associated with lower-level thinking, and they are often learning this knowledge in fragmented chunks within the context of the tests alone. In this way, high-stakes testing is effectively restricting the way knowledge itself is structured in teachers' practices in U.S. schools.[9]

Nowhere was the efficiency movement more elevated in importance and more misunderstood in public debate than in the conservation of natural resources. Many leading environmentalists of the day were hoping to preserve the natural beauty of the wild for aesthetic purposes and to preserve ecosystems to allow America's native species of plant and animal life to flourish alongside an increasingly industrialized environment.

However, professional societies and industries aligned with President Theodore Roosevelt's administration around repositioning conservation as an efficiency agenda. While they argued that natural resources were a critical asset responsible for much of the country's steep rise to world dominance as the premier industrial power, they also warned that the rush to own, expropriate, and exploit the nation's treasure trove of natural resources was killing the goose that was laying the golden eggs and urged a more efficient exploitation of the country's natural heritage to advance American industries and the economy as a whole. Since questions of resource use were of a technical nature, the oversight ought to be put in the hands of the experts who knew best how to efficiently manage the nation's natural wealth.

Environmental historian Samuel P. Hays summed up the nub of the conservation movement this way: "The apostles of the Gospel of Efficiency subordinated the aesthetic to the utilitarian. Preservation of natural scenery and historic sites, in their scheme of things, remained subordinate to increasing industrial productivity."[10]

Were anyone to think that the approach to the use of the nation's public lands has changed in the course of the past century, consider this. Currently, ninety percent of public lands "are available to oil and gas drillers while only ten percent are for a focus on conservation and other values including recreation and wilderness."[11] Worse, 42 percent of all coal mined in the U.S. is on federal lands as well as 22 percent of all crude oil and 15 percent of natural gas, accounting for 23.7 percent of the country's CO_2 global warming emissions, according to a recent survey of federal land use by the U.S. Department of Interior.[12]

The efficiency narrative in the opening decades of the 20th century became a convenient tool to sidestep fundamental questions around issues of equity, gender and racial equality, political disenfranchisement, morality, and even humankind's responsibility for the natural world. Efficiency was extolled as a neutral force. Just as Charles Darwin rewrote the book of nature arguing that the process of species selection guaranteed that the most fit would survive, neutering any question of divine purpose, the principle of scientific management came with its own rationale that efficiency rides above the din of conflicting and competing interests. To challenge efficiency is to bump up against the impenetrable laws of science and the workings of the natural world. How wrong we were.

MISREADING HOW THE WORLD WORKS:
How Revered Minds Led Our Species Astray

One-third of the world's topsoil has been degraded during the industrial era, and scientists tell us we may have only sixty years of topsoil left to feed the human population of the planet.[13] It takes upward of five hundred years to replenish one inch of topsoil.[14] Our scientists are also warning us that climate change is triggering a mass extinction and that we could lose up to fifty percent of all existing species over the course of the next eighty years.[15]

Meanwhile, the oxygen on the planet is being snuffed out at an alarming rate, unparalleled in two billion years. Plant phytoplankton from the oceans, which account for half the oxygen production on Earth, are now threatened by the rising ocean temperature brought on by global warming emissions. New studies project that as early as 2100, phytoplankton losses could deplete ocean oxygen on a global scale.[16] Equally harrowing, floods, hurricanes, droughts, and wildfires are now fast increasing in intensity as the earth's temperature rises from global warming emissions, destabilizing ecosystems, making large areas of the planet uninhabitable, and leading to 19 percent of the earth becoming "a barely livable hot zone" by 2070.[17]

The impact our species is having is staggering to behold. While a century ago, approximately 85 percent of the earth's surface was still characterized as wilderness, today less than 23 percent of landmass remains unmodified by humans, with projections that over the next several decades this last remnant is likely to disappear after 3.5 billion years of life on the planet.[18]

How could this have happened? Why did we not see this coming? There are plenty of opinions on this subject. But, the indisputable truth is that much of the blame lies at the feet of the scientific community, the economics pro-fession, and the business community that served up the narrative for how the global economy functions under optimal conditions to further the interests and secure the well-being of humanity.

That story begins with the French mathematician and scientist René Descartes, often regarded as the first modern philosopher. Born in La Haye en Touraine, France, in 1596, the young Frenchman excelled as a student in mathematics and physics. In his youth, Descartes marveled at all of the new mechanical inventions that were extending man's power over nature and opined that these must be part of a much bigger picture, a mechanical universe—that is, a rational universe operating by mechanical laws. Des-cartes argued that these laws could be discovered and put to use to better the lot of humankind.

Descartes recalled that on the night of November 10, 1619, then only twenty-three years old, he went to bed and had three dreams in succession in which the divine spirit revealed to him a new philosophy unlike any other that preceded him. Upon waking, he had grasped the elements of what came to be known as analytical geometry and the concept of applying mathemat-ics to philosophy. Descartes mused "that it makes no difference whether it be in numbers, figures, stars, sounds or any other object that the question of measurement arises. I saw consequently that there must be some general sci-ence to explain that element as a whole, which gives rise to problems about order and measurement. . . . This, I perceived, was called universal mathe-matics . . . and its province ought to extend to the eliciting of true results in every subject."[19]

Descartes came to believe that human thought, unconstrained and armed with mathematics, could create an orderly, predictable, and self-perpetuating mechanical analogue of existence here on Earth just as the godhead has done in the cosmos at large. "Give me extension and motion," Descartes is said to have stated, "and I will construct the universe"—perhaps the most audacious sentence ever uttered.[20] Yet, it fell on receptive ears, especially among the in-telligentsia of the time.

Descartes's description of a mechanical universe was not meant as an analogy or metaphor. He meant it. Descartes described human emotions—memory, imagination, passions—as functions that follow from the arrangement of "its counterweights and wheels" and characterized our fellow creatures as "automata."[21] In a letter he posted to the British philosopher Henry More in 1649, Descartes wrote, "It seems reasonable since art copies nature, and men can make various automata which move without thought, that nature should produce its own automata much more splendid than the artificial ones. These natural automata are the animals."[22]

But Descartes still faced an impassable stumbling block with his vision of a mechanical universe: every machine ever invented is confronted by gravity in its operations. Although Descartes was able to describe the components of the machine, he didn't have an answer for how the external force of gravity affects it. That answer would have to wait for another sixty-eight years and the musings of a young university student.

Isaac Newton was twenty-two years old and in his third year of studies on a scholarship at Trinity College at the University of Cambridge in 1664 and a devotee of René Descartes. At the time, the Black Plague was wreaking havoc in London, killing one hundred thousand inhabitants—25 percent of the population—and was spreading quickly across the countryside. Cambridge University closed its doors and sent its students home to quarantine. Newton returned to his family's rural estate in Woolsthorpe. He remained there in quarantine for nearly two years.

During that time, he worked on the laws of motion and universal gravitation, and the creation of infinitesimal calculus. Historians have called his time in quarantine the "Year of Wonders."[23] He returned to Cambridge in the fall of 1667 with notebooks brimming with insights. He became a professor of mathematics in 1669. His masterwork, *Principia Mathematica*, was published by the Royal Society in 1687 and became an overnight sensation in Britain and soon thereafter in France and the rest of Europe.[24]

Newton uncovered the mathematical formula for describing gravitation. He argued that the phenomena of nature "may all depend upon certain forces by which the particles of bodies, by some causes hitherto unknown, are either mutually impelled towards each other, and cohere in regular figures, or are repelled and recede from each other."[25] Newton posited that a single law could describe why the planets move in a certain fashion and why an apple falls from the tree in a particular way. His law of universal gravitation states that "the force of attraction between two masses is directly proportional to the product of their masses and inversely proportional to the square of the distance between their centers."[26]

According to Newton's three laws, a body at rest remains at rest, and a body in motion remains in motion in a straight line unless acted upon by an external force; the acceleration of a body is directly proportional to the applied force acting upon the object and inversely proportional to the mass of the object; and for every force, there is an equal and opposite force in reaction. Newton's three laws deal with how all the forces in the cosmos interact and settle back into "equilibrium."

Adam Smith was a fan of Newton's equilibrium theory and the systemiza-tion of physics, calling his work "the greatest discovery that ever was made by man."[27] Smith even went so far as to use the term "the invisible hand" to describe how the process of supply and demand in the marketplace oper-ates in a manner that, at least on the surface, is remarkably similar to the way Newton describes his third law of gravity—that for every action there is an equal and opposite reaction. Smith, and a legion of economists who followed over the next two and a half centuries, argued that self-regulating markets act in a likewise fashion, with supply and demand continually react-ing and adjusting to each other on the price of goods and services, eventu-ally leading to an agreement, a transaction, and a return to a Newtonian-like equilibrium.

Newton's universe of matter and motion was orderly and calculable and made no room for spontaneity or unpredictability. It was a world of quanti-ties without qualities. Newton supported his insights with mathematical proof rather than just relying on deductive reasoning—making mathematics the go-to science for both understanding the world and expropriating it. Newton mathematicized the Age of Enlightenment and mathematics, in turn, pro-vided the scaffolding for the ensuing Age of Progress.

It's also worth noting that Newton's three laws of matter in motion are without time's arrow. In Newton's universe, all processes are time reversible. But in the real world of nature and, by extension, the economy, no event is time reversible. By embracing Newton's atemporal schema as a tool to model economic activity, generations of economists would be led astray, further dis-tancing themselves from reality.

Adam Smith and the early economists weren't the only ones to draw par-allels between Newton's thesis of how the universe operates and their own interests. His theory was enthusiastically embraced at the time by the pow-ers that be in Britain, especially the Anglican Church and the British gov-ernment, both of which were deeply concerned over the increasing social unrest and economic disruptions brought on by a rapidly changing economy and society. The British Crown saw in Newton's description of an orderly, predicable, and self-regulating universe a model that the church, the gov-ernment, and the academic establishment could use to enlist the allegiance of the educated elite and, through them, put Newtonism to work educating and taming the masses while quieting the unruly mob of anti-monarchy and anti-church intellectuals who were increasingly challenging state authority. The implicit and often explicit message was that opposing the British govern-ment was futile because it would be flying in the face of the natural order of things—that is, a predictable, orderly, and self-regulating world of which the Crown was its earthly defender.

THE LAWS OF THERMODYNAMICS:
The Rules of the Game

It's not that the economics profession didn't know that relying on the Newtonian schema—and its time reversibility—to explain the workings of a capitalist economy was a poor choice to hang their hat on.

The economists knew. By the last half of the 19th century, a new set of scientific laws were discovered whose scope and reach were so broad, inclusive, and uncontestable that they would come to provide an overarching frame for all of the other scientific laws—including Newton's laws of matter and motion, Darwin's theory of the evolution of life, and even Albert Einstein's theory of relativity. These new scientific principles of how the universe is organized are the first and second laws of thermodynamics.

A century after they were first enunciated, Albert Einstein would make note of the overriding importance of the laws of thermodynamics in an unequivocal acknowledgment . . . one that would go unchallenged by his fellow scientists. Regarding the laws of thermodynamics, Einstein wrote,

> "A theory is the more impressive the greater the simplicity of its premises is, the more different kinds of things it relates, and the more extended is its area of applicability. . . . [The laws of thermodynamics] is the only physical theory of universal content concerning which I am convinced that, within the framework of applicability of its basic concepts, it will never be overthrown."[28]

While the shortcoming of Newton's laws governing matter and motion is that they don't account for the passage of time and the irreversibility of unfolding events, the laws of thermodynamics are all about the passage of time. The first law of thermodynamics, often referred to as the conservation law, states that all the energy in the universe is constant, and has been so since the Big Bang brought it into existence—the point being, energy can neither be created nor destroyed. The total energy of the universe will remain until the end of time. However, while the total energy of the universe is constant, that energy is always changing form, but only in one direction, from available to unavailable. This is where the second law of thermodynamics enters the picture. That law tells us that energy always flows from hot to cold, from concentrated to dispersed, and from order to disorder, marking the irreversible passage of time.

For example, if one burns a piece of coal all of the energy remains, but is no longer concentrated but, rather, dispersed. The energy is released in the form of carbon dioxide, sulfur dioxide, and nitrogen oxide dispersed into the atmosphere. Although the sum total of that energy remains, it will never be reconstituted again into a piece of coal. The German scientist Rudolf Clausius coined the term "entropy" in 1865 to refer to expended energy that remains, but is largely unusable.[29]

Some would argue that the sun is the universal source of energy bathing the earth and via photosynthesis continues to provide ample stores of energy, at least until our sun burns out, which is likely billions of years into the future. True, but there are other stores of material bounded energies—metallic ore, rare earths, and even all the minerals embedded in rocks, that have been here since the earth blew off the sun, cooled off, and formed the material substance of the planet. These materials, in the form of bounded energies, are fixed and finite. While meteorites—ranging from a few grains of dust to asteroids—enter the atmosphere in meteor showers during any given year, scientists estimate the total weight of meteoric material falling on the earth each day is only about 48.5 tons, too little to make much difference.[30]

There are three types of systems that we know of in the universe: open systems, which exchange both energy and bound energy in the form of matter with the outside world; closed systems, which exchange energy but not matter with the outside world; and isolated systems, which exchange neither energy nor matter with the outside world. The earth, in relation to our solar system, is a closed system. We enjoy a continuous flow of energy from the sun, but exchange very little bound energy in matter with the outside world. For an example, let's circle back to fossil fuels.

Coal, oil, and natural gas deposits buried deep beneath the land surface and the ocean floor are the dead remains of life from three hundred fifty million years ago in the Carboniferous Era—they are bound energy. Although it's theoretically possible that sometime in the far distant future in another geological era, with similar plant and animal life, their dead remains might metamorphose into coal, oil, and gas, it's highly unlikely that this might come to pass. We might say the same about the rare earths that are becoming increasingly valuable inputs in technologically driven society, embedded in a wide range of products including LED screens, smartphones and tablets, batteries, and electric vehicle motors. A brief explanation is due on what is meant by bound energy. As Brian Greene, professor of physics and string theory at Columbia University, points out in a *New York Times* opinion piece:

Mass and energy are not distinct. They are the same basic stuff packaged in forms that make them appear different. Just as solid ice can melt into liquid water, Einstein showed, mass is a frozen form of energy that can be converted into the more familiar energy of motion. . . . In the far, far future, essentially all matter will have returned to energy.[31]

The fatal flaw of conventional economics is that it is still bound to the Newtonian equilibrium worldview in which time is reversible. By boxing in all economic exchange of goods, services, and property between sellers and buyers in a timeless vacuum—to wit the atemporal point of the transaction—economists and the business community conveniently dismiss any relevant side effects over time that might accompany the extraction of natural resources and all the many interactions that intersect, accompany, or in some way affect their journey through their various stages of conversion into goods and services. At every stage in the conversion process effects are rippling out and affecting other phenomena, which are not factored into the market transaction.

It wasn't until the 1920s that economists even began to address the question of spillover effects. Henry Sidgwick and Arthur C. Pigou are credited with formalizing the concepts of these unanticipated impacts as "positive" or "negative" externalities.[32] By externalities, they meant the unrecognized effects of a market exchange in either inducing greater profit or cost somewhere else and at some other time that was not factored into an efficient cost-benefit analysis. But even up until now, economists have continued to treat externalities as a narrow sidebar to the economics of market exchange, and of only marginal relevance. Account for the entire trail of economic activity before, during, and after the journey of an economic product or service and we begin to understand how feeble the economics discipline is in determining the real long-term costs of the short-lived benefits gained at the moment it is exchanged and consumed.

So what if Newton's equilibrium theory still has a hold on economics? Granted, the elimination of time from the economic equation allows economists to use ever more arcane mathematical models in their craft. How damaging could this be? Besides, it was long believed that the thermodynamic laws deal only with energy flows and entropy sinks, arguably of great interest to chemists and physicists but irrelevant to explaining the biology of life on Earth. The consensus was that these laws applied only when energy is used to power machines, allowing engineers to better calculate the ratio of energy output to energy input and, by so doing, improve their efficiency.

Therefore, the thinking was that these laws were not as universal as the physicists and chemists claimed. Life, it was thought, must not be entangled in the entropic web. After all, evolution tells us of a world overflowing with new life forms, each more complex and ordered.

This last wall of resistance came tumbling down in 1944, when Austrian physicist and Nobel laureate Erwin Schrödinger explained that biology, like physics and chemistry, is ruled by the same laws of thermodynamics. Schrödinger argued that "what an organism feeds upon is negative entropy . . . continually sucking orderliness from its environment."[33] Every living being is continually taking in available energy when eating and excreting waste and, by doing so, depleting the available energy on Earth and adding to the entropic bill. Were we to stop consuming available energy, we would die, and what remains would turn to dust—the final entropy bill. It's only after that last breath that every human being and every other creature reaches the state of equilibrium.

Rarely do we step back and reflect on the sheer amount of the earth's natural endowment that is required to maintain each of us in a non-equilibrium state away from death. The chemist G. Tyler Miller refers to a simplified food chain to help us fully appreciate how much of the earth's available energy needs to flow through our body for each of us to maintain a nonequilibrium state. His food chain is made up of grasshoppers who eat the grass, the frogs who eat the grasshoppers, the trout who eat the frogs, and the human beings who eat the trout. It turns out that three hundred trout are required to support one human for a year. The trout, in turn, must consume ninety thousand frogs that must consume twenty-seven million grasshoppers that live off one thousand tons of grass.[34]

Why does so much of nature's wealth need to be expropriated and consumed at each higher level of the food chain? It turns out that in devouring prey—for example, a lion chasing, killing, and devouring an antelope—"about 80–90 percent of the energy is simply wasted and lost as heat to the environment at each step. In other words, 10–20 percent of the energy is stored in the living tissue available for transfer to the species at the next level [of the food chain]."[35] The cultural historian Elias Canetti captured the grim specter of our own aliveness, remarking that "each of us is a king in a field of corpses."[36]

Economics is wedded to an equilibrium paradigm and is woefully unprepared to address nonequilibrium thermodynamics in which every expropriation of available energy provides a short-term gain, but at the expense of a greater long-term entropic loss, including the energy embedded in the product itself. The efforts by economists to factor in a few easily recognizable positive and negative externalities that might accrue in the life cycle of a product are a pitiful attempt to come to grips with the reality that every economic exchange has a long entropic tail that spreads in every possible direction, affecting other phenomena.

The laws of thermodynamics are a stark reminder of how utterly absurd a metric like gross domestic product (GDP) is for measuring a nation's growth and wealth on an annual basis. GDP measures only the momentary exchange value of economic activity. Clearly, the value of the products and services at the moment of sale does not begin to account for the costs in terms of the depletion of the earth's energy reserves and other natural resources and the entropic waste that accompanies each step in the value chain.

The economic profession wasn't altogether off track at the beginning. The very first economics philosophers, called physiocrats, emerged in the mid-to-late 18th century, mostly in France. They argued that all economic activity derives its value from nature's storehouse. More canonical economists, including Adam Smith, David Ricardo, and Thomas Malthus, were of a like mind, and even if they didn't go as far as the physiocrats in believing that all wealth comes from nature, they at least realized its importance as the seed stock of all economic activity.

The physiocrats' short-lived prominence was the victim of historical circumstances. Their heyday coincided with the peak of the earlier proto-agricultural Industrial Revolution—the precursor to modern industrial capitalism, which was just emerging in the late 18th century with the development of coal-powered steam technology and factory production of textiles and other manufactured products. As agriculture retreated from the front lines in the wake of the Industrial Revolution, becoming more of a necessary sidebar, manufacturing took to the fore and attention turned to the importance of capital and labor in creating wealth. Nature, in turn, was reduced to merely a raw material input. And, as natural resources were abundant, especially with the discovery of vast open land in the New World, harnessing nature was relatively cheap and increasingly seen as just a factor in production, rather than as a substantial generator of wealth.

James Watt installed his first two coal-powered steam engines in 1776, the same year that Adam Smith published *An Inquiry into the Nature and Causes of the Wealth of Nations*.[37] Over the course of the next century, the steam engine became an overarching presence across Europe and the Americas. Although the steam engine was a critical element in capital formation, the coal that powered it was relatively cheap and also came to be regarded as an almost inconsequential factor in production.

Like other thinkers at the time, Adam Smith was awed by the efficiencies brought on by the invention of the steam engine and was particularly taken with how every machine is comprised of individual components that have to work in synchronicity to ensure optimal performance. Smith found a similar principle at work in the manufacturing process, which he described as division of labor. In *The Wealth of Nations*, Smith used the example of how in a pin factory, the production of a pin is divided up into eighteen distinct operations, all performed by different workers, resulting in a vast increase in the efficiency of producing pins en masse.

Mass production became the other great leap in efficiency that would catapult industrial capitalism to the forefront of economic life. Eli Whitney introduced the idea of mass-producing identical standardized and interchangeable parts that could be easily assembled by relatively unskilled workers and applied the process to the production of muskets. Division of labor and mass production were to become the indispensable processes at the heart of the new industrial efficiencies.

With the advent of industrial production, the economists set their sights on expanding capital and making labor more efficient, regarding both as key elements to generating productivity and profit. The new capitalist industrial system and the economists who described its workings strayed far afield from the early vision of the physiocrats, giving less consideration to nature's wealth and more to the role of capital and labor in advancing efficiency gains, productivity, and revenue—but with a hitch. The early economists came to understand that the invisible hand had failed to consider the principle of diminishing marginal utility.

At the inception of classical economics, Anne Robert Jacques Turgot was the first to discover the law of diminishing marginal returns on the supply side. He argued that producers invariably faced the prospect of reaching an optimal level of capacity utilization after which each individual factor of production yields a decrease per unit of incremental returns of profit. A century later, in the 1870s, a new generation of neoclassical economists—William Stanley Jevons, Carl Menger, and Léon Walras—discovered a similar process at work on the demand side that they described as the diminishing marginal utility of consumption.

The principle states that the first unit of consumption of a good or service yields greater utility—or pleasure—than the second, and each additional unit of consumption yields diminishing utility and pleasure. For example, a consumer is willing to pay more for her first ice-cream cone because of the initial pleasure it brings but is likely to pay less for each additional cone because of the decreasing marginal satisfaction or pleasure.

The nexus where diminishing marginal returns on production and diminishing marginal utility of consumption meet determines the agreed-upon price for the exchange. An increase in the price will lower buyers' consumption while raising the production part of suppliers. A decrease in the price will do the opposite—in either instance facilitating the appropriate market exchange and bringing the system back to equilibrium.

The new emphasis on the diminishing marginal utility of consumption had a huge impact on the field of economics. The classical economists—Adam Smith, David Ricardo, and John Stuart Mill—looked to the cost of labor as the distinctive element in establishing exchange value, while the neoclassical economists shifted the focus to the role of the consumer in determining exchange value. This cooled the debate over how much of the profit of production ought to go to the workers who produce the product or service versus the owners who provide the capital, leaving the process of market exchange devoid of equity issues—at least in the eyes of the new generation of neoclassical economists.

The principle of diminishing marginal utility also gave neoclassical economists what they needed to mathematize the discipline and join the ranks of Newtonism with the aspiration of becoming a bona fide science. Two of Jevons's contemporaries, Francis Ysidro Edgeworth and Philip Henry Wicksteed, went on to devise the appropriate mathematical calculus in the form of "indifference and contract curves, Lagrangian multipliers, and production coefficients," which are still used to this day.[38]

With all the enthusiasm generated around mathematizing economics, the neoclassical economists stubbornly remained committed to a mechanical universe made up of forces and counterforces, attracting and repelling, and always settling back into equilibrium. Listen to Jevons: "Just as the gravitating force of a material body depends not alone upon the mass of that body, but upon the masses and relative positions and distances of the surrounding material bodies, so utility is an attraction between a wanting being, and what is wanted."[39]

In fairness, Jevons was well aware of the difficulty of squaring the use of equilibrium theory of forces attracting, repelling, and always returning to equilibrium with a dynamic market where every single sale changes the milieu, forcing a new set of relationships, no matter how small the shift. He observed in his *Theory of Political Economy* that "the real condition of industry is one of perpetual motion and change."[40] Jevons acknowledged that the dynamic marketplace is difficult to study. He conceded that "it is only as a purely statical problem that I can venture to treat the action of exchange." Even more telling is his lament:

The Theory of Economy thus treated presents a close analogy to the science of Statistical Mechanics, and the Laws of [economic] Exchange are found to resemble the Laws of Equilibrium of a lever as determined by the principle of virtual velocities. . . . But I believe that dynamical branches of the Science of Economy may remain to be developed, on the consideration of which I have not at all entered.[41]

Jevons realized that his ardent belief in Newtonian physics and a mechanical universe in equilibrium didn't square with the reality of an ever-evolving economic marketplace, and reluctantly admitted that his economic theory was but a "close analogy." Even so, he hoped to reconcile a static mechanical universe in equilibrium with a dynamic economic marketplace self-evolving moment to moment—an impossible task.

The economists remained mute on the overriding importance of the laws of thermodynamics in defining not only the way the universe operates but also the evolution of life on Earth and the workings of the economy. However, many of the world's leading scientists in the fields of physics, chemistry, and biology continued to emphasize the importance of positioning the thermodynamic laws at the very center of the story of the nature of existence, further isolating the economics profession from a reality check.

Einstein was not the only eminent figure in science to explain that the first and second laws of thermodynamics are the overarching frame that governs the workings of the universe. In 1911, the Nobel laureate chemist Frederick Soddy, in his book *Matter and Energy,* admonished the economics profession for its blind disregard for the laws of thermodynamics and its slavish attachment to a Newtonian-centered equilibrium theory of economic activity that was not only contrary to the real underpinnings of economic practice but also a potentially deadly course that would imperil both civilization and the natural world. He reminded his economist colleagues that it is the laws of thermodynamics that "control, in the last resort, the rise or fall of political systems, the freedom or bondage of nations, the movement of commerce and industry, the origin of wealth and poverty, and the general physical welfare of the race."[42]

The Belgian chemist Ilya Prigogine, who was awarded a Nobel Prize in chemistry for his work on dissipative structures in chemistry and biology and the laws of thermodynamics and nonequilibrium thermodynamics, also spent a lifetime appealing to economists to eschew the Newtonian equilibrium model. In 1982, Prigogine delivered the Tanner Lecture at Jawaharlal Nehru University in India, reminiscing on what he had learned in his lifetime of work in the field of chemistry. He noted that "all of chemistry corresponds to irreversible processes" that obey the laws of thermodynamics—so too, in biology and physics.[43] How then could economics exist outside the realm of these basic laws that govern the universe?

Alluding to the economics profession, Prigogine explained that the laws of thermodynamics:

"[Lead] to a new view of matter in which matter is no longer passive, as described in the mechanical worldview, but is associated with spontaneous activity. This change is so deep that I believe we can speak about a new dialogue of man with nature."[44]

Prigogine suggested that:

the idea of an unchanging, permanent substrate for matter has been shattered . . . [thermodynamics] leads to a conception of matter as active, as in a continuous state of becoming. This picture deviates significantly from the classical description of physics, of change in terms of forces or fields. It is a momentous step to leave the royal road opened by Newton. . . . But I believe that the unification of dynamics and thermodynamics paves the way to a radically new description of temporal evolution of physical systems. . . . We now overcome the temptation to reject time as an illusion. Far from that . . . time is to be constructed.[45]

Prigogine concluded that "all these theoretical constructs have one element in common: they indicate some limit to our manipulation of nature."[46]

The economists disagree. Their assumption is that the economic process itself, if left relatively unfettered, will generate increasing wealth to be shared by the capitalist owners, the workforce, and consumers, with no upper limit except the creative inventiveness of the entrepreneurial class.

What, then, have been the consequences of living under an economic system wedded to a timeless mechanical universe, consumed by the expropriation of nature, obsessed with finding new technical means to increase the efficiencies in transforming "natural resources" into a short-lived orgy of consumption, always with a nod to cost-benefit analysis and increasing revenue? To put it in thermodynamic terms, the short-lived economic gains reaped over the two-and-a-half-century reign of industrial capitalism are both minuscule and fleeting in the wake of the long-term entropic bill whose imprint and negative externalities will be felt for eons to come. Knowing this, how do we rethink our notion of what constitutes wealth?

3

THE REAL WORLD

NATURE'S CAPITAL

I n actuality, the "real wealth" upon which the entire life process depends, and without which the economic system would not exist, remains remarkably unconsidered among economists and business leaders, and that is where negative externalities begin.

Net primary production—the production of plant biomass—is all of the carbon dioxide taken up by vegetation during photosynthesis minus the carbon dioxide lost by respiration. Net primary production is the generator of all wealth and the source upon which species feed up the food chain to secure their survival. The human race has been living off the net primary production of the earth over the past two hundred thousand years of its existence. Yet, during the course of the industrial era in the past two centuries our species gathered up an increasing amount of the planet's net primary production, transforming it into short-term productive wealth, allowing for a vast increase in human population and longevity.

There were approximately seven hundred million human beings on Earth at the dawn of the Industrial Revolution.[1] By the year 2000, there were more than six billion human beings populating the planet and we were appropriating 24 percent of global terrestrial net primary production.[2] Moreover, current projections suggest that with increasing population, human-appropriated net primary production could top 44 percent by 2050, leaving as little as 56 percent of the net primary production to be shared by the other species inhabiting the planet.[3]

But net primary production is not possible without nature's base capital, soil. No soil, no vegetation, no photosynthesis. The soil is a highly complex microenvironment. Its parental material is rock. Over a long period of time, rock is subjected to physical weathering and natural erosion brought on primarily by rain, wind, temperature, gravity, earthquakes, and volcanoes. Given enough time, the rock disintegrates into ever-smaller particles, which eventually become sand and sediment. Lichens mix with the sand and sediment, breaking it down to even smaller particles. Fungi and bacteria, burrowing insects, and animals also assist in the degrading of the rock into soil. The elements and minerals in the degraded rock are the critical ingredients of the soil.

Plants, in turn, grow in the soil. Animals eat the plants and contribute their feces to the soil. Worms and bacteria break down plant litter and animal waste, adding to the soil base. The average soil sample is composed of 45 percent minerals, 25 percent water, 25 percent air, and 5 percent organic matter. There are more than seventy thousand types of soil in the United States alone.[4]

GREAT EXPECTATIONS:
The Green Revolution in Agriculture

Part of the reason why the earth's topsoil is disappearing is directly related to the new efficiencies in plant genetics and industrial agriculture that gave rise to fast-growing, high-yield variety crops (HYV), the practice of monoculture, the use of more toxic pesticides and insecticides, new irrigation practices, and a three-crop planting season per annum, where before there was only one. All of these elements together dramatically increased agricultural production over a period from the 1960s to the mid-1980s, especially in India, China, and Southeast Asia, but also in Africa, Europe, the United States, and other regions.

It was called "The Green Revolution" and was the brainchild of Dr. Norman Borlaug, who was later awarded a Nobel Peace Prize for alleviating hunger in the developing world. When all is said and done, however, he left behind a degraded soil base too far gone to restore in time to prevent a critical shortage in food production in many regions.

Here's how it unfolded. An ambitious plan was established to dramatically increase the efficiency of agricultural production in India and, shortly thereafter, all of Southeast Asia, and later Africa and the rest of the developing world, to mitigate the growing problem of hunger. The plan was made up of several components, each of which was to complement the others and together create a great leap forward in agricultural production and output.

The first component was the planting of a new generation of HYV seeds that could produce higher yields per acre. The seeds were developed by Dr. Borlaug, and the funding was provided by the Ford and Rockefeller Foundations beginning in 1954. The seeds covered the basic crop staples of rice, wheat, corn, soybeans, and potatoes produced in developing countries. The high-yielding seeds were more responsive to petrochemical fertilizers, but dependent on extensive irrigation to ripen. The high-yield varieties of plants were also resistant to many diseases and matured quicker than conventional varieties of the same plants.

The goal was to optimize agricultural production in ever-shorter time intervals with the increased efficiencies leading to more profit and greater stores of food to feed a hungry and growing population in the poorest countries. Unfortunately, the efficiencies built into the HYV seeds came with a heavy environmental price, which left agricultural regions in Asia and elsewhere more impoverished, and their land and soil seriously degraded.

For starters, the HYV seeds were more expensive, making them less accessible to the poorer famers in developing countries. The high initial capital costs encouraged vertically integrated agricultural companies to sweep in and wrest control over immense tracts of unused land while buying out smaller plots of land from farmers and consolidating them into larger producing fields. The high costs were compounded by the need to introduce petrochemical fertilizers on a large scale. The intensification of production was accompanied by elaborate new irrigation systems to ensure a quicker maturation of the crops. The increase of the moisture in the soil brought with it more insects, requiring an increased use of pesticides and herbicides. The speedup of agricultural production also necessitated a greater outlay of expenditures to acquire tractors, threshers, and tillers as well as the erection of enlarged storage facilities to house the surplus and improved logistics and transport to more quickly move the grains to market.

In the first fifteen years of the Green Revolution in Asia, rice yields rose from 2.1 percent per annum to 2.9 percent.[5] More land was brought into cultivation during that period, further increasing rice yields. However, by the early 1980s, it was becoming evident that the Green Revolution was beginning to stall, and even backslide, with ever-declining yields. Something had gone wrong.

Here's what backfired. The increased efficiencies of fast-maturing HYV crops allowed farmers, who traditionally grew only one crop per annum—letting the soil lie fallow the rest of the year and renew its nutrient content—to grow two and even three crop plantings per year. And the new year-round growing season meant year-round irrigation, resulting in flooded fields and more soil runoff.

It was estimated that in India alone, six thousand million tons of topsoil was being leached annually.[6] The soil runoff, in turn, required more inputs of petrochemical fertilizers to replace the native soil, and more pesticides to ward off insects drawn to the flooded plots. To add to the misery, the plowing of the soil by tractors and the use of combines during harvest three times a year further damaged the microorganisms in the soil, reducing its fertility. These multiple interacting disruptions depleted the chemical and biological properties of a soil system that evolved over thousands of years.

When the assessments began to come in, it became apparent that the efficiencies of using quickly maturing high-yield variety seeds and extensive irrigation networks to stimulate their growth were resulting in the depletion of nutrients in the soil, giving rise to the term "nutrient stripping." The attachment of this term to the new agricultural practices marked a turning point in the aggrandizement of the Green Revolution and the beginning of a rethink of how to approach the future of agricultural production across not only the developing world but also the developed countries.

By the 1980s, the data on yields began to show a failed experiment on a massive global scale. The once lauded Green Revolution, heralded as a great scientific advance in the agricultural sciences that would vastly increase the efficiency of crop yields and revenue for farmers while providing cheaper food for a hungry world, had faltered. Farm data coming in from the principal rice-producing nations of Southeast Asia and the Pacific—central Luzon in the Philippines, Thailand, and West Java in Indonesia—showed that from 1980 to 1989:

> The rate of growth in yields was lower than the rate of growth in input use. In Central Luzon, a 13 percent yield increase over a ten-year period was achieved with a 21 percent increase in fertilizers, and a 34 percent increase in seeds. In the Central Plains, for the same period, yields increased by 6.5 percent, while fertilizer levels increased by 24 percent and pesticides by 53 percent. Similarly, for West Java, yields increased by 23 percent, while fertilizer use increased by 65 percent and pesticide use increased by 69 percent.

Lest we think that this is occurring only in the developing countries in Asia, and only with rice production, we need to think again. This change in agricultural practices was happening then and it is still happening now in all of the major farm producing regions of the world.

The Union of Concerned Scientists in the United States weighed in with "The Hidden Cost of Industrial Agriculture" in the American corn belt. The same HYV seeds and accompanying high inputs of irrigation, petrochemical fertilizers and pesticides, and large-scale monoculture of crops have resulted in similar negative externalities of massive soil loss, threatening the viability of the American farm belt and the U.S. economy.[7]

Like a growing number of reports on the state of global agriculture, the Union of Concerned Scientists puts the blame on increased scientifically based efficiencies.

> From its mid-20th century beginnings, industrial agriculture has been sold to the public as a technological miracle. Its efficiency, we were told, would allow food production to keep pace with a rapidly growing global population, while its economies of scale would ensure that farming remained a profitable business. But too often, something crucial was left out of this story: the price tag. In fact, our industrialized food and agriculture system comes with steep costs, many of which are picked up by taxpayers, rural communities, farmers themselves, other business sectors, and future generations. When we include these "externalities" in our reckoning, we can see that this system is not a cost-effective, healthful, or sustainable way to produce the food we need.[8]

The series of unintended missteps that took the once promising Green Revolution from the great hope of humankind to a dangerous depletion of the earth's topsoil and the prospect of global hunger on an unprecedented scale is what might be called the "pile-on effect." It is particularly striking how each component of the Green Revolution doubled back on the others and created still new unanticipated negative externalities in a cascading positive feedback loop.

Like it or not, each of us is caught up in a giant biosphere classroom where we are learning the lesson that each and every act we engage in requires some change, no matter how trifling, in the natural world we inhabit. None of us are ever autonomous but agents engaged in extractive and symbiotic relationships with the world that surrounds us. Ever greater efficiencies in everything we do increase our ecological footprint and our entropic bill. The only issue is how lightly we choose to tread.

The more efficient we become, the more negative externalities and positive feedback loops we can expect. Most of us have come to believe in the simplistic notion that an exchange of a good or service between a seller and a buyer in the market affects only the two parties involved, with little or no appreciable entropic effect that spreads out, touching off other negative externalities along the way. This is more than a bit naïve.

That's not to say that positive externalities can't also ripple out in our various acts of exchange, but the laws of thermodynamics and nonequilibrium thermodynamics are a hard taskmaster. Even positive externalities come with an entropic tail, certain to create their own negative externalities somewhere during their passage.

BEWARE SYNDEMICS

Apparently, we are beginning to get the message. A new term has surfaced that captures the emerging consciousness of what it means to live in a world governed by the laws of thermodynamics. It's called "syndemics," and was coined by Merrill Singer, a medical anthropologist at the University of Connecticut in the mid-1980s, who described how epidemics overlap with one another, creating positive feedbacks and spiraling negative externalities. In 2017, *The Lancet*, one of the oldest peer-reviewed medical journals in the world, gave the term credence in the publication of a series of reports describing the term in a much more expansive and detailed fashion. Then in 2019, *The Lancet* published a study entitled "The Global Syndemic of Obesity, Undernutrition, and Climate Change."[9]

In the study, *The Lancet* took on three global pandemics circling civilization—obesity, undernutrition, and climate change—and analyzed how each is playing off and affecting the other, taking us into a vicious cycle, similar to the one encountered by the Green Revolution. Interestingly, the negative externalities of the Green Revolution actually play a principal role in the unfolding of the new super syndemic.

The Lancet argues that the conjoining of obesity, undernutrition, and climate change "constitute[s] a syndemic, or synergy of epidemics, because they co-occur in time and place, interact with each other to produce complex sequelae, and share common underlying societal drivers."[10] Obesity, a little-known marginal issue a half century ago, has exploded, becoming the leading human health threat in the world, at least before the COVID-19 pandemic struck. By 2015, two billion human beings were characterized as obese. The illness results in four million deaths annually and a loss of one-hundred-twenty million disability-adjusted life years.[11] Equally stunning, the estimated cost attached to obesity has jumped to 2.8 percent of global GDP.[12] Add cardiovascular disease, lung disease, and diabetes resulting from obesity and the statistics leap off the chart.

The flashpoints for this disease trace back to the transition into petrochemically based agriculture in the 1950s, its extension in the 1960s with the onset of the Green Revolution and high-yield variety crops, and the late 1990s with the emergence of genetically engineered crops. Petrochemical agriculture accounts for upward of 23 percent of all greenhouse gas emissions and, as *The Lancet* report notes, if the downstream part of the food system is included—for example, transport, logistics, and waste management—food and agriculture is responsible for 29 percent of all global warming emissions.[13]

Moreover, with each one-degree rise in temperature attributed to global warming emissions, the water holding capacity of air increases by approximately 7 percent, leading to more concentrated precipitation in the clouds and the generation of more extreme water events: frigid winter temperatures and blockbuster snows; devastating spring floods; prolonged summer droughts and horrifying wildfires; and deadly category three, four, and five hurricanes into the fall, with unprecedented loss of life and property and destruction of ecosystems.[14]

The earth's biomes, which developed in tandem with a fairly predictable hydrological cycle over the 11,700 years since the end of the last Ice Age, cannot catch up with the runaway exponential curve currently driving the hydrological cycle, and they are collapsing in real time.[15]

Petrochemical agriculture also induces additional negative externalities that are little considered, but enormous in their impact. The application of petrochemical fertilizers atop a deteriorating soil base and the leaching of pesticides and insecticides into the soil is killing off the nutrient composition that is essential for healthy plant growth. And here is where the syndemic is triggered. The diminished nutrient value in the crops is transferred into a variety of food products eaten by nearly eight billion people. This means our species is not consuming enough nutrients required for healthy bodily functions over a lifetime. The Food and Agriculture Organization of the United Nations put it best with its motto "healthy soils are the basis for healthy food production."[16]

Industrial agriculture operates with the same overriding goal of other industrial sectors: that is, increasing efficiency across its value chains, in this case with the monoculture of crops, the heavy use of petrochemicals to speed the process, and the production and sale of low-nutrient and highly processed foods that will guarantee a long shelf life to enable product lines to be shipped globally and stored in inventories over longer periods of time. Processed foods are "high in calories, fats, sweeteners, and other carbohydrates," and are consumed by billions of people, triggering a runaway global epidemic of obesity, resulting in a rise in heart disease, diabetes, and other life-threatening illnesses.[17]

The change in the global food diet has had a massive impact on the health and well-being of billions of people who suffer from obesity-related life-threatening

diseases. As to how this has come to pass, it all goes back to the increasing rationalization of a global food industry controlled by a small number of multinational corporations dedicated to increasing efficiencies across their value
chains and improving their revenues. James Tillotson, an emeritus professor
of food policy and international business at the Friedman School of Nutrition
Science and Policy at Tufts University, sums up the matter, pointing out that
"you have a whole regime here that works to increase agricultural efficiency."[18]

Highly processed foods—which are energy dense and nutrient poor—
are cheaper and bought and consumed mainly by low- and moderate-income
families whose children are often already preconditioned metabolically from
birth to obesity because their parents are obese.

According to a study authored by Dr. Peter Dolton, a professor of economics at the University of Sussex, in the journal *Economics and Human Biology*,
"the intergenerational transmission mechanism is both a biological process . . .
and also shared environmental process . . . we find that the joint effect of the
family and its associated genetic makeup accounts for around 35–40 percent
of the child's likely BMI [Body Mass Index]."[19] The genetic predisposition to
pass on obesity generation after generation is a marketing dream for the food-
processing industry, ensuring them a strong consumer base for their product
lines, but unfortunately at the price of plunging successive generations into
deteriorating health by this inherited negative externality.

The food industry has accelerated its efficiencies with the introduction
of "fast foods," conditioning generations of consumers to a diet of processed
foods with low nutrient content. By adding massive doses of high-fructose
corn syrup, sugars, and fats—to what is euphemistically called "comfort" foods
and drinks—each generation becomes addicted over a lifetime to a diet that
all but guarantees threatening health issues and costly health bills. The fast-
food culture brought the processes of rationalization and efficiency into the
heart of food preparation and consumption while simultaneously addicting
the public to a more fattening and less nutritious diet.

Quick-service restaurants favor processed foods and rarely serve fresh fruits
and vegetables. It's all designed around efficiency. After all, fresh fruits and vegetables have a shorter shelf life compared with processed foods. Fruits and vegetables require additional logistics to ensure they are made available on a timely
basis, while processed foods require less attention due to their longer shelf life.

The United States Department of Agriculture (USDA) found that food
away from home's "share of total average daily energy intake increased from
17 percent in 1977–78 to 34 percent in 2011–12, and consumption of QSR
[quick-service restaurant] foods was the largest source of this growth."[20] The

USDA concludes that food away from home "contained more saturated fats and sodium, and less calcium, iron, and fiber."[21] Notwithstanding, efficient eating has been sold to the public as a pleasurable experience.

The Lancet's study on the syndemic of obesity, undernutrition, and climate change, although nuanced, didn't cover the many other negative externalities that at first glance may seem unrelated. In recent months, the scientific and medical community has become alarmed by the discovery of a relationship between the COVID-19 pandemic and the syndemic of obesity, malnutrition, and climate change. The COVID-19 data shows that among the most at-risk in contracting the virus and dying are the chronically obese, that part of the population who suffer most from diabetes, heart disease, and lung disease, the same global cohort that was birthed and courted by the global food industry during the Green Revolution and subsequent biotech agricultural revolution.

Many negative externalities are simply difficult to foresee. For example, consider the relationship between antibiotics, obesity, and the COVID-19 pandemic. Antibiotics were among the wonder drugs of the 20th century, saving millions of lives. My sister and I were among the first babies in the U.S. to be treated with penicillin. We were born in January 1945 and were extremely premature, with each of us weighing less than 2.5 pounds and not expected to live. Penicillin saved our lives.

Antibiotics went into large-scale use after World War II, first in America and then virtually everywhere else. There are more than one hundred antibiotics in use today for treating bacterial infections. What worries the medical community is that many of these antibiotics are no longer effective because of overuse. Bacteria have successfully mutated and become resistant to the drugs.

According to the U.S. Centers for Disease Control and Prevention (CDC), forty-seven million antibiotic prescriptions are written up each year in the United States for infections that don't require them or as a cautionary preventative.[22] A similar pattern of overprescribing antibiotics is seen in veterinary and agricultural use. The CDC reports that "more than 2.8 million antibiotic-resistant infections occur in the U.S. each year."[23] Globally, about seven hundred thousand people die each year from drug-resistant diseases.[24]

The World Bank warns that drug-resistant bacterial infections are the next great pandemic and "could cause global economic damage on par with the 2008 Financial Crisis."[25] In a study issued in 2017 titled *Drug-Resistant Infections: A Threat to Our Economic Future*, researchers report that antimicrobial resistance (AMR) results in increased hospital stays and deaths, and we could see a drop in global GDP by as much as 3.8 percent by 2050 in the developed nations, and by 5 percent or more in low-income nations.[26] The value of global trade could plummet by as much as 3.8 percent while health care costs could reach $1.2 trillion per year.[27]

What keeps the medical establishment up at night with COVID-19 is lung disease. It turns out that in the Spanish flu pandemic of 1918–20, the majority of the deaths were not caused by the virus itself but rather from secondary bacterial pneumonia infections in the lungs, according to Dr. Anthony Fauci of the U.S. National Institutes of Health (NIH).[28] The concern is that the dramatic increase in the use of antibiotics to treat lung-related bacterial infections brought on by the COVID-19 epidemic could accelerate the mutation of resistant strains of bacteria, making the existing arsenal of antibiotics useless, with calamitous consequences for humanity.

Our overly simplified notion of limited cause and effect in measuring benefits and costs, although appearing to be benign, can unleash a firestorm of interactive and interconnective negative externalities with long life spans.

WE ARE THE FOSSIL FUEL PEOPLE

The whole of the Age of Progress is but a misnomer for a deeper narrative that until recently remained tucked away. It can be said, without overstatement, that the modern era is the Age of Fossil Fuels. If our species survives this moment in Earth's history, future generations will know of us only by our remaining carbon footprint in the geological record. Just as we characterize our distant ancestors as the Stone Age people, Bronze Age people, and Iron Age people, future generations eons from now will think of us as the Carbon Age people.

Although we normally associate fossil fuels with the energy that powers our vehicles, heats our homes and workplaces, generates our electricity, and is used in synthetic fertilizers and pesticides, in fact they also provide the heat to produce the vital material components of our economy—for example, steel. Fossil fuels are found in innumerable products, including construction materials, plastics, packaging, pharmaceuticals, food additives and preservatives, lubricants, synthetic rubber, synthetic clothing, cosmetics, detergents, furniture, and electronics.

The bulk of our economic activity is either comprised of fossil fuels or transformed and moved by them. What goes into our bodies, homes, businesses, offices, and factories is to a large extent mediated by and/or made up of fossil fuels.

The negative externalities and syndemics wrought by petrochemical ag-riculture, the Green Revolution, and biotech farming, while devastating, are not a one-off. Every industry and sector of the global economy tells a simi-lar story. Although these negative externalities all differ in degree, they are alike in kind.

Consider the global fashion industry. When we think of the big polluters responsible for global warming emissions and other negative externalities affecting the environment, the global fashion industry, until recently, was under the radar and given a pass. Not anymore. The industry generates 10 percent of all global warming emissions, more than all the international flights and maritime shipping combined. It's also the second-largest pol-luter of water.[29]

The fashion industry's huge carbon and water footprint has everything to do with its increasing efficiencies in production and savvy advertising and marketing campaigns to convince consumers to stay up with fashions each season by throwing out last season's purchases and buying new. Much of the efficiency gains have come from outsourcing parts of the production process to developing nations with lax or nonexistent environmental standards, and whose labor forces receive bare subsistence wages and work under Dicken-sian conditions in unsafe factories.

These increased efficiencies have dramatically reduced the cost of apparel and increased consumer purchases. In 2020 in the European Union, the av-erage consumer of clothes and footwear tallied more purchases, but with less expenditure than a decade ago. In the United States, the average consumer purchases an item of clothing every 5.5 days.[30] It's no wonder that the lifetime use of a garment has also been substantially reduced by 36 percent compared to fifteen years ago.[31] The fashion industry projects that "if demographic and lifestyle patterns continue as they are now, global consumption of apparel will rise from sixty-two million metric tons in 2019 to one hundred and two million tons in 10 years."[32]

More purchases and less use time translates into more waste. The indus-try is responsible for ninety-two million tons of waste generated per annum and some estimates suggest that 25 to 30 percent of the fabric used is wasted in just the manufacturing of the garments.[33] In the European Union alone, upward of one-third of the garment inventory goes unsold each season and ends up being discarded. Adding textiles damaged and discarded during the manufacturing process puts fashion at 22 percent of all the mixed waste going into the global environment annually (less than 15 percent of post-consumer textile waste is recycled).[34]

Textile manufacturers also use more than 2,500 chemicals in the manufacturing process, and one study found that 10 percent of those chemicals were
of "high potential concern for human health." Finally, the fashion industry
uses approximately forty-four trillion liters of water a year for irrigation, or
about 3 percent of all irrigation water use.[35]

For most of the Industrial Age, fossil fuels were so cheap that we paid little attention to how critical they were to increasing efficiencies. As discussed
earlier, although economists included energy along with time, capital, and
labor as the principal inputs that determine efficiencies, with the exception
of engineers, businesses usually ignored it in determining productivity because it was so cheap. They focused almost exclusively on the cost/benefit of
capital and labor in increasing efficiencies.

In hindsight, the naïveté, especially among economists, is telling. Rarely
does one find even a passing mention in the literature acknowledging that
most human capital in the industrial era is the stored wealth generated, one
way or another, by fossil fuels that keep every worker alive and healthy.

The reality that the very existence of our civilization is intertwined with
fossil fuels only became obvious in the face of the sudden increase in the price
of oil on world markets in the first decade of the 21st century. In the 1960s,
oil was selling at a mere $3 per barrel. Oil prices began to rise in fits and starts
with the imposition of the Organization of the Petroleum Exporting Countries oil embargo in 1973. In the first decade of the 21st century, oil continued to spike ever higher, reaching a record peak of $147 a barrel in July 2008.

When oil went over $100 a barrel, the global economy began to slide, be-
cause so much of the things we manufacture and produce are made out of and
moved by fossil fuels. By the time oil capped at $147 a barrel, the entire global
economy had ground to a halt, because the price of virtually every good and
service in the economy is intrinsically connected to fossil fuels.

July 2008 marked the beginning of the end of the fossil fuel–based Industrial Age. It was the seismic earthquake from which society has never fully
recovered. The collapse of the financial market mired in subprime mortgages—
which is akin to a giant Ponzi scheme—was the aftershock. It was impossible to maintain the fictional economy of mortgage price manipulation when
the hard-core fossil fuel economy shut down every corner of economic life.

Our global business community, governments, and certainly our economists have yet to fully understand that the steep upward climb in efficiencies
and productivity that generated unparalleled material wealth would not have
been conceivable were it not for the exhumation and transformation of the
fossil fuels of a distant geological period in history. The flip side of animating

the Carboniferous burial ground with its storehouse of bounded energy and dissipating it in less than two hundred years to create the Age of Progress is that we have been left with an entropy bill in the form of global warming emissions that is now threatening the future of life on Earth.

Given the shortcomings of market equilibrium theory and the rationalization process that puts efficiencies at the center of the equation while steadfastly refusing to acknowledge the thermodynamic implications of negative externalities, what's needed is a complete rethinking of economics and, more important, the nature of human agency. That rethinking first requires coming to grips with the way we have perceived the very notions of time and space.

Admittedly, our long-held ideas of time and space seem far removed from the crisis we find ourselves in. Yet reassessing the way we have come to understand and know these primal coordinates of human consciousness is essential to extricating our collective humanity from the toxic brew of rationality and efficiency, euphemistically referred to as the Age of Progress, and helping us find our way to a more adaptive and empathic way to live that is more befitting of the coming Age of Resilience. Rethinking our very existence in time and space is likely our species' last best chance to change course and learn how to thrive on an unpredictable and rewilding Earth.

Part Two

PROPERTIZING THE EARTH AND PAUPERIZING THE WORKFORCE

4

THE GREAT DISRUPTION

THE PLANETARY ENCLOSURE OF TIME AND SPACE

It was May 24, 1844. Members of the U.S. Congress assembled to witness an extraordinary event. Years earlier, the U.S. Congress had agreed to finance the development of a device by an American inventor, Samuel F. B. Morse, who promised he could perfect a machine—an electric telegraph—that would tap into electric currents and send an encoded communication to a location forty miles away instantaneously and receive the coded response in a matter of seconds on a paper tape. It was a promise that would have been difficult to even contemplate previously.[1]

Morse dispatched a message to his assistant, Alfred Veil, forty miles away at a railroad station in Baltimore, requesting a response. Seconds later, the response came back to the U.S. Capitol. The returned message read, "What Hath God Wrought?" That moment marked the virtual annihilation of spatial distance and the compression of temporal duration to near simultaneity, signaling the beginning of the electronic age. The saying was pirated from the Bible and appears in the Book of Numbers: a more than fitting utterance that captured the moment.

Recall in the book of Genesis that God brought the world into existence with the command of "Let there be light" and without any passage of time "it was so," the perfection of efficiency. Morse's near simultaneous communication was met with awe by members of Congress, conjuring up the kind of efficiency that previously might have been reserved for the Lord Almighty.

The story of how we came to this juncture in history and a fundamental transformation in our notion of time and space begins rather innocently in the 14th century in medieval Europe with two developments that would later come to define the modern age. The first was the invention of the mechanical clock and the rigorous scheduling of time by Benedictine monks in their daily liturgies. The second was the invention of linear perspective in painting by artists during the Italian Renaissance.

THE MECHANICAL CLOCK AND LINEAR PERSPECTIVE IN ART:
The Unintentional Consequences That Changed History

The Benedictines were a Christian monastic order founded in 529 by Benedict of Monte Cassino. The Benedictines were dedicated to strenuous manual labor and strict religious observance. Their cardinal rule was "idleness is the enemy of the soul." The brothers believed that continuous manual activity was a form of penitence and a path to securing eternal salvation. St. Benedict cautioned his brothers that "if we wish to escape the pains of hell and attain eternal life, we must hasten to do such things only as they profit us for eternity, now while there is still time."[2]

The Benedictines were the first to perceive of the passage of time as "a scarce resource" and because time belonged to God, they had to use it to the fullest to pay homage to the Lord. To this end, every moment was to be given over to organized activity. There were appointed times to pray, labor, eat, read, bathe, and sleep.[3]

To ensure that all the brethren adhered to the prescribed routines and activities in concert, the Benedictines reintroduced the Roman hour, which had been virtually abandoned after the fall of Rome. Literally every activity was assigned an appropriate hour of the day, and to make sure everyone showed up on time, they introduced bells to announce each activity. The most important bells summoned the faithful to the eight canonical hours, when the monks celebrated the divine office. But, even the most ordinary of activities were given a time slot during designated weeks and even seasons, including head shaving, mattress refilling, and bloodletting. No time was left to chance.

The Benedictines were perhaps the first cohort in history to rationalize time by what we call "the schedule" in the modern era. For that reason, they are often regarded as "the first 'professional' of Western civilization."[4] The group synchronization of highly correlated routines, with each member ascribed a specific role, has not gone unnoticed by historians of a later period. Sociologist Eviatar Zerubavel said the Benedictines "helped to give the human enterprise the regular collective beat and rhythm of the machine."[5]

Despite the fanatical zeal to be on time, the Benedictines faced the problem that human bell ringers were not always reliable. The answer was the invention of the mechanical clock circa 1300—an automated machine that ran by a device called an escapement, a mechanism that "regularly interrupted the force of a falling weight," controlling the release of energy and the movement of the gears.[6] The new device allowed the brethren to standardize the length of hours so they could schedule their daily activities with precision and supervise their efforts with greater reliability.

This technological marvel was so extraordinary that the word soon spread from the monastery to the urban communes, where clocks became the centerpiece of every town square and the coordinator of daily commercial and social life. Commercial life, and life in general, was becoming increasingly efficient and not only required greater punctuality but also precision. In 1577, the minute hand was introduced, and, shortly thereafter, the second hand.[7] Calibrating time became a fetish and pastime. With the incipient rise of the Industrial Age and market capitalism, "Time is money" became the new adage of the era. By the 1790s, timepieces, once a spectacle and luxury, had become affordable necessities in every home, and workers were even beginning to wear pocket watches.

In Jonathan Swift's *Gulliver's Travels*, the wise men of Lilliput reported to the emperor that the alien giant they had shackled was continually reaching into his pocket, taking out a shiny object that made an incessant noise like a windmill, and putting "this engine to his ear." Their conjecture was that: "It is either some unknown animal, or the god that he worships; but we are more inclined to the latter opinion; because he assured us . . . that he seldom did anything without consulting it."[8]

The clock and pocket watch were steadily reorienting the public to draw away from nature's time, calculated by the sunrise, high noon, and sunset, and toward the steady beat of mechanical time on the factory floor. The adjustment to the factory production system that required unerring attention in the synchronization of activity was a milestone on the way to a hyperefficient civilization.

Parenthetically, the Benedictines had no intention of seeing their invention used to promote a more efficient secular life that would eventually undercut the theological worldview of medieval Christendom. Henceforth, time itself would be perceived as standard measurable units operating in a parallel universe unbeholden to the rhythms of the earth. It would be dedicated to the mechanistic vision of increasing efficiencies in expropriating and consuming the whole of the natural world—all in the name of economic progress. The repercussions would come to wreak havoc in the closing decades of the modern era.

Just a century later, a Florentine architect and artist, Filippo Brunelleschi, became the first European to paint a picture using linear perspective. Other artists quickly followed. Linear perspective in art would become the tool that changed the way humanity perceived space. The imaginative turning point in spatial orientation would inspire the birth of the scientific method and the mathematization of space and provide the tools and techniques by which modern cartography would enclose and privatize the earth's spheres.

In feudal Europe, place mattered, and the idea of empty space would have been inconceivable. In the world of Christendom, the faithful conceived of every place in God's kingdom as occupied by an ascending order of God's creation—a ladder reaching up from the lowliest creatures that "crawlith upon the earth" to human beings, the angels, and the Lord on high. God's kingdom is a plenitude, without any spatial vacuum. Why would God have left his creation with a vacuum to be filled at some future date? Alfred W. Crosby, a professor of history and geography at Harvard University, put it best, pointing out that "vacancy had no authenticity or autonomy for a people who rejected vacuum as a possibility."[9]

Perched high up on the ladder that made up the Great Chain of Being and just below the angels are the heirs of Adam and Eve, whose eyes are always focused upward to heaven. There would be little reason to gaze outward to the horizon in a fallen world, perceived as a temporary stayover in anticipation of their ascendance to heaven and eternal life.

When American tourists visit Europe, they are often put off upon seeing the great medieval cathedrals. They expect to capture the cathedral's majesty from a distance and to "gaze" on its overwhelming presence in space, only to be disappointed that it is densely embedded in the center of concentric circles of medieval and modern habitats blocking their view. That's because in feudal Europe, the empty horizon beyond the city gates and surrounding fields lurked with dangers. Collective security came from being nestled close to the bosom of God's cathedral. When one walks through the imposing doors, eyes immediately look up into the overarching vaults and toward heaven above, where their eternal life awaits.

As to the paintings and tapestries that adorn cathedral walls, they depict God's creation on a flat plane with all the living forms ascending upward toward heaven. To the eye of the visitor, the paintings appear dreamlike and childish. While beautiful, the paintings lack depth—they are without perspective. They don't appear "realistic."

Brunelleschi tore up the church's script by using linear perspective to depict the baptistery in Florence from the front gate of the cathedral while it was still under construction. The linear perspective projected the illusion of three-dimensional depth by use of a "vanishing point" to which all lines converge, at eye level, on the horizon.[10] His brushstrokes touched off one of the great revolutionary transitions in world history, which changed the very way our species has come to perceive space and our relationship to it. Michelangelo, Leonardo da Vinci, Raphael, and Donatello soon put brush to canvas, painting their own masterpieces depicting perspective.

The artist Masaccio was the first of the Renaissance painters to demonstrate a mature command of the use of perspective and the rules that accompany it. His paintings have volume and the habitats and landscapes recede into the distance the same way the naked eye perceives them. Art historians refer to the new artistic style as "realism."

Try to imagine the herculean forces let loose by this simple artistic maneuver. Previously, for the untutored and illiterate masses, what they learned about the reality of existence was to be found in the paintings that adorned their great cathedrals. It was their only classroom. The faithful had long been comforted by paintings that depicted a huddled humanity—a community of believers—anxiously awaiting the return of Christ to Earth and their eternal salvation of being lifted up to heaven. From now on they would be looking at paintings that repositioned the eye to gaze out at a horizon, much of which still remained unfilled and ready to be transformed.

Perhaps the most transformative aspect of the use of perspective in art is that it led the way to a shift in human consciousness. It prepared successive generations to conceive of the world from the point of view of the "seeing eyes" of the observer. Everything in one's gaze becomes a potential "object" to assess, size up, capture, expropriate, and privatize.

To see the world as a detached observer is to remove oneself from the fray of one's surroundings and assume the role of a voyeur. It's not coincidental that many of the master paintings of the Renaissance depict a lone observer looking out a window at what exists beyond. The very notion of an autonomous self took wings in the Italian and later northern European Renaissance.

Many of the early artists applying linear perspective in their paintings were also architects by trade and used their knowledge of perspective to make architectural drawings. The lessons learned in their artworks carried over to the field of mathematics with the development of projective geometry.

Galileo, the father of modern science, banked the whole of his scientific pursuits on the lessons he learned from artists and architects on the mathematics of perspective. Born in 1564 near Florence, Galileo took up the study of mathematics, where he was introduced to perspective in art. Not unexpectedly, mathematicians at the time, both in Italy and in Germany, were immersed in the art of using perspective to advance their discipline. After all, both fields were about measurement and calculations. There was regular interplay during this fertile gestational period of modern science among artists, architects, and mathematicians, all of whom were using lessons learned in both perspective and the study of geometry.

Galileo himself toyed with becoming an artist and aspired to become the official artist of the Medici. Like Descartes, Galileo helped introduce mathematics into science, transforming scientific exploration into mathematical measurement of observable phenomena, within which it still remains today. In his book *Il Saggiatore*, published in 1623, Galileo writes:

> Philosophy is written in this grand book, the universe, which stands continually open to our ["gaze"]. But the book cannot be understood unless one first learns to comprehend the language and read the letters in which it is composed. It is written in the language of mathematics, and its characters are triangles, circles, and other geometric figures without which it is humanly impossible to understand a single word of it; without these, one wanders about in a dark labyrinth.[11]

Philipp Lepenies, director of the Environmental Policy Research Center at the Free University of Berlin, observes that Galileo's use of the word "gaze" in his scientific observations harks back to the widespread application of linear perspective in art. The scientist, like the artist, is a detached observer, gazing out at the object of his or her inspection, using mathematics as a means of measurement to objectify and know phenomena being studied.[12]

To be "objective," which translates to being detached and rational, has maintained its hold as much on popular culture as in the rarefied world of science for more than half a millennium of history, and alongside it the notion that every one of us is an autonomous agent gazing out on the world, objectifying and expropriating it to secure our selfhood.

The shift to linear perspective in art wasn't just about painting more realistically, or even advancing geometry and mathematics and elevating the scientific method to become the gold standard for discovering the truths of all phenomena in the world. On a deeper level, the elevation of sight came at the expense of the depreciation of aurality. So accustomed are we to the idea that "seeing is believing" that it is difficult to imagine that in earlier cultures, orality figured more prominently in validating reality. In feudal Europe, where oral cultures ruled, learning was in the way of apprenticeship and the passing on of knowledge by word of mouth. Contractual arrangements, for example, were mostly made by way of oral agreements.

While the visual sense is detached and removed, hearing is close up and intimate. And sound surrounds, it envelops. Oral cultures are localized. When travelers visited traditional societies, at least until the 20th century, they often noticed how close people would nestle up to each other, often all talking at the same time. To a Western observer, this display often seemed invasive and disrespecting of each other's space and individuality. What's missed is that oral cultures are deeply participatory and communal for the simple reason that oral communication has limited spatial reach.

SILENT COMMUNICATION:
A New Approach to Socialization

If the schedule and clock enclosed time and perspective in art sped the process of expropriating and enclosing space, the invention of the printing press was an equally transformative force in enclosing both temporality and space, like the invention of the telephone in the late 19th century and the internet in the late 20th century. The printing press was instrumental in advancing mass literacy across Europe and eventually around the world. It allowed millions of people far distant from one another in time and space to silently share communication on the written page.

Learning by reading was also a more solitary and cerebral experience compared with oral culture. Reading is meant to be done in privacy. Although oral communication is fleeting, print is permanent, allowing us to hold on to the words and thoughts, storing them and returning to them to reference. In oral cultures, communication must be stored in one's memory, offering only limited ability to recall. That's why oral cultures relied on mnemonics and rhyme to store their memories.

Print exercised the mind in other novel ways, particularly in nurturing reflection. A reader could reflect on or even turn back the pages to revisit information, opening up the human imagination to wholly new ways of thinking.

Print also created the idea of individual authorship—the ability to claim one's words as property in the form of copyrights. Claiming sentences as property would have been absurd in earlier periods of history. The premodern philosophers didn't think of their musings as "original thoughts," but rather as "revelations" that came to them from the ether often through dreams or in awestruck moments. Authorship, by contrast, reinforced the belief in autonomous selfhood—that each individual is the proprietor of his or her unique communications with others.

Commercial life was similarly transformed by print. Bookkeeping in the feudal era relied mainly on oral agreements. The limited spatial reach meant that commercial agents generally acted locally, relying on knowing each other firsthand. Written bookkeeping records were less trusted, and the numbers and terms on the ledger were read aloud to the parties to ensure their authenticity. The term "audit" has survived the centuries, hearkening to an earlier, more oral culture. In the Gospel of Luke, Ambrose of Milan cautioned that "sight is often deceived, hearing serves as guarantee."[13] Today, we have come to trust the written word as gospel.

Books capture and sequester time itself. A book has an aura of permanence attached to it. Even today, in the electronic age, most people would be appalled at the act of tearing up a book or throwing it in the garbage. Time is frozen in space inside the pages of a book, just as a photograph would become frozen in time in the 19th century. The change in consciousness brought on by the printed word would come to condition the way scientists and economists freeze time and claim space in their respective disciplines.

We often hear the terms scientific point of view, economic point of view, psychological point of view, ad nauseam, only subliminally aware that the word "view" is endowed with truth and the only way to "envision" what's real—"the only way to look at a thing." The oral sense of what is real and true has been marginalized during the course of the modern era.

The print revolution was instrumental in enabling the great wave of exploration across the oceans and the discovery of new spaces to enclose. New discoveries of oceanic trade routes and descriptions of coastlines and landmasses could be standardized in printed maps, allowing seafarers more accurate navigation. Standardized maps dramatically increased the temporal efficiency of ocean travel, colonization of new lands, and commercial trade from the 16th century onward.

Print also furthered the new idea of nationhood. The nation-state would have been impossible to conceive without a common language to bind its citizenry together as an extended social family. Consider the problem that on the eve of the French Revolution, barely 50 percent of the population in what we now call France spoke French.[14] At the moment Italy was unified in 1861, only 2.5 percent of the population spoke standard Italian.[15] The prime minister of Piedmont was said to have declared, "We have made Italy. Now we must make Italians."[16]

It was the printers who came to the rescue. Printers were anxious to increase their efficiencies, sales, and revenues by mass-producing books, but were stymied by literally hundreds of local languages and dialects, the markets being too small to warrant the printing of books. To remedy the situation and establish a more efficient means of marketing, printers began to combine elements of the various idioms spoken in a region and then standardized the grammar in a singular vernacular language, generally the most dominant in a region, and ensured its adoption by the young nation-states as their official language.

Adopting a common language came with the added value of forging a sense of common national identity. Individuals began to experience one another as an extended family of citizens wedded to common loyalty to their state. Reducing the number of spoken and written languages to only a single vernacular language in each nation-state also vastly increased the efficiencies in commerce, social life, and governance.

EXHUMING COAL AND BLOWING OFF STEAM

The revolution in print communication was followed by equally powerful revolutions in energy and mobility. The dramatic diminution of forestlands across Europe to make room for agriculture, pastoralization, and urban development led to a continental energy crisis. Forests, after all, were the main source of energy and building materials in European society before the Industrial Revolution. The British found an alternative in the mining of coal. The problem was that at a particular depth, the water level was reached, making drainage an impediment to bringing the coal to the surface.

In 1698, Thomas Savery gave Europe the solution with the invention and patenting of a steam pump to remove water from the depths of mines. However, once brought to the surface, coal presented a second problem. It was much heavier and bulkier to transport than wood, difficult to ship across unsurfaced roads (especially in rainy weather), and horse teams were too expensive to employ. The answer came with James Watt's patenting of the steam engine in 1776. First used in the production process in the cotton industry in the 1780s, coal-fired steam engines soon spread to other industries, and became a tour de force with the first deployment of a steam-powered locomotive on rails in Britain in 1804.[17]

The sheer speed of the steam locomotive mesmerized the British public. By the 1830s, steam locomotives were operating at a breathtaking speed of sixty miles per hour. By 1845, "forty-eight millions of passengers already used the railways of the United Kingdom in a single year."[18] Steam locomotives were obliterating time barriers and compressing distances traveled and, in so doing, creating a powerful new dynamic in transportation and logistics whose hyperefficiencies would reverberate across the world, laying the basis for continental trade on a scale hitherto unimaginable.

Locomotives were also virtually impervious to seasonal swings in the weather and could operate year-round. In terms of speed of delivery, a steam-powered locomotive could make several trips back and forth in the time it took a canal barge to make one. Steam locomotives could also handle three times the freight as barges at an equivalent price, all of which added up to a historic acceleration in speed and efficiency in time and space.

As early as the 1830s, steamships were operating in open seas, with costs that were 15 to 20 percent lower than sailing ships. By 1900, steamships were carrying 75 percent of the global tonnage of cargo. Steamships were also ferrying millions of European immigrants to American shores. The name of the game was efficiencies—all made possible by exhuming coal from the burial grounds of the Carboniferous era.

The compression of time and space occasioned by the coming together of new forms of communication, a new source of energy, and new modes of mobility and logistics to communicate, power, and move economic activity, social life, and governance enthroned efficiency as the dominant theme of society by the 1890s, at least in Europe and America.

THE STANDARDIZATION OF WORLD TIME

There was only one fly in the ointment. Every locality set its clocks to its own time preferences, causing a logistics nightmare for the railroads. In 1870, a rail passenger traveling from Washington, D.C., to San Francisco would have to set his or her watch more than two hundred times to stay current with local time zones along the route.[19] If localized time zones were allowed to remain in place, the potential efficiencies in logistics and trade that came with steam locomotives and steamships would be forever lost. The clear need was to bring rationalization into the flow of transportation and logistics to enable the potential new efficiencies and accompanying productivity that steam locomotives and steamships offered an emerging Industrial Age.

Creating national, continental, and global markets for commerce and trade required a transition in the organization of time and space. The proposed solution was daring. The plan was to desocialize and delocalize time by establishing standard universal time zones across the entire world.

The British and American governments were the first to divide their countries into standardized time zones to accommodate rail services and by the 1880s other nations were clamoring for the implementation of a single world time. In October 1884, the International Meridian Conference voted to make Greenwich, near London, as the marker to locate zero longitude for the implementation of a universal time system. The French government opposed the siting at Greenwich, in favor of making the Paris observatory the timekeeper. The squabble dragged on for decades.

In 1912, however, Paris hosted the International Conference on Time, attended by various nations, and made it official. Greenwich would be marked as zero longitude, and hereafter participating nations agreed to abandon their local times for a world timing system. With this single stroke, time was separated from local temporalities and the rhythms of the earth to serve commerce, logistics, and trade in a newly globalized economy.

The abstraction, rationalization, and compression of time and space continued on into the 20th and 21st centuries with the subsequent discoveries of vast deposits of oil and natural gas, the introduction of electricity, the invention of the telephone, the coming of the auto age and air travel, the advent of radio, television, the computer, the internet, artificial intelligence and algorithm governance, and GPS interconnectivity, with long-lasting impacts on how our species perceives time and space and the very nature of existence.

With these new temporal and spatial coordinates, humanity has successfully enclosed, partially privatized, and expropriated the great spheres of the earth and the other agencies that make up the intimate geochemistry, physics, and biology of the planet. All have been captured, pillaged, and consumed with a hedonistic zeal driven by efficiencies unparalleled in the short existence of our species. Unfortunately, this history has been circumscribed in most accounts of the modern age and deserves to be aired.

5

THE ULTIMATE HEIST

COMMODIFYING THE EARTH'S SPHERES, GENE POOL, AND ELECTROMAGNETIC SPECTRUM

P roperty in the feudal society meant something different from what we understand it to be today. The church's view was that the earth is God's creation and entrusted to the descendants of Adam and Eve. God grants his flock the right to use parts of his domain in a descending hierarchy of obligations and responsibilities reaching down from Heaven on high to God's emissaries in the church and from there to the kings, princes, lords, and serfs. In this scheme of things, proprietary relations rather than property relations reigned. No one owned property the way we think of it today but only exercised proprietorship over those parts of the Lord's creation that he bequeathed in descending order. Buying and selling land did not play a prominent role in feudal Europe.

PROPERTIZATION OF THE EARTH'S SPHERES

By the 18th century, the feudal regime of proprietary relations had begun to collapse, giving way to the modern notion of private ownership astride an incipient capitalist system. The English philosopher John Locke provided the philosophical foundation for a wholesale rethinking of property in his *Two Treatises on Civil Government* that was published in 1690.

Locke argued that private property is an unalienable natural right, affirming God's promise to Adam in the Garden of Eden that he and all his progeny would have dominion over his earthly kingdom and all of the creatures that dwell therein, as well as the bountiful fruits the earth brings forth. Locke makes clear that:

> When [God] gave the world in common to all mankind, [He] commanded man also to labour, and the penury of his condition required it of him. God and his reason commanded him [humankind] to subdue the earth—i.e., improve it for the benefit of life, and therein lay out something upon it that was his own, his labour. He that, in obedience to this command of God, subdued, tilled, and sowed any part of it, thereby annexed to it something that was his property, which another had no title to, nor could without injury take from him.[1]

More disturbing, however, is Locke's categorization of nature as waste until man harnesses it and transforms it into valuable property.

> He who appropriates land to himself by his labour, does not lessen, but increases the common stock of mankind. For the provisions serving to the support of human life, produced by one acre of enclosed and cultivated land, are . . . ten times more than those which are yielded by an acre of land of an equal richness lying waste in common . . . it is labour then, which puts the greatest part of value upon land, without which it would scarcely be worth anything.[2]

Locke transformed dominion over the earth's commons from a mutually shared obligation on God's Great Chain of Being to a right of each individual to possess parts of the planet unencumbered by the community of humankind.

The life force of the planet is bound up in the interchanges of its principal spheres—the hydrosphere, lithosphere, atmosphere, and biosphere. The biosphere, which receives the most attention, is the nineteen kilometers from the ground and ocean depths to the upper edge of the atmosphere within which the hydrosphere, lithosphere, and atmosphere interact to enable life to flourish.

During the Age of Progress, our species captured each of these vital spheres that make up the planetary infrastructure from which life emerges and evolves and, in the name of efficiency, turned them into manipulable property for commercial exploitation. Now, we are reaping the whirlwind. Here is an abbreviated history of the wreckage inflicted on the lithosphere and hydrosphere, both of which play a critical role in sustaining life on Earth.

THE LITHOSPHERE:
The Ground We Walk On

The lithosphere is the solid part of the earth, and includes its upper mantle and crust. The surface of the lithosphere contains the soil and is called the pedosphere. Soil covers most of the earth's landmass and its thickness varies between a few centimeters and several meters. This ultraslim veneer of the lithosphere is often referred to as the Critical Zone, and for good reason. The U.S. National Science Foundation points out that:

"It is a living, breathing, constantly evolving boundary layer where rocks, soil, water, air, and living organisms interact. These complex interactions regulate the natural habitat and determine the availability of life's sustaining resources, including our food products and water quality."[3]

The soil anchors and grows our plants and purifies our water. Soil not only contains vital minerals but is also teeming with life—it's a mini-ecosystem. The Earth Institute at Columbia University states that an acre of soil "may contain nine hundred pounds of earthworms, twenty-four hundred pounds of fungi, one thousand five hundred pounds of bacteria, one hundred thirty-three pounds of protozoa, eight hundred ninety pounds of arthropods and algae, and even sometimes small mammals . . . one grain of soil may hold one billion bacteria, of which only 5 percent have been discovered."[4]

Why is the scientific community suddenly focusing so much on the soil we have long taken for granted? Because the emergence of the mechanical revolution of farming in the late 19th century, chemical farming in the 20th century, and now genetically engineered farming in the 21st century have taken an enormous toll on the soil base across every continent. For the first time in history, "the rate of top soil loss from erosion [has] surpassed the rate of soil formation. The International Soil Reference and Information Center warns that soil is a "threatened, natural resource."[5] The repercussions are wide-ranging. As mentioned, soil formation is a slow process. It takes nature five hundred years or more to create a single inch of topsoil.

But it is not just high-tech, superefficient petrochemical farming that is degrading the soil. Livestock grazing is another driver in the diminution of the soil. Twenty-six percent of the earth's ice-free landmass is taken up by livestock, mostly cattle, but also including sheep, goats, and other species.[6] Widespread cattle grazing has inflicted serious damage to the planet's soil base. The United Nations' Food and Agricultural Organization (FAO) warns of "the detrimental effects on groundwater availability, soil fertility, and biodiversity" brought on by cattle grazing. The UN agency points out that "20 percent of the world's grasslands are degraded."[7]

This trend is only going to accelerate, mainly due to the intensification of animal grazing per acre as the human diet becomes increasingly fixated on beef and a meat-based diet. If this weren't enough, cows emit methane, a global warming gas that is twenty-five times more potent in trapping heat than CO_2 emissions. Livestock—mostly cattle—are responsible for 14 percent of all greenhouse gas emissions.[8]

Were cattle and other livestock to continue to increase in numbers, that alone would likely tip the scale with the loss of much of the earth's remaining precious soil base, but there are other factors at work as well. A 2020 study by the World Economic Forum found that 95 percent of the earth's surface "has been modified by humans."[9] Among the other major contributors to soil loss are deforestation, human settlement, mining, and transport and road systems.

The most damaging of the remaining categories responsible for soil erosion is deforestation. The principal drivers in deforestation are four commodities: beef, soy, palm oil, and wood products, according to the Union of Concerned Scientists.[10]

It's no secret that large areas of the Amazon rain forest and other tropical rain forests the world over are being burned to the ground for cattle grazing. But there's more to the cattle connection than meets the eye. Much of the additional clearing of tropical forests is to make way for growing soy. What the public is not aware of is that 70 percent of the world's soy production goes to feeding cattle and other livestock.[11] Palm oil, for its part, has become a widely used ingredient of processed foods. What ties all of this together is market efficiency. The entropy bill comes due with the loss of much of the earth's remaining topsoil—at the present rate, potentially in the lifetime of today's toddlers.

Unfortunately, the entropy bill doesn't stop with the diminution of the topsoil. The lithosphere extends from the upper crust to the treetops above. With deforestation to make room for cattle grazing, soy and palm oil crops, and the provisioning of lumber and other wood products—alongside a warming of the climate from CO_2, methane, and nitrous oxide emissions—entire forests around the world are disappearing. This has climate scientists panicked.

Forests, especially tropical forests, like soil, are carbon sinks. Both capture CO_2 from the atmosphere and store it. Now, a dangerous reverse trend has set in. A new study published by the journal *Nature* in 2020 involving one hundred of the world's leading scientific institutions and carried out over thirty years shows that tropical forests are taking up one-third less carbon than in the 1990s because of warming temperatures, drought and, in particular, deforestation. The study projects that the typical tropical rain forest may become a carbon source by the 2060s, according to Simon Lewis, a professor of geography at Leeds University and one of the principal authors.[12]

The report noted that tropical forests were taking up around 17 percent of CO_2 emissions from human activity in the 1990s, but by the last decade they were taking up only 6 percent of atmospheric CO_2.[13] The rate of decline in trees absorbing CO_2 emissions from the atmosphere is intensifying global warming and acting as a positive feedback loop, killing off even more trees. Lewis says the speed of the shift of the world's tropical forests from carbon sinks to net emitters of CO_2 "is decades ahead of even the most pessimistic climate models."[14]

There are also 2,300 billion tons of carbon embedded in the earth's soils, compared to approximately 790 billion tons of CO_2 locked into the atmosphere. If the soils continue to degrade and the diminishing forests absorb less CO_2 emissions from the atmosphere, and release what carbon they currently store, the runaway feedback loop is likely to take the earth's temperatures far higher than currently projected by the UN Panel on Climate Change.[15]

Let's do a side-by-side cost-benefit analysis comparing a year's revenue in the industries most responsible for depleting the earth's soil base and forests to see how little short-term commercial gain was achieved in the global economy relative to how much long-term damage was inflicted on the earth's lithosphere. Revenue in the global cattle industry was $385 billion in 2018.[16] The forest industry logged in at $535 billion in revenue in 2020.[17] The soy industry reaped $42 billion in 2020, and the palm oil industry came in at $61 billion in 2019.[18] Mining tallied at $692 billion in revenue in 2019.[19] The total comes to $1.7 trillion. Line these statistics up against the eradication of the earth's soil and the erosion of the remaining forests on a dying planet. Worth it?

THE HYDROSPHERE:
Privatizing Water

The hydrosphere encompasses all of the liquid water on Earth and includes the oceans, lakes, rivers, underground aquifers, ice, and the fog and clouds in the atmosphere. Our forager-hunter ancestors regarded water as a common resource for more than 190,000 years. With the advent of agriculture and pastoralization some ten thousand years ago, feuds over access to water along rivers and lakes increased, although generally the resource was shared as there were ample reserves to go around in a world with a human population still in the low numbers. Today, with a population of about 7.9 billion, the battle over water rights has become a defining issue—aggravated by climate change and the increasing desertification of huge regions of the earth's landmasses.

The oceans, on the other hand, have generally been regarded globally as open to navigation and fishing by everyone. While there is a record of struggle and open warfare over control of the seas in trade, enclosing parts of the ocean and claiming sovereignty over it is a relatively new phenomenon.

The first titanic struggle over enclosing the earth's oceanic commons pitted Spain against Portugal in the 1400s, both of whom at that time were the premier ocean powers. They each claimed sovereignty of the whole of the Atlantic Ocean, Indian Ocean, and Pacific Ocean—a presumptuous claim to say the least. In the Treaty of Tordesillas, signed in 1494, they divided the world's oceans into sovereign enclosed spaces "between the north and south poles that ran 370 leagues west of Cape Verde Islands."[20] Spain was given exclusive jurisdiction of all the ocean west of the demarcation line, including the Gulf of Mexico and the Pacific Ocean, and Portugal was given control over everything east, including the Atlantic and Indian Oceans.

By the 17th century, their tidy arrangement had been torn asunder as Britain, France, and other European powers asserted their sovereignty over the high seas. The prize was worth fighting for. The English explorer Sir Walter Raleigh captured the importance of the gambit, suggesting that "whosoever commands the sea commands the trade; whosoever commands the trade of the world commands the riches of the world, and consequently, the world itself."[21]

With the prospect of any one nation gaining sovereignty over the oceans being an unlikely scenario, nations began to nibble away at parts of the ocean stretching from their coastal waters. The Italians claimed a hundred-mile zone from their shoreline out to sea, the measure being the distance a ship could sail in two days. Other countries sought sovereignty out onto open waters as far as the visual horizon. Some nations ambitiously suggested extending sovereignty as far as the telescope could see. The Dutch preferred extending sovereignty over the oceans as far out as a cannonball could be propelled. By the time of Napoleon, the range of fired artillery was three miles. That new demarcation became the standard until the eve of World War II.

After the war, the United States, now the world's dominant superpower, claimed jurisdiction over all the gas and oil deposits and minerals along the seabed of its continental shelf. By the late 1960s, many nations were claiming sovereignty over coastal waters extending twelve miles out to sea.[22]

In 1982, the United Nations established a Law of the Seas Convention signed by nations around the world, granting each country sovereignty twelve nautical miles out to sea, but also including the granting of exclusive economic zones (EEZs) up to two hundred nautical miles offshore, giving each nation "sovereign rights for the purpose of exploring and exploiting, conserving and managing" the living and nonliving resources of the oceans, seabeds, and subsoil.[23] This extraordinary giveaway allowed coastal nations to enclose a large portion of the world's ocean areas, containing 90 percent of the marine fisheries and 87 percent of the offshore oil and gas reserves along continental shelves.[24]

The big prize in recent decades is the enormous wealth in oil and gas that lie at the bottom of the oceans and seas. The oceanic seabed is also a storehouse of valuable minerals and metals including copper, manganese, cobalt, aluminum, tin, uranium, lithium, and boron. To date, 57 percent of the entire ocean floor has been doled out to nations for their exclusive use, enclosing the last great commons on Earth and much of the hydrosphere that governs the watery planet.[25] And the oceans make up over 70 percent of the earth.

Bringing up oil and gas from the ocean floor to the surface is big business, reaping riches for nations fortunate enough to extend their sovereignty onto these fertile fields. Smaller countries like Norway have become among the leading oil nations in the world from the extracting rights they enjoy in taking up fossil fuels from the depths of the North Sea. The United States is among the leaders, with offshore oil platforms lining the western seaboard and the Gulf of Mexico.

Open sea fishing has been the other lucrative business opportunity, at least until recently, as overfishing has depleted much of the fishing stocks. Five countries account for 64 percent of the high seas fish catch, with aggregate revenues of $7.6 billion in 2014—China, Taiwan, Japan, South Korea, and Spain.[26]

Using digital technologies, satellite surveillance, seabed mapping, sonar, radar, and GPS devices to locate deep-sea fishing fields has transformed the fishing industry into the "strip miners" of the ocean depths. The big players deploy massive trawler ships weighing upward of fourteen thousand tons that stretch the lengths of football fields. The trawlers are equivalent to giant floating factories that kill, process, and package their catch on board. The trawlers, which can store up to eighteen million servings of frozen fish in their holds, sweep the ocean floor with nets large enough "to swallow twelve jumbo jets" and so powerful they can shove aside twenty-five-ton boulders. The trawlers can lay out "eighty miles of submerged longlines or forty-mile drift nets."[27] The super efficiencies of high-tech ocean fishing have so depleted the global fish stock that about one-third of fishing revenues now come from government subsidies just to keep the industry afloat.[28]

The fresh water on the planet—the basic substance of life on Earth—is likewise being enclosed and privatized. It was perhaps inevitable, given the enclosure, rationalization, and privatization of time and space, that water would be branded as a scarce resource and similarly enclosed and privatized, serving the pecuniary interests of a handful of global companies. They argue that they are best positioned to maintain and disseminate this vital resource to humanity.

The privatization of freshwater sources followed on the heels of the Margaret Thatcher–Ronald Reagan political consensus during their respective administrations in the United Kingdom and the United States in the early 1980s. Both governments advocated for turning over the leasing and/or ownership of such assets as public road systems, railroads, the postal service, deepwater ports and airports, public television networks, electricity grids, prisons, public-school systems, and others to the private sector. They embraced what was called "neoliberalism," popular at the time, which argued that government bureaucracies were slow to innovate, unresponsive to public demands, and above all, highly inefficient. The rationale was that by letting the private sector take over public goods and services, market forces would ensure that the most efficient operating practices would be put in place and deliver the best market prices, all to the advantage of consumers.

Notably, there was little evidence at the time that government administration of public services was inefficient or unresponsive to the needs of the citizenry. At least in highly industrialized nations, railroads ran on time, postal services delivered mail, road systems were maintained, public schools were adequate, and public health services were professionally administered. Nonetheless, champions of the neoliberal economic agenda succeeded in catching the ear of political leaders and subsequently global mediating institutions, including the United Nations, the Organization for Economic Co-operation and Development (OECD), the World Trade Organization (WTO), and the World Bank, all of whom introduced policies to dismember and privatize public services globally, handing them over, for the most part, to some of the world's biggest multinational corporations.

The WTO declared water to be a tradable commodity and classified it as a "commercial good," a "service," or an "investment," and locked in provisions that would constrain governments that attempted to prevent the private sector from engaging in the water business in the marketplace. The World Bank became the principal institution in championing the privatization of public water systems, especially in the developing world, mandating that nations enact legislation to foster the privatization of fresh water and sanitation systems as a quid pro quo for securing loans. The World Bank and other lending institutions encouraged so-called public–private partnerships (PPPs) that would allow governments to lease their water infrastructure to private companies to manage for a designated period of time.

The World Bank, the WTO, the OECD, and other global institutions failed to recognize that there is little incentive on the part of private companies to continually upgrade the public infrastructures and services they are managing or lower prices. Unlike markets where consumers have a choice in providers and can transfer their allegiance to competitors (who can offer them a better price and improved service), public infrastructure—roads, airports, et cetera—are natural monopolies. Consumers have no alternative but to use them.

Public–private partnerships with long-term leases encourage companies to engage in "asset stripping"—that is, not adding improvements to the infrastructure and services knowing that their users have little or no alternative to the service rendered. Unlike publicly administered infrastructure services, private companies have to show a steady improvement in their revenue streams and profit, although their consumer base remains relatively flat. In other words, the potential market is often tapped from the start. The end result is continuous asset stripping to save on costs and ensure that profits continuously flow. This is particularly so with water and sanitation systems, where the poorest communities have no choice but to accept whatever conditions private companies impose—hardly a case study of how the invisible hand at work guarantees the best price.

In the early years of the privatization of water, the World Bank encouraged public–private partnerships through generous loans to governments, and through its public sector arm, the International Finance Corporation, whose mission, in part, is to invest in privatization projects.

Even as evidence mounted on the shortcomings of the privatization of water, the World Bank continued to finance its privatization. Between 2004 and 2008, for example, "52 percent of World Bank water services and sanitation projects—78 projects totaling 5.9 billion dollars—provided some form of privatization, and 64 percent of them provided some form of cost recovery."[29] The hold on market efficiency and market forces is still strongly adhered to in official circles within global institutions like the World Bank, the International Monetary Fund (IMF), OECD, and others, and among national governing institutions.

The privatization process has yet to be quelled. Ten global corporations dominate the water market and the top three—Suez, Veolia, and RWE AG—

provide water and sanitation services to customers in more than one hundred countries.[30] These giant global corporations push a privatization agenda, benefiting from generous government incentives and subsidies while raking in massive profits by charging high prices for water while risking reducing the quality of water services, all in the name of increased efficiencies duly recorded in cost-benefit reports and quarterly statements.

Privatizing water systems is only one side of the burgeoning water market. On the other side, global companies have found a growing market in selling bottled water. By the 1970s, one billion liters of water were being sold in the global marketplace. Forty years later, in 2017, bottled water sales had skyrocketed to 391 billion liters and by 2020 the bottled water market was expected to increase to $300 billion in revenue. The water divisions of companies like Coca-Cola and PepsiCo were outpacing their soft drink sales by 2016.[31]

Thirty years into the privatization of fresh water and accompanying sanitation services, the World Health Organization and UNICEF issued a report in 2019 and found that 2.2 billion people in the world still go without safely managed drinking water services and 4.2 billion people without safely managed sanitation services. Three billion people lack even basic handwashing services.[32]

Nor is inadequate access to water and sanitation services an issue only in developing countries. A study conducted on water services in the United States found that industry-owned utilities typically "charge 59 percent more for water service than local government utilities" and "charge 63 percent more for sewer service than local government utilities."[33] The study reviewed eighteen municipalities that ended contracts with private companies and found that "public operations averaged 21 percent cheaper than private operations for water and sewer services." Moreover, privatization "can increase the cost of financing a water project by 50 percent to 150 percent." To minimize their losses, private water companies cut costs by asset stripping using "shoddy construction materials, delaying needed maintenance, and downsizing their workforces, all of which translates into poor and unreliable service." The report's conclusion is straightforward: "Multinational water companies are primarily accountable to their shareholders, not the people they serve."[34]

The human right of access to water and sanitation services is going to face an even more uncertain future with the ascent of climate change. Some areas of the earth will become uninhabitable as ecosystems collapse from the dramatic changes in the circulation of water, forcing unprecedented mass migrations from unlivable regions. Those who relocate will need to radically rethink how to safeguard a reliable water regime by introducing resilience practices to guarantee access to sufficient water to maintain life.

MARKETING THE GENE POOL

In recent years, even the diverse gene pool that constitutes the blueprints of life has been swept up in the commodification frenzy in the name of efficiency. The scientific community, the life sciences industry, biotech companies, the pharmaceutical industry, agribusiness, and the medical community have all staked claims over various aspects and properties of the genetic map in pursuit of enclosing the most intimate interior of the natural world. The "gene rush" to reconfigure the genetic programs of the life-world for commercial ends represents the final stage in the pacification of the wild.

In 1972, Ananda Mohan Chakrabarty, a microbiologist then employed by General Electric, applied to the U.S. Patent and Trademark Office (PTO) for a patent on a genetically engineered microorganism designed to consume oil spills on the oceans. The PTO rejected the claim, arguing that with the exception of asexually reproduced plants, which were granted special status as patentable by an act of Congress, all other life-forms are not patentable because they are products of nature.

Chakrabarty appealed the decision to the Court of Customs and Patent Appeals, where in a narrow 3–2 decision the justices overruled the PTO. The majority of judges argued that "the fact that microorganisms . . . are alive [is] without legal significance" and that a microorganism is "more akin to an inanimate chemical composition such as reactants, reagents, and catalysts than to horses and honeybees, or raspberries and roses."[35]

The PTO appealed the case to the U.S. Supreme Court and was joined by my organization, the People's Business Commission, which filed an amicus curiae brief arguing that "manufactured life—high and low—will have been categorized as less than life, as nothing but common chemicals" and that if the patent were granted by the U.S. Supreme Court it would open the way to patenting all forms of life and their constituent parts in the future.[36]

In 1980, the U.S. Supreme Court, by a slim 5–4 margin, ruled in favor of Chakrabarty, granting a patent on the first genetically engineered life-form. The chief justice, Warren Burger, referring to my office's amicus curiae brief, called it "the gruesome parade of horribles."[37] Just months after the Supreme Court ruling, Genentech (a young start-up biotech company) issued a million shares of its stock, and by the end of the first trading day, the company had doubled the price of its shares—a stunning feat in Wall Street history—despite the fact that it had yet to introduce a single product into the marketplace.[38]

In 1987, the PTO, which had originally argued that patents on life were inadmissible, reversed its stance and issued a ruling that all genetically engineered multicellular living organisms, including animals, are potentially patentable—a ruling that signaled the beginning of the biotech century. To counter public concerns, Donald J. Quigg, the commissioner of the Patent and Trademark Office, issued a statement that while patents could conceivably be granted to every genetically modified species on Earth, human beings were excluded because the Thirteenth Amendment to the U.S. Constitution forbids slavery.[39] On the other hand, human embryos, fetuses, genes, cell lines, and tissues and organs are all potentially patentable if genetically modified, if not the whole human being.[40]

A year after the new PTO guidance, the PTO granted a patent on the first mammal, a genetically engineered mouse containing human genes that predisposed it to developing cancer. Somewhat later, a Scottish research team received a U.S. patent for the method used to clone the famous Dolly the sheep.[41] Since then, thousands of patents have been granted by patent offices around the world on both the methods used and the modified components of genetically engineered seeds and animals, including modified human genes and cell lines.

Plant geneticists and farmers were particularly incensed, as global agricultural and life science companies including Monsanto, W. R. Grace, Bayer, and Syngenta began securing patents on genetically engineered seeds, gaining a lock on the basic food sources that sustain human life. For thousands of years, farmers gathered up the new seeds at harvest time to plant the following season, but now they were not able to do so with the purchase of genetically engineered seeds. In subsequent decades, thousands of farmers on every continent were kept under constant surveillance by life science companies, and if found using the next generation of genetically engineered seeds for planting the following year, were brought to court and charged with a breach of the companies' patent and related rights.[42]

With few exceptions, biologists actively supported the commercial patenting of life. A study conducted by Dr. Sheldon Krimsky, professor of urban and environmental policy and planning at Tufts University in the late 1980s, found that 37 percent of biotechnology scientists, who were members of the prestigious National Academies of Sciences, a body that advises the U.S. Congress and the executive branch of government on science policy, had "industrial affiliations."[43]

After decades of growing opposition to granting patents on genetically modified life by farm associations, public health authorities, university researchers, and the general public, the U.S. Supreme Court ruled in a case brought against Myriad Genetics that received patents on two genes implicated in curing breast and ovarian cancer, backtracking only slightly. The court agreed that while genes themselves could not be patented, simply because they were identified, the synthetic DNA used in the screening of women could be patented because it does not occur naturally in nature, keeping the door wide open to commercial exploitation of our species' genetic makeup.[44]

The biotech companies argue that genetic engineering is a force for good by pursuing more efficient means of growing healthy plants and raising animals. A growing number of scientists also support eliminating harmful genetically inherited genes in the human population, and even adding enhanced genes that improve physical and mental health.

Short-term efficiency gains touted by the biotech industry inevitably come with more serious negative externalities. At the top of the list is the chilling atmosphere created in university research laboratories. Big pharma, life science companies, and global agrobusiness companies have seized hold of university research laboratories by financing much of the biotech research, and even issuing shares of their company's stock to the scientists involved, creating a veil of secrecy in university laboratories.[45]

Graduate and postgraduate students and their professors are often required to enter into nondisclosure agreements with biotech companies to ensure that research is not shared with colleagues. Researchers are also prohibited from publishing in a timely manner in peer-reviewed scientific journals, muffling the sharing of data among scientists and their students. Many younger scientists have begun to establish a counter-agenda of not accepting industry-financed biotech research, arguing that the short-term financial gains reaped by global companies should not be at the expense of shackling the free and open exchange of scientific research and data.

Nowhere has the efficiency banner been more flagrantly displayed than in the emergence of a new gene-splicing technique that goes by the name of CRISPR. CRISPR is being touted as "the most versatile genomic engineering tool created in the history of molecular biology to date."[46] The 2020 Nobel Prize in chemistry was awarded to its two inventors, Emmanuelle Charpentier of the Max Planck Unit for the Science of Pathogens and Jennifer Doudna of the University of California at Berkeley. The two scientists transformed a bacterial immune mechanism called CRISPR into "a tool that can simply and cheaply edit the genomes of everything from wheat to mosquitoes to humans."[47] This cheap-to-use and amazingly efficient tool, which acts as a "genetic scissors," has given birth to a new biotech industry across the fields of medicine, agricultural products, pest control, and other fields.

Pernilla Wittung-Stafshede, a chemical biologist at the Chalmers University of Technology, speaks to the promise of this incredibly efficient tool, noting that "the ability to cut DNA where you want has revolutionized the life sciences."[48] But the exponential increase in efficiencies in cutting out genes in the germ lines of plants, animals, and humans to eliminate so-called damaging traits, with little understanding of the complex and subtle genetic relationships within each species that has evolved and adapted over eons, portends untold negative externalities. Those negative externalities are likely to outweigh any short-term efficiency gains and revenues generated by the pharmaceutical, agricultural, medical, and life science industries.

Case in point: I coauthored a book in 1978 with Ted Howard entitled *Who Should Play God?* on the promises and perils of the then rudimentary biotech revolution. We argued at the time that scientists would one day have at their disposal the very scissor techniques that won the two scientists the 2020 Nobel Prize in chemistry. We warned against cutting so-called monogenic traits from the germ line. These are single gene traits that cause chronic diseases and even premature death.

For example, the sickle cell recessive trait, found mostly in individuals of African American origin, is a potential marker of early morbidity. But the same trait has also been found to ward off malaria. Similarly, the recessive trait for cystic fibrosis, which, too, is debilitating and life-threatening, has been found to correlate with greater resistance to cholera. The fact is, we have little knowledge of why these and other recessive traits in the human genome exist and what might possibly be the evolutionary advantage that has enabled them to persist in the human genome over time.

In the late 1970s, I was invited to debate Dr. Bernard Davis, a prominent biology professor at Harvard University, on the issue of germ line genetic engineering. I asked him, if gene-splicing tools were available, would he eliminate all of the recessive gene traits in the human germ line, and his answer was a crisp "yes." But, I cautioned that since some of these recessive traits have continued to exist in the human genome over evolutionary history, it is possible that by eliminating them we might inadvertently monoculture our own species as we have done with plants and animals, with deleterious impacts on our fitness and even survival, making human beings more vulnerable and less resilient to new potential assaults from the environment that these recessive gene traits might have been able to fend off.

The reality is that somatic cell genome editing—that is, cutting out a potentially crippling or deadly trait after birth—would likely be far more efficacious because doing so would not affect the passage of that trait into the germ line, keeping options open for generations not yet here while ensuring a healthy life for those individuals who carry that gene. Unfortunately, these reservations and alternative options have received short shrift from the biotech industry.

The ethical conundrum around using CRISPR to intervene in the human germ line surfaced in November 2018 after a Chinese scientist announced the birth of twin girls with edited genes: the first germ line genetic engineering of a fetus. The scientist, He Jiankui, reported that he had modified a key gene in a number of embryos that would confer resistance to HIV before implanting them in a mother's womb.[49]

Scientists were both horrified and excited by the announcement. Like so many breakthroughs that were previously considered to be unacceptable, once the redline was crossed, the majority of scientists and life science companies were quick to jump on the bandwagon, only raising the procedural question of whether the scientist adhered to the appropriate vetting protocols in advance of the experiment, side-stepping the deeper ethical and ecological implications of ever conducting such an experiment.

The biotech industry heralded the development of CRISPR while also cautioning that proper procedures needed to be put in place to ensure the success of the new enhancive medical technology. A study on the commercial prospects of genome editing technology pointed to the quick embrace of CRISPR within the biotech industry, noting that in just the year 2015–2016 alone, CRISPR resulted in a "five-fold increase in genome editing bio-enterprise investment," a clear indication that the new gene-editing tool "has spurred a global bio-technology revolution." The authors of the report expressed confidence that "the global shift in bio enterprise will continue to grow as the demand for personalized medicine, genetically modified crops, and environmentally sustainable biofuel increases."[50]

While commercial interests were quick out of the gate, it must be acknowledged that many scientists are motivated as much by humanitarian concerns as commercial interests when it comes to the health of human beings and understand the dangers that eliminating gene traits may pose to future generations of our species and other species. But, in the long run, they view CRISPR's ability to increase the efficiencies of gene editing as a tool too seductive to pass by and, despite misgivings about future negative externalities, are nonetheless keen to use the technology for improving, if not perfecting, the human genome to the betterment of our species.

In journal articles describing the potential long-term negative effects of CRISPR editing of genes, researchers continually emphasize how efficient this new tool makes the process of reengineering the human genome, as if efficiency is an overriding moral imperative in and of itself.

Take, for example, an article that appeared in the *Journal of Molecular Biology* written by Carolyn Brokowski of the Department of Emergency Medicine at Yale School of Medicine and Mazhar Adli, professor in the Department of Biology and Molecular Genetics at the University of Virginia, entitled "CRISPR Ethics: Moral Considerations for Applications of a Powerful Tool." Like so many other pieces written by scientists and doctors in the field, the authors ran in the same lane of equating morality with efficiency.

They explain that given the "technical limitations and the complexities of biological systems, making precise predictions about the future of an edited organism and gauging potential risks and benefits, might be difficult if not impossible." They then fall back on the reality that "technology is evolving at an unprecedented pace," and conclude that "as more efficient and sensitive CRISPR tools are developed, many of these concerns may become obsolete." They ostensibly take the default position that efficiency trumps unknown future potential perils—a clear sign that efficiency remains the highest moral ground of a dying Age of Progress.[51]

RIDING THE ELECTOMAGNETIC SPECTRUM:
GPS, the Earth's Global Brain and Nervous System

The rationalization of time and space to the end of enclosing, expropriating, privatizing, and consuming the largesse of the earth with ever greater quanta of technological efficiencies came to a head on February 14, 1989. On that day, the U.S. government launched the first satellite of the Global Positioning System (GPS) into orbit.

The GPS system, which reached full operational capability on July 17, 1995, is made up of thirty-three satellites orbiting the earth 20,000 kilometers above the planet. Each satellite transmits a GPS signal carried by radio waves in the microwave part of the electromagnetic spectrum. The system, with headquarters at the Schriever Air Force Base in Colorado Springs, Colorado, employs eight thousand military and civilian personnel dispersed across 16 monitoring stations around the world.[52] GPS oversees what is the largest surveillance system ever devised, monitoring and coordinating virtually every aspect of daily life that much of the human race relies on to mediate their very existence.

Each satellite is outfitted with an atomic clock, which is synchronized in nanoseconds with the atomic clock in the other GPS satellites, and all of these clocks are guarded by the master clock at the U.S. Naval Observatory in Washington, D.C. Greg Milner, author of the book *Pinpoint: How GPS Is Changing Technology, Culture, and Our Minds,* explains in laymen's terms how the GPS system operates, for example, when someone uses a mobile phone or any other digital device, anywhere in the world:

> The satellites broadcast a continuous radio signal that carries information about where the satellite was and will be—and also the exact time the signal left the satellite. The signal makes a 20,000-kilometer journey, taking an especial pummeling as it pushes through the earth's ionosphere. When it reaches us, sixty-seven milliseconds later, it is even fainter. Nearly every spot on Earth has a line of sight to at least four GPS satellites at all times. By noting each signal's origin and its arrival time, the receiver can compute the latitude and longitude of the phone, and express it as a point on a map. The receiver can also provide the correct time. Four satellites, four dimensions. A pinpoint calculation of space and time.[53]

The GPS positioning and navigation system is a real-world equivalent to Isaac Newton's machine-like universe, or on the dark side, Jeremy Bentham's universal panopticon. Its atomic clocks and signals pulsing down to the earth's surface act much like a global brain and nervous system, coordinating economic activity, social life, and governance in time and across space. Milner explains the importance of GPS as an organizer of temporal and spatial relationships throughout the human environment:

> We use GPS to track the movements of criminal suspects, sex offenders, wild animals, dementia sufferers, and wayward children. GPS guides planes to the ground and orients ships at sea. We wear watches with GPS. We buy specialized GPS sporting applications for golfing and fishing. We use GPS to locate oil deposits. GPS has helped grow a significant amount of the food you will eat today. GPS is itself one of the world's most accurate clocks—and also a clock that unites other clocks. The components and nodes of the world's complex systems require time synchronization, often linked to GPS time. GPS timekeeping helps regulate the electrical grid in all its transnational complexity, bounces your mobile phone conversation from tower to tower, and orders billions of transactions through financial trading networks, where millisecond discrepancies can affect billions of dollars. GPS helps predict the weather. GPS surveys land, and builds bridges and tunnels. It knows how much water is in the ground and in the ash plume rising from a volcano, and how the oceans help redistribute the planet's center of mass.[54]

There are currently 6.4 billion devices that receive signals from GPS and the other satellite navigational systems.[55] The market size of global satellite navigation systems as of 2019 was \$161.27 billion, and is projected to more than double by 2027 to \$386.78 billion.[56]

The European Union launched the Galileo positioning system, equivalent to the GPS system, in 2011. Russia has its GLONASS satellite positioning system in orbit around the earth, and China has its BeiDou Navigation Satellite System.

On the upside, GPS could potentially connect the whole of the human family with our fellow creatures and the lithosphere, hydrosphere, atmosphere, and biosphere in a metaglobal organism, re-conditioning the human race back into the intimate inner workings of a dynamic Earth. In a way, GPS is the supreme choreographer and coordinator of the activity taking place on our planet.

On the downside, there is also growing evidence that GPS choreography of temporal and spatial relations is severing our species from the once intimate relationship we shared with the agencies and rhythms of the earth, while infantilizing our sense of personal and collective agency. To take one example, a growing number of clinical studies are finding that increasing reliance on the GPS brain and nervous system to manage our daily routines is reducing our cognitive ability to map spatial relations and synchronize our bodily rhythms to the world around us.

In June 2019, Noam Bardin paid a visit to my office in Washington, D.C. Noam is the founder and former CEO of Waze, the widely popular GPS guided tracking system that directs drivers on the road to their points of destination. Noam and I spent several hours together talking about the ups and downs of the GPS guidance system that enables millions of drivers to take the fastest route to their destination and, by so doing, save gasoline and reduce CO_2 emissions.

During the conversation, I mentioned that my wife, Carol, and I use Waze and are real enthusiasts. But, I shared our personal cautionary tale with Noam. We have close friends—husband and wife—whom we visit throughout the year. Several years ago, they changed residences and moved to another neighborhood in a different suburb of Washington, D.C. This was around the same time we began using Waze, since the directions for getting to their home were complicated, requiring many twists and turns. Several months passed by, and on one particular day we set out to visit our friends, and after several blocks realized that we had left our cell phone with the Waze app behind, and had no idea where we were, or how to get to our destination. As we peered through the window, we were unable to identify any markers—roads, homes, stores, that looked familiar.

It dawned on us that we were without a mental map on how to get to our friends' house, even though they lived only twenty-five minutes away. We suddenly realized that Waze had streamlined our travel, making it much more efficient, but at the expense of us losing personal agency in our ability to recognize and map our physical surroundings. We had been infantilized. Our sense of movement in space had become the charge of Waze and GPS spatial and temporal guidance.

There is a term for this phenomenon. It's called "developmental topographical disorientation" (DTD). It's a rare disorder in which an individual is "unable to form mental representations of surrounding spaces."[57] Individuals suffering from this disorder have normal memory recall, but simply can't create "a spatial representation of their individual surroundings that contains information about the environment's layout, the objects (i.e. landmarks) available within it and, most important, the spatial relationship between these objects."[58] These are individuals who are without navigational skills. To date, there is no treatment for this particular disorder. To be clear, these are individuals who often cannot find their way from their bedroom to their kitchen on any given day.

Our experience, which is only a very weak "acquired" version of DTD, is apparently quite common. Researchers in the field of cognitive science have begun to ponder the question of increasing reliance on the GPS brain and nervous system for not only mapping travel directions but also a host of other ordinary spatial mapping activities. Scientists believe that the parts of our brain responsible for spatial navigation are no longer being exercised and are atrophying. Again, like so many other avenues of life in an increasingly technologically mediated and digitally connected world where GPS guidance can assist, ease, and make more efficient decisions for us, we risk the atrophying of our cognitive abilities.

Lest we dismiss this loss of personal agency as being more anecdotal and without serious consequence, consider the new phenomenon called "death by GPS." Travelers using GPS become so reliant on the tracking device and so skittish about cross checking it by actually looking out their side windows, that they continue on, sometimes plunging over cliffs or drifting into rivers or lakes, or crashing into dead ends. They have surrendered all sense of personal agency to the GPS.

While we have come to think of GPS as the master global clock, Milner makes the point that it is more correctly described as "the world's most powerful stopwatch, a perfect way to manage time."[59] I recall back in the 1980s when digital watches, which display the current time only numerically, began to replace analog watches that show a hand that moves around a circle.

In my presentations, I would remind students that the hand moving around the circle was meant to be an analogue of the rotation of the earth over a twenty-four-hour daily cycle, while the digital watch is more like a timer informing the wearer of the current moment in isolation, with no reference to the past from which it came, and the future to which it will go. Digital time is frozen in space.

GPS digital timing operates in a similar fashion. It is a timing mechanism (channel Frederick Taylor). And its most important application is the timing and synchronization of the key elements of an emerging smart digital infrastructure that's beginning to transform all of society in both the physical and virtual worlds. Its presence is being met with enthusiasm from some corridors and angst from others. Both attitudes are critical to understanding the different possible paths that await us with this fundamental change in the way we communicate, power, and move our collective economic life, sociability, and governance in the centuries ahead as we leave the Age of Progress behind and cross into the Age of Resilience.

REWIRING THE HUMAN BRAIN

The loss of agency in a virtual universe has been a bone of contention for more than two decades. Much of the controversy is centered around whether the first two generations of digital natives—millennials and Gen-Zs—who grew up in cyberspace, think differently. And we are not just talking about points of view but, rather, whether the new immersive world they inhabit for much of their lives and that has become indispensable to their cognitive development has actually changed the way their brain is wired. If so, what might be the consequences for the way our species will navigate its future?

The first inkling that prolonged immersion in the virtual world might be affecting human cognition and perhaps even the wiring of the brain came with the precipitous decline recorded in vocabulary and literacy among a younger digital generation fixated on interfacing on the screen. Because the internet is primarily a visual medium in which "a picture is worth a thousand words," each successive digital generation is being exposed to fewer rare words. Then too, while the internet contains virtually every word that exists in all the major languages, its emphasis on efficiency via browsing, multitasking, and quick links to other pieces prioritizes skimming over words and whole paragraphs, shortening attention to text.

Text messaging, emails, and more recently Instagram and Twitter have resulted in even fewer rare words and more abbreviated communications, and ever-increasing reliance on acronyms and emoticons. That being so, virtual communications of every kind accommodate the shorter attention span of users. By shortening and simplifying the text and the choice of words, especially when accompanied by visual material, users are exposed to a much-abbreviated vocabulary and therefore "lose their way" with a corresponding loss of agency in their ability to effectively communicate with others and express complex thoughts, not unlike what befalls Waze users in losing their way on the road. By contrast, every other communication revolution in history has both broadened the range and usage of vocabulary and increased the storage, giving human beings more nuanced ways to communicate with one another.

Dr. Patricia Greenfield, a professor of psychology at the University of California, Los Angeles, and director of the Children's Digital Media Center, published an extensive report on the effects that the use of computers, the internet, multitasking, and video games were having on personal agency in the journal *Science* in 2009. She analyzed fifty different studies on the interface of learning and the new digital communication technologies. She reported that while visual skills had improved, there was a commensurate decline in reading texts, and especially literary reading, which has possibly contributed to a decline in critical thinking.[60]

Greenfield noted that "by using more visual media, students will process information better," but was quick to add that most visual media are real-time media that do not allow for reflection, analysis, or imagination so important to critical thinking.[61] The efficiency gained in quicker access to more simplified visually represented media with diminished text is at the expense of a deeper learning experience. Greenfield took particular aim at multitasking, suggesting that "if you are trying to solve a complex problem, you need sustained concentration . . . if you are doing a task that requires deep sustained thought, multitasking is detrimental."[62]

A decade later, scientific studies were beginning to come in, showing that the numerous efficiencies triggered by "the interface with the internet" were affecting changes in the neural wiring of various parts of the human brain, with unknown consequences, effecting a loss of personal agency. A mammoth report prepared by a global team of researchers from Harvard University, Oxford University, King's College, the University of Manchester, and Western Sydney University was published in the journal *World Psychiatry* in May 2019. The findings show that the human brain is an extremely plastic organ subject to rewiring by the way it's used.[63] It's particularly sensitive to radical transformations in the technological means by which human beings communicate. This suggests that the great historic shifts from oral communication to script, print, electronic, and digital not only change the way we communicate but also the way the brain operates.

Among the findings, researchers report that in a randomized controlled trial involving six weeks of interacting in an online role-playing game, there were significant reductions in gray matter within the orbitofrontal cortex—the specific region of the brain involved in impulse control and decision-making.[64] Researchers also report that prolonged internet usage accompanied by media multitasking was associated with "decreased grey matter in prefrontal regions associated with maintaining goals in face of distraction."

Another meta-analysis of forty-one studies found that multitasking correlated with "significantly poorer overall cognitive performance."[65] In a study of the internet versus encyclopedia information searches, magnetic resonance imaging showed that "the poorer recall of Internet-sought information compared to encyclopedia-based learning was associated with reduced activation of the ventral stream [in the brain] during online information gathering," supporting the possibility that "online information gathering, while faster, may fail to sufficiently recruit brain regions for storing information on a long-term basis."[66] Other studies of high-functioning analytical thinkers with higher cognitive capacities document that they rely less on storage and retrieval of information from the internet, and more on personal memory of the information.[67]

These and other reports on the trade-off of increased efficiencies versus loss of cognitive agency in interfacing with the internet are unsettling and suggest the need for a comprehensive rethink on how current and future generations use the new communication medium.

The new hyperefficiencies that come with working, playing, and living more of our lives in the virtual worlds of cyberspace have not only begun to infantilize a digital generation's sense of personal agency and even changed the wiring of their brains, but have also begun to rob humanity of its own future. Recall that efficiency is a restless force whose modus operandi is to optimize every future output, expending ever less time, energy, labor, and capital. The lifeblood of efficiency is the annihilation of the passage of time and the optimization of all futures in an ever-present now, eliminating time's arrow altogether. Of course, that's not what human beings have in mind when striving in everyday life to be more efficient. Rather, the subtext that comes with the relentless drive for ever more efficiency is the fear that each moment expended is a moment lost, bringing all of us closer to our inevitable demise. Efficiency is the surrogate plan to buy more time and secure a bit of immortality here on Earth.

Now, it appears that the efficiency crusade has entered a final phase. It's called "algorithm governance." The corporate world and government are increasingly pinning their commercial and political fortunes on the amassing of historical data of every stripe and kind across cyberspace and examining the information using analytics. The objective is to create algorithms that can help them describe, predict, prescribe, and even preempt futures, with the intent of controlling or at least affecting events in markets, social movements, and governance in futures not yet here.

ALGORITHM GOVERNANCE:
Known Knowns, Known Unknowns, and Unknown Unknowns

On June 6, 2002, at the North Atlantic Treaty Organization's headquarters in Brussels, Belgium, U.S. Secretary of Defense Donald Rumsfeld held a press conference to discuss NATO efforts in support of the global war on terrorism. After briefing the press corps on what was discussed at the conference, Rumsfeld opened the floor for questions.

The first question from the press corps: "Regarding terrorism and weapons of mass destruction, you said something to the effect that the real situation is worse than the facts show. I wonder if you could tell us what is worse than generally understood?"

Rumsfeld responded:

I have . . . done a great deal of work and analysis on intelligence information and . . . probed deeper and deeper and kept probing until I found out what it is we knew, and when we learned, and when it actually had existed. And I found that, not to my surprise . . . [that we] did not know some significant event for two years after it happened, for four years after it happened, for six after it happened, in some cases eleven and twelve and thirteen years after it happened. Now what is the message there? The message is that there are known "knowns." There are things we know that we know. There are known unknowns. That is to say there are things that we now know we don't know. But there are also unknown unknowns. There are things we don't know we don't know. So, when we do the best we can and we pull all this information together, and we then say well that's basically what we see as the situation, that is really only the known knowns and the known unknowns. And each year, we discover a few more of those unknown unknowns.

It sounds like a riddle. It isn't a riddle. It is a very serious, important matter. There's another way to phrase that and that is that the absence of evidence is not evidence of absence. . . . Simply because you do not have evidence that something exists does not mean that you have evidence that it doesn't exist. And yet almost always, when we make our threat assessments . . . we end up basing it on the first two pieces of that puzzle, rather than all three.[68]

The press corps, usually unflustered at formal government press conferences, experienced their own "shock and awe" over what they just heard. Had the U.S. secretary of defense lost his marbles? Or was he saying something so utterly profound that one might expect to hear it in a university philosophy seminar? The Rumsfeld tongue twister shot across the world and became the subject of comic relief and endless intellectual banter as to its meaning. In all fairness, Rumsfeld wasn't the first to mouth what is a truism. The known unknowns and unknown unknowns were common parlance around the National Aeronautics and Space Administration (NASA) headquarters for years when discussing what might go wrong in space flights. American psychologists Joseph Luft and Harrington Ingham used the term *unknown unknowns* in the 1950s as a therapeutic technique. These bundled truisms have a long trail dating far back in history. However, in the wake of the unexpected 9/11 terrorist attacks that downed the World Trade Center, leaving 2,977 dead, unknown unknowns suddenly became chillingly real and on the minds of every American and people everywhere.

The grand prize in artificial intelligence is the amassing of data and the use of analytics to unmask the known unknowns and unknown unknowns: that is, to know the future before it knows itself . . . to be clairvoyant. One of the least considered impacts of a hyperefficient, technically driven society is how the speed of occurrences increases the risk of things going utterly wrong—with potentially catastrophic impacts. Scholars across a variety of academic fields, business leaders, and overseers of government are understandably consumed with mitigating future risk.

This is where AI and analytics come in. Much of the primary work in this field has focused on prediction, especially in the commercial realm. The goal is to anticipate potential wants before a consumer is even aware of them, based on past wants and predispositions. The music and film industries have been using data mining to analyze and predict the commercial success of any given song or film in advance of its release for nearly two decades. Companies like Platinum Blue Music Intelligence and Epagogix have flourished. Businesses across the commercial spectrum have been doing the same with the rollout of consumer products and services using analytics and algorithms in their advertising and marketing to reach specific demographics made up of likely customers whose past interests and purchases best match the item or service being marketed.

There has been a lively debate among scholars on how predictive analytic practices narrow the window to the future by precluding new genres of art, entertainment, product offerings, and services from getting into the game and breaking the conventional mode of what is desirable. Predictive analytics often shrink the personal agency of prospective entrants by locking them into an ecosystem based on past preferences and proclivities.

John Cheney-Lippold, a digital studies professor at the University of Michigan, describes predictive analytics for the purpose of directing, managing, and usurping the public's personal agency. He writes:

"Cybernetic categorization . . . tells us who we are, what we want, and who we should be . . . and ultimately requires us to conceive of freedom . . . much more differently than previously thought. We are effectively losing control in defining who we are online, or more specifically we are losing ownership over the meaning of the categories that constitute our identities."[69]

The Pew Research Center reached out to experts across society on the issue of "the pros and cons of algorithms," seeking their advice and opinions in a 2017 survey. While acknowledging the many benefits of amassing data and using analytics to create algorithms to better understand how millions of people define their lives, three overriding qualifications crept into the dialogue at every turn of the conversation.

First, algorithms reflect the biases of programmers and data sets; second, algorithmic categorization deepens divides; third, algorithms create filter bubbles and silos shaped by corporate data collectors—they limit people's exposure to a wider range of ideas and reliable information and eliminate serendipity.[70]

What's particularly interesting is the number of times that efficiency, profits, and loss of personal agency came up in conversation among the experts. Pew found widespread agreement "that algorithms are primarily written to optimize efficiency and profitability without much thought about the possible societal impacts of the data modeling and analysis."[71] Many of the respondents agreed that "humans are considered to be an 'input' to the process and they are not seen as real, thinking, feeling, changing beings."[72] One respondent went to the depth of the problem, noting that "algorithms value efficiency over correctness or fairness, and over time their evolution will continue the same priorities that initially formulated them."[73]

Predictive analytics, while narrowing the future agency of billions of human beings, is rather tame compared with preemptive analytics. Here's the arena where hyperefficiency becomes a danger to the passage of time on a scale never before witnessed.

PREEMPTION:
Eliminating Futures Before They Happen

On June 1, 2002, at the U.S. Military Academy/West Point graduation ceremony, President George W. Bush of the United States spoke to the graduating class, in the wake of the 9/11 terrorist attack. The president cautioned the graduating cadets that:

"If we wait for threats to fully materialize, we will have waited too long . . . we must take the battle to the enemy, disrupt his plans, and control the vast threats before they emerge . . . our security will require all Americans to be forward-looking and resolute, to be ready for preemptive action when necessary."[74]

Few journalists, and even less of the American public, paid much attention at the time to President Bush's speech. Yet, this formal introduction of "preemptive action" marked not only a fundamental change in military strategy and foreign policy but, also, of governance that would quickly trickle down into the affairs of commerce and even the workings of civil society, affecting the public's well-being and social doctrines.

On that day, the president took the United States, and soon other countries and peoples, into the murky realm of the Unknown Unknowns where the only way to confront future risks that are unknowable is by preempting potential "imagined events" that might happen sometime in the near or distant future and intervene in the present to thwart their occurrence.

First off, there is a rift built into the logic of preemption. AI analysts search reams of past data for clues that might help them unmask an unknown unknown in an imagined detrimental occurrence that could happen somewhere along the future time horizon and then initiate a present response before the event even exists. Yet, past data is unlikely to detect futures that have never occurred, and therefore don't provide an adequate trail of information that might be helpful in uncovering an unknown unknown. Second, since the preemption is in the form of an action against an imaginary occurrence, "it" becomes the only event. But, in doing so, the preemption creates the conditions for an actual retaliatory response rather than being the response. Ironically, in the name of preempting future risks, preemption creates the very risk it hopes to prevent, sowing chaos in the here and now.

Since the 9/11 terrorist attacks, the use of big data and analytics to create algorithms that can be used to discover unknown unknowns and trigger preemptions has taken wing. Cities, in particular, are increasingly relying on "anticipatory security calculus" to identify unknown unknown future risks. The protocol establishes 24/7 algorithm surveillance to provide massive up-to-the-moment data on the proclivities, activities, and comings and goings of their citizens. They then use that data and accompanying analytics to intervene and preempt risks before they occur, reasoning that preemption is a more efficient means to thwart criminal and antisocial activity.

Government-directed surveillance and preemption is mostly aimed at potential criminal activity and social protests deemed dangerous and a risk to public safety. However, sociologists have pointed out that the determination of who is a risk and which type of activity poses a threat is often biased by the analysts who collect the data and program the algorithms. Stereotyping is primarily aimed at surveilling racial and ethnic minorities and disadvantaged communities, liberal and left-wing social protest movements, and even animal rights organizations.

Preemptive governance rides under the banner of what analysts call "futuring"—a new type of "anticipatory governance" organized generally around urban preemption interventions. A range of commercial apps have been introduced sporadically in recent years to enlist the public in providing real-time surveillance on conditions that might pose risks requiring preemptive intervention. The apps inform users while they are walking through or driving in neighborhoods that are high crime areas or poorly lit or have abandoned buildings or are populated by large numbers of homeless people living in the streets and advise them that these are "unsafe neighborhoods." App users are encouraged to text to the platform their impressions and observations while traveling through these neighborhoods that can be added to the database.

Several years ago, Microsoft patented the Pedestrian Route Production system, a navigation-centric app that reroutes pedestrians around "dangerous" neighborhoods.[75] Many of the apps have raised the ire of the public, and especially minority communities in the most disadvantaged neighborhoods, forcing the platforms' voluntary withdrawal or redesign to eliminate, or at least mask, any overtly discriminatory footprints.

Preemption is particularly cued to unknown unknowns that pose potential contagion threats including protests, rioting, and looting. These cohorts and the spaces they occupy are earmarked for greater surveillance, increased police patrolling, and other measures like early curfews or closing off specific streets to preempt potentially adverse activity.

The fact that governments and the public at large have come to put more emotional trust on preempting future risks than promoting present opportunities signals a fundamental change in the emotional and social mindset. But, the political consequences of this shift in governance raise troubling questions that go to the heart of democratic jurisprudence. Writing in the *Stanford University Law Review*, Ian Kerr, the research chair of ethics and technology of the faculty of law at the University of Ottawa, argues:

> A universalized preemption strategy could challenge some of our most fundamental jurisprudential commitments, including the presumption of innocence. . . . Big data enables a universalizable strategy of preemptive social decision-making. Such a strategy renders individuals unable to observe, understand, participate in, or respond to information gathered or assumptions made about them. When one considers that big data can be used to make important decisions that implicate us without our even knowing it, preemptive social decision-making is antithetical to privacy and due process values.[76]

Preemption represents the ultimate usurpation of power by holding the future of others in an extended lockdown, preventing segments of the population from exercising agency over their own time horizon.

Taylorism's promethean reach over the past century is unquestionable. Virtually every operative agency that makes up the earth's complex systems has been expropriated, commodified, and put on life support in the name of efficiency and profits. Now, the Gospel of Efficiency is even leading to the implosion of the capitalist system as we've come to know it . . . a look next at the last act.

6

THE CATCH-22 OF CAPITALISM

INCREASED EFFICIENCY, FEWER WORKERS, AND MORE CONSUMER DEBT

The proselytizers of efficiency, for all of their professional acumen, were blind to a contradiction so glaring that it should have been readily apparent from the very beginning of the process of applying the principles of scientific management to industrial production. The so-called dumb workforce that Taylor deemed incapable of understanding even the simplest workings of either tending the machines or the elementals of commerce, did at least understand the consequences of speeding up the churning out of ever-cheaper goods while reducing the labor costs. Workers everywhere realized that producing more in less time, although more efficient, invariably meant fewer workers were needed, leading to smaller workforces and long unemployment lines.

By the mid-1920s, American industry had become hyperefficient, producing ever more goods at ever-cheaper manufacturing costs while saving on labor costs by pink-slipping redundant employees and maintaining a tight lid on the compensation for those still working.

THE CONSUMPTION CRISIS

Workers' concerns were not unfounded. The euphoria of scientific management and the doctrine of efficiency ran head-on into a consumption crisis as fewer workers with smaller paychecks left manufacturers with overstocked inventories and retailers with closed cash registers. Henry Ford was the first to wake up to the "consumption deficit" brought on by the efficiency of the modern assembly line, suggesting to his fellow capitalists the unheard-of notion that American companies provide a generous increase in pay and a reduction in the workweek or otherwise, he asked, "Who would buy my cars?"[1]

To his credit, Ford put his plea into practice by instituting an eight-hour workday—other corporate heavyweights begrudgingly followed his lead. Ford also increased the wages of his workforce, which still remained anathema among other corporate leaders wedded to accelerated efficiency with its emphasis on introducing ever-cheaper and more efficient technologies to reduce labor costs and return more revenue to the company.

The National Association of Manufacturers pleaded with the public to "end the buyers' strike" while their members continued to replace "less productive" and "expendable" workers with cheaper, more efficient machines. The U.S. Congress intervened in 1925, holding hearings before the Senate Committee on Education and Labor on the issue of endemic unemployment, and concluded that "technology improvements" were the primary cause. Moreover, according to the Senate Committee report, those who were let go remained unemployed for longer periods of time and when rehired received less remuneration in their paychecks.[2]

In the meantime, while the business community was begrudgingly willing to go along with an eight-hour day to defuse the growing militancy of the labor movement, they balked at increasing wage compensation and continued to replace human labor with more efficient machines, further weakening consumer demand. Instead, they looked to new ways to entice workers to buy.

It was at this time that the modern advertising industry emerged in full force, borrowing insights from the new field of psychology to draw workers away from the long-cherished Christian value of frugality—living within one's means—by offering up visions of "the good life" in the here and now, the future be damned. Popular magazines painted a picture of a new man and woman living the American Dream in the present. Advertising took on the task of redefining selfhood more by one's material possessions and surroundings than by one's traditional responsibilities and relationships. An individual's "character" became less defining than his or her "personality," and the latter was increasingly dressed up and surrounded by ever more possessions, celebrating a lifestyle once only available to the superrich.

The advertising industry realized that it needed to create "the dissatisfied consumer," which, in turn, would make people want new, more, and better things. This is where the automaker General Motors, long playing second fiddle to the Ford Motor Company, pulled ahead by being the first to embrace the new advertising strategy. When Henry Ford announced the introduction of his Model T to the public he remarked, "Any customer can have a car painted any color that he wants so long as it is black."[3] By contrast, GM realized that it could increase sales and even overtake Ford by offering different types of vehicles in different colors and change the models each year, making customers dissatisfied with their outmoded vehicle and hungry for the newest version coming off the assembly line. General Motors' Charles Kettering argued that the key to economic prosperity was to "keep the consumer dissatisfied."[4]

The business community came to understand that the best way to gin up sales was to debut new models and versions, even if the changes were merely cosmetic and marginal. The advertising pitch transformed consumer purchases from a mundane task to a seductive experience. Companies positioned their products as "new and improved," turning consumption into a game of "keeping up with the Joneses" to be the most modern and up-to-date in their daily life.

Still, mass advertising needed a second prong to seal the deal on increasing consumption. They found their willing prey in new immigrant families streaming into America at the time. The first generation of American-born children of immigrant parents were eager to experience the American Dream. The advertising industry played on both their aspirations and the embarrassment they felt about their immigrant parents' frugal lifestyles and old-world customs by enticing a younger native-born generation with store-bought clothes and the newest laborsaving appliances. The advertising industry used the new media of film and radio to showcase a more sensual and materialist culture, preparing America's newest progeny to become part of what would come to be called the "gospel of consumption."

By 1929, advertising had utterly transformed the very notion of consumption from a bare necessity to a hedonist craving. That year, President Herbert Hoover's Committee on Recent Economic Changes published a report on the change in human psychology that had occurred in just a few decades at the hands of a savvy advertising industry. Here are the findings:

> The survey has proved conclusively what has long been held theoretically to be true, that wants are insatiable; that one want satisfied makes way for another. The conclusion is that economically we have a boundless field before us; that there are new wants which will make way endlessly for newer wants as fast

as they are satisfied. . . . By advertising and other promotional devices . . . a measurable pull on production has been created. . . . It would seem that we can go on with increasing activity. . . . Our situation is fortunate, our momentum remarkable.[5]

The only thing standing in the way was how to afford entrance to the American Dream. The capitalist system provided it in the form of buying on credit. It was called installment buying. In the 19th century, furniture, an expensive item, was increasingly purchased on credit via installments. The Singer sewing machine was among the first appliances purchasable in installment payments. The company introduced the new financing mechanism as far back as 1850. By the 1920s, installment loans had taken off. At the top of the installment payment ladder was the purchase of automobiles, the most expensive and prized possession of the time and which, more than any other, came to be seen as the very epitome of experiencing the American Dream. As early as 1924, 75 percent of all the automobiles purchased were financed by installment loans.[6]

Mass advertising extolling a vision of glamour and the good life ushered in what social critic Christopher Lasch called the "culture of narcissism."[7] The new era would compensate for declining wages and underemployment by extending credit via installment buying, providing a pathway to mass consumption, allowing industry to breathe life back into the cult of efficiency and accelerate production to keep the industrial machine churning and revenue accruing.

This consumer binge crashed along with the stock market in 1929. While installment credit limped along during the whole of the Great Depression in the 1930s, there were too few workers employed and, even then, they were taking home smaller paychecks. Frugality roared back, this time not to put away income in the form of a nest egg for the future but, rather, just to ward off being put out on the street.

Despite the precipitous fall in consumer demand, American industry continued to replace workers with cheaper and more efficient technology during the whole of the Great Depression. A 1938 study found that although 51 percent of the decline in man-hours worked was due to a fall in production, a startling 49 percent was traceable to rising productivity and labor displacement.[8]

Given that more efficient technology and rising productivity required fewer workers, society had two choices: reduce the workforce or reduce the workweek. Most companies continued to favor the former course, although it was tantamount to "cutting off one's nose to spite one's face" as fewer workers meant fewer paychecks and dwindling purchasing power, even with installment credit.

A few companies did decide to bite the bullet and move to a six-hour day and a thirty-hour workweek to share the work and keep people employed, hoping it would rejuvenate consumption and boost the economy.

Some of America's leading companies, including Kellogg's; Sears, Roebuck; Standard Oil; and Hudson Motors, shifted to a thirty-hour workweek. Kellogg's went a step further, raising the minimum wage of its male workers by four dollars per day, an increase that offset the loss of two hours of work each day.[9] Federal legislation mandating a thirty-hour workweek passed the Senate and secured sufficient potential votes to pass in the House of Representatives, only to be nixed by President Franklin Delano Roosevelt.

With employers continuing to replace workers with more advanced technologies, the incoming Roosevelt administration launched a series of high-profile government-sponsored and government-financed programs to put people back to work, boost consumer spending, and stimulate the economy. Though each of these New Deal efforts provided a modicum of relief, it was not enough to revive consumption spending to the level that matched the productive capacity of American industry. The result was that many businesses failed and declared bankruptcy.

Through it all, technologies continued to remake the workplace, increasing productive capacity, but industries could not find sufficient demand to clear inventories. For all of the bold initiatives that went into the New Deal, America remained mired in depression until its entrance into World War II and the remobilization of the U.S. economy for wartime production. Millions of Americans joined the armed forces and millions of others, especially women, went to work in well-paid defense industry jobs.

While incomes of workers in war-related industries climbed back up, price controls and rationing prevented families from buying and consuming at the same level they enjoyed prior to the Great Depression. Scores of basic goods, accounting for one-seventh of all consumer buying, were subject to rationing, stymying consumer spending.[10] With widespread rationing placing life in general on hold during the war effort, family savings grew. The pent-up savings of American families would soon come in handy after the war.

Returning soldiers, anxious to make up for lost years, rushed to purchase homes with Federal Housing Administration (FHA) mortgages in the suburban tracts being laid out along the exits of the new Interstate Highway System beginning in the late 1950s. The Interstate Highway System would become the most expensive public works project in all of history. The suburbs brought with them a rebirth of the American Dream—this time along the lines of what would come to be called "suburban domesticity."

THE SUBURBAN CAMELOT

American industry ramped up the suburban economy with the same vigor it had mobilized for the war. It should be noted that families living in the suburbs were twice as likely to own one or more automobiles as their counterparts still living in the cities.[11] The suburbs also brought a new public life with the introduction of fast-food chains, shopping malls, and theme parks. The interstate highways opened up America to a new iteration of travel—auto tourism—which boosted automobile sales. Motels and tourist attractions popped up everywhere as Americans took to the road to enjoy the vast expanse and cultural diversity of the country.

With suburban life, the gospel of consumption became a tidal wave. For a short period of time, paralleling the thirty-year construction of the nation's interstate highway infrastructure—jobs were plentiful and salaries were generous. Workers of every kind were recruited for the build-out of suburban America. But even the new prosperity enjoyed by millions of Americans was not enough to keep up with an insatiable suburban appetite, fed by massive consumer advertising via the new medium of television. Only 9 percent of Americans owned televisions in 1950, but by 1978, 91 percent of homes had TVs.[12] For most Americans, the medium had become an addiction. According to the Nielsen Report, in 2009 an average sixty-five-year-old American had watched the screen for nine entire years, averaging four hours a day and twenty-eight hours per week. And what's more, the average sixty-five-year-old had watched more than two million TV commercials in his or her lifetime.[13]

The enticement with television was that the programming was free. The catch was that local TV stations and TV networks made their revenue on advertising. In a very real sense, television was first and foremost an advertising medium putting "a salesman in every living room" and only secondarily an entertainment medium that served as a lure to draw in prospective consumers. It worked. If millions of Americans became addicted to watching TV, the medium conditioned them to become equally addicted to buying more things and experiences. The gospel of consumption enjoyed a second life.

Even the increase in take-home pay during the short-lived suburban dream couldn't keep up with the addiction to buy. The financial community saved the day with revolving credit and credit cards. Department stores were the first to introduce the system of revolving credit. A customer could defer paying back the balance owed on purchases by being charged interest on whatever balance was left unpaid. The giant department stores, in effect, became bankers and often made as much profit on the interest charged to customers' revolving credit accounts as they made on the sale.[14]

Banks and large finance companies began to take notice of the revolving credit scheme used by department stores in the 1960s. While the experimentation a decade earlier in the issuing of credit cards had proven largely unsuccessful, the banks considered stepping in a second time, sensing the possibility of a huge credit market. Although there were potential risks, they reasoned that while middle-class suburban families were racing into consumer debt to finance their new lifestyles, they were generally successful in paying off the principal over time.

Bank of America was the first to jump in with its BankAmericard in 1958. A decade later the card was renamed Visa. In 1966, a consortium of California banks introduced the Master Charge card. Credit cards proliferated in the 1970s. They quickly replaced cash and checks for many goods and services. Unlike department stores, the banks and financial institutions had the deep pockets to finance consumer credit on a macro scale. The credit card was a game changer in the debt market.

Revolving credit without limits gave the consumer command and control over how much they would borrow, rather than the banker setting the limits, fundamentally changing the relationship between lenders and borrowers. The banks were happy to make the accommodation, realizing that the more consumers extended their revolving credit lines, the more revenue would accrue to the credit card companies. And, as long as the banks were maintaining a tight control on background checks to ensure that their largely middle-class base of potential card users were creditworthy, the risk seemed manageable.

It was during this period, however, that the financial community took a gamble by extending consumer lending to millions of Americans who previously would not have been eligible for loans or credit cards. The new departure was called "subprime lending." Anxious to increase their profitability, banks and credit card companies made credit cards available to the 26 percent of Americans who were previously excluded because they were poor, generally underemployed, mostly from disadvantaged communities, and with little or no credit history by which to judge their credit risk. The new credit card holders were labeled as "thin file" customers.[15] Despite the inherent risk that came with subprime credit card lending, the financial community and American industry were determined to stimulate more and more consumer spending.

THE END OF WORK

Meanwhile, the three decades spent on completing the Second Industrial Revolution infrastructure and the well-paid jobs that came with it masked a very different phenomenon that was quietly unfolding across industries, affecting both the blue- and white-collar labor forces, whose ranks were thinning. Entire job categories were disappearing, threatening the livelihood of millions of Americans with troubling implications for the future of the economy and society.

The new wrinkle in employment could be traced back to 1943, when a mathematician from the Massachusetts Institute of Technology, Norbert Wiener, published a scholarly article in the journal *Philosophy of Science* on the new theory of cybernetics, which provided the technical description of how machines can think, learn, and adjust their behavior via feedback. Wiener's description of cybernetics provided the scientific and technical framework for the age of computerization and later, artificial intelligence. He argued that "the physical functioning of the living individual and the operation of some of the newer communication machines are precisely parallel."[16]

Wiener was aware of the profound consequences that would come with more efficient smart machines in industry and commerce and warned that "the automatic machine . . . is the precise economic equivalent of slave labor. Any labor which competes with slave labor must accept the economic conditions of slave labor."[17]

His prescient prophecy was soon realized. The first generation of numerical control technologies were introduced into factories in the late 1950s, marking the beginning of the automation of industrial production. The computerization and automation of every facet of economic life followed quickly in the ensuing decades, first eliminating unskilled labor, then skilled labor, white-collar labor, and professional and knowledge labor. By the 1990s, it was becoming obvious that a revolution in the nature of work was beginning to eliminate jobs across many sectors of the economy (see my book *The End of Work*, 1995).

Since then, the replacement of millions of workers with robotics, computerization, and AI has dramatically accelerated efficiencies while beggaring and devastating workforces in every country, forcing a crisis in consumption of such profound proportions that palliatives offered up in the way of extending ever more consumer debt to encourage buying were becoming a social time bomb. The average family's savings rate, which in the early 1990s was around 8 percent, took a nosedive in the years to follow, shrinking to 1 percent in 2000.[18]

MORTGAGING THE FUTURE

Just at the time that the automation revolution was shifting into high gear, another knockout force was amassing—the introduction of subprime mortgages into the housing market in 1997. This newest iteration of subprime lending took the American economy and society on a wild ride and quickly passed into other countries to become a historic bubble, before bursting in the late summer of 2008. Although Wall Street and the banking community were at least subliminally aware that the subprime mortgage lending had all the earmarks of a giant Ponzi scheme, their "animal spirits" took over, as economist John Maynard Keynes might suggest, snuffing any worries or reckonings that might lie ahead. Virtually everyone in the financial community, Wall Street, and the housing industry, almost to a person, were on board for the ride.

Subprime mortgages required little money down, with interest rates only increasing over time, encouraging millions of new buyers whose income and creditworthiness would not have qualified them previously to take the bait and purchase homes beyond their means. The housing stampede was on. Just between the years 2000 and 2006, the percentage of subprime mortgages rose from a historical baseline of about 8 percent of the market to approximately 20 percent.[19] Speculation skyrocketed. Investors—those individuals buying homes as investments rather than domiciles—rose from 20 percent to 35 percent in just the span of 2006–7.[20] New homebuyers also became speculators, often purchasing a home and as the value of the property rose with more bidders entering the market, flipping the house and purchasing another, higher-priced home, only to flip that one as the value of the new home increased, and so on. Home values doubled and tripled in some regions of the United States.

The real estate bubble burst in 2008.[21] Housing prices plummeted. Millions of Americans, who had been riding high on the runaway housing market bubble, spending more and going deeper into debt, never suspected that there would be a day of judgment, when they would find themselves unable to pay the interest on their mortgage that was now coming due. Foreclosures spread across America. Banks and other lending institutions faced bankruptcy. Some of the big players on Wall Street went down, beginning with Lehman Brothers. AIG, the company that held subprime mortgage bonds and loans in the billions of dollars, faced a meltdown. Banks froze lending and the American economy slowed to a halt in the most significant economic collapse since the Great Depression. The collapse was branded forever as the "Great Recession."

The federal government came to the rescue of Wall Street with a $700 billion bailout, arguing that the giants of American finance were "too big to fail." While the Wall Street firms that created the bubble came away largely unscathed, millions of American families and workers were abandoned. Unemployment soared to 10 percent of the workforce by the end of 2009—17 percent of the labor force if accounting for discouraged workers who left altogether and marginally attached workers who were working only part-time but desiring full-time employment. Adding it all up, the housing bubble left 27 million Americans unemployed or underemployed and saddled with debt and 2.9 million homeowners receiving foreclosure notices in 2010 alone.[22] To appreciate the depth of the toll on American workers and their families, by 2008 accumulated household debt was nearing a whopping $12.7 trillion.[23] To put things into perspective, the U.S. GDP in 2008 was only slightly higher at $14.7 trillion.[24] Clearly, the capitalist system was broken.

More frustrating still, apparently no lessons were learned from the carnage of the Great Recession. It is true that America bounced back in an economic recovery between 2010 and 2020. But, that recovery is, to some extent, a mirage made possible by the buildup of still another consumer debt bubble. In the first quarter of 2020—before the economic downturn brought on by the coronavirus—total household debt had climbed back over the past decade, totaling $14.3 trillion, eclipsing the previous debt peak in 2008 by $1.6 trillion.[25]

Why don't companies just raise wages commensurate with productivity gains and reduce the workweek in line with the increased efficiencies brought on by robotics, automation, and AI—which seems eminently more reasonable? The answer is it flies smack in the face of accounting procedures and accompanying quarterly statements issued by companies to shareholders. Publicly traded companies walk a tightrope that critics call "short-termism," having to show their shareholders increasing revenues each quarter of the year or risk a drop in the value of their stock, or worse, replacement of their CEO.

Increasing efficiency and productivity with the introduction of cheaper technology and AI allows companies to let workers go and keep wages low for the existing workforce. Cutting costs looks good on the books and allows them to show gains in revenue, making shareholders happy. In the long run, the financial community and American industry would be better off sharing their gains brought on by new and more efficient technologies with the American workforce, but unfortunately it contradicts the way the system operates. Efficiency, measured in terms of cost-benefit analysis, drives the system.

THE EFFICIENCY GAME GOES MENTAL

While the gospel of consumption has been kept alive with more intricate ways of keeping consumers buying into debt, the efficiency paradigm has likewise morphed in more refined directions since the birth of Taylorism. Taylor's more blunt approach to applying the principles of scientific management that were taken up in the early years by the Ford Motor Company and soon thereafter by other companies and industries across America and economies abroad was experiencing diminishing returns by the 1950s. It was around that time that the Japanese company Toyota began experimenting with its own modified version of Taylorism, which it branded "lean production." This new more enlightened version, at first blush, seemed so different in application from Taylor's original vision, as to be an entirely new management model. In practice over the past half century, the new approach to the management of the workforce, more often than not, bore a closer resemblance to Taylorism than one might suspect.

Like Fordism, Toyota's goal was similarly skewed toward producing more output with fewer resources and workers. Where it differed is in the nature of the production process and the "handling" of the workforce. Toyota executives came to believe that Fordism, predicated on mass production of high-volume standardized products, was far too inflexible and lacked the agility to respond in real time to changes in market preferences and consumer demand.

Companies relying on mass production of standardized product lines also tend to run their operations at full throttle to reduce costs. Because of the enormous expense of the machinery, downtime is avoided at all times to optimize amortization. To ensure continuous operations, management has "buffers" in the form of extra inventory and workers to avoid running out of inputs or slowing down the flow of production. Lastly, the high cost of investment in the machinery precluded retooling for new product lines. The trade-off is the customer benefits from cheap prices at the expense of fewer new offerings and less variety.

Lean production, often called just-in-time manufacturing, is designed rather for agility and flexibility. The objective is to produce only what the market is demanding at the moment and to make available a wide variety of products to meet customers' individual preferences while simultaneously increasing efficiencies across its value chains. In their 1991 book *The Machine That Changed the World,* management professors James Womack, Daniel Jones, and Daniel Roos argued that lean production is lean because:

> It uses less of everything compared with mass production—half the human effort in the factory, half the manufacturing space, half the investment in tools, half the engineering hours to develop a new product in half the time. Also, it requires keeping far less than half the needed inventory on site, results in many fewer defects, and produces a greater and ever-growing variety of products.[26]

The Japanese approach to lean production tempers Taylorism's top-down approach to command and control of the workforce with its rigid division of labor into ever smaller prescribed tasks and assignments by organizing its workforce into teams that collaborate. Design engineers, computer programmers, and factory workers interact face-to-face in sharing ideas, problem solving, and implementing joint decisions on the factory floor. The rationale is that troubleshooting problems in multidiscipline teams operating on the ground in real time results in less downtime.

Workers are even invited to share their ideas on the development of new cars, including questions around design, production, distribution, marketing, and sales, in a process called "concurrent engineering" to ensure a more seamless systemic approach to the manufacturing and sale of the vehicle. This team process is less about giving employees a feeling of being counted and more about the bottom line. A delay of just six months in moving a new product to market can reduce profits by up to 33 percent.[27] Inviting everyone into the design stage holds down costs and avoids delays.

The lean production system is built around what is called the Five Zeroes Strategy: zero defects, zero breakdowns, zero delays, zero paper (reduction of bureaucracy), and zero inventory. This is what is meant by lean . . . using just what you need, just at the time, to produce just what the customer is asking for.

The theory of lean production sounds almost too good to be true and a far cry from Taylorism. In practice, the exercise of authority is always from the top down, though more subtle and even more demanding of its workforce, and less democratic than what might meet the eye. That's not to say that it isn't more efficient. Quite the contrary. By demanding more of every worker—harnessing both their mind and their body—companies using lean production have, in fact, increased their efficiencies, optimized the use of resources, and quickened the process of producing and delivering their product lines while saving on operational costs.

A study of three decades of lean production by sociologist Christopher Huxley of Trent University in Canada drawing on research in lean production practices in the United States, Canada, and Mexico is revealing. The study found that lean production in Japan "emphasized the intensification of work . . . and speedup for hourly production workers" and "was exacerbated by a deliberate technique of managerial control described as 'management by stress.'"[28] Furthermore, the "principle of Kaizen [the Japanese term for continuous improvement] and the quest to reduce non-value added labor time suggest a relentless campaign to reduce recovery, or down time, for the worker on the job."[29]

Huxley concludes that "thirty years of lean production in North America provide scant evidence to support the enthusiastic initial claims made that the new system would fundamentally transform for the better the quality of work life for those working in the new workplaces."[30]

Lean production, as it turns out, is merely a more veiled form of Taylorism, designed to increase workers' performance using psychological manipulation to condition and extract ever more efficiency, all to the service of optimizing output at minimum expense.

THE ENDGAME

Over the course of the 20th century and into the 21st century, industries' approach to managing the workforce became ever more veiled. Whether applying a strict behavioral approach of rewards and punishments, appealing to participation and engagement, or nurturing emotional intelligence, the goal was and remains adjusting the workers to become efficient appendages to the machines they attend.

Now, the digital revolution has taken commercial life to a new level of accelerated economic activity with its emphasis on big data, analytics, algorithms, and surveillance, making the Taylorism of the early 20th century seem like child's play. The mental stress of attending a digitally sped up economy is taking workers in every category to the limits of human endurance. The efficiency imperative is now evolving at such warp speed that it's unlikely that masses of human beings will be able to keep up physically, emotionally, and mentally, and might well fall by the wayside as robots, automation, and AI replace mass employment and even much of professional labor over the course of the next several decades.

Every industry has its own favorite guiding principle. For example, in real estate it's "location, location, location." For management, "what gets measured, gets managed." That's the Taylorist legacy handed down over the past six generations, reprocessed over and over again to fit the prevailing social narrative.

If Fordism and lean production dominated the 20th century, the Amazonians have carried the Taylorist vision into the 21st century. Amazon, the largest logistics company in the world, is all about measurement, management, and hyperefficiency. The company delivered 3.5 billion packages globally in 2019, and jumped up to the number one spot in the Global Fortune 500 in late 2020.[31] Its founder, Jeff Bezos, is now the second-richest human being in the world, worth $170 billion.[32] His sprawling logistics empire is easily the most efficient industrial machine ever put online. If Frederick Taylor were alive today, he would no doubt be in awe of the sheer breadth and scope of Bezos's accomplishments using the principles of scientific management.

But one person's utopian dream is often another's dystopian nightmare. Bezos's gigantic warehouses with their automated control systems, ubiquitous surveillance, and thousands of mobile robots all synchronized via algorithmic logistics guidance networks are an immense technological achievement. But a closer look reveals the dirty truth that with all of the high-tech appurtenances, the entire system succeeds or fails on the shoulders of 1.2 million employees, most of whom work at low wages in modern-day sweatshop conditions—although the fulfillment centers are air-conditioned and fire-resistant.[33]

Amazon prides itself on measures and management and at tasking employees beyond their comfort zone—both mentally and physically. When they "hit the wall" because of the inhumane pace and workloads, they are admonished rather than consoled by supervisors and warned to "climb the wall." Its management and white-collar workforces are often expected to be on call 24/7—literally at times working past midnight and taking text messages in the middle of the night. New employees quickly learn that only the fittest survive.[34]

In management sessions, colleagues are expected to rip into the shortcomings, faults, and ineptitudes of their cohorts with the saving grace that it will energize them to excel and exceed beyond their limits. While some do survive and even flourish, many others have bailed out, unable to take the constant pressure to improve performance and efficiency. One former executive told of his enduring image of watching colleagues weeping in their offices as he walked by. "You walk out of a conference room and you'll see a grown man covering his face. Nearly every person I worked with, I saw cry at their desk."[35]

Frugality is the watchword at Amazon facilities—no frills, no little extras, be it subsidized lunch or more spacious offices. The look is spare and lean. And across the workforce, from initial screenings of new recruits to advancements up the chain of command, every single worker is continually being assessed on his or her "performance improvement algorithm." From top to bottom, employee activity, regardless of how trivial, is subject to measurement of performance, with the data duly registered in algorithms that keep a moment-to-moment account of every efficiency gained or lost. In this sense, the efficiencies of the one million–plus Amazon employees are tallied, appraised, and adjusted, keeping a running tab on every aspect of their work in the same manner that the company applies to its retail operations and its customers.

Freelance journalist Emily Guendelsberger went undercover to work in an Amazon warehouse in Indiana and recounts her personal work experience in vivid detail in her book *On the Clock: What Low-Wage Work Did to Me and How It Drives America Insane*. Guendelsberger was a "picker," assigned to locate items from the stockroom, pick them off the shelves, and send them down the line on automated robots. She characterizes the work at the bottom of the Amazon pyramid in the fulfillment centers as "cyborg jobs." She was outfitted with a scanner gun worn on her waist that monitors her location at every moment and guides her to the item she is to pick from the shelf. The scanner also tells her how much time is allotted to accomplish the task. A sliding bar counts down the seconds remaining to make the pick, scan the item, and send it along.

After each item is picked on the floor of the fulfillment center, the next assignment appears immediately on the scan. The timing of each task is so tight that it leaves virtually no room for rest. Many of the items being picked by Emily and her cohorts in the Indiana warehouse are oversized and heavy and take a toll in back injuries. In 2020, the high injury rate at one of Amazon's facilities was found to be nearly double the rate of non-Amazon warehouses in the United States.[36]

With few bathrooms, often remotely placed in the giant warehouses, it often took Guendelsberger and fellow coworkers ten minutes at a minimum on their toilet breaks. She reports: "You're only supposed to have eighteen minutes per eleven-hour shift, *maximum*. And they do notice—a manager *will* come and find you and give you a talking-to if your scanner reports you're taking too much Time Off Task."[37] Many employees report that they abstain from drinking water or any other liquid before and during their shifts as their only recourse.

Although Amazon is the benchmark in the new era of digital neo-Taylorism, it's unfair to suggest that it's unique. It's only that Amazon is the most successful of the new companies in the neo-Taylorist era. Electronic sensors, browser history retention, phone apps, network records, and facial recognition systems are just the beginning of a digital surveillance culture.

Does all of this surveillance yield efficient results? Absolutely! In 2009, United Parcel Service affixed two hundred sensors onto its delivery trucks that track everything along the route, from driving speed to stops, to assess the optimum number of deliveries that could be made per day. The company found that within four years of introducing surveillance monitoring of its workforce, 1.4 million more packages were delivered by carriers every twenty-four hours by one thousand fewer drivers. The surveillance was a stimulus for some to outperform and an intimidation to others who feared demotion or being fired.[38]

GAMIFICATION:
Making Servitude Fun

Using digital platforms to collect massive amounts of data and employing analytics to mine that data and create algorithms and apps to impose increasing demands on workers with the aim of improving efficiency has reached dizzying proportions, numbing employees' personal sense of agency—a kind of mentally enforced servitude that's unique in history. But there's one more twist of the screw that takes Taylorism and the efficiency agenda to new heights. It's called gamification and it's the most sophisticated form of command and control designed to elicit greater performance and efficiencies from every worker.

The Dutch historian Johan Huizinga coined the phrase Homo Ludens in his book of the same title, published in 1938. Huizinga suggested that while Homo faber and Homo economicus tell us much about the social orientation of our species, at a deeper level, society arises out of play—"It is through this playing that society expresses its interpretation of life and the world."[39] The many aspects of human activity—language, myth and folklore, art, dance, philosophy, the law, and most of all, the stories we tell each other that make up our collective narrative and worldview—emerge from deep play.

The basic elements of play are very different from those of work. Play is enjoyable. People can't be coerced or forced into play. It has to be engaged in freely. Although a certain amount of deep play exists at the high end of professional employment, the vast majority of jobs across society are dull, repetitive, and if not necessary to survive, would be abandoned without so much as an afterthought. And finally, play often exists in a timeless state without a rigid beginning and end. Being spontaneous, play is often open-ended, and when caught up in the sheer joy of it, players tend to lose all sense of time. Instead of time being a constraint to feed a utilitarian goal in the most efficient manner possible, time often becomes suspended during play.

Contrast the attributes of play to work, often described as tedious and exploitative. But now, even play is being harnessed by industry, embraced by management consultants and extolled by business schools to the service of unrelenting efficiency. Workers are now referred to as "talent." Performance has become the stand-in for achievement and play has been bastardized by a dark surrogate called gamification.

The unspoken purpose of gamification is to use play to inculcate the workforce with the rationalized rules and procedures management requires to bind them to the task of becoming ever more efficient in their thoughts and actions in order to keep pace with the machines and technological processes they are attending. Gamification has established itself as the last and most efficient rite of passage in the long road traveled by the forces of production.

Writing in the *Journal of Gaming and Virtual Worlds*, Jennifer deWinter, Carly A. Kocurek, and Randall Nichols argue that gamification serves as the "reconditioner" of a global workforce emerging in the network-based economy and has become an essential feature in the next stage of capitalism. The authors contend that:

> The computer games successfully look and act as a type of scientific management as advocated by Frederick Winslow Taylor; however, because of the computerized medium itself, gamified training serves as an expansion of scientific management into new spaces. . . . This engagement dangerously collapses the domains of labor and leisure by combining the domains of play space and the real world . . . the problem with institutionalizing alternative realities in art or in games is that they become co-opted by the system, subordinated to the prevailing world view. . . . Players subject themselves to the logic of the game, and through participating in the algorithmic processes of the game, those same players become trained.[40]

A study done by Tracey Sitzmann, a management professor at the University of Colorado, examining sixty-five different academic samples to determine the efficacy of simulation games in teaching employees to improve their performance and efficiency, found that declarative knowledge "was 11 percent higher for trainees taught with simulation games than a comparison group; procedural knowledge was 14 percent higher; retention was 9 percent higher; and self-efficacy was 20 percent higher."[41]

DeWinter et al. cite the example of a training game used by Coldstone Creamery, an American ice-cream parlor chain designed to be fun while, at the same time, teaching new employees how to successfully serve their customers under different shift scenarios. The game features a very sophisticated ice-cream parlor simulation, making it more fun. The trainees compete with each other in the simulation in customer service, accuracy of portion size, and correct recipe recognition, all of which determine their overall scores. Upon completion, the game tells the player "to the penny how much his mistakes would cost the store."[42]

The game is so entertaining that trainees often spend far more of their leisure hours on "the assignment" than they might otherwise do in "studying" a traditional training manual. Simulation games are an efficient way to train workers for their assignments and tasks and because the games are fun, the workers are more likely to think of their real work in the same way. In other words, it will pay off in terms of increased efficiency and a motivated workforce, or better yet, "playforce."

What ties traditional Taylorism with gamification is that both employ rationalized processes to train workforces. The difference is that with traditional Taylorism the workers are on guard to resist or, at least, offer up only the minimum of effort to get by, while gamification masks the rationalized manipulation, making the player feel that he or she has used their own agency to master the game, and later the work process itself.

The data being collected in gamification throughout the employee's tenure has a second life, providing rich information that can be mined with analytics to revise, embellish, and adapt their workers to the changing market environment. The data is also a means to evaluate the workers' performance, thus making ongoing surveillance an integral part of the gamification experience.

Widespread corporate gamification in the future will almost assuredly shrink the domain of leisure. Perhaps the most insidious aspect of gamification is the capture of play by commercial forces who use it to recondition millions of people to accept a life of unrelenting work, cued to increased efficiency and returns on investment.

❊   ❊   ❊

While Frederick Taylor's impact on the workings of commerce has been singular, his influence has extended far deeper into virtually every aspect of society over the course of the 20th century and to this day. His obsession with efficiency has permeated the depths of human agency, changing the very way humanity has come to see itself, with deleterious effects not only on the human psyche but also on the natural world.

Harvard Business School professor Gary Hamel's glowing assessment of Taylor's accomplishments and impact is widely shared by some, and equally reviled by others. He writes:

"With his emphasis on research, planning, communications, standards, in-centives, and feedback, it is possible to track Taylor's influence to every sector. Business, government, health care and education have all incorporated the principles into the fabric of their operations. One hundred years after the pub-lication of his most famous work, Frederick Winslow Taylor's subtle influence is as persistent as the ticking of his ever-present stopwatch."[43]

Peter Drucker, long regarded as the father of modern business management, is even more effusive in his adoration, suggesting that Taylor's work has been "the most powerful as well as the most lasting contribution America has made to Western thought since the Federalist Papers."[44]

But it's not over yet. Taylorism may be on the cusp of its ultimate success because of efficiency advances in robotics and AI that are beginning to eclipse the ability of even the best and brightest workforces to keep pace and stay rel-evant. In the executive suites of high-tech companies there is growing talk over what's called the approaching singularity—the point at which smart technology becomes more intelligent and efficient than the human race—forcing a funda-mental paradigm shift in the role of our species in managing our own destiny.

The public's wake-up call came in 1997 when IBM's Deep Blue computer defeated world chess champion Garry Kasparov in a match, igniting a global debate on whether robots and AI might one day outmatch human intelligence and become the dominant species. A spate of new studies by leading univer-sities and management companies, including Oxford Economics, McKinsey, and the World Economic Forum, project millions of jobs lost to the new smart technology.[45]

The insatiable appetite for more efficient and ever cheaper technology drives every industrial sector. Terry Gou, the head of China's Foxconn, the world's largest contract manufacturer, whose clients include Apple and other corporate giants, delivered a searing rebuke of the world's human workforce that others in corporate boardrooms prefer to keep shuttered behind closed doors. He notes that "Hon Hai (Foxconn) has a workforce of over one million, and as human beings are also animals, to manage one million animals gives me a headache."[46] Gou is putting teeth to his ambition. Foxconn replaced sixty thousand workers with robots by 2016 alone, and more since, with the goal of reaching 100 percent automation in "lights out factories" in the very near future. An Oxford economic study found that 8.5 percent of the global workforce will likely be displaced by robots by 2030.[47]

What the prognosticators are missing is that the Age of Resilience will bring hundreds of millions of people into the new categories of "resilient em-ployment," engaging in meaningful work in eco-stewardship that is too complex for even the most intelligent technology. The new epoch will change our very notion of agency, taking future generations away from a "work ethic" centered on production and consumption of things to a "stewardship ethic" of tending to the natural world. We will address the changes in the nature and functions of the workforce in part four, as we delve deeper into the economic makeup of the Resilient Revolution.

If the human family is to have a future, it will depend, to a great extent, on whether we can come together as a species facing a common threat to our survival and the survival of our fellow creatures who travel with us and to whom we are beholden in ways we are just beginning to understand and appreciate. How, then, do we reconceive our existence both temporally and spatially in a way that will allow us to adjust to a planet that is quickly heating up from global warming? All around us we witness with both awe and dread as the planet's spheres struggle to readjust to the damage our species has inflicted during the fossil fuel–driven Industrial Age. We begin to sense how misguided we've been in ever believing that our own species' agency was sufficient to master the powerful planetary forces that govern life on Earth.

Thinking and acting as a planetary civilization might have seemed over the top and even silly a generation ago. Not now. Though the future seems bleak, we have a last card to play that could allow our species and many of our fellow creatures to weather the storms and fires that are coming. To understand how this last hand will play out, we need to rethink what life on Earth is all about in a wholly new way and how our species fits into it.

When Charles Darwin published his book *On the Origin of Species* in 1859, it altered our ideas on how life evolved over history. While many of his premises continue to bear weight, even today, the picture he drew falls far short of telling the whole story. Dramatic developments in the fields of chemistry, physics, and biology in recent years have begun to describe a far more expansive narrative of how life came to be and how it evolves and sustains itself. Although not yet widely shared in the public domain, the new broader description of evolution shatters our most basic assumptions about the forces that have shaped life.

What the new discoveries tell us will fundamentally change what it means to be a human being on an animated Earth comprised of a manifold of interactive agencies that together dictate the terms by which we exist and flourish. It's this new understanding, if properly absorbed, that provides the insight that will allow our species to change course at this moment in history and redirect our journey, hopefully in time to save our species and our extended evolutionary family.

Part Three

HOW WE
GOT HERE

RETHINKING EVOLUTION
ON EARTH

7

THE ECOLOGICAL SELF

WE ARE EACH A DISSIPATIVE
PATTERN

When most of us think about selfhood, we consider it to be a rather uncontroversial subject. We're each born with a genetic profile that partially conditions what we become and the rest is filled in by our individual drives, passions, experiences, and relationships that make each of us unique. We like to think of ourselves as autonomous agents, although subject to the serendipities of life and the good fortune and bad luck that come our way. We're willing to accept the notion that not everyone else thinks and feels the same way, and acknowledge that there are even some among us who live in various alternative realities that can even border on the psychotic. The rest of us, however, generally agree about what being a conscious human being is all about. And that's the way it has always been.

BECOMING HUMAN

Not really. In just the short half millennium of history that marks the passage from the medieval to the postmodern era, twenty-five generations of our species have entertained a wide assortment of beliefs about what it means to be a conscious self. Our Christian forebears believed that every baby is born in original sin and lives a desperate life of gnawing fear as to whether he or she will be granted eternal salvation in heaven or burn in hell for all eternity after death. In the modern era, Charles Darwin took exception to original sin, arguing that human consciousness is more of a crapshoot and that the random selection of traits passed on by parents to offspring largely establish not only one's physical being but, to some limited extent, one's consciousness as well. Sigmund Freud was convinced that babies are born into this world with an insatiable appetite to extinguish their libido, and that every living moment is cued to quenching their sexual desires. But what binds together all of the more contemporary ideas about the human makeup, at least since the Enlightenment in the 18th century, is the notion of one's unique character as a relatively "free" agent continually bumping up against myriad forces but generally returning to an equilibrium—just as Newton predicted—all the while maintaining a very clear sense of autonomous personhood.

The 18th-century philosopher Immanuel Kant argued that autonomy is humanity's highest calling but requires a lifelong struggle to ensure that one's actions are purely rational and unencumbered by emotions or any external considerations that might taint the natural proclivity to employ pure reason in one's worldly experience.

In the past, thinking of oneself as an autonomous agent would have been incomprehensible. Our forager-hunter Paleolithic forebears had little notion of the kind of individuality we take for granted today. Their migratory lives were organized around very little differentiation of skills and few means to store and divide surpluses by which to distinguish one individual's status from another's. The anthropologist Lucien Lévy-Bruhl points out that the very idea of "I" does not exist among primitive people—only "we."[1] Life was lived collectively and what differentiation did exist was in the form of cohort groups organized by age and gender with identity bound up in the temporal rites of passage into different stages of their life cycle from early childhood to elders.

A primitive social order did exist in every forager-hunter group. The elders of the community, who retained the stored memories and collective wisdom of the ancestors, were looked to for guidance, but again life was far more egalitarian than in any other subsequent period of history. There was little to distinguish anything resembling individual personhood, and they had even less awareness of their uniqueness as a species. Forager-hunters lived in an undifferentiated world of forms and forces continually intermingling in what Lévy-Bruhl described as "a mist of unity" in which other animals were not distinguished as "the other" but rather as animated beings in different guises. Even mountains, waterfalls, and forests were thought of as alive and full of agency.

Darwin noted in his travels that forager-hunters were constantly observing other animals and would mimic their behavior, in a sense embedding their spirit into their own. Historian Lewis Mumford observed that incorporating the agency of other living creatures gave our early ancestors clues to how better to survive:

"Being imitative as well as curious, he may have learned trapping from the spider, basketry from the birds' nests, dam building from beavers, burrowing from rabbits, and the art of using poisons from snakes. Unlike most species, man did not hesitate to learn from other creatures and copy their ways; by appropriating their diet[s] and methods of getting food he multiplied his own chances for survival."[2]

In their rituals our Paleolithic ancestors wore antlers, dressed in pelts, and adorned their bodies with feathers, while mimicking the behavior of other animal spirits. This seamless intertwining of the living world and the spirit world is the essence of animism. This ancient cosmology holds the belief that all phenomena, be they material or immaterial, of the flesh or the spirit, have agency and interact temporally in a spatial dimension that is interconnected and boundaryless. The sense that everything around one's self—not only other creatures but even nonliving beings—are animated spirits not unlike ourselves is what one observes in almost every toddler and child up to the age of five or six who likewise inhabit a magical world surrounded by a field of life forces, many of which are inanimate.

Paleolithic people lived in a temporal world of seasons and cycles that historian Mircea Eliade describes as an "eternal return."[3] Just as their migratory life was wedded to the birth, life, death, and rebirth of the seasonal cycles, so too did they come to understand their own passages in life. Upon death, one's spirit remains in limbo only to eventually find its way into other forms of life, be it human or other creatures, or even embedded in the inanimate world. The 19th-century anthropologist Sir Edward Tylor was the first to categorize such societies as animist cultures.

The social reorientation that came with the rise of the great hydraulic agricultural civilizations in the Middle East, North Africa, India, China, and later, the emergence of marauding empires, and finally the advent of the Industrial Age would each be marked by a relentless disseverment of the animist worldview. The expropriation, enclosure, and propertization of what our earlier ancestors regarded as an animated Earth has been the central theme of what we call civilization. Only recently, however, has the academic community come to grips with this underlying dynamic of civilization.

A heated discussion is currently unfolding among the world's geologists and other academics on the issue of naming a new geological epoch as the Anthropocene. The new proposed epoch signals a period where the human input in sequestering, consuming, and transforming the geology of the earth has been so consequential that it will leave a unique historical footprint in the geological record that many geologists argue will be discernable hundreds of millions of years from now. A growing number of geologists believe that the Anthropocene begins with the extraction of fossil fuels from the earth's depths two hundred–plus years ago. Other geologists suggest that the Anthropocene dates as far back as the rise of the hydraulic civilizations and the cumulative impact humankind has had ever since on enclosing and exploiting the earth's spheres and diminishing the environment.

As to where blame might be placed, it's true that Western theology has at least been up front in flaunting "mankind's" mastery and exploitation of the earth, arguing that it's a gift of an all-knowing God who granted Adam and Eve and their heirs dominion over it. The Eastern religions and philosophies are more nuanced and maintain a strong whiff of inclusion, positing that humanity is not the master of nature but an intricate part of it, and must continually harmonize the workings of civilization with the numerous other agencies that exist on Earth and to which every species is beholden. In practice, however, the great Asian civilizations have often strayed, and while their impact on the rest of the earth's agencies, until late, has been gentler, their usurpation and exploitation of the earth's spheres has increased with the second rise of Asia in the course of the past half century.

Regardless of exactly where on the timeline of human history we mark the beginning of the Anthropocene, the reality is that the increasing enclosure of the earth's agencies at the hands of our species has shaped the way we have come to define ourselves in relation to the rest of nature. As the human expropriation and propertization of the earth's spheres evolved and intensified during the long passage of the agricultural era and, more recently, the short duration of the Industrial Age, communal life gave way to public life, and public life, in turn, gave way to private life, and with each passage personhood turned in on itself.

As the Age of Progress matured, individual autonomy hardened as vast swaths of humanity retreated behind closed doors surrounded by their personal possessions on a "possessed Earth." The human race has become increasingly boxed in, with each individual becoming more autonomous and isolated, while crowding together in dense cities and sprawling suburbs of millions and even tens of millions of human beings, all closed off from an increasingly desolate external environment. The year 2006 marked a historic passage for the human race. That was when a majority of the 6.6 billion human beings living at that time were cloistered in dense urban spaces, signaling the final ascent of Homo urbanus.[4]

Nevertheless, there is a sense of hope emerging from the hard lessons learned from climate change and the soft lessons learned from new discoveries of our true biological makeup that might bring our species back full circle to a new beginning and another chance to rewrite the future. That new inspiration begins with a fundamental rethinking of what it means to be a human being in the deepest biological sense. Much of what we thought we were as a biological entity is deeply mistaken and has taken us to this despairing moment in our species' history.

Waking up to who we really are, as a species, in the strictest physiological sense is the liberating relief that can steer us on a new path back into the folds of an animated and evolving Earth. This time, we rejoin the planetary community with a very different sense of agency from the one bequeathed by the Abrahamic God to Adam and Eve and their progeny.

RETHINKING EXISTENCE:
From Objects and Structures to Processes and Patterns

If credit is to be paid to the architects of the digital revolution and information theory, Norbert Wiener, the father of cybernetics, and his contemporary Ludwig von Bertalanffy, the father of general systems theory, would both be high up on the list. They were the inspiration for their respective fields, whose theories have taken humanity into the Information Age, artificial intelligence, and the virtual worlds of cyberspace and beyond. Each came to understand, through their own work, that humanity's long-held assumptions about time, space, and the nature of existence were tragically misconceived, to the detriment of our species' survivability.

In 1952, von Bertalanffy wrote, "What are called structures are slow processes of long duration, functions are quick processes of short duration."[5] Two years later, in 1954, Wiener took a more intimate approach to looking at our own species, although his remarks were meant to be applicable to all of life and the whole of the material world. He wrote of human life that:

> It is the pattern maintained by this homeostasis, which is the touchstone of our personal identity. Our tissues change as we live: the food we eat and the air we breathe become flesh of our flesh, and bone of our bone, and the momentary elements of our flesh and bone pass out of our body every day with our excreta. We are but whirlpools in a river of ever-flowing water. We are not stuff that abides, but patterns that perpetuate themselves.[6]

Bertalanffy, Wiener, and others, including the chemist Ilya Prigogine with his theory of dissipative structures and nonequilibrium thermodynamics, and

Nicholas Georgescu-Roegen with his complementary thermodynamic recon-ditioning of economic theory and practice, were each beginning to reconcep-tualize the very meaning of existence in their respective fields, reshaping our species' understanding of temporality and spatiality, giving humanity a new way to comprehend the nature of life.

Their pathbreaking ontological journeys owe much to the thinking of the iconoclast philosopher Alfred North Whitehead. Whitehead's early work was in mathematics. He coauthored with Bertrand Russell *The Principia Mathematica*, a three-volume series on the foundations of mathematics, a work in formal logic that became math's undisputed bible in the 20th century. His interests shifted to physics and philosophy in the second part of his career. His principal work, *Process and Reality*, was published in 1929 and went on to influence many of the leading thinkers in science and philosophy over the course of the century.

Whitehead took aim at Isaac Newton's description of matter and motion devoid of the passage of time:

> which presupposes the ultimate fact of an irreducible brute matter, or ma-terial, spread through space in a flux of configurations. In itself such a mate-rial is senseless, valueless, purposeless. It just does what it does do, following a fixed routine imposed by external relations which do not spring from the nature of its being.[7]

Whitehead deeply opposed Newton's description of existence as made up of "durationless" instants "without reference to any other instant," argu-ing that "velocity at an instant" and "momentum at an instant" was, to put it bluntly, simply absurd.[8] Whitehead argued that the idea of isolated matter having "the property of simple location in space and time" left "Nature still without meaning or value."[9]

What irked Whitehead was that the prevailing worldview of Nature in the scientific community "omits any discrimination of the fundamental activities within Nature."[10] The historian and philosopher Robin G. Collingwood of Ox-ford University points out that relationships and rhythms only exist in "a tract of time long enough for the rhythm of the movement to establish itself."[11] For example, a note of music is nothing without the notes that precede and follow it.

To be fair, Whitehead didn't come to this new epiphany without a ground-work being laid. Other ruptures were already occurring along the fault lines of classical physics. By the early decades of the 20th century, physicists began to realize that their earlier suppositions about the physicality of atoms as solid matter taking up a fixed space had been "misplaced." They came to the realization that an atom was not a thing in the material sense but, rather, a set of relationships operating at a certain rhythm, and that being so, "within a given instant of time the atom does not possess those qualities at all."[12]

As the physicist Fritjof Capra explains:

> "At the subatomic level, the solid material objects of classical physics dissolve into patterns of . . . probabilities of interconnections. Quantum theory forces us to see the universe not as a collection of physical objects, but rather as a complicated web of relations between the various parts of a unified whole."[13]

The conventional notion of separating structure from function gave way with the coming of age of the new physics. It is literally impossible to separate what something is from what is does. Everything is pure activity and nothing is static. Things do not exist in isolation, but only through time. Whitehead summed up the new view of physics:

> The older point of view enables us to abstract from change and to conceive of the full reality of Nature *at an instant*, in abstraction from any temporal duration and characterized as to its interrelations solely by the instantaneous distribution of matter in space. . . . For the modern view process, activity, and change are the matter of fact. At an instant there is nothing. Each instant is only a way of grouping matters of fact. Thus, since there are no instants, conceived as simple primary entities, there is no Nature at an instant.[14]

It was not only the new physics that was deconstructing the old. A new approach to biology was emerging in the late 19th century that would also rewrite the history of time and space. Charles Darwin introduced temporality into biology, arguing against the orthodox proposition that species emerged as wholes, and were parts of a grand creation, and existed without change over time. Darwin's revolutionary thesis, by contrast, stated that ever more complex species evolve over time by way of natural selection. Although new traits are random, those that confer an advantage to a species, allowing it to better adapt to a changing environment, are most likely to survive.

Although Darwin's theory of evolution brought temporality into the equation of biology, transforming our understanding of nature, biologists continued to be more interested in probing the "structure" of each organism to assess its fitness to the environment, keeping at least a part of the new biological profession fixated on taxonomy.

This limited view of the temporality of biological evolution began to change when a German naturalist, Ernst Haeckel, introduced the new field of ecology in 1866. An emerging generation of biologists were more interested in "the science of the relations of living organisms to the external world, their habitat, customs, enemies, parasites, etc."[15] Ecology marked a partial departure from the field of biology with its focus more concentrated on the science of how living communities develop and adapt themselves to changing circumstances over time.

The new field of physics and the emerging field of ecology were reinventing time and space, and Whitehead became their voice. He summarized the new sensibility about the nature of nature in a mere sixteen words: "There is no Nature apart from transition, and there is no transition apart from temporal duration."[16]

While the shift in thinking about the relationship between time and space, and being and becoming, might be intellectually stimulating to scientists and philosophers, what significance might it have for the rest of us who think of ourselves as unique and relatively autonomous physical beings continually enhancing and protecting our personhood in a world of competing agencies? It's difficult to even imagine that each of us is more like a vessel and medium, with the swirling elements of the world—its forces, fields, atoms, and molecules—continually flowing in and out of us, challenging our sense of autonomy at every moment. Here's the reality.

WE ARE EACH AN ECOSYSTEM

Let's begin with water. Although the scientific community has yet to understand the deep connection between water and the emergence and evolution of life on Earth, it's a fact that every species is mostly composed of water from the hydrosphere. In some organisms, upward of 90 percent of their body weight comes from water, and in humans, water makes up approximately 60 percent of an adult body.[17] The heart is about 73 percent water, the lungs are 83 percent water, the skin is 64 percent water, the muscles and kidneys are each 79 percent water, and the bones are 31 percent water.[18] Plasma, the pale-yellow fluid that transports blood cells, enzymes, nutrients, and hormones throughout the body, is 90 percent water.[19]

Water plays an essential role in managing the most intimate aspects of living systems. The list of particulars is impressive. Water is:

A vital nutrient in the life of every cell [and] acts first as a building material. It regulates our internal body temperature by sweating and respiration. The carbohydrates and proteins that our bodies use as food are metabolized and transported by water in the bloodstream. [Water] assists in flushing waste mainly through urination. [Water] acts as a shock absorber for [the] brain, spinal cord, and fetus. [It] forms saliva [and] lubricates joints.[20]

Water is flowing in and out of our bodies every twenty-four hours. In this sense, our semipermeable open systems bring fresh water from the earth's hydrosphere into our very being to perform basic life functions, after which it is returned to the hydrosphere. If there's a case to be made that the human body—and all other living creatures—is more like a pattern of activity than a fixed structure, and operates as a dissipative system feeding off energy and excreting entropic waste, rather than a closed mechanism importing energy to secure its own autonomy, the cycling and recycling of H_2O is an appropriate point of departure.

The average male body is made up of approximately thirty trillion cells.[21] Although every cell harbors the hereditary genetic blueprint of the organism, specific cells perform specialized functions across the body. In 2005, a research team led by Dr. Kirsty Spalding, a researcher at the Karolinska Institute in Stockholm, Sweden, published a study in the journal *Cell* entitled "Retrospective Birth Dating of Cells in Humans."[22] *The New York Times* science writer Nicholas Wade wrote an article on the findings entitled "Your Body Is Younger than You Think," which created a stir.[23] It is possible that the "average age of all the cells in an adult's body may turn out to be as young as 7 to 10 years." While a few of the cells we are born with remain until death—in particular some of the cells in the cerebral cortex—most are replaced over and over again, suggesting that from a physical perspective we live in several different bodies over a single lifetime.[24]

We are aware that skin cells, fingernails, toenails, and hair cells come and go. Yet, we've long assumed that vital organs stay with us through our lifetime, giving us the assurance that we are each a unique and enduring self. This isn't so.

Red blood cells have a lifetime of around four months; cells from the muscles of the ribs of adults in their late thirties have an average lifetime of 15.1 years; the cells that line the stomach turn over in five days; gastrointestinal colon crypt cells are replaced every three to four days; bone osteoclast cells are replaced every two weeks; intestine Paneth cells are replaced every twenty days; trachea cells every one to two months; fat cells every eight years; skeleton cells have a 10 percent turnover every year; and liver hepatocyte cells every six months to one year. The average adult human liver has a turnover time of three hundred to five hundred days. The central nervous system remains the same for a lifetime, as do the lens cells.[25]

About 3 percent of the near surface layers of one's skeletal bones and up to a quarter of porous bones in the limb joints are replaced every twelve months, and one's near entire skeleton is replaced over a decade or so. The enamel in one's teeth, however, lasts a lifetime.[26]

When we scale down from the cells to the molecules and atoms that make up our bodies, the turnover is even more rapid. An adult human being is made up of approximately seven octillion atoms.[27] So while organs are made up of cells, and cells are made up of molecules, and molecules are made up of atoms, when we get to this most basic level of atoms, what makes up a human being starts to look more like "a pattern of activity" that exists over time than an autonomous structure existing in space. Let's consider why.

Whenever we breathe air, drink water, and consume food, massive numbers of atoms are ingested into the body from the earth's biosphere. And conversely, whenever we exhale, sweat, urinate, and defecate, atoms return to the biosphere, where many of them eventually become embedded in other human beings and/or our fellow creatures.

By weight, the human body is 65 percent oxygen, 18.5 percent carbon, 9.5 percent hydrogen, and 3.2 percent nitrogen, and the remaining weight includes calcium, phosphorus, sodium, potassium, sulfur, chlorine, and magnesium. When we add up all of the atoms that make up these different molecules, it turns out that there may be more atoms in a single human being than there are stars in our universe.[28] Equally telling, in the passage of a year, over 90 percent of the atoms in one's body are no longer there and have been replaced by new ones.[29]

Most of the oxygen and hydrogen taken into our bodies come from the atmosphere, hydrosphere, and lithosphere that together make up the biosphere within which all of life dwells. When those molecules return to the biosphere, they spread easily through the air currents and water currents across the earth. With every single human body having upward of 4×10^{27} hydrogen atoms and 2×10^{27} oxygen atoms, it's a sure thing that some of those atoms were at one time or another in the bodies of other human beings and other creatures that preceded us throughout history. Likewise, some of those hydrogen and oxygen atoms that were once in our bodies will likely find their way into other human beings and fellow creatures that will come after us.[30]

From a scientific point of view, our bodies are not relatively closed off autonomous agents but, rather, open dissipative systems. Every human body is wrapped up in a semipermeable membrane selectively allowing the passing of chemical elements through its interior—oxygen, hydrogen, nitrogen, carbon, calcium, phosphorus, potassium, sulfur, sodium, chlorine, and so on—that come from across the biosphere.[31] Our bodies, then, are just one among the multitude of mediums that host the earth's elements.

But chemical elements aren't the only agencies churning through our cells, organs, and the earth's multitude of systems. Consider bacteria, the tiniest form of life on Earth. In 2018, researchers from the Weizmann Institute of Science and the California Institute of Technology published a study in the *Proceedings of the National Academy of Sciences* entitled "The Biomass Distribution on Earth." They reported that the sum of the biomass across all taxa is approximately 550 gigatons of carbon, of which plants make up 450 gigatons, while surprisingly bacteria are next at 70 gigatons. Other groups in descending order are fungi at 12 gigatons, archaea at 7 gigatons, protists at 4 gigatons, animals at 2 gigatons, and viruses at 0.2 gigatons. In this vast species category, human beings represent less than .06 gigaton of the biomass on Earth.[32]

When it comes to the human body, we share much of our physical being with various strains of bacteria. According to another Weizmann Institute report, "the number of bacteria in the body is actually of the same order as the number of human cells, and their total mass is about 0.2 kg."[33] While the vast number of bacteria live in the colon, they also take up residence in the stomach, skin, saliva, oral mucosa, and throughout the body. We are not alone in our own bodies, but rather cohabitants living with our earliest relatives, the bacteria. Bacteria in the digestive system help break down food, especially plant fiber. They also supply the digestive system with important vitamins including B-complex and vitamin K.[34] Bacteria also prime the immune system to ward off pathogenic invaders.[35]

Most of us are familiar with the fact that bacteria cohabit our body. However, there are other species of microorganisms living inside our body as well, including fungi, archaea, and protists. Although researchers have yet to calculate the number of fungal cells in the human body, it's a magnitude smaller than the bacteria.[36] Some fungal organisms, like *Candida albicans*, can be deadly in immunocompromised individuals. This particular organism also plays a significant role in diseases of the stomach, vaginal tract, and mouth. *Cryptococcus neoformans* in the lungs can seize up and bloom, causing life-threatening illness. *Pneumocystis* can cause pneumonia in immunocompromised individuals. Other fungi species also play a role in maintaining overall body health. *Saccharomyces cerevisiae var. boulardii*, a probiotic, helps relieve gastroenteritis in some people.[37] A recent study found 101 different fungal species in a sample of human beings, with each individual hosting between nine and twenty-three species, including *Cladosporium*, which triggers asthma, and *Aureobasidium*, which can cause fungal infections in organ transplant patients.[38]

Archaea is perhaps the least known and studied microorganism living within our bodies. Archaea are single-celled organisms that lack a cell nucleus and are classified as a prokaryote. Recent studies have found archaea present in the human gastrointestinal tract, the skin, the lungs, and the nose. So far, four species of methanogenic archaea have been cultivated and isolated from human bodies. Upward of 96 percent of people carry *Methanobrevibacter smithii* in their gut. Another archaeon, *Methanosphaera stadtmanae*, is found in about 30 percent of subjects tested. *Methanomassiliicoccus luminyensis* is less prevalent and shows up in approximately 4 percent of people.[39]

Archaea are prevalent in the human colon and are suspected of playing a role in contributing to obesity. Other studies suggest they are associated with chronic constipation. They may also be a marker for cardiovascular disease and associated with periodontal disease.[40] Their presence throughout the human body suggests that archaea play a major role in the regulatory processes of human physiology.

Protists are also abundant in the human body. These eukaryotic organisms contain a single cell nucleus, but are not an animal, plant, or fungus but, rather, a separate category of life. Protists include *Plasmodium*, amoebas, ciliates, and *Giardia*. Free-living protists in nature occupy environments that contain water and constitute a significant portion of the marine and terrestrial biomass. Seaweed, an important component in the human diet, is a protist. Plantlike protists—phytoplankton—produce half the oxygen on the planet via photosynthesis.[41] Protists are used in medical and biomedical research. Between seventy and seventy-five species of protists live inside various parts of the human anatomy including the skin, teeth, eyes, nostrils, digestive tract, circulatory system, sex organs, and brain tissue. Some protists are virulent and others are relatively harmless.[42] Protists are responsible for a number of deadly human diseases including malaria, amebic dysentery, trichomoniasis, and sleeping sickness.

And then there are the viruses. We have come to think of viruses as invaders who steal into our bodies, create disease, and spread contagion and death, as with the COVID-19 virus. Karin Mölling, of the Max Planck Institute for Molecular Genetics, points out in a journal article entitled "Viruses More Friends than Foes" that they "are the most successful species on Earth . . . they populate the soil, the oceans, the air, our human body, and even our genome." Although viruses are generally categorized as pathogens, and are immediately identified with deadly diseases like Ebola, SARS, HIV, AIDS, Zika, and MERS, Mölling reminds us that "most viruses are, however, not enemies or killers but play important roles in the origin, development, and maintenance of life of all species on our planet." Mölling goes on to point out that "viruses built our immunity: viruses protect against viruses . . . they are the drivers of evolution and adaptation to environmental changes."[43]

While there are 38 trillion bacteria living inside of us, they pale in comparison to the 380 trillion viruses inhabiting us—a living community so ubiquitous and diverse that it has been formally named the "human virome."[44] Fortunately, though many of these viruses are not harmful, the fact of the matter is that while scientists know quite a bit about the various strains of bacteria and what functions they perform in the human body, there is sparse information about what roles these viruses play in either regulating or destabilizing human health.

Viruses are found to inhabit all of the spaces of the human body. They are in the blood, lungs, skin, urine, and virtually everywhere else. Viruses live to kill bacteria. That is their single mission in life. Scientists have begun to turn their attention to the viruses in the human virome for clues of how certain viruses protect human beings from disease-causing bacteria, especially those that precipitate serious and deadly infections, and are increasingly becoming resilient to most antibiotics.[45] Figuring out all of the numerous relationships that affect the side-by-side existence of trillions of bacteria and even more viruses throughout the human body, with the goal of discovering new approaches to ward off bacteria-related diseases, is at the moment a daunting undertaking.

When we add up all of these cohabiting species that live inside of the human body, it turns out that human cells make up only 43 percent of the body's overall cell count. The other 57 percent of cells come from the microorganisms that dwell within us. Were we to get more granular and assess the makeup of the human being at the genomic level, we would find that each of us is made up of twenty thousand genes that provide the instructions that comprise our physiological makeup while the genes that comprise the totality of microorganisms that inhabit the same human space come in at between two and twenty million.[46]

Microbiologist Sarkis Mazmanian at Caltech tells us something we never before considered: biologically speaking, "We don't have just one genome . . . the genes of our microbiome present essentially a second genome which augment the activity of our own," adding that "what makes us human is, in my opinion, the combination of our own DNA, plus the DNA of our gut microbes."[47]

From a biological perspective, the human part of what we have come to think of as a human being makes up less than half our body, which raises the question of whether we should consider our species as a chimera, which, in a sense, it is. As unsettling as the thought might be to our long-held belief that human beings are a unique specimen within the family of species, the scientific reality is more complicated than that. Dr. Prabarna Ganguly of the National Human Genome Research Institute of the U.S. National Institutes of Health provides a new paradigmatic description of what constitutes a human being:

> There is a mighty but invisible kingdom of microbes present within your body. Small yet incredibly powerful, these thousands of species and trillions of inhabitants live in all parts of your body and make up the diverse human microbiome. These microbiomes support and maintain your health but also, when the microbiome is disturbed in some fashion, have been linked to hundreds of ailments such as cancers, and autoimmune and cardiovascular diseases . . . researchers don't yet know if a change in a microbial community leads to a disease or if a microbial community changes in response to the development of a disease.[48]

In 2014, the National Institutes of Health Human Microbiome Project (HMP) was launched with the intended purpose of both characterizing the types of microbes that live in the human body and describing the role they play in co-choreographing human life. Up to that time, little was known about the ubiquitous presence of other forms of life cohabiting the human body, and many of the microbes living inside of us had yet to be identified and characterized.

The Human Microbiome Project marked the first time that a world-renowned scientific institution, and the leading medical research arm of the U.S. government, recognized the human body as a biome (a biome is a "large naturally occurring community of flora and fauna occupying a major habitat").[49] By acknowledging that the human body—and by extension the bodies of other species—is a microbiome, the NIH was formally asserting that the human species and every individual human being is an ecosystem. An ecosystem is "a biological community of interacting organisms and their physical environment."[50] The redefining of human physiology as a microbiome is a historical event that is yet to be fully grasped. The project leaders describe the initiative:

> The HMP will address some of the most inspiring, vexing, and fundamental scientific questions today. Importantly, it also has the potential to break down the artificial barriers between medical microbiology and

environmental microbiology . . . questions about the human microbiome are new only in terms of the system to which they apply. Similar questions have inspired and confounded ecologists working on macroscale ecosystems for decades.[51]

The scientific revelation that every human being is a biome and, by inference, that the ecosystems of the planet don't stop at the body line of our species but continue down into the microbiome of every individual signals the emergence of the ecological self. We are each a biome that reaches deep into the bowels of our being and out to the borders of the biosphere and even beyond. The new paradigm shift in the nature of what constitutes a human being is already beginning to change the way researchers approach diseases and secure the health of patients.

Professor Rob Knight, of the University of California, San Diego, makes the point that "these tiny creatures totally transform our health in ways we never imagined until recently."[52] Researchers are exploring the role microbes play across the human microbiome in digestion, regulating the immune system, protecting against disease, and manufacturing vital vitamins. Dr. Knight and others believe that monitoring the microbiome will become standard medical practice, and we will come to think of one's stool as a "data dump" of microbial DNA information that can be mined to assess a patient's state of health or disease.

Dr. Trevor Lawley of the Wellcome Sanger Institute says it's not a stretch to think that in the future cures for diseases and ways of promoting health will depend on prescribing the administering of ten to fifteen bugs into the patient's microbiome.[53]

What's so noticeable now, but for so long ignored, is that the innards of every human being and all of our fellow creatures are simply extensions of the biomes, ecosystems, and spheres that make possible a planet thronged with life. Each creature and every cell therein are open systems wrapped in semipermeable membranes, allowing the elements of the earth's systems to filter through and sustain the patterns of life. The very idea of an Earth filled with fixed structures is a misnomer. Ilya Prigogine put it most succinctly, noting that in biology, as in chemistry, what are identified as things are really processes. Every living creature is a dissipative system whose becoming depends on feeding off the available energy on Earth with the consequence of always adding to the entropic waste.

But surely, not everything is a pattern of activity. What about the solid rocks that make up much of the physicality of the earth? Certainly they don't fit the idea that everything is an evolving pattern rather than a fixed thing. Well, actually they do. Recall Bertalanffy's observation that "what are called structures are slow processes of long duration [while] functions are quick processes of short duration."[54] At first glimpse, we marvel at the great mountain ranges— the Alps, Himalayas, Rocky Mountains, and Andes. Their majesty incites a sense of awe and their solitude conjures up the sublime. We are comforted by their eternal presence. Unfortunately, our experience is an illusion. These seemingly inert structures are forever in motion. They, too, are patterns of activity metamorphosing over time.

If we could take a time-lapse film and focus on Mt. Everest over millions of years and speed it up, we would witness its patterns evolving at every moment. Anyone that's ever taken a geology course learns about the great changes in the earth's crust over time. For example, 320 million years ago, there existed a single supercontinent—called Pangaea—surrounded by the great oceans. And it began to break apart two hundred million years ago, eventually becoming the continental landmasses we know today.[55] But one doesn't have to go that far back in time to experience rocks as processes unfolding moment to moment in real time.

Recall the mention in chapter 3 on how rocks disintegrate into ever smaller particles by weathering and the burrowing of tree roots, plants, insects, and animals, which degrade the rock into soil. The minerals in the degraded rock become the essential ingredients of the soil. Plants take up the minerals, and when we eat those plants the minerals transfer into our bodies. Two of those minerals, phosphorus and calcium, are elements that make up our skeleton and teeth. Of equal importance, the semipermeable membranes that wrap around every cell and act as a doorkeeper, letting nutrients in and flushing entropic waste out, are also made of phosphorus.[56]

We are, in fact, partially composed of minerals from rocks that play a key role in maintaining the processes that sustain our own pattern of becoming. These slivers of rock have slowly journeyed over distant times, finding their way into our human ecosystem and, from there, will travel elsewhere.

We are each a pattern in which multiple agencies operating at different times and scales become participants in our becoming, only to travel on and participate in still other patterns. But this is not the whole of the story. There are two other principal agencies that help orchestrate all the patterns of all of the species on the planet—biological clocks and electromagnetic fields— which together provide crucial missing links on how life has evolved amid the various other agencies on Earth, and to which we now turn.

8

A NEW ORIGIN STORY

THE BIOLOGICAL CLOCKS AND ELECTROMAGNETIC FIELDS THAT HELP SYNCHRONIZE AND SHAPE LIFE

It was noon on February 28, 1953, at the Eagle Pub, a hangout visited by faculty and students at the University of Cambridge, in England. As the tale goes, two research scientists burst into the tavern. The older gentleman was Francis Crick, a thirty-seven-year-old British physicist, and his younger colleague was James Watson, a twenty-five-year-old American molecular biologist. Crick blurted out to the assembled patrons the words, since immortalized, "We have discovered the secret of life." The two would go on to win a Nobel Prize in physiology or medicine for the discovery of the double helix structure of deoxyribonucleic acid, or DNA.[1] Not so fast. There may be more to the story.

BIOLOGICAL CLOCKS:
The Choreographers of Organisms

Flash back to 1729. It was known that plants extend their leaves during the daylight hours, and fold them back at night. The French astronomer Jean-Jacques d'Ortous de Mairan, however, was curious whether plants would unfold and refold their leaves when placed in a darkened room. He stored a mimosa plant in a darkened cupboard, and observed that the plant continued to unfold and refold its leaves over a twenty-four-hour period, even though tucked away in total darkness, suggesting that there must be some force at work independent of light cues to account for the plant's activity.

In 1832, a French-Swiss biologist, Augustin Pyramus de Candolle, verified Mairan's findings but added another intriguing layer. While Mairan's experiments eliminated the possibility that the mimosa plant unfolded and refolded its leaves only because of its exposure to light, Candolle thought perhaps the process was tied to the plant's response to temperature. He exposed the plants to continuous light and found that even absent the light-dark cycle, the plants unfolded and refolded every twenty-two to twenty-three hours "like clockwork," suggesting that there must be some internal clock.[2]

In the 1960s, Curt Richter of Johns Hopkins University attempted to break the circadian cycle of rats in a series of cruel experiments by subjecting them to freezing, shocking them with electrical currents, blinding them, stopping their heartbeat, and even removing sections of their brains. They continued to exhibit their twenty-four-hour circadian activity cycle.[3]

Ueli Schibler, a chronobiologist at the University of Geneva in Switzerland, describes how biological clocks oversee the temporal patterning of mammalian species:

> In most mammalian species, physiological processes undergo daily oscillations that are controlled by the circadian timekeeping system. This system consists of a master pacemaker located in brain's suprachiasmatic nucleus (SCN) and peripheral slave oscillators in virtually all body cells. The SCN, whose phase is entrained by daily light-dark cycles, imposes overt rhythms in behavior and physiology by a variety of neuronal, humoral, and physical outputs. While some of these SCN outputs have direct consequences for circadian behavior, others serve as inputs to synchronize the countless circadian oscillators in peripheral cell types. Daily feeding-fasting cycles are the major Zeitgebers (timing cues) for the synchronization of oscillators in many peripheral organs.[4]

While it's been well established that DNA codes for circadian biological clocks, it is not the only source. In January 2011, the journal *Nature* published a study conducted by John S. O'Neill and Akhilesh B. Reddy, of the Department of Clinical Neurosciences at the University of Cambridge Metabolic Research Laboratories, entitled "Circadian Clocks in Human Red Blood Cells." The study used human red blood cells specifically because they are without a nucleus and, therefore, no DNA is present. Nonetheless the researchers detected a strong circadian rhythm of approximately twenty-four hours operating in the cells.

This means that the circadian rhythm had to be generated by the cytoplasm. The study, and other similar studies, does not suggest that DNA clocks don't exist. They do and have been meticulously identified and catalogued across the animal and plant kingdoms. What the study does tell us is that genes are not the only source of body clocks as the upholders of the neo-Darwinian synthesis previously thought.[5]

Internal body clocks are continually adjusting to circadian cues—especially the light and dark cycles and cold and warmth changes. Being able to anticipate and respond to changes in the external environment is critical in maintaining a healthy organism. During an active phase, and especially when foraging and hunting for food, an organism requires a temporal readiness to trigger either a fight or flight response. Scheduling and organizing digestion, immune system functions, and regeneration happens during rest and sleep cycles that require altogether different temporal scheduling and deployment. There are also all of the other internal activities that are continually adjusting to changes in the external environment over the course of a circadian day that need continuous temporal management and synchronization including the heart rate, hormone levels, and the like.

An accumulated body of evidence also ties human diseases with desynchronization of biological clocks. Consider, for example, artificial light. For two hundred thousand years or so, our species and our fellow creatures lived mostly with natural light emitted directly by the sun and indirectly by its reflection on the moon. Today, electric lighting has created artificial daylight throughout the night hours, subjecting millions of people to interrupted sleep and affecting millions of others who work night shifts.

Entire generations living in dense urban environments partially lit up twenty-four hours a day have never experienced the starlit universe and the nine galaxies visible to the naked eye in a dark sky.[6] Sadly, the newest attraction in the travel and tourism industry is flying tourists to the handful of "dark sky parks" in the few uninhabited places on Earth so they can experience the awe of the universe.

New studies in recent years show that artificial light at night throws off our biological clocks by suppressing pineal melatonin production, which is suspected to play a role in the increased risk of prostate and breast cancer.[7]

Other studies into adult attention deficit hyperactivity disorder find that it is associated with impaired sleep, which can exacerbate the illness.[8] A spate of research reports have documented that shift workers tend to have higher rates of heart disease, diabetes, infections, and cancer. Equally alarming, numerous studies suggest that an impaired circadian system plays a role in triggering major psychiatric disorders including schizophrenia and bipolar affective disorder.[9]

These and other findings trace an increasing number of human illnesses directly to the circadian master clock lodged in the suprachiasmatic nuclei of the brain. Russell Foster, a professor of circadian neuroscience at the University of Oxford, suggests that the deep connection between a range of serious diseases and the circadian-directed wake cycle "represents a truly remarkable opportunity to develop novel evidence-based treatments and interventions that will transform the health and quality of life of millions of individuals across a broad spectrum of illnesses."[10] Unfortunately, temporally related illnesses are barely touched on in the medical training of future doctors.

Scientists have discovered that species also have internal clocks synchronized to the lunar/tidal and circannual cycles. For example, the palolo worm reproduces only during neap tides in the last quarter moon in October and November.[11] Kenneth C. Fisher and Eric T. Pengelley segregated a squirrel in a windowless room and provisioned continuous food and water, while setting the temperature at the freezing point. The squirrel maintained its body temperature at 37 degrees Celsius and, right on time, in October stopped eating and drinking and began hibernating, as it would have outdoors, and later resumed its normal activity just as it would have done in the early spring.[12]

Aside from circadian, lunar/tidal, and circannual rhythms, scientists have discovered ultradian rhythms. These rhythms appear within a twenty-four-hour cycle and vary in length—for example, a heart rate that lasts less than a second. What we know now is that hundreds of processes in animal species—less in plant species—that maintain their bodily dissipative patterns are totally dependent on endogenous biological clocks operating in every cell, all synchronized in an elaborate symphony that we call a "being" or, more accurately, a "becoming."

Microbiologist David Lloyd of the Cardiff School of Biosciences in the United Kingdom summarizes the current state of our scientific knowledge on the primal role played by our endogenous clocks, saying that "strict internal timekeeping is intrinsic to the coordinated control of our every biochemical, physiological and behavioral function, as to our moods and vitality."[13]

The most common ultradian clocks are called circahouralian clocks. Our species has a well-documented basic activity/rest rhythm of around ninety minutes.[14] A half century ago, Nathaniel Kleitman, an American psychologist teaching at the University of Chicago, discovered that human beings are temporally attuned to concentrated activity lasting about ninety minutes, after which rest sets in.

Ultradian rhythms schedule the daily routines of each species' pattern of activities including: "synchronizing compatible processes and preventing the simultaneous activation of incompatible processes; preparing biological systems to respond to stimuli such as cell–cell communication, and the maintenance of neuronal integrity and alertness; interacting with circadian rhythms."[15]

For example, ultradian rhythms manage the timing of the ovarian cycle and synchronize reproductive activity with changes in both the internal and external environment.[16] Ultradian rhythms alert an organism to threats of a predator attack by increasing the body's temperature and organizing the phases of reaction and response.

One of the most important roles of biological clocks is synchronizing the functions going on over a twenty-four-hour period. For example, the space in the cell, and even an organ, is very limited, and, therefore, requires temporal compartmentalization in scheduling to ensure that the proper time is allotted for each activity taking place in the right order.[17] Maximilian Moser, of the Institute for Physiology at the Medical University of Graz, stresses the central role temporal scheduling plays in maintaining an organism's pattern of activity:

"Temporal compartmentalization allows polar events to occur in the same space unit: there are polarities in the universe of our body, which cannot happen simultaneously. Systole and diastole, inspiration and expiration, work and relaxation, wakefulness and sleep, reductive and oxidative states cannot be performed . . . at the same time and place."[18]

What biological clocks are teaching us is that a healthy cell remains in sync with its biological clocks and its metabolic processes. That is, the cell stays on schedule to the time allotted by the ultradian and circadian clocks for performing each metabolic function. In short, regarding the internal dynamics of every organism, the timing is set for each function over a twenty-four-hour circadian cycle to ensure the proper functioning of the organism as a whole.

Although learning that our increasing detachment and isolation from the circadian cycle of day and night by which our own species has been able to secure its pattern of existence is unnerving, a far more profound calamity is unfolding across the living kingdom from which there may be no escape if we fail to act in time.

Here's the problem. There are other specialized prewired biological clocks embedded in every cell of every organism that allow species to flourish by enabling them to anticipate coming seasonal changes and prepare the appropriate response. These other rhythms that adjust each species to seasonal changes are called photoperiodism, and they measure the length of daylight as a cue by which to time seasonal events, including the best times to migrate, forage and hunt, reproduce, and sleep and wake.

If, for example, an animal is at the wrong place at the wrong time, it might be subject to predation by competitors. Or, if a species arrives too early or too late in a new habitat, it might miss foraging and hunting opportunities, or the optimum time to reproduce or migrate, or hibernate, narrowing its chance of survival. All of these activities have to take place just at the right time and if missed narrow other future options that follow in sequence, like storing up fat for dormancy or molting feathers in preparation for migrational flights. The dilemma is that the earth's spheres are radically rewilding in the midst of a changing climate, forcing a disconnect in the internal biological rhythms of every species that orient them to the changing seasons.

Just as the SCN regulates circadian clocks, allowing the organism to cue the twenty-four-hour wake/sleep cycle, it also regulates the organism's queuing of seasonal changes by producing a neuro signal of the day length. Psychiatrist Thomas A. Wehr, a research scientist emeritus at the U.S. National Institute of Mental Health, explains that "the day-length signal is encoded reciprocally in the duration of nocturnal melatonin secretion, which becomes longer in winter and shorter in summer. Sites that respond to the melatonin signal induce changes in behavior and physiology that are programmed to occur during the season that is indicated by the duration of the signal."[19]

For those who insist that they experience a change in their physiology and mood during the changing of the seasons, for example, seasonal affective disorder (SAD), a feeling of sadness, depression, and tiredness in the winter months because of fewer hours of daylight, their experience is not in their imagination but, rather, in their physiology.

Wehr notes that "nearly all of the elements of the anatomical and molecular substrates of photoperiodic seasonal responses in monkeys and other mammals have been found in humans."[20] Researchers in the field suggest that human responses to seasonal changes have likely been dampened during the industrial era as our species retreated into more artificial environments.

The growing fear among climate scientists, biologists, and ecologists is that the relatively reliable seasonal patterns that have characterized the temperate climate on Earth during the past 11,700 years of the Holocene era are dramatically changing in the wake of global warming. Because the changes in the hydrological cycle brought on by climate change are already wreaking havoc on local ecosystems with more unpredictable weather events, species' inherited photoperiodism conditioned to a climate regime that's now radically changing in ways that are unpredictable is placing every species at risk.

To sum up, our species and our fellow creatures are physiologically equipped with a labyrinth of biological clocks that continually adjust every cell, tissue, and organ to the circadian, lunar, seasonal, and circannual rhythms cued to the rotation of the planet every twenty-four hours and its passage around the sun every 365 days. Ultradian clocks choreograph the daily internal processes in an organism that allow it to survive. Other biological clocks that measure the length of the day allow a species to adjust to seasonal changes in order to survive and flourish. All of these biological clocks are proof that our species and all of our fellow creatures are, at their core, temporal patterns that allow them to continually adjust to the rhythms of multiple agencies on a dynamic living planet.

The call from the Nobel Committee came in at 5:10 AM on an October morning in 2017. When he heard the phone ring before dawn, Dr. Michael Rosbash, a professor of biology at Brandeis University, said that his first thought was that someone had died. When he picked up the phone and heard that he won the Nobel Prize in Physiology or Medicine along with Dr. Jeffrey Hall, another professor of biology at Brandeis University, and Michael Young, a professor of genetics at Rockefeller University, his initial utterance was "You are kidding me."[21]

While the discovery of the structure of DNA that contains the code and instructions for making an organism was a significant milestone in the history of science, no less so was the recognition by the Nobel Committee of the accomplishment of these three biologists. An unsolved mystery had baffled biologists for nearly three centuries, ever since Jean-Jacques d'Ortous de Mairan first discovered that a mimosa plant would unfold and refold its leaves, even in a darkened room, over a twenty-four-hour period.

Then, in 1971, American neuroscientist Seymour Benzer and his student Ronald Konopka noticed, quite by accident, that a batch of mutant fruit flies appeared to have faulty internal clocks, which they subsequently traced to a specific gene that they called the "period" gene.[22] In 1984, Hall and Rosbash began studying the period gene. They were particularly interested in the protein the body makes from the gene, called PER. What they found is that the protein builds up in the cell over the nighttime hours and breaks down over the daytime hours. The PER gene protein rose and fell like clockwork every twenty-four hours. Eureka! They discovered the first biological clock, but more would follow.

In 1994, Young discovered a second body clock, called TIM. When TIM proteins join up with PER proteins in the cells, they stick together, and enter the nucleus where they shut the period gene down. By the late 1990s, other scientists were discovering even more biological clocks and have continued to do so.

In awarding the prize, the Nobel Committee noted that "with exquisite precision, our inner clocks adapt our physiology to the dramatically different phases of the day" and by doing so "the clock regulates critical functions such as behavior, hormone levels, sleep, body temperature, and metabolism."[23] The Nobel Committee, as expected, emphasized the practical health implications in the discovery of biological clocks. They failed to mention the more fundamental importance of the discovery that every living creature is a dissipative pattern—its atoms, molecules, cells, and organs—perpetually coming and going, and that pattern is maintained by an array of intricately interconnected biological clocks, which we've just begun to discover.

I suppose that when future generations of students are introduced to biology, equal importance will be attached to the scientific discoveries of life's temporal nature as well as the genetic instructions carried by the genes. When children grow up thinking of life as temporal patterns interacting with the earth's spheres and its daily rotation, the changing of the seasons, and the yearly passage of the planet around the sun, they will be comforted by the notion that our species is neither autonomous nor alone, but a pattern within patterns, all interconnected and mutually interdependent on an indivisible Earth.

While biological clocks orchestrate the internal pattern of activity of each creature and synchronize its relationship to the circadian, lunar, seasonal, and circannual rhythms of the earth, there is still another force that we are just now learning plays a critical role in establishing the temporal as well as spatial pattern of each species—electromagnetic fields.

THE ARCHITECTS OF LIFE:
Electromagnetic Fields and Biological Patterns

Rütger Wever was an obscure physicist working at the famed Max Planck Institute in Munich, Germany. In 1964, he installed an underground bunker with two experimental rooms isolated from all outside environmental cues—sunlight, wind currents, rainfall, sound, and so on. He provisioned the rooms with food, water, and comfortable living arrangements that could allow volunteers to remain there in isolation for up to two months at a time. One of the experimental rooms had an electrical shield placed over it that reduced geomagnetic rhythms from the outside world by 99 percent.[24]

All the volunteers' daily rhythms were monitored twenty-four hours a day—temperature, wake/sleep cycles, urinary excretion, and other physiological activities. Day-in and day-out, from 1964 to 1989, Wever monitored volunteers in more than 450 experiments living under every conceivable condition and summarized his final data in a 1992 study entitled "Basic Principles of Human Circadian Rhythms."[25]

This is what he found: In the unshielded bunker isolated from sunshine, but still exposed to exogenous electromagnetic fields, circadian sleep and wake patterns fell off only slightly, averaging 24.6 hours. However, in the room shielded from the outside electromagnetic field, the circadian cycle slipped demonstrably with more irregular physiological desynchronization. In fact, the subjects cut off entirely from the exogenous electromagnetic field not only lost their circadian rhythm altogether but also began to careen toward a loss of timing across a range of metabolic functions.

In some of the experiments, Wever pulsed artificial electric and magnetic rhythms into the room with the electromagnetic shield still around it. Then it happened. At one point, a very weak 10 hertz of electromagnetic field was introduced into the electromagnetically sealed off room, and it immediately restored the circadian rhythm of the volunteers, showing, for the first time, that an exogenous electromagnetic field plays a role in regulating the circadian clocks of human beings.[26]

James Clerk Maxwell was the first to propose a formal theory of the workings of electromagnetic fields covering the earth. His theory set the basis for modern physics in the 20th century and established an outline for a new explanation of the nature of existence that would come to overshadow Newton's physics as the prevailing scientific but also philosophical paradigm.

During the 1860s, he wrote his two most influential papers theorizing that the earth was animated by what he termed an "electromagnetic field." Maxwell's contribution was to show, through a series of equations, that the speed of an electromagnetic field is approximately the same as the speed of light, and that being true:

"We can scarcely avoid the conclusion that light consists in the transverse undulations of the same medium which is the cause of electric and magnetic phenomena . . . the agreement of the results seems to show that light and magnetism are affections of the same substance, and that light is an electromagnetic disturbance propagated through the field according to electromagnetic laws."[27]

His magnum opus, *Treatise on Electricity and Magnetism*, was published in 1873 and set the course that would lead to Albert Einstein's special theory of relativity in the 20th century.

Electromagnetic fields are crucial to the workings of the universe and life on Earth. The earth's core is made up of a mix of molten nickel and iron and is an electromagnet. Its magnetic field is charged by electricity that flows in the molten core. These powerful currents stretch over hundreds of miles at speeds of thousands of miles per hour as the planet rotates. The magnetic fields pass out of the core and through the earth's crust and enter the atmosphere.[28]

The portion of the earth's magnetic field that enters outer space is called the magnetosphere and it plays a critical role by creating layers of magnetic plasma that act as a shield to protect the earth from solar and cosmic particle radiation and prevent solar winds from stripping away the atmosphere that's indispensable for maintaining life on Earth.[29]

Maxwell's theory of electromagnetic fields spawned a new way to think of physics and inspired everything that's come since in that field. Still, it was the deeper cosmological implications that touched a nerve with Alfred North Whitehead in the 20th century. As alluded to in chapter seven, Whitehead was chagrined by Newton's insistence that nature is simply made up of isolated autonomous bits of matter existing in a timeless location and found an intellectual soul mate in Maxwell and his theory of electromagnetic fields.

Whitehead realized that the theory of electromagnetic fields "involves the entire abandonment of the notion that simple location is the primary way in which things are involved in space-time," for it suggests that "in a certain sense everything is everywhere at all times."[30] Whitehead wrote those words in 1926 in his book *Science and the Modern World*. By 1934, Whitehead's thoughts on the ontological significance of Maxwell's theory of electromagnetic fields had matured into a fully developed philosophy that today is reshaping our understanding of life as temporal patterns. In *Nature and Life*, he pondered the significance that electromagnetic fields might have on rethinking the nature of existence. He wrote that electromagnetism tells us that:

> The fundamental concepts are activity and process. . . . The notion of self-sufficient isolation is not exemplified in modern physics. There are no essentially self-contained activities within limited regions. . . . Nature is a theatre for the interrelations of activities. All things change, the activities and their interrelations. . . . In the place of the procession of [spatial] forms (of externally related bits of matter) modern physics has substituted the notion of the forms of process. It has thus swept away space and matter, and has substituted the study of the internal relations within a complex state of activity.[31]

Whitehead was convinced of the relatedness of nature or what he termed the "togetherness of things." In Whitehead's world "each happening is a factor in the nature of every other happening."[32] Whitehead was onto something but was unable to translate the cold physics of electromagnetic field theory into the warm world of biology and life, leaving his own intuition about the meaning of life unresolved.

During the same decades that Whitehead was ruminating about physical fields, a Russian scientist, Alexander Gurwitsch, was rethinking the nature of morphogenesis, the biological process that causes "the shaping of an organism by embryological processes of differentiation of cells, tissues, and organs."[33] In 1922, Gurwitsch first introduced the concept of a biological field to describe the process by which an organism develops shape and form. It wasn't until the 1940s, however, that he developed a fully articulated biological field theory. Gurwitsch argued that:

> A cell creates a field around itself: that is to say, the field extends outside the cell into extracellular space. . . . Therefore, at any point . . . within a group of cells there exists a single field being constituted of all the individual cell fields. . . . The field employs the energy released during exothermic chemical reactions in living systems to endow molecules (proteins, peptides, etc.) with ordered, directed movement. . . . A point source of a cell field coincides with the center of the nucleus; hence, the field is in general, a radial one.[34]

Gurwitsch's biological field theory still held on to the conventional belief that the field was tied to elemental components and that when an embryo took shape, each stage was derived from the preceding less complex stage directed outward from the center of the nucleus. In other words, there was no separate force field independent of the embryo playing a role in establishing the pattern of the embryo's development and final form. Gurwitsch's field theory was still mired in the orthodox idea of the evolving embryo as an assemblage of components—a classical machine metaphor with just a splash of field theory thrown in.

Other biologists were more eager to fully explore the implications of field theory in physics as a way of rethinking biology. Paul Weiss, an Austrian biologist with a background in physics and medical engineering who taught at Rockefeller University, brought with him an understanding of electromagnetic field theory, the vital knowledge that would make possible the next step in postulating a fully developed field theory of biology. After years of research into the workings of biology and the evolution of species, he concluded that "the patterned structure of the dynamics of the system as a whole coordinates the activities of the constituents" rather than the orthodox notion that the organism is an aggregate of the separate parts that somehow assemble themselves together in a working whole—the classical machine metaphor.[35]

Weiss used the face as a point of departure to make his argument. He asked, how could the face be assembled by all of the little genes that make it up? Rather, he suggested that the face is an invisible pattern that somehow coordinates the parts. Just like iron filings line up against the invisible and immaterial force of the magnet, the appropriate cells line up in the correct place of the face by an invisible field that choreographs the activity. In his 1973 book *The Science of Life*, Weiss describes experiments in which researchers take a limb bud in a developing embryo and transplant it to different locations within the sac. What they discovered was whether the bud developed into a right or left limb depended "essentially on its orientation relative to the main axes of the body, or more correctly, of the axiate pattern of its immediate surroundings."[36]

Similarly, a severed antenna of a praying mantis can sprout either another antenna or a leg depending on the region of the organism to which it is transplanted. Weiss makes clear that "which of the two alternatives is to prevail depends on where the cell group stands within the larger complex."[37]

Still unanswered is: What is the nature of the biological field and can it reveal the greatest mystery—how an organism comes to be? A first tentative answer came from decades of field research by Harold Saxton Burr, a professor of anatomy who taught at Yale University from 1914 to 1958. Burr studied the relationship between the development of living organisms and electromagnetic fields. He published his findings in 1972 in a book entitled *Blueprint for Immortality*. He was the first to propose—based on field research—an electromagnetic field theory for the evolution of life. He wrote:

> The pattern or organization of any biological system is established by a complex electro-dynamic field . . . this field is electrical in the physical sense and by its properties relates the entities of the biological system in a characteristic pattern.[38]

Unlike earlier purely theoretical speculations on biological fields, Burr backed up his claim with decades of field studies. For example, in a study conducted jointly with the Connecticut Agricultural Experiment Station, Burr examined the electrical pattern in seven strains of corn—four of the corn seeds were prize strains, three were hybrids. His study showed a direct "correlation between the electrometric activity of the seeds and their growth potential." These and other similar experiments with trees and other organisms that he conducted over the years led him to suggest that "the conclusion seems to be inescapable that there is a very close relationship between the genetic constitution and the electrical pattern."[39]

As to the age-old question of what makes up a particular organism or species, Burr suggests that "the chemistry provides the energy, but the electrical phenomena of the electrodynamic field determine the direction in which energy flows within the living system."[40]

In the subsequent decades since Weiss and Burr tentatively suggested a partial rewrite of Darwin's theory to make room for the integration of both an organism's genetic code and its electrodynamic fields, lab and field studies began to fill in some of the remaining unanswered questions concerning the dynamics that compose life. In the process, a new generation of biologists and physiologists have begun to bring together the fields of physics, chemistry, and biology in a new synthesis that's beginning to look like a historic paradigm shift in our understanding of the meaning of life and, in particular, how we come to perceive our relationship to a vibrant, alive, and evolving Earth.

The blowback from within the field of biology by the standard-bearers of the neo-Darwinian synthesis has been, at best, largely dismissive. For the most part they have closed ranks until late in defense of the neo-Darwinian synthesis, and have shunned newcomers in the field who dare to suggest that physics, particularly endogenous and exogenous electromagnetic fields, might play a part in establishing the patterns by which the cells, organs, tissues, and whole bodies are organized. If they were to acknowledge the role that bioelectromagnetic fields play in the development of an organism, it would mean that while the genetic code is the "instructions" for creating cells, organs, tissues, and bodies, an endogenous and exogenous electromagnetic code may be the indispensable agent in orchestrating the "patterns" that determine how genes are arranged to form the body parts and the whole of the organism.

The reluctance to consider the radical new notion of the role that electromagnetic fields play in the evolution and programming of life took a sudden turn in the first decade of the 21st century. The reason is that a promising commercial field of electromagnetic diagnostic tools and disease therapies was emerging, raising the possibilities of extraordinary medical advances, challenging the long-held notion that new ways of managing and curing diseases fall mainly under the purview of breakthroughs in genetic therapies and genomic medicine. The use of non-ionizing electromagnetic fields for medical treatment has proliferated over the past two decades. Here's a partial list of some of the EMF applications currently in widespread use or in experimental trials: Magnetic resonance imaging (MRI); Cancer treatment; tumor treatment; diathermy for treating muscle pain; stimulation of the *nervus vagus* for the treatment of epilepsy; pulsed EMF in bone fracture healing; electroporation to increase the permeability of cell membranes to deliver drugs or genes into tumor cells; treatment of pathological conditions related to the nervous system; electroconvulsive treatment; the treatment of neurological conditions including deep brain stimulation; treatment of Parkinson's disease and other tremors; treatment of chronic pain; treatment of therapy resistant depression; treatment of nerve regeneration, migraines, and neurodegenerative disorders; treatment of osteoarthritis; wound healings; immune system modulation; dermatological treatment of cancerous lesions and other skin conditions.[41]

How close are we to a fundamental rethinking of the evolution of life on Earth? A series of experiments over the past decade have taken society ever nearer to a new understanding of the nature of living systems. While Watson and Crick's accomplishment of breaking the "genetic code" with the discovery of the double-helix structure of genes in 1953 set off what some believe would be a genomics era, today a new generation of biologists, often cross-trained in physics and AI, are coming ever closer to cracking what they call the "bioelectric code." The bioelectric code refers to electromagnetic fields that permeate every living creature and that may play a role in determining the shape, pattern, and form of every cell, organ, tissue, and organism. A growing number of scientific experiments suggest that electromagnetic fields may be "the first mover" that establishes the pattern and form of each organism.

Daniel Fels of the Department of Environmental Sciences at the University of Basel, Switzerland, provides a shorthand description of how bioelectric fields operate in organisms:

> EMFs play essential roles in cell dynamics. . . . Cell internal EMFs not only oscillate within cells, but also within a tissue . . . leading to pattern formation. . . . [For example,] when a sperm encounters the ovum, successful fertilization only occurs after what is called a zinc spark. Only after an enormous membrane voltage change associated with this zinc spark event occurs, can embryonic development start successfully. This membrane voltage dependency for life processes to occur continues in the development of multicellular organisms, and is found as a trigger for gene activation and epigenetic control, as well as for regeneration or stem cell differentiation. . . . Electromagnetic fields

external to the organism have measurable effects on life, too, and therefore belong to the environment of cells and organisms.[42]

Several scientific discoveries of late have brought forth tantalizing evidence of how bioelectric fields operate on and in living systems. A trailblazing report was made public in July 2011 by Dany Adams, a biology professor at the Tufts School of Arts and Sciences. Adams made a fascinating discovery. She found that in the early stages, when a frog embryo is developing and before it gets a face, "a pattern for that face lights up on the surface of the embryo"—an electric face. What's unusual is that the discovery was made quite by accident. On one particular evening in September 2009, Adams left a camera on overnight that had been filming a developing frog embryo. The next morning, she and her team watched a time-lapse video in which a bioelectrical signal formed an electrical pattern of a face taking shape that would then be filled in with living matter. She says it was:

Unlike anything I had ever seen . . . The imagery revealed three stages, or courses, of bioelectric activity. First, a wave of hyperpolarization (negative ions) flashed across the entire embryo, coinciding with the emergence of cilia that enable the embryos to move. Next, patterns appeared that matched the imminent shape changes and gene expression domains of the developing face. Bright hyperpolarization marked the folding in of the surface, while both hyperpolarized and depolarized regions overlapped domains of head patterning genes. In the third course, localized regions of hyperpolarization formed, expanded and disappeared, but without disturbing the patterns created during the second stage. At the same time, the spherical embryo began to elongate.[43]

In subsequent experiments, the Tufts team found that if they disrupted the bioelectric signaling by inhibiting ductin—a protein that transports hydrogen ions—the embryos would develop craniofacial abnormalities, with some embryos growing two brains rather than one, and others developing abnormal jaws and other distorted facial features.[44]

Laura Vandenberg, a postdoctoral fellow on the team, summed up the importance of what they had discovered:

Our research shows that the electrical state of a cell is fundamental to development. Bioelectrical signaling appears to regulate a sequence of events, not just one. . . . Developmental biologists are used to thinking of sequences in which a gene produces a protein product that in turn ultimately leads to development of an eye or a mouth. But our work suggests that something else—a bioelectrical signal—is required before that can happen.[45]

It's becoming increasingly clear that the 160-year reign of the Darwinian worldview, in all of its incarnations, is being at least partially amended by an expanded narrative. That doesn't mean that all of Darwin's insights and the various modifications, appendages, and amplifications of his theory that have since emerged are being cast aside. Some are proving to be false, while others continue to have currency. What's happening is that a far more complex understanding of what life is all about is surfacing with each new discovery along the way, leading toward breaking the bioelectric code.

The scientific initiatives that are fast zeroing in on breaking the bioelectric code are bringing physics, chemistry, and biology together in a new synthesis that speaks to an animated Earth, not in terms of analogy or metaphor, but rather, as a verifiable organism—perhaps unique in the universe.

By 2014, the upholders of the neo-Darwinian synthesis were under siege by the publication of a rash of experiments by physicists, physiologists, and biologists in leading scientific journals that challenged the long-held notion that the genetic code alone held the secrets to the evolution of life. In June of that year, the journal *Physiology* published a special issue with the provocative title *The Integration of Evolutionary Biology with Physiological Science*.

In the editorial introducing the special issue, five leading scientists dared to ask the question of whether "the modern synthesis is to be extended or replaced by a new explanatory structure, [and if so] what is the role of physiology in the development of this structure?" They challenged the central theme of Darwin's theory, writing that "the mechanism of random change followed by selection becomes only one of many possible mechanisms of evolutionary change." They went even further, boldly challenging the idea of the supremacy of the genetic code, asserting:

Physiology in a broad sense, therefore, now moves to center stage in evolutionary biology as we are finally in a position to step conceptually and technologically out of the narrow frames of the Modern Synthesis and take explanatory responsibility for a much wider set of evolutionary phenomena and patterns across time and space.[46]

Charles Darwin presented a novel new theory of the evolution of life—natural selection—to explain how species emerge, evolve over time, and give rise to new species that share common ancestors. He argued that random, incremental changes in inheritable biological traits that confer an advantage to an individual in his or her struggle for survival pass on to their offspring, conferring the same advantages. Over a period of time, these incremental trait changes build up and result in the emergence of new species that share common ancestors. Darwin admitted, however, that he was particularly troubled about how the buildup of such incremental traits could result in the formation of an organ as complex as an eye. He wrote, "To suppose that the eye, with all its inimitable contrivances for adjusting the focus to different distances, for admitting different amounts of light, and for the correction of spherical and chromatic aberration, could have been formed by natural selection, seems, I freely confess, absurd in the highest possible degree."[47]

One hundred forty-eight years later at the Tufts Center for Regenerative and Developmental Biology, a team led by Michael Levin, a professor of biology and the director of the center, performed an experiment that would shake the world of biology and offer another piece of evidence of the role that electromagnetic fields play in orchestrating the assembling of organs, tissues, and whole organisms. And they used the eye to make their case.

In December 2007, Levin's research team announced that "for the first time, scientists have altered natural bioelectrical communication among cells to directly specify the type of new organ to be created at a particular location within a vertebrate organism." Tufts postdoctoral fellow Vaibhav Pai, the lead author of the report, entitled "Transmembrane Voltage Potential Controls Embryonic Eye Patterning in *Xenopus laevis*," describes the process.[48]

The team changed the voltage gradient of cells in the tadpole's back and tail to match the voltage gradient of the location where the eye cells normally develop. The result, "the eye-specific gradient drove the cells in the back and tail—which would normally develop into other organs—to develop into eyes."[49]

"The hypothesis," according to Dr. Pai, is that for every structure of the body there is a specific membrane voltage range that drives organogenesis. "By using a specific membrane voltage, we were able to generate normal eyes in regions that were never thought to be able to form eyes. This suggests that cells from anywhere in the body can be driven to form an eye."[50]

Although Levin's team was quick to point out the vast potential medical benefits of using a specific membrane voltage range that drives the development of each organ, tissue, and limb in repairing birth defects and in a range of regenerative medical practices, Levin was not unmindful of the bigger picture, concluding that this single experiment "is a first step to cracking the bioelectric code."[51]

9

BEYOND THE SCIENTIFIC METHOD: COMPLEX ADAPTIVE SOCIAL/ ECOLOGICAL SYSTEMS MODELING

What we are discovering about the nature of nature is so at odds with the conventional scientific narrative underlying the Age of Progress that it's not altogether surprising that our long-held approach to scientific inquiry is under siege. This deeply flawed scientific paradigm to wresting nature's secrets didn't just emerge pell-mell or by chance. It was forcefully introduced into the public arena by a single individual over four centuries ago and became the rule of thumb not only for understanding nature but also for commandeering it for near-exclusive use by the human family.

Francis Bacon, born in London in 1561, has long been regarded as the patron saint of modern science. In his opus the *Novum Organum*, Bacon excoriated the ancient Greek philosophers. Looking over the history of Western civilization since Platonism was introduced into the social space, Bacon concluded that its central themes had done nothing to improve the human lot. He argued that the Greeks, for all their musings, had not "adduced a single experiment which tends to relieve and benefit the condition of man."[1]

Bacon cut new ground by championing the "how" of things as the cornerstone of philosophy and cast his lot with secular power over divine revelation. He believed that a human being's most basic agency was the ability to separate oneself from nature, observe it impartially from a distance, and wrest its secrets to amass "objective knowledge" about the world, "enlarging of the bounds of Human Empire to the effecting of all things possible."[2]

For Bacon, the mind is a nonmaterial agency whose raison d'être is to have dominion over the material world. He pursued reason while crusading to restore the Lord's initial pledge to Adam and Eve that they shall have dominion over nature. In his own words, "the world is made for man, not man for the world."[3] Bacon outlined the rudiments of what would become the scientific method, boasting that with this new approach, human beings have "the power to conquer and subdue" nature and "to shake her to her foundations."[4] The goal, he prophesied, is to "establish and extend the power of dominion of the human race over the universe."[5]

Bacon's reputation as the father of modern science continued to grow and his scientific method would become a reality with the establishment of the Royal Society in London in 1660 followed by similar scientific societies and academies across Europe and later around the world.

Bacon's naïvely simplified, inductive, objective, detached, and linear approach to scientific inquiry that has accompanied the Age of Progress seems so sophomoric in hindsight in how to approach the natural world. The ever-evolving dissipative patterns and processes of intermingling self-organizing systems that make up our Earth's life force—now beginning to be understood—have spawned a new scientific method more attuned to our awakening understanding of the world.

A NEW SCIENCE FOR A REWILDING EARTH

Crawford Stanley Holling was a Canadian ecologist who served on the faculty of the University of British Columbia and later at the University of Florida. In 1973, he published a new theory on the emergence and workings of the natural environment entitled "Resilience and Stability of Ecological Systems." Holling introduced the concept of "adaptive management" and "resilience" in ecological systems theory and, along with other pioneers, laid the foundation for a radical new scientific method that would fuse ecology and society and come to challenge the guiding principles of conventional economic theory and practice.[6] The theory is called complex adaptive social/ecological systems (CASES).

We use the acronym CASES as an apt description of the type of inquiry used in complex adaptive social/ecological systems. A case is a situation that calls for an "investigation and/or a question to be settled" and is more descriptive of the new approach to scientific inquiry that is far more adaptive to the coming era than "experiments."[7] Although a mouthful to digest, the new theory and practice is beginning to reshape the way society thinks about time and space and how our species relates to the natural world.

Holling proposed that "the behavior of ecological systems could be defined by two distinct properties: resilience and stability."[8] His thesis was simple and elegant while not shying away from exploring the complexity of relationships that animate the natural world and our own species' interaction with it. His resilience theory has since spread into virtually every discipline: psychology, sociology, political science, anthropology, physics, chemistry, biology, and the engineering sciences. The commercial sectors and industries have also begun to follow suit: particularly in the fields of finance and insurance; manufacturing; ICT and telecom; electric utilities; transport and logistics; construction; urban planning; and agriculture.

But, most important, ground zero of the "New" Great Disruption lies at the intersection of economics and ecology. Holling explains that:

> Resilience determines the persistence of relationships within a system and is a measure of the ability of these systems to absorb changes of state variables, driving variables, and parameters, and still persist. In this definition resilience is the property of the system and persistence or probability of extinction is the result. . . . **Therefore, a major strategy selected is not one maximizing either efficiency or a particular reward, but one which allows persistence by maintaining flexibility above all else.** A population responds to any environmental change by the initiation of a series of physiological, behavioral, ecological, and genetic changes that restore its ability to respond to subsequent unpredictable environmental changes. . . . The more homogeneous the environment in space and time, the more likely is the system to have low fluctuations and low resilience. . . . A management approach based on resilience . . . would emphasize the need to keep options open, the need to view events in a regional rather than a local context, and the need to emphasize heterogeneity.
>
> Flowing from this would be not the presumption of sufficient knowledge, but the recognition of our ignorance; not the assumption that future events are expected, but that they will be unexpected. The resilience framework can accommodate this shift of perspective, for it does not require a precise capacity to predict the future, but only a qualitative capacity to devise systems that can absorb and accommodate future events in whatever unexpected form they may take.[9]

Over the next thirty years, Holling's initial foray into resilience and adaptation theory was modified, amplified, and qualified by others, adding increasing sophistication to the doctrine. In 2004, he coauthored a revised rendition of the theory of resilience and adaptation cycles entitled "Resilience, Adaptability and Transformability in Social-Ecological Systems." In the modified schema, Holling and his colleagues placed increasing attention on the "transformability" of natural systems. That is, the system may not be able to maintain itself, forcing a transformation to a new self-organizing system.

This revised interpretation of resilience is important because the early consideration of the word may have mistakenly given the impression that resilience is a measure of how much disruption a complex adaptive social/ecological system can take and still recover its original state. While that is certainly a consideration, resilience covers a more expansive temporal span in the lifetime of a biological community that extends far into the future and includes a succession of ecological transformations. Ecologists use the term *ecological succession* to describe the birth, maturation, demise, and transformability of biological communities.

The earliest stage of an ecological community is often referred to as the pioneering stage where life begins to bud in a region that has been left barren after cataclysmic events like volcanic eruptions and lava flows, wildfires, floods, and a shift in the climate, for example, between glacial and interglacial periods. New pioneering stages in ecological communities also occur in the wake of human exploitation of environments, for example, via logging, strip-mining, and the spread of toxic waste in the groundwater. In these early stages of ecological succession, we see the emergence of soil, plants, lichens, and mosses, followed by grasses, shrubs, and shade trees. Herbivores follow, eating off the vegetation, and later carnivores appear, eating the herbivores. Each new stage forces an adaptation by all of the previous elements in the evolving biological community in an emerging self-organizing system.

The last stage of succession in the life cycle of a biological community is called the mature stage or the climax community. In a climax community, there is little yearly accumulation of organic matter. The annual production and use of energy are relatively balanced and the climate is relatively stable across the seasons. There is a diversity of species interacting across complex food chains. There is close to a 1:1 ratio between gross primary production and the overall respiration of the community and between energy captured and used from sunlight and released in decomposition, as well as a delicate balance between the capture of soil nutrients and the return of nutrient litter back to the soil. Each species is continually adapting over time to the changing adaptations of every other species, not purposefully but by necessity.

An ecological community's resilience rests in "the diversity of the drivers, and in the number of passengers." Lance H. Gunderson, of the Department of Environmental Sciences at Emory University, makes the telling observation that the resilience of an ecological community depends on overlapping influences by multiple processes, "each one of which is inefficient in its individual effect but together operating in a robust manner."[10]

Resilience, then, be it in human or ecological communities, has, since Holling penned his initial theory, been generally misconstrued as the ability of the system to respond to massive disruptions with sufficient robustness to allow it to bounce back to its initial equilibrium. But what we have learned in previous chapters is that in nature, society, and the universe, when agencies interact, they never return to where they were because the interactions themselves change the dynamic regardless of how slight they may be. Every interaction changes the relative relationship of each actor to the other, as well as affecting the multiple systems in which they are embedded. At best, one can talk of a relative "bounce-back" to a new state whose actions, agencies, and relationships are roughly comparable as to be able to identify the ecological community as more or less similar in its attributes, processes, dynamics, and populations as before.

The point is that resilience never means reestablishing the exact status quo. The passage of time and events is always changing the patterns, processes, and relationships, no matter how small the footprint, in nature as in society. Resilience should never be thought of as a "state of being" in the world, but rather a way of acting on the world. Adaptivity, in turn, is the temporal agency by which an individual organism, an entire species, or a larger biological community embed themselves in all of the interacting processes and patterns that make up the earth's microbiomes, ecosystems, and biomes on an interactive planet.

Much of the confusion here lies with the way resilience has come to be defined by society—especially in the social sciences disciplines. Learning to be resilient has come to be associated with a therapeutic means of adjusting to trauma that undermines a person's sense of agency, often with the unstated hope of retrieving one's personal and collective life to a semblance of what it was before the disruption. But as anyone who has ever experienced trauma of this sort can attest, the road to recovery and resilience is never backward. One can never go back, but only forward to a new sense of agency that comes from the emotional and cognitive lessons learned.

To complicate matters, resilience is often seen as a way to overcome vulnerability. Yet, to be vulnerable does not always mean being endangered. It also speaks to our ability to be open to the other. To be vulnerable can also mean to take risks, to leave one's comfort zone, and enrich one's sense of personal agency by experiencing the unknown and nurturing more diverse relationships and patterns of living. Resilience is never simply about regaining control but rather of openness to establishing new venues of embeddedness.

Fiona Miller of the Department of Research Management and Geography at the University of Melbourne points to the difficulty of living in the Age of Resilience: "The challenge from a [social] resilience perspective is to learn to live with change and develop the capacity to deal with it instead of trying to block it out."[11] This is the juncture where humanity lets go of efficiency and grabs hold of adaptivity as the temporal means to reestablish its relationship with the earth from one of expropriation to reharmonization. It is the dividing line that takes us from the Age of Progress to the Age of Resilience.

Although not yet acknowledged from within the profession, the economics citadel is collapsing, mostly because of two factors: first, the threat of climate change and increasing pandemics have taken command on a scale that eclipses whatever metrics remain in the economics arsenal to tackle these crises; second, a bewildered humanity has lost faith in the willingness of the business community to right the wrongs that have plunged the human race and our fellow creatures into the throes of an environmental holocaust.

The economics discipline, if it is to survive, will need to metamorphize into a wholly new way of thinking of its relationship to the natural world. That makeover will require, in part, a reassessment of some of the long-held tenets of the discipline, including general equilibrium theory, cost-benefit analysis, the narrow definition of externalities, and its misleading concepts of both productivity and GDP. At the root of this transformation will be the need to temper and even challenge the profession's overriding preoccupation with efficiency and begin to develop tools and business models that bring the discipline in line with adaptivity. Above all, the business community will need to walk back the whole of its relation to and understanding of the natural world as a "resource" and, instead, reenvision nature as a "life force" of which our species is only one of a legion of species whose own journey on Earth is of commensurate value to our own.

More difficult still, our species would need to acknowledge that it's not "all about us" and that if truth be told, all the other species who inhabit the planet with us would be better off if humans were to disappear into the long list of species who have descended into the fossil record before us. Admittedly, this is a tough assessment to confront but an honest evaluation of where things stand. Humbling for sure, but necessary if we are to rewrite our species' future. The question is: How do we begin anew?

Where better to start remodeling economic theory than to follow the science that accompanies the Age of Resilience and that is extricating other academic disciplines from the doldrums of conventional scientific inquiry that conditioned the Age of Progress. Complex adaptive social/ecological systems offer up far more than a new theory of scientific inquiry. The new science amounts to an ontological leap in the way we think about the meaning of existence. The best way to appreciate the significance of this cognitive transformation is to compare this new mode of scientific inquiry with the accepted scientific method to which generations were trained.

Although defining the scientific method has been a slippery and even murky process, there are a number of common denominators that are generally agreed upon. Here is how the *Stanford Encyclopedia of Philosophy* describes the nature of scientific methodology: "Among the activities often identified as characteristics of science, are systemic experimentation, inductive and deductive reasoning, and the formation and testing of hypothesis and theories." The scientific method is accompanied by a set of goals, including "knowledge, predictions, or control" as well as a set of overriding values and justifications known to every student: "objectivity, reproducibility, simplicity, or past success."[12]

The approach that CASES takes to scientific inquiry differs fundamentally from the conventional scientific method. To begin with, the scientific method, as touched on earlier, often focuses on isolating a single phenomenon and observing the workings of its components and parts in order to understand the assemblage of the whole. Second, the conventional approach to scientific inquiry, though long touted as unbiased in its investigation of nature, is anything but. Students come to the lab armed with a set of preconceived notions about the nature of nature and human beings' relationship to the natural world. For example, every student is told to always be "objective" and leave preconceived biases at the door, not realizing that objective comes from the word "object." The unspoken bias is to examine the world as made up of an assortment of objects that are passive and even inert in nature and with little or no agency. Third, nature is often viewed as "resources" to be exploited for societal gain.

By contrast, in the complex adaptive social/ecological systems approach, nature is experienced as "open dynamical systems that are able to self-organize their structural configuration through the exchange of information and energy."[13] Complex adaptive systems also learn to be adaptive to new circumstances, patterns, and environments, and the processes by which they transform themselves into new states—known as emergence.

Researchers Rika Preiser, Reinette Biggs, Alta De Vos, and Carl Folke, in a 2018 journal article entitled "Social-Ecological Systems as Complex Adaptive

Systems," summarized the state of the art of complex adaptive social/ecological systems as reflected in the hundreds of studies, reports, and articles by scientists and researchers across multiple disciplines. The following are some of the defining characteristics that distinguish complex adaptive systems inquiry from the traditional scientific method:

> From characteristics of parts to systemic properties: This involves a shift from studying the characteristics of parts in isolation to looking at systemic properties that emerge from the underlying patterns of organization. Systemic properties are destroyed when dissected because emergent properties cannot be decomposed into the properties of their constituent parts.
>
> From objects to relations: Systems properties emerge through dynamic patterns of interaction. Thus, the underlying organizational processes, connections, and emergent behavioral patterns are important to understand.
>
> From closed to open systems: Complex phenomena are embedded in networks and hierarchies through which there is a continuous exchange of information, energy, and material. Therefore, there is no clear inside or outside of SES [Social Ecological Systems] because all entities are connected through processes of organization on different spatial and temporal scales.
>
> From measuring to capturing and assessing complexity: Complex phenomena are constituted relationally through dynamic interactions that form emergent patterns of behavior. Thus, a perceptual shift is necessary that enables us to capture and understand relationships that cannot be measured in terms of material causes. Moreover, through the dynamic mapping and assessing of relations, connections, and multiple complex causal pathways, we can trace configurations and characterize networks, cycles, and cross-scale interactions. These efforts can elucidate how SES are constituted relationally and how patterns of behavior emerge. This can in turn facilitate our ability to anticipate adaptive and transformative behavior and pathways.
>
> From observation to intervention: CAS [Complex Adaptive Systems] are contextualized and constituted relationally, and information about systems properties and dynamics cannot be separated from the organizational properties defining a system. The study of SES implies a process of framing the boundaries of the system that is observer-dependent and entails intervention that is quite different from that of objective observation.[14]

A CASES approach to scientific inquiry falls short of the kind of predictability that science has hitherto sought. Any attempt to establish a boundary on a self-organizing system misses the underlying truth that all self-organizing systems are patterns among other patterns that spread out in time and space and across the earth's operating spheres, impacting one another in subtle and profound ways that rarely can be foreseen. The most important lesson of applying CASES thinking is to partially let go of the obsession with "prediction" and settle for "anticipation" and "adaptation."

Even many of the findings on the future of climate change are generally after the fact. Scientists in the field admit that changes in the earth's spheres and ecosystems brought on by global warming are difficult to forecast before the effects are seen. That's because the positive feedback loops on a warming planet are so pervasive, with cascading effects rippling out in every direction, that forecasting becomes problematic.

For example, for decades climate scientists paid no attention to the permafrost that covers 24 percent of the entire northern hemisphere landmass until they noticed the effect that global warming was having on the melting of the ice.[15] They realized that under the ice lay vast carbon deposits—the remains of lush animal and plant life that flourished in the northern climes before the beginning of the last Ice Age. Even more troubling, they noticed that the melting of the ice was accelerating because the opaque white layer of the ice that had previously reflected the sun's energy back into space upon melting was leaving behind large swaths of exposed black earth that was absorbing more of the heat from global warming emissions and hastening the melting process—again, another positive feedback loop.

They began measuring the CO_2 and methane emissions that were seeping up from under the ground and realized that the leakage was increasing at an exponential rate, threatening a dramatic increase in global warming emissions that might rival the CO_2 emissions from industrial activity over the past two hundred years. Here was a new reality that had not previously been predicted—an unknown unknown. We finally began to grasp the difficulty of predicting the course of evolving self-organizing complex systems in a radically changing climate and how they might affect society.

The way forward, then, is to at least "partially" shift the focus of scientific inquiry from prediction to adaptation. There is still a significant role to play in making predictions, although that path is narrowing with the cascading rewilding of the earth in the throes of global warming. At the same time, the science of adaptation is ripe to play a role in redirecting society's response to climate change. After all, adaptation is the way every other species adjusts to the unpredictable changes in an ever-evolving world. Adaptivity is not a new concept in science. It's only that it's getting a second life because of the increasing risks facing society.

FROM PREDICTION TO ADAPTATION

John Dewey was one of the founders of the philosophy of pragmatism and among the first to shine a light on the merits of adaptivity as an approach to scientific exploration and problem solving. Dewey had little patience with scientific orthodoxy with its emphasis on objectivity and detachment. He was even less disposed to the deductionist approach of scientific inquiry, which often starts with predetermined hypotheses followed by experiments to test their validity. He also had a particular aversion to the researcher as a spectator. For Dewey, the seeker of knowledge always starts his or her inquiry into a problem by being an active participant, experiencing the issue up close and being affected by it.

The early pragmatists, who included Charles Sanders Peirce and George Herbert Mead, were interested in "actionable" knowledge that could be used to solve a problem and set a new course. Dewey and the other pragmatists were also predisposed to the interconnectedness of experience, understanding that problems are never isolated events that can be easily separated from the many relationships to which they are attached and therefore need to be taken up in a holistic manner.

Dewey eschewed the very notion of the duality of theory and practice and instead "viewed knowledge as arising from an active adaptation of the human organism to its environment."[16] Dewey and other early pragmatists gave fresh life to the importance of adaptivity as a keystone attribute of all living creatures.

While adaptivity gained some traction during the Progressive Era at the onset of the 20th century, it was soon overrun by the efficiency crusade. Managing the future by optimizing the use of time struck a more powerful chord in the heyday of the Industrial Revolution with its mania for managing future outcomes. Now, with a fossil fuel–driven industrial revolution in a death throe and insiders even questioning its guiding principles, adaptivity is suddenly experiencing a revival.

Efficiency, on the other hand, which until recently seeped into every business conversation, has become more muted of late as society reels from crisis to crisis and now faces the prospect of escalating pandemics and climate-related disasters. Talk of unlimited opportunities has given way to discussions on mitigating risks, and efficiency has begun to take a backseat to adaptivity on a rewilding Earth. The Age of Progress, which provided an overarching frame for modernity and a narrative by which successive generations planned and lived their lives, has quietly receded from the public discourse, without so much as a requiem. Everywhere, the talk is of adaptivity and resilience, particularly in the scientific magazines and journals.

In the depths of the COVID-19 pandemic, *National Geographic* magazine thought it fitting to run a piece on "Adaptation and Survival" in nature. The article cited the various types of adaptation flora and fauna take on to enhance their own resilience, reproduction, and survival. These examples offer creative approaches to adaptation that might spur imitative practices in the business community and society at large.

The *National Geographic* editors led off with everyone's favorite wild animal, the koala, noting that they have adapted to eating only eucalyptus leaves, which happen to be very low in protein value in addition to being toxic to many other species, giving them a noncompetitive source of nourishment.

Some adaptations can be structural, in the form of a physical attribute. For example, succulent plants have adapted to hot dry desserts by "storing water in their short, thick stems and leaves."[17]

Other adaptations are behavioral. Gray whales travel thousands of kilometers each year from the cold waters of the Arctic to the warm waters of Mexico to give birth to their calves and then double back to the Arctic to feed in its nutrient-rich waters.

England's peppered moth, *Biston betularia*, is a classic example of an animal's adaptation to a change in environment. Before the Industrial Revolution in the 19th century, most peppered moths were cream colored with dark spots and only a small number were either black or gray. But, as the soot from industrial activity began to settle on trees, the darker-colored moths came to dominate in numbers because they blended into the darker surface. Birds couldn't see the dark moths and settled for eating the white moths, which resulted in black moths becoming the dominant type.

Sympatric speciation is where a variety of near-identical species share the same habitat because each is adapted to a special diet and therefore is not competitive with others. A variety of orchids live in Lake Malawi in Tanzania. One variety of orchid feasts on algae, another on insects, and a third on fish.

Harvard Business Review was among the first to give a shout-out to adaptivity as the new defining business value moving forward. In a provocative article entitled "Adaptability: The New Competitive Advantage," the authors, Martin Reeves and Mike Deimler of the Boston Consulting Group, noted that the most successful corporations have built their businesses "around scale and efficiency—sources of advantage that rely on an essentially stable environment."[18] But, as they explained, in a world of increasingly unpredictable risks and instabilities, these tried-and-true values become an albatross. Rather, adaptivity becomes the intrinsic value if an enterprise is to survive. This means the willingness to experiment and accept failures, even if it chokes off short-term revenue. It is the way to regroup and stay in the game.

As well, adaptivity favors leaving centralized bureaucracies behind with their vertically integrated economies of scale, noting that they are too rigid and brittle to survive a world hurtling from crisis to crisis. The authors favor "creating decentralized, fluid and even competing organizational structures" and suggest that such an approach "destroys the big advantage of a rigid hierarchy." They argue that the switchover to seeding an expansive set of alternative business platforms gives a company a diverse number of options, allowing the enterprise the agility it needs to adapt to the fast-changing circumstances in a high-risk environment.[19]

Although the flurry of excitement around rethinking the business model more along the lines of adaptivity and resilience has been more glib than substantive, there are a few green shoots emerging that portend the vast changes ahead. Make no mistake about the significance of complex adaptive thinking applied to social/ecological systems. This is a systemic change in the way society understands, approaches, and reintegrates our species back into the rhythms of a living planet as adaptive agents seeking resilience. The hope is to be counted among the species that survive and flourish in the Anthropocene.

Conventional economics and the workings of the capitalist system, in both theory and practice, won't survive in their current form with the transformation brought on by initiating complex adaptive systems modeling. The profession's guiding assumptions are deeply at odds with the way an animated Earth operates. Some of industrial capitalism's values and ways of provisioning communication, energy, mobility, and habitats will remain as our species readapts to the earth's plethora of agencies and systems, but much of the remnants that make up the bulwark of neoclassical and neoliberal economic theory will disappear, along with the current model of industrial capitalism and the narrative of the Age of Progress.

Complex adaptive system modeling will also require a remake of what we've come to think of as academia. The academic and professional disciplines that emerged in the Enlightenment and matured alongside the Age of Progress were each an end to themselves with their own narratives, language, metrics, and rules of engagement. And each, to some extent, attempted to understand the whole of reality from their own limited perspective.

In regard to pedagogy, virtually every school system and institution of higher education, at least until recently, have been tightly defined by academic silos. Scholars are penalized for wandering beyond the confines of their academic disciplines in their published studies and books, and often ridiculed for being "generalists" and soft in their erudition.

Admittedly at the university level, and even in some progressive secondary school systems, interdisciplinary studies have become a marginal part of the curriculum, but are still generally taught as an optional course or seminar rather than being embedded into the heart of the academic experience, signaling a pedagogic transformation that would bring teachers, scholars, and students together under the aegis of complex adaptive systems modeling. In recent years, the realities of climate change and the resulting public awareness of the interconnectivity of all phenomena on Earth, as well as a growing understanding of the multiple planetary agencies that affect and adapt to one another, have taken our collective humanity into a historic crisis. This state of affairs can only be understood by adopting complex adaptive systems modeling, which, in turn, requires an interdisciplinary approach to knowledge in the academic community and across curricula.

So, is a resilient economy governed by adaptivity just the newest fad with a limited life span? Unlikely, because the risks and realities associated with a warming climate is not a temporary phenomenon. All of the collective effort of humanity to forestall climate change, at least up to now, has been largely for naught. And now, our scientific community is warning us that a dead planet is no longer an impossibility. While our species will need to continue to push toward mitigation of global warming emissions, it will also have to find ways to continually adapt to the existential change brought on by the warming climate. Laying the foundation for a resilient society is, perhaps, the only surety our species can confidently embrace and take into the future.

All of which brings us back to the question of how best to learn to adapt, become resilient, survive, and perhaps flourish in ways quite different from what we have been accustomed to when we think of a life well lived. Public awareness has only just begun to own the terms adaptivity and resilience, but with little attempt to dig below the surface and rethink what life would be like in this kind of future.

Our forager-hunter ancestors might provide some guidance as they proved to be highly adaptive and resilient through ice ages and interglacial flows, the conditions that would challenge even the hardiest of our species today. Scientific research over the past twenty years has brought to light the eye-opening evidence that *Homo sapiens* may be one of the most adaptive species on Earth.

THE *HOMO SAPIENS* MIND:
Wired for Adaptivity

In the mid-1990s, biologists, cognitive scientists, and anthropologists unearthed new data suggesting that "the evolved structure of the human mind is adapted to the way of life of Pleistocene hunter-gatherers and not necessarily to our modern circumstances."[20] In 2014, scientists from New York University and the Smithsonian National Museum of Natural History published a study on the evolution of our early ancestors that amended earlier theories. For a long time, the consensus among evolutionary biologists was that the genus *Homo* emerged at "the onset of African aridity and the expansion of open grasslands."[21] The savannas favored adaptive traits, including large, linear bodies, elongated legs, large brain sizes, reduced sexual dimorphism, increased carnivorism, and unique life-history traits, including longevity, extensive toolmaking, and increased social cooperation.[22]

New fossil discoveries have further revised the theory of *Homo* origins. According to the scientists involved in the study, "new environmental data sets suggest that *Homo* evolved against a background of long periods of habitat unpredictability that were superimposed on the underlying aridity trend." The study found that "the key factors to the success and expansion of the genus rested on dietary flexibility in unpredictable environments, which, along with cooperative breeding and flexibility in development, allowed range expansion and reduced mortality risks."[23] The researchers came to their conclusion by refining a detailed climate model of the past, and compared it to the *Homo* fossil record, and what they discovered is that the *Homo* lineage did not originate during a calm, cool, stable climate period, as previously thought.

Richard Potts, one of the researchers and the director of the Human Origins Program the Smithsonian Institution, summed up their findings, saying that it was unstable climate conditions that "favored the evolution of the roots of human flexibility in our ancestors," adding that the "origin of our human genus is characterized by forms of adaptability."[24] The use of the term *unstable climate* does a disservice to how destabilizing was the period, which covers the most recent 2.3 million years on Earth. This is the era in which our hominin ancestors evolved, ending with *Homo sapiens*.

During this period, ice ages followed by thaws were the norm. The *National Geographic* reminds us that "by eight hundred thousand years ago, a cyclical pattern had emerged: Ice Ages last about one hundred thousand years, followed by warmer interglacials of ten thousand to fifteen thousand years each.

The last ice age ended about ten thousand years ago," taking our species into the relatively temperate climate of the Holocene and the advent of an agricultural way of life.[25]

Potts said in an interview with the magazine *Scientific American* that in this geological period of wild extremes in the weather, it was human ingenuity, the ability to think of creative ways to adapt to these harsh conditions, that was key to our species' survival. Potts is convinced that "the evolution of the human brain is the most obvious example of how we evolved to adapt."[26]

Summing up his research on human origins, Potts suggests that:

Our brains are essentially social brains. We share information, we create and pass on knowledge. That's the means by which humans are able to adjust to new situations, and it's what differentiates humans from our earlier ancestors, and our earlier ancestors from primates. You had *Homo sapiens* going into colder environments than even the Neanderthals could tolerate, at the same time that they were migrating into deserts, tropical forests, steppes and glacial environments. . . . How this thin, long-limbed hominid could make it in all these different environments, to me that is a story about how you become adaptable.[27]

Whether our species' adaptive capacities can adjust to the speed at which global warming is changing the hydrological cycle of the earth is the underlying question of our age.

Human adaptability to wildly changing climate regimes is our strong suit. It's what has made us one of the most resilient species on Earth. This is perhaps the most heartening news of our time and should be acknowledged and embraced with gusto at the outset of the Age of Resilience, with a qualification. The same adaptability that allowed our species to prevail during wild gyrations of the climate has been our undoing as well.

The cognitive attributes that allowed us to adapt to wildly changing climates during long stretches of the Paleolithic era, when we were forager-hunters, have been put to use over the past 11,700 years in the relatively predictable temperate climate of the Holocene to reverse course and force the natural world to adapt to our desires. This, too, is about adaptation. Beginning with the Agricultural Revolution, and more recently transitioning into the Industrial Revolution, we retooled our adaptive instincts from living with the changing seasons to storing surplus. That surplus multiplied exponentially during the two hundred years that marked a fossil fuel–based industrial civilization, or what we call the Age of Progress.

That is not to say that the fruits of the Industrial Revolution weren't a boon for large numbers of people, especially in the Western world. Arguably, most of us in the highly developed nations are far better off than our ancestors were before we began the industrial age. It's also fair to say that nearly half the population of the world (46 percent), living on less than $5.50 per day, the dividing line that defines poverty, is at best only marginally better off than their ancestors, and perhaps no better off.[28] Meanwhile, the wealthiest human beings have triumphed. By 2017, the accumulated wealth of the eight richest individuals in the world equaled the total wealth of half the human beings living on the planet—3.5 billion people.[29] Gandhi best captured the choice before us. He put it this way: "Earth provides enough to satisfy every man's need but not any man's greed."[30]

Part Four

THE AGE OF
RESILIENCE

THE PASSING OF THE
INDUSTRIAL ERA

10

THE RESILIENT REVOLUTION INFRASTRUCTURE

E very great shift in the way our species interacts with the natural world
since the dawn of civilization is traceable to the epochal infrastructure revolutions in history. Although most historians have thought
of infrastructure simply as scaffolding to bind large numbers of people together in collective life, it plays a far more fundamental role. Every transformative infrastructure paradigm brings together three components that
are indispensable to maintaining a collective social existence: new forms
of communication, new sources of energy and power, and new modes of
transportation and logistics. When these three technical advances emerge
and congeal in a seamless dynamic, they fundamentally change the way a
people "communicate, power, and move" their day-to-day economic, social, and political life.

THE SOCIOLOGY OF INFRASTRUCTURE TRANSFORMATIONS

Infrastructure revolutions are analogous to what every organism requires to
maintain an earthly existence: that is, a means to communicate; a source of
energy to stay alive; and some form of mobility or motility to maneuver in
their environment. Human infrastructure revolutions provide a technological prosthesis that enables large numbers of people to come together in more
complex economic, social, and political arrangements performing more differentiated roles, in what is best described as large-scale "social organisms"—
self-organizing systems that act as a whole.

Just as every organism requires a semipermeable membrane—for example, a skin or shell—to orchestrate the dynamic relationship between its inner life and the external world to which it is interconnected and dependent for its survival, so too, infrastructure revolutions come with changes in buildings and enclosures of all sorts. These artificial semipermeable membranes allow our species to survive the elements, store the energies and other necessities we need to maintain our physical well-being, provide secure and safe places to produce and consume the goods and services we require to enhance our existence, and serve as a congregating place to raise our families and conduct social life.

The great infrastructure revolutions also change the temporal-spatial orientation brought on by the new collective arrangement as well as the nature of economic activity, social life, and forms of governance to cohere with the opportunities and restraints that come with the new more differentiated collective patterns of life made possible by the new infrastructures.

In the 19th century, steam-powered printing and the telegraph, abundant coal, and locomotives on national rail systems meshed in a common infrastructure to communicate, power, and move society, giving birth to the First Industrial Revolution and the rise of urban habitats, capitalist economies, and national markets overseen by nation-state governments. In the 20th century, centralized electricity, the telephone, radio and television, cheap oil, and internal combustion transport on national road systems, inland waterways, oceans, and air corridors converged to create an infrastructure for the Second Industrial Revolution and the rise of suburban habitats, globalization, and global governing institutions.

Today, we are in the midst of a Third Industrial Revolution. The digitized broadband communication internet is converging with a digitized continental electricity internet, powered by solar and wind electricity. Millions of homeowners, local and national businesses, neighborhood associations, farmers and ranchers, civil society organizations, and government agencies are generating solar and wind electricity where they live and work to power their operations. Any surplus green electricity is being sold back to an increasingly integrated and seamless digitized continental electricity internet using big data, analytics, and algorithms to share renewable electricity just as we currently share news, knowledge, and entertainment on the communications internet.

Now these two digitized internets are converging with a digitized mobility and logistics internet composed of electric and fuel-cell vehicles powered by solar- and wind-generated electricity from the electricity internet. Over the coming decade, these vehicles will be increasingly autonomous on road, rail, water, and in air corridors and managed by big data, analytics, and algorithms just as we do with the electricity and communications internets.

These three internets will increasingly share a continuous flow of data and analytics, creating fluid algorithms that synchronize communication, the generation, storage, and distribution of green electricity, and the movement of zero-emission autonomous transport across regions, continents, and global time zones. All three internets will also be continuously fed data from sensors embedded across the terrain that are monitoring activity of all kinds in real time, from ecosystems, agricultural fields, warehouses, road systems, factory production lines, and especially from the residential and commercial building stock, allowing humanity to more adaptively manage, power, and move day-to-day economic activity and social life from where they work and live. This is the Internet of Things (IoT).

In the coming era, buildings will be retrofitted for energy savings and climate resilience and embedded with IoT infrastructure. They will also be equipped with edge data centers, giving the public direct control over how their data is collected, used, and shared. Smart buildings will also serve as green micro power-generating plants, energy storage sites, and transport and logistics hubs for electric and fuel-cell vehicles in a more distributed zero-emission society.

Buildings in the Third Industrial Revolution will no longer be passive, walled-off private spaces but, rather, potentially actively engaged nodal entities sharing their renewable energies, energy savings, energy storage, electric mobility, and a wide range of other economic and social activity with one another at the discretion of their occupants. Self-reliant, smart buildings are a critical component of the emerging resilient society.

For those who are justifiably alarmed about the possibility that this digital planetary infrastructure will only be captured by dark forces to centralize and concentrate power in the hands of new elites, while siphoning agency away from much of the human race to the end of pillaging the earth, there is a more compelling path forward. The backstory begins with the overlap as the Second Industrial Revolution peaked and began to slowly decline, and many of the innovative components that would come to make up the Third Industrial Revolution began to surface.

MORPHING BEYOND CAPITALISM

As the digital Third Industrial Revolution infrastructure rolled out in the EU, China, and elsewhere, a curious phenomenon emerged that the capitalist system was unprepared for. It became increasingly apparent that data, analytics, and algorithms that manage the digital platforms were creating novel new ways of organizing economic activity, social life, and governance, and were undermining many of the critical elements of capitalist theory and practice that had accompanied the previous two industrial platforms.

There is a popular expression, attributed to the American biochemist Lawrence Joseph Henderson, that "science owed more to the steam engine than the steam engine to science"—meaning that it was by studying the workings of a steam engine and how it generated power that scientists were able to abstract its operating principles and posit the laws of thermodynamics. In a similar vein, capitalism, both in theory and practice, owes more to the operating principles of its industrial infrastructures than those industrial infrastructures owe to capitalism.

The first two industrial revolution infrastructures were engineered to be centralized, operating pyramidically from the top down, and performed best if enclosed in layers of intellectual and physical property rights. The centralized infrastructures also favored vertically integrated economies of scale by the industries plugging into them to create sufficient economies of scale to secure returns on investments. This allowed a handful of first movers to gain control over emerging markets and dominate each industry or sector.

There was no other way to organize the business model. That's because the technologies that made up the infrastructure spokes—the railroads, the telegraph and telephone systems, electricity transmission, oil pipelines, and the automotive industry—were so expensive to develop, deploy, and operationalize that they were beyond the capacity of even the wealthiest families and governments alone to finance. They required the growth of the modern stockholding corporation, finance capital, and a nascent capitalist class. As well, every other industry attached to the fossil fuel–driven industrial revolution infrastructure was constrained and compelled to accept the capitalist shareholding business model and establish sufficient vertical economies of scale to succeed. The result is that, as of 2020, the Fortune 500 largest global corporations in the world accounted for $33.3 trillion in revenue and made up one-third of the total global GDP, with a workforce of only 69.9 million out of a global workforce of 3.5 billion people.[1]

Both of the industrial revolution infrastructures, powered largely by fossil fuels, also required expansive geopolitical and military commitments to secure their uninterrupted operations. And each industrial revolution infrastructure was designed to optimize efficiencies in order for companies to return increasing increments of profit to their shareholders. Increasing efficiencies, in turn, resulted in unlimited material growth with few safeguards built in against negative externalities resulting from their operations. Lastly, these engineering features of the First and Second Industrial Revolutions operated nearly the same way, regardless of whether they were deployed in either capitalist or socialist countries.

The Third Industrial Revolution infrastructure, by contrast, is designed to be distributed rather than centralized. It performs best if it remains open and transparent, rather than privatized, to optimize the network effect. The more people who share the networks and platforms, the more "social capital" is amassed by all the participants. Unlike the First and Second Industrial Revolutions, the Third Industrial Revolution infrastructure is engineered to scale laterally rather than vertically. Tim Berners-Lee designed the World Wide Web to allow anyone to share information with anyone else from the edges without asking permission or paying a fee to agents at the center.

Moreover, while the First and Second Industrial Revolution infrastructures were engineered more to reward a few over the many in a zero-sum game, the Third Industrial Revolution infrastructure is engineered in a way that, if allowed to operate as it was designed to, would distribute economic power more broadly, fostering a democratization of economic life.

Of course, it's true that a first generation of start-up companies—Apple, Google, Facebook, et cetera—succeeded in creating dominant global platforms that, in the short run, garnered control over the operating systems of at least the communication internet by allowing free and open access to their platforms but at the expense of bundling the personal data of billions of their users and selling it to third parties who would use it to gain access to consumers for the purpose of advertising and selling their goods and services.

But it's unlikely that these global oligopolies will prevail in the long run. Already, the EU and other governments are beginning to lock horns with these new digital giants, imposing restrictions on how they can access the data of their users and, equally important, increasingly focusing efforts on antitrust legislation to break their monopoly holds on what was designed to be a distributed, open, and democratic infrastructure.

More important, global monopolies will likely be corralled, if not sidelined altogether, because the TIR infrastructure is continually self-evolving into new iterations that make centralized command and control of the platforms far less likely. The introduction of billions, and soon trillions, of sensors in an evolving Internet of Things infrastructure is quickly spreading across every neighborhood and community and throughout the world and is already generating massive amounts of data.

This is forcing a spatial shift in the collection and storage of data and the

management of analytics and algorithms away from traditional giant vertically integrated global companies to locally situated and distributed high-
tech small- and medium-sized enterprises (SMEs) spread laterally around
the planet.

Many in the information and communications technology (ICT) industry are
projecting that the sheer volume of IoT data will soon vastly outstrip the data
storage capacity of centralized data centers and their ability to utilize the data
in real time. Already, small "edge data centers" are appearing alongside IoT infrastructure, collecting data on-site and sharing it across multiple platforms.

ICT industry leaders are also coming to understand that cloud computing—
sending locally generated data along to remote giant data centers—is too
slow to react in real time to locally unfolding events. This is called the "la-
tency factor." If, for example, an autonomous vehicle were about to crash,
the response time in sending up-to-the-moment data to the cloud and receiving back instructions on the ground would be too slow to react and avoid
a collision. Given this reality, a new term has entered the ICT lexicon. It is
"fog computing."

Over the course of the next several decades, millions of ever-cheaper edge
data centers embedded in homes, offices, local businesses, neighborhoods, communities, and in the environment will lateralize the collection and storage of
data on-site and allow populations to use analytics and algorithm governance
in real time in regionally connected networks, increasingly bypassing the vertically integrated and centralized ICT networks that characterized the first generation of digital enterprises.

The new digitized and distributed infrastructure brings with it the prospect of a vast democratization of commerce and trade on a planetary scale.
Many global companies will survive the transition and flourish, but their new
role will be more along the lines of aggregating supply chains, aligning tasks,
and providing technical expertise and training for local and more agile SMEs
that will do much of the economic deployment.

While the First and Second Industrial Revolution infrastructures were
largely owned and operated by governments or, in some instances, privatized
and put in the hands of large corporate players, many of the components that
make up the Third Industrial Revolution infrastructure are distributed in nature and owned by the people. Wind turbines, solar roof panels, microgrids,
IoT-equipped buildings, edge data centers, storage batteries, hydrogen fuel
cells, electric charging stations, and electric vehicles are part of the distributed infrastructure owned by hundreds of millions of families and hundreds
of thousands of local businesses and neighborhood associations.

As this highly distributed infrastructure rolls out over the next twenty years, billions of people will be able to deploy, aggregate, disaggregate, and reaggregate their particular components of the infrastructure in fluid blockchain platforms, at will, in their communities and connect across regions, continents, and oceans. This is "power to the people," literally and figuratively.

The complex but highly distributed and integrated nature of the infrastructure makes the system operate more like an ecosystem made up of numerous interactive nodes and agencies. Anyone who has ever used smart platforms knows that the very notion of contributing one's social capital is more in the nature of an adaptive contribution than an efficient expropriation. Each increment of social capital is an input that allows the platform to evolve and become more interdependent in ever more self-organizing ways, while enhancing the overall social capital of all of its contributors . . . think wikis.

The interconnectivity of the critical components of the infrastructure—communications, energy, mobility and logistics, and the IoT—facilitates circularity. Unlike the earlier two industrial revolutions that were linear, the TIR is circular, with every element and input feeding back to every other, much like the processes in a climax ecosystem, creating an economic process that favors regenerativity over productivity while mitigating negative externalities.

It's instructive to think of the TIR infrastructure as a cohort of smart, nonlinear self-organizing ecosystems that communicate, self-power, and manage their mobility, constantly learning from their many feedback loops, and ever evolving and transforming themselves as they interact with one another. This emerging infrastructure dynamic is so unlike the static centralized equilibrium-based economic system that characterized the business practices of the First and Second Industrial Revolutions as to be noncomparable. The Third Industrial Revolution infrastructure is giving rise to a new economic system with completely different operating principles and objectives.

The change from an analog to a digital infrastructure eviscerates one of the anchors of capitalist theory—the value of market exchange transactions. Every would-be entrepreneur is in search of ever-cheaper technology and streamlined business practices that can reduce fixed costs and, even more important, reduce the marginal cost of manufacturing goods and delivering services. By doing so, the proprietor is able to increase revenue per unit sold and return sufficient profit to investors. The optimum market is selling at marginal cost. But in the two hundred years of capitalist expansion, no one dreamed of a technological revolution so powerful in reducing marginal cost that it plunges ever closer to near zero. When marginal costs drop that low, it is near impossible to make a profit by the "exchange" of certain goods and services in markets. That is what the digital revolution is doing.

Markets become too stodgy to accommodate a digital infrastructure. Think about it. Sellers and buyers have to find each other and settle on an exchange price, after which they part. It is the downtime between market exchanges that is the killer. In the interim, the seller still has costs to contend with: inventories, rent, taxes, salaries, and other overhead expenses. In addition, the seller has to recharge its marketing, advertising, and soliciting, all of which add more time and expense between market exchanges.

The start/stop mechanism of market exchanges is literally an anachronism in a digitized economy. Markets are transactional. Networks, on the other hand, are digitally driven and cybernetically connected, operating as flows rather than exchanges. This allows commercial life to move away from start/stop transactions in markets to continuous flows in networks. There need be no downtime in networks. Because of this fundamental change, the economy is beginning to make a historic leap from ownership to access and from sellers and buyers in markets to providers and users in network.

Even though the marginal costs are lower with digital interconnectivity, it's the continuous feed of services in provider-user networks that allows the networks to make up for the steep decline in marginal costs by the uninterrupted flow of the traffic. In the new economic era of provider-user networks, every economic activity is potentially a service, from knowledge sharing to energy sharing to vehicle sharing. Because the providers of the service generally own the assets, they have every interest in manufacturing high-quality and high-performance machinery with a long life span and deploying supply chains and logistics with built-in redundancies that make the system more resilient in order to save on downtime costs and ensure dependable operability in the face of unexpected disruptions.

Some marginal costs are plunging so low to near zero that they are becoming nearly free, taking the new digital economy into a new economic system best described as a resilient sharing economy. Some of the sharing services have given rise to capitalist networks like Uber and Airbnb that connect providers and users at near zero marginal cost, but exact a toll for access to the service. That's not likely to hold in the long run. Already, for example, drivers who own their own vehicles, pay for their own gasoline, insurance, and maintenance, and provide all of the labor are beginning to organize in regional—and soon countrywide—digital cooperative platforms providing their own services, allowing them sufficient revenue to make a living without having to hand over a significant portion of their income to a third party. Other sharing services like

Wikipedia are free, and exist as nonprofit platforms that are financed by small donations. Then too, people are taking free online college courses taught by the best professors at world-class universities and often receive college credits. Millions are also creating and freely sharing news blogs, music and art, and many other goods and services on digital platforms. None of these activities are included in the GDP, but they contribute to improving the quality of life in society.

Cynics may scoff, but the reality is that as broadband, renewable energies, and autonomous car-sharing services become cheaper, the more distributed economy will continue to expand. Some of the sharing economy will remain attached to a corporate model and payment of fees for access, while even more will turn toward high-tech cooperatives, bringing providers and users together in seamless services, and still other provider-user activity will be nearly free.

The digitally interconnected and distributed sharing economy, though still very much in its infancy, is the first new economic system to enter the world stage since capitalism in the 18th century and socialism in the 19th century—another sign of how different the new economic order that's emerging is from what we've known under industrial capitalism. For example, in the digitally connected economy, GDP is quickly losing its hold as a marker of economic performance. It was never a good metric. GDP is a crude tool that measures every economic output, whether it is life-affirming or damaging to the well-being of society. Cleaning up toxic waste dumps, manufacturing more deadly weapons systems of mass destruction, building more prisons, increasing hospitalizations to treat lung disease because of exposure to CO_2 emissions from burning fossil fuels, having to rebuild neighborhoods and communities because of climate disasters, all show up in the GDP.

In recent years, GDP has begun to fall from grace as global institutions, including the OECD, the United Nations, and the European Union, have turned to quality-of-life indicators (QLI) to measure economic well-being. The new metrics measure such things as infant mortality, life expectancy, education levels, access to public services, air and water quality, leisure time, volunteer activity, the availability of commons resources, and living in safe communities, transforming the very way a younger generation has begun to appraise the good life.

By 2020, billions of human beings had smartphones, each with more computing power than sent our astronauts to the moon.[2] With the fixed cost plummeting and the marginal costs of smartphones now near zero, the human race is connecting on a multitude of platforms for play, work, and social life. This emerging global interconnectivity is opening new channels of communication that bypass the traditional gatekeepers—national governments and global corporations. The result is that the new digital infrastructure is democratizing temporal and spatial relations, allowing new affiliations to flourish around the world for the purposes of commerce, trade, and civic and social life. This takes society from globalization to glocalization.

A more glocal economy shifts production—in part—from offshoring to onshoring as communities begin to pay more attention to self-sufficiency and stewardship of their biosphere. At the same time, the plummeting fixed and marginal costs of production and distribution of goods and services with lateral economies of scale allow small- and medium-sized high-tech cooperatives to engage in commerce with one another—region to region—across the globe, often with more agility and competitiveness than global corporations.

The transformation from a global to a glocal paradigm, accompanied by a shift from an analog to a digital infrastructure to communicate, power, and move the economy, social life, and governance will require a wholesale reorientation of the human workforce. While the industrial workforces of the 19th and 20th centuries were dedicated to the exploitation and consumption of the earth's resources, the workforce of the 21st century will increasingly center on stewarding the biosphere. New employment categories and millions of new jobs will be generated in eco-stewardship. Robots and AI will play only a secondary role in monitoring and stewarding ecosystems, while the heavy lifting will require human engagement on a massive scale to address an increasing array of climate related disasters utilizing imaginative new ways to adapt to an unpredictable rewilding Earth.

The Brookings Institution has already identified 320 unique job categories across all the major sectors that will be dedicated to the deployment and operation of a zero-emission resilient economy.[3] These new job categories will run the gamut from vocational to professional skills. A detailed study, published by TIR Consulting Group, LLC, projects fifteen to twenty-two million net new jobs between 2022 and 2042 in the United States alone, with the robust deployment of the continental Third Industrial Revolution infrastructure and the accompanying new businesses and employment opportunities that will feed into and off of the new TIR digital platforms.[4]

Communities are also beginning to share their locally generated solar and wind electricity with neighboring communities and within the next twenty years they will be sharing green electricity across regions and around the world, connecting the whole of humanity. The sharing of sun- and wind-generated electricity ends the long nightmare of a fossil fuel–driven industrial civilization whose stored energies were fought over in regional wars and, in the 20th century, two world wars in which millions perished.

The Age of Resilience liberates our collective humanity from militarized geopolitics fetishized around the command and control of concentrated deposits of coal, oil, and natural gas and takes us into a new era of "biosphere politics," which incentivizes the sharing of sun and wind energies on a digital Pangaea that stretches across continents, oceans, and time zones. For those who worry that one or more of today's superpowers might try to gain control of a glocal energy internet and bend the whole of humanity to its will, that's unlikely to happen. In the Age of Resilience, literally billions of families, millions of businesses, and hundreds of thousands of communities—big and small—across every continent, will capture the sun and wind where they work and live, store the new energies in microgrids, and share any surplus of green electricity across the emerging glocal energy internet.

Unlike fossil fuels, which are found in abundance in only a few places, the sun and wind are distributed energies and found everywhere, but because they are intermittent they force a sharing of electricity in tandem with the weather and daily rotation of the earth, and the changing seasons of the planet as it travels around the sun.

Any attempt by a single nation or a cabal of nations to act as a gatekeeper would likely fail, as any locale could, at a moment's notice, disaggregate from the glocal energy internet and reaggregate onto community and regional microgrids that will soon cover all of the continental landmasses, keeping the lights on and the electricity flowing, locally and regionally. The highly distributed nature of the glocal energy internet would make it virtually impossible for any nation to control millions of locally sited microgrids across every continent.

When we begin to compile all of the economic changes brought on by the shift to a Third Industrial Revolution smart digital infrastructure, the enormity of what's transpiring suggests a fundamental transformation in the way we conceive of economic life: from ownership to access; seller-buyer markets to provider-user networks; analog bureaucracies to digital platforms; zero-sum games to network effects; growth to flourishing; finance capital to natural capital; productivity to regenerativity; linear processes to cybernetic processes; negative externalities to circularity; vertically integrated economies of scale to laterally integrated economies of scale; centralized value chains to distributed value chains; GDP to QLI; globalization to glocalization; global corporate conglomerates to agile high-tech SMEs blockchained in fluid glocal networks; geopolitics to biosphere politics; and so on. The Third Industrial Revolution infrastructure is a transitional economic paradigm—partly still locked into an older industrial economic model and partly exhibiting many of the defining features of an emerging Resilient Revolution.

Over the past seventy years, the Third Industrial Revolution has evolved from the marketing of the first commercial computers and the introduction of numerical control technologies, robotics, and automation to a fully integrated digitized global interface stretching from GPS guidance in outer space to ubiquitous IoT sensors across landmasses and oceans. In the unfolding of this process, the internal dynamics of this self-organizing system and all of its spinoffs have metamorphized into something quite different from what had been expected at the outset. That is, we are witnessing an extraordinary leap into a new economic paradigm that by the mid-2040s will likely no longer be considered a Third Industrial Revolution operating by a strictly capitalist economic model. Our global society is beginning to exit the two-hundred-fifty-year span of the Industrial Revolution and looking ahead to a new era best characterized as the Resilient Revolution.

If the medieval era put a premium on piety and the dream of heavenly salvation and the modern age on being industrious and advancing unlimited material progress, the coming era is punctuated by resilience at every turn and the prospect of realigning our species back into the rhythms and flows of the planet. The prime markers of the transformation are the shifts in temporal and spatial orientation brought on by the deployment of a resilient infrastructure, with efficiency giving way to adaptivity, and detachment and commodification of nature giving way to deep reparticipation with an animated Earth. The Age of Resilience lies before us.

A BEACHHEAD IN AMERICA

While the EU and China are both moving ahead on a transition into a digitally integrated resilient infrastructure, the United States has remained mostly on the sidelines, with the exception of a handful of states and big-city mayors who are moving in step with the world's other two superpowers. The rest of the country, however, is still deeply mired in a Second Industrial Revolution carbon-centric paradigm. By happenstance, in January 2019, a "climate friend" in the business community whom I had been informally advising was interrupted during a meeting we were having to take a call from then-Democratic minority leader and now majority leader of the U.S. Senate, Charles Schumer.

After the call, I asked about his relationship with the senator and he said that they were lifelong friends.

I was aware that Senator Schumer was a longtime advocate of dealing with climate change. But what made his voice particularly unique is his public announcements on addressing climate change have consistently been entwined with building out a smart green infrastructure revolution that could bring together ICT/broadband, renewable electricity generation, and electric and fuel-cell transportation in a resilient society—a similar approach to what was already being taken up in both the EU and China. I asked if it would be possible to arrange a meeting with the senator and was told it was easy to do.

On March 11, 2019, the senator and I met at the U.S. Capitol and I told him of our work in the EU and China on conceptualizing and deploying a climate-related Third Industrial Revolution infrastructure transformation. The senator expressed his enthusiasm for a "uniquely American approach" to advance the same end and asked if our global team might work directly with him and his legislative staff to develop a resilient 3.0 infrastructure plan for the United States. I agreed, and we were off and running.

Senator Schumer and I met on ten occasions between March 2019 and March 2020. Five of those meetings took place at his office, and four of the meetings were virtual teleconferences and phone conversations. In addition, Senator Schumer hosted a dinner for the two of us and seven senatorial colleagues who he thought would be important to enlist in a smart, 3.0 resilient infrastructure rollout. Over the course of twelve months, and at the senator's request, my office delivered three iterations of a strategic memorandum on the conception and deployment of the proposed new infrastructure. The senator signed off on each iteration and we continued to move forward.

After the last memorandum, I suggested we take a more granular approach and lay out a detailed infrastructure plan with all of the accompanying metrics that would cover a twenty-year nationwide infrastructure transformation, taking America into a new zero-emission green economy. Senator Schumer agreed and our office went to work.

A rider is in order at this point. There have been numerous proposals in the United States on transitioning to a green zero-emission future. But, virtually every one of them has been in the form of a laundry list of stand-alone proposals and initiatives only loosely connected, if at all, to creating a seamless resilient infrastructure of the kind we had helped deploy in the EU and China. And the few initiatives that touched on infrastructure came mostly from academic circles with little to no real-world experience in the field in actually deploying a long-term construction site for the kind of infrastructure revolution we had in mind. Even the progressive governors in keystone states and mayors of several of the country's green cities were focusing more on siloed projects without a clear plan to lay out the kind of infrastructure that could take the country forward to a new economic paradigm and post-carbon era.

We brought together some of the world's leading players in industries with whom our office had intimately worked over the years, along with professional staff from their organizations. We began by asking the question: What would it take and what is possible to move the United States to a fully operational and resilient 3.0 infrastructure, free of CO_2 emissions, by the year 2040? The task we set out was based squarely on what was technically possible and commercially feasible to do, given the existing state of the art and widely agreed upon industry standards and projections of future costs, savings, and revenues, over the two decades between 2020 and 2040. The result was a 237-page detailed plan covering a historic infrastructure transformation for the United States. It became clear that the report represented a systemic shift from a still evolving Third Industrial Revolution Infrastructure to a nascent Resilient Revolution Infrastructure by the end of the first half of the 21st century.

Senator Schumer reviewed the plan, after which our global team of partners met with him in a Zoom conference on August 25, 2020, to go over highlights, details, projections, and how best to move forward on this new vision for the country. The senator said that he thought the plan "was great" and that he was "very enthusiastic" about marshaling support in the Democratic Caucus and across the political aisle at the congressional, state, and local levels, and suggested that our team work alongside his team to flesh out the particulars on a fast track, including briefings with key senators, in preparation for the incoming administration and Congress in January 2021.

The following details the highlights and projections in the report.

THE AMERICA RESILIENT 3.0 INFRASTRUCTURE TRANSFORMATION (2020–2040)

- A $16 trillion investment to scale, deploy, and manage a smart digital zero-emission third industrial revolution infrastructure for a 21st-century economy
- The creation of 15 to 22 million net new jobs over the period 2022 to 2042

- Every dollar invested in the America 3.0 infrastructure is projected to return 2.9 dollars in GDP between 2022 and 2042
- An increase in the annual growth rate of GDP from a business as usual 1.9% GDP to 2.3% GDP, and a $2.5 trillion larger GDP in 2042 (moving from $29.2 to $31.7 trillion in that year)
- $377 billion to lay 22,000 miles of underground cable and install 65 terminals to build out and manage a state-of-the-art high-voltage direct current continental electricity internet across the country
- $2.3 trillion to install and maintain 74,000,000 residential microgrids, 90,000 commercial/industrial microgrids, and 12,000 utility-scale microgrids in communities across America for the generation and sharing of renewable electricity
- $97 billion to install fiber-based broadband in all 121 million homes across the United States
- $1.4 trillion to build out and maintain a nationwide EV charging infrastructure to power the millions of electric vehicles coming into the market between 2020 and 2040
- $4.4 trillion to retrofit the nation's commercial and industrial buildings
- $4.3 trillion to install solar PV on or around commercial buildings
- $1.8 trillion to retrofit residential buildings
- $1.61 trillion to install PV on or around residential buildings
- A roughly doubling in aggregate efficiency—the ratio of potential work (amount of real GDP) compared to useful energy—across the American economy
- The avoidance of $3.2 trillion in air pollution and health care costs and $6.2 trillion in cumulative climate-related disaster costs
- Prioritization of the America 3.0 infrastructure in the nation's designated 8,700 opportunity zones—the poorest and highest-risk disadvantaged communities
- The shift in the business model from ownership to access, markets to networks, sellers and buyers to providers and users, productivity to regenerativity, GDP to quality-of-life indicators, and negative externalities to circularity across the value chains

The report delves into virtually every technical and commercial aspect in the conceptualization and phase-by-phase deployment of the resilient infrastructure over a twenty-year rollout. The study also goes into greater detail on the manufacturing, procurement, and assemblage of the various components and their integration into the infrastructure across a continental construction site. The technical aspects are accompanied by the cost projections of the infrastructure spokes and their returns on investment (ROI) over time.

The hundreds of professional and technical skills that will need to be deployed are discussed, along with the specialized training that will be required to prepare a smart, 21st-century infrastructure workforce to manage the buildout.

While the study is designed to provide a template for the purpose of launching a nationwide construction project on a scale comparable to the buildout of America's two prior infrastructure revolutions in the 19th and 20th centuries, its implementation will be less centralized and more distributed in nature and customized to the needs, aspirations, and goals of each of the fifty states and their localities. These state-by-state contributions will provide a mosaic of diverse tributaries feeding into and off of one another in a seamless but fluid continental digital interface befitting a complex adaptive social-ecological system. The entire 237-page report prepared for Senator Schumer, entitled *America 3.0: The Resilient Society a Smart Third Industrial Revolution Infrastructure and the Recovery of the American Economy*, is open-source.

During the First and Second Industrial Revolutions, the infrastructures favored short-term efficiency gains and quick profits over long-term resilience and steady and reliable returns on investments. The result is that we now live in a highly fragile and vulnerable society subject to unexpected massive disruptions—increasingly severe climate disasters, pandemics, and malware incursions—crippling whole parts of society, destroying the natural environment, damaging the economy, and undermining the health and well-being of millions of American citizens.

Nowhere is the expediency of short-term efficiency versus long-term resilience more apparent than in our nation's crumbling Second Industrial Revolution infrastructure. For example, we built out our national telecommunication and electricity grid infrastructures aboveground to save on the expense of placing cable underneath the earth. Now, rarely a season goes by without downed telephone and electricity transmission lines, leading to massive telecom disruptions and power outages, caused by global warming–induced floods, droughts, wildfires, and hurricanes, racking up billions of dollars in losses to the American economy and society.

Our nation's residential, commercial, and industrial building stock has similarly been erected with the intent on cutting corners to secure quick short-term profits, making our homes, offices, and factories more fragile and less resilient

to an ever-escalating wave of unrelenting climate disasters and the concomi-
tant loss of lives, homes, businesses, and property. Then too, our continental
electricity grid, made up of a patchwork of local electric utilities and a largely
archaic electricity grid, is becoming the target of cyberterrorist probes whose
mission is to shut down parts of the national grid, throwing regions and communities across the country into pandemonium.

Moreover, the massive privatization of public infrastructure over the last
forty years—roads, water systems, prisons, schools, et cetera—has been at
the expense of shaving costs to ensure short-term efficiency gains and profits,
undermining the resilience of critical infrastructures the public relies on to
communicate, power, and move economic activity and social life.

A future punctuated by increasing climate disasters, cybercrime, and cy-
berterrorism can quickly disrupt supply chains, putting communities and even
the entire society in jeopardy. In turn, global pandemics can shut down supply chains virtually overnight. When the logistics system is compromised, the
basic necessities of life—food, water, and medicine—can't be delivered and
entire populations are at risk. This lesson has come home in the wake of the
COVID-19 pandemic, which paralyzed the U.S. and world economies, shut-
ting off the supply of vital medical equipment, medicines, and food supplies,
and leaving local economies helpless and unable to secure the basic necessities to maintain their health and well-being.

It is essential that resilience be built into logistics systems and supply chains
by relying on more onshoring of regional manufacturing centers and sourcing
of rare earth metals. In addition, it will be especially important as we move
to autonomous electric passenger vehicles and hydrogen-powered fuel-cell
freight trucking on smart road systems, that backup power be available across
the entire system to ensure supply chains and logistics. This will require that
fueling stations at travel centers along interstate highways are equipped with
dedicated on-site or nearby solar and wind installations to generate electricity for charging stations and hydrogen fuel-cell pumps that can keep electric
vehicles and long-haul hydrogen-powered freight trucks on the road. Warehouses and distribution centers will also need similar solar and wind power
generated on-site or nearby to provide electricity for lighting, heating, air conditioning, and mechanical and robotic services to ensure that basic necessities can be properly logged in, stored, and sent on their way.

The America 3.0 infrastructure prioritizes resilience built into every facet
of the nation's infrastructure. For instance, consider what would happen were
a catastrophic wildfire, flood, or hurricane to shut down parts of the national
and regional power grid and cell towers, leaving millions without power for

their computers and cell phones. Were this to happen, homes, local businesses, neighborhoods, and municipalities could quickly transfer off the central power grid and onto literally millions of solar- and wind-generating microgrids lodged in or around homes, offices, factories, neighborhoods, or nearby open fields and reaggregate in distributed networks to keep the electricity flowing and computers and cell phones powered up, ensuring uninterrupted connectivity to the outside world until the regional or national grid comes back online.

In a like manner, retrofitting building stock to harden homes, offices, and factories to be more resilient to withstand climate disasters is fast becoming a necessity for survival. A vast number of existing buildings will have to undergo a complete retrofit to seal interiors, minimize energy loss, optimize energy savings, and buttress structures to be resilient to climate-related disruptions. Gas and oil heating, which are big sources of global warming emissions in buildings, will need to be replaced by electrical heating across the residential, commercial, industrial, and institutional building stock. The return on a building's retrofit investment in energy savings takes place over relatively few years, after which the owner or renter enjoys a reliable stream of savings on energy costs for decades.

A water internet made up of IoT sensors is also being embedded in water reservoirs and in the pipelines that bring fresh water to consumers and remove wastewater, sending it back to treatment plants for repurification. The IoT sensors continually monitor pressure on the pipes, the wear and tear of the equipment, potential leakages, and the change in water clarity and chemistry, and use the data and analytics to anticipate, intervene, and even remotely fix trouble spots along the line. Smart meters and sensor monitoring also provide just-in-time data on water flow, including the volume and time of usage, to more effectively manage water resources, from provisioning and ensuring clean water distribution to recycling and purifying wastewater that can then be reused by consumers, thus saving water in a virtuous circular system. The embedding of a water internet throughout our water systems becomes particularly apt when we consider the fact that nearly six billion gallons of treated water are wasted every day because of leaking pipes, metering inaccuracies, and other errors, according to the American Society of Civil Engineers.[5]

The IoT nervous system of the America 3.0 resilient infrastructure is also becoming an indispensable technology for monitoring climate change impacts. For example, sensors are being embedded across the earth's biosphere, monitoring flood and drought conditions and wind currents to both measure the impact of climate change and to alert authorities to potentially dangerous hot spots that can flare up and unleash raging floods or wildfires, giving first responders advance notice to intervene with appropriate mitigation.

Other IoT sensors are being placed along ecosystem corridors, tracking wildlife and providing data on endangered species, including the thinning of herds and flocks. The data is mined with analytics to assess avenues of intervention for protecting wildlife and maintaining biodiversity in various eco-regions. IoT has also become helpful in monitoring air pollution by providing up-to-the-moment readings on the air quality of the atmosphere, which is a serious health issue for at-risk populations suffering from asthma and other pollution-related illnesses. Sensors are even being inserted just below the earth's crust to monitor the condition of the soil—the pedosphere—to inform scientists of the "nutrient health" in the "Critical Zone," which all of life on Earth depends on for survival.

In a sense, the IoT is analogous to a planetary nervous system that is beginning to monitor the health of the critical organs of the earth—the hydrosphere, the lithosphere, the atmosphere, and the biosphere—and what we are discovering is that changes to any one of the earth's spheres spill over and affect every other sphere and every species, including our own. This profound realization is likely to fundamentally change humanity's worldview, teaching us that all phenomena on Earth, be they biological, chemical, or physical, are intimately connected to every other, and whatever happens anywhere along the earth's complex gradients and nervous system intimately affects everything else, including the well-being of our own species. This fundamental new understanding takes us into the resilient society and a new social contract for our species.

All of the above changes are transformational in nature and collectively retire to history the short 250-year saga of the Age of Progress. We are ushering in what's likely to be an open-ended temporal and spatial reorientation in the way we come to understand and navigate the world around us in the emerging Age of Resilience. The key will be our ability to unearth the known unknowns and the unknown unknowns that lie before us in the Anthropocene and create new forms of adaptive governance that will foster a deep participation with the life forces here on Earth.

Where, then, do we go from here?

11

THE ASCENDANCE OF BIOREGIONAL GOVERNANCE

R
epresentative democracy proved to be a viable political compromise at the beginning of the industrial era, capable for a time of maintaining a delicate if not contentious balance between nationality and locality. However, on a rewilding Earth of horrifying disasters that afflict regions arbitrarily and without notice, governance becomes much more of a community affair in which the entire populace is often engaged—protecting, rescuing, restoring, and preparing for the next wave or assault. "All hands on deck" reflects a new kind of commons governance that is far more personally charged.

Not unexpectedly, climate disasters cross governing jurisdictions and affect entire ecoregions. We are waking up to the new reality that old political boundaries are of little avail and often an impediment to seeking solutions in a climate disaster–prone world. Local governments in the United States and elsewhere are beginning to understand that their well-being is intimately tied to a more fundamental governing jurisdiction—the ecoregions in which they dwell. For example, in America the states that make up the Great Lakes ecoregion all experience more intense flooding annually. In the Cascadia region of the Pacific Northwest, drought and summer wildfires sweep through, forcing a regional response. In the Gulf of Mexico ecoregion, the population is pummeled by relentless hurricanes from June through November each year. Everyone in the ecoregion is affected.

The shifting awareness that one's political identity, affiliation, and allegiance are dependent on the environmental well-being of one's ecoregion will only deepen and ripen in the years, decades, and centuries to come. Our species is beginning to find its way back to the natural world, to which we've always been attached, whether acknowledged or ignored. This political repatriation with nature is already underway. But there is no guarantee we will get there in time. Destabilizing political forces in America and other countries could undermine or expedite the journey.

THE SECESSION FEVER

The secession fever is spreading all around the world. National governments are under siege from the inside as regions begin to demand their independence. What's most worrying is that this once rare political phenomenon has begun to shake the foundations of political stability in the United States of America, long held up as the most stable of national governments and the epitome of representative democracy.

A national opinion poll conducted on the eve of the presidential election in 2020 found that nearly 40 percent of likely voters would support state secession if their candidate loses.[1] Much of the fervor stems from the belief of millions of Americans that their vote doesn't count. In two recent presidential elections, the loser received more of the popular vote but lost in the Electoral College. Immediately after the 2020 election, 77 percent of Republicans said they "believe that there was widespread fraud" in the presidential election, and only 60 percent of registered voters "believe that Biden's victory was legitimate."[2]

While the growing alienation of American voters is politically inspired, the more fundamental problem that lies at the heart of the crisis can be laid at the door of geography. The problem is that America, like other countries, has experienced a depopulation of rural areas and has become increasingly urbanized and suburbanized, leaving its rural communities decimated, but not without political clout. Likewise, the divide between urban and rural voters in terms of educational attainment, income, upward mobility, social values, and worldviews has deepened, leaving the country polarized and living in alternative universes. A similar political divide is unfolding in highly urban and industrialized nations all around the world. The divide is leading to a proliferation of extreme populist movements and growing political unrest in small towns and the countryside, often resulting in violent protests aimed at urban centers.

The Industrial Revolution and a cosmopolitan narrative favored urban settlement over rural life, with the result that rural communities became impoverished backwaters. Agriculture, like other components of the economy, became increasingly vertically integrated, with a handful of corporate giants controlling virtually every aspect of production and distribution, from the patenting of genetically engineered seeds to warehousing fiber and grain to distributing finished products to retail markets. The family farm, at least in the highly industrialized countries in the West, became increasingly marginalized and small towns shriveled, leaving millions of rural citizens desolate.

THE COUNTER MIGRATION:
A Flight Back to Rural Communities

The Resilient Revolution changes the dynamic. In the emerging Anthropocene, rural communities will likely be revived and ascendant, along with smart midlevel cities and town centers with populations of between fifty thousand and one hundred thousand. There are a number of causative factors underlying this historic geographic transformation.

In the first place, in a digitally interconnected and glocalized world where the fixed and marginal costs of production and distribution are rapidly falling, vertically integrated economies of scale, the hallmark of the industrial era, are fast giving way to lateral economies of scale favoring small- and medium-sized high-tech SMEs rather than the global corporations that dominated in the 20th century. Mario Carpo, a professor of architecture theory and history at Bartlett School of Architecture, University College, London, explains the transformation:

> The technical logic of the industrial world is based on mass-production and economies of scale. Most tools of industrial mass-production use casts, molds, dyes [sic] . . . the more identical copies we make, the cheaper each copy will be. Digital fabrication . . . does not use mechanical matrixes, casts, or molds. Without mechanical matrixes, there is no need to repeat the same form in order to amortize the cost of the production set-up, hence every piece, when digitally made (milled or 3D printed, for example) is a one-off: making more identical copies of the same item will not make any of them cheaper. . . . The marginal cost of production is always the same. Economies of scale do not apply to digital manufacturing.[3]

This means that smart high-tech start-up companies can set up shop operating in small cities and towns in rural areas where real estate is less expensive and overhead costs are lower and still be competitive in glocal markets.

Even logistics costs begin to plunge toward near zero as fabricated 3D printing allows an SME to create the program for printing out a product and then send the instructions digitally to a manufacturer, wholesaler, or retailer instantaneously anywhere in the world, where the product can be printed out and delivered to the end-user. A more geographically distributed commerce extending across rural areas will continue to trend as the resilient smart digital infrastructure encompasses continents.

The coronavirus pandemic has also accelerated the repopulation of rural areas, with a younger generation seeking open space and a return to a more inviting natural environment to raise families, conduct business, and work. Moreover, an increasing number of younger digital natives raised in smaller towns in rural areas who would normally have migrated to the cities for employment opportunities are making the decision to stay put as employment options improve. A 2018 Gallup survey asked a cross-section of Americans from every age cohort which of five geographic locations they would prefer to live in—big city, small city, suburb of a big city, suburb of a small city, or rural area. The highest percentage, 27 percent, chose rural milieus, and another 12 percent preferred towns generally nestled in or near rural areas.[4]

There may be a growing sense—although largely unconscious—that vast urban centers of millions of inhabitants walled off from the natural world in hermetically sealed artificial environments is a doomed prescription for the collapse of civilization. Meanwhile, rural regions surrounding urban and suburban corridors will increasingly be the front line in both restoring the earth's ecosystems and reimagining civilization.

Climate change brings together urban, suburban, and rural communities under a common tent, where everyone's political affiliation shifts upward to their nineteen kilometers of the biosphere—the collective habitat in which we are all intimately ensconced. This is the expansive community that our species will increasingly call home. This new sense of space, place, and affiliation comes with a reprioritization of what is regarded as the mainstays of the economy. The livelihoods in the Age of Resilience are less attached to the production of things and consumption and more engaged with the regeneration of the earth's ecoregions and spheres. This is the juncture where what constitutes essential economic services changes. A resilient economy wrapped around ecosystem businesses and services signals the emergence of a highly educated and ecologically oriented rural workforce and a potential rapprochement between rural and urban populations that have long been at odds.

While life is lived temporally, we've come to learn that geography—one's attachment to place—in large part determines one's worldview and the narrative by which each of us lives out our lives. Understanding how rural populations and communities relate to their environment and to the natural world, in contrast to suburban and urban populations, is important in establishing an esprit de corps around a shared ecoregional governance. A study published in 2020 by the Nicholas Institute for Environmental Policy Solutions at Duke University entitled "Understanding Rural Attitudes toward the Environment and Conservation in America" is instructive of the talking points for a potential healing of the urban-rural divide and the coming together around a collective stewardship of ecoregions in America and elsewhere in the world. The study involved in-person interviews with rural leaders and focus groups and phone surveys in largely rural states.

The research revealed that the rural population in the United States tends to be highly critical of what is perceives to be federal government meddling in rural affairs, is distrustful of environmental organizations, and is skeptical of global warming prognostications. The rural population is also more religiously conservative in its views and less open to changes in social mores relative to urban and suburban populations. At the same time, the rural citizenry is deeply attached to the land and to stewardship of the environment.

When rural citizens were asked to prioritize their motivations for adopting strong environmental policies in a national survey, 62 percent of the respondents cited their strong moral responsibility to steward the natural environment for future generations as their top concern—which makes a strong case for rural communities assuming a leadership role in protecting ecoregions.[5] Understanding the cultural dynamics at play with a historic depopulation away from cities of millions of people to a more distributed repopulation along ecosystem lines, accompanied by a more flexible ecologically driven form of governance, is crucial to our species' future prospects on Earth.

The likelihood of rural communities becoming the front line in preparing America for the Age of Resilience and a new era of ecological services is not just a hope but is fast becoming a reality and is coming about in a most unexpected way. It turns out that the regions with the greatest wind and solar potential as energy sources for generating utility-scale green electricity are in red Republican states—the Southeast states, the Great Plains states, and the Southwest desert states. Six of the ten leading states currently producing wind energy boast strong rural bases and are Republican strongholds, as are five of the ten largest solar power–generating states. Thousands of new businesses and jobs are mushrooming across rural regions with their rich veins of solar and wind energy potential.

Equally impressive, the American auto industry, the bulwark of the Second Industrial Revolution and the commercial sector that uses the most fossil fuels and accounts for the most CO_2 emissions, is quickly exiting its traditional home base in the Northeast and Midwest and resettling in strong Republican states in the near central South, the southern region, and the prairie and western regions of the country. In October 2021, Ford Motor Company stunned the country and the world, announcing that it was building mega-plants in rural Kentucky and Tennessee to manufacture its next generation of all-electric F-150 series trucks and the electric batteries that will go into the vehicles. The $11.4 billion 21st century truck campuses will create 11,000 new net jobs. These new high-tech green manufacturing facilities are the biggest single investment in the history of Ford.[6]

Ford's decision to manufacture a new generation of electric F-150 trucks to replace its existing line of internal combustion trucks will not only change the very nature of the auto industry but also the sociopolitical dynamic in America. The F-150 series trucks are the most popular-selling vehicles in America and the company's runaway cash cow with $42 billion in revenue in 2021—the second-highest revenue for a branded product in America, behind only iPhones.[7]

But the new electric truck line is only the beginning. In making the announcement, Ford said it "expects 40 percent to 50 percent of its global vehicle volume to be fully electric by 2030."[8] Left unsaid, but immediately apparent is that Ford trucks are the vehicle of choice among rural drivers and stereotypically identified with Republican voters. According to a recent survey of automotive buyers, Republicans buy eight pickup trucks to every one purchased by Democrats, and many of those vehicles are F-150 Ford pickups.[9]

Nowhere will the effects of these changes be more poignantly felt than in the political arena. That's already beginning to happen. To lure Ford and other companies to its state, the Kentucky General Assembly passed a $410 million economic incentive package that would allow Ford to be able to take advantage of $250 million in forgivable loans. In addition, $36 million is being made available for skills training. Tennessee government officials, not to be outdone, said the state will offer similar incentives of more than $500 million to lure other companies and industries to the region.[10]

The green business wave is coming on strong and the states with the most wind and solar potential are gearing up to do business. The power and electricity industry and the automotive industry are first movers. Other industries making the transition to green infrastructure, product lines, and ecological services are likely to follow. Rural areas in these first mover states and soon elsewhere across the midwestern, southern, and western regions of the country are likely to change not only the business landscape but also the social, cultural, and political milieu over the course of the next thirty years. Time will tell.

The changing cultural dynamic that comes with the economic and political realignment of rural regions toward a greener orientation is likely to have the biggest impact on the nature of governance itself. As states, counties, and municipalities become more deeply engaged in ecological businesses and services, attention will invariably be drawn to how best to govern their regional ecosystems. In the United States and other countries, we are already beginning to witness a shift in governance that goes beyond the urban, suburban, and rural divide to embrace a more inclusive governing domain—the local ecoregions in which the citizenry abides and to which their future and fate is intricately tied. The impacts of climate change are felt differently in each ecoregion, which means extending the old political borders, at least in part, to allow neighborhoods and communities that share a common ecoregion to steward it collectively. This embryonic political awakening is giving rise to a new concept of governance loosely defined as "bioregional governance" in communities across America and countries around the world.

THE COMING OF BIOREGIONAL GOVERNANCE

The scientific community has established the context and timeline for bioregional governance with the call to rewild half the earth. E. O. Wilson, the famed Harvard biologist, issued a jeremiad in his 2016 book, *Half-Earth*. He argued that to prevent a full-blown sixth extinction of life, there would need to be a massive mobilization over the coming decades to redesignate half of the planet's surface as natural reserves to preserve the existing biodiversity.

At first, Wilson's plea attracted little attention, mostly within the scientific and academic community. But, as the data began to pour in from every quarter of the earth of the loss of species and ecosystems, the idea took off in the European Union, China, and the United States. In 2019, scientists from around the world published a study entitled *A Global Deal for Nature: Guiding Principles, Milestones, and Targets*, providing a detailed account on how to approach and deploy a mission of this magnitude and scale. The authors of the scientific report began with the target goal: to forestall a mass extinction of life, it will be necessary to hold the line on global warming emissions to ensure that the rise of temperature on Earth does not exceed 1.5 degrees Celsius, the point at which the collapse of the earth's ecosystems and the die-out of species on a mass scale would be all but inevitable. They argued that "the most logical path to avoid the approaching crisis is maintaining and restoring at least 50 percent of the earth's land area as intact natural ecosystems in combination with energy transition measures."[11]

The researchers pointed out that "intact forests and especially tropical forests sequester twice as much carbon as planted monocultures" and that "two thirds of all species on Earth are found in natural forests, [and that being the case] maintaining forests is vital to preventing a mass extinction." They noted that "carbon sequestration and storage extends far beyond rainforests: Peatlands, tundra, mangroves, and ancient grasslands are also important carbon storehouses and conserve distinct assemblages of plants and animals" and need to be included in the preservation game plan.[12] The authors of the report also turned their attention to marine ecosystems, reminding policy makers that marine protected areas cordoned off as protected marine reserves "have proven much more effective than other actions in protecting and restoring biodiversity, increasing yields in adjacent fisheries and enhancing ecosystem resilience."[13]

While the talk of preserving the planet's ecosystems is not new, it has suddenly leapt from the ecological sciences to center stage in the political arena. President Joe Biden caught the country by surprise, announcing just after winning the presidential election that the United States would adopt the goal of conserving 30 percent of its lands and oceans by 2030. To date, 26 percent of U.S. coastal waters are protected in line with the 30/30 target, but only 12 percent of the U.S. landmass is protected. Ensuring an additional 18 percent of America's land is put under protection by 2030—an area twice the size of Texas—is a significant commitment, but doable with an all-out effort. To get there, the federal government would have to team up with the states to reverse the trend.[14]

The elimination of natural ecosystems has only been increasing in recent decades in the United States. The human footprint grew by twenty-four million acres from just 2001 to 2017, equivalent to a football field of natural ecosystem eliminated every thirty seconds.[15] The global statistics on the loss of open land to human development are equally dismaying, putting more than one million plant and animal species at risk, with ominous implications for the future survival of our own species.[16]

There is robust public support for the 30 by 30 agenda. A 2019 survey found that 86 percent of Americans support the plan, and that 54 percent strongly support the initiative. Only 14 percent oppose the effort.[17] By any account, a ringing public endorsement. Yet, the devil is in the details. There is general agreement that while the federal government should establish the goals, targets, and timeline and offer incentives and mandates, along with the appropriate reset of codes, regulations, and standards to facilitate the transformation, the states and their communities will need to be the front line in strategizing and deploying the 30 by 30 plan, tailored to the ecological, cultural, and political realities and aspirational guidelines best suited to their locale. There is also widespread public support for the idea that any such plan must prioritize the disadvantaged communities whose loss of ecosystem services—unpolluted water and clean air, to name just two—are most at risk.

Although 28 percent of the landmass in America is owned by the federal government, an additional 12 percent is owned by the states, counties, and municipalities. Moreover, 75 percent of the natural environment in the forty-eight continental states that was lost to development just between 2001 and 2017 was on private lands.[18] Even more important, 56 percent of the 751 million acres of forested land in the United States is privately owned, which means that the citizenry will need to be heavily engaged in every ecoregion in determining the path to reach the 30 by 30 goal or it will fail.[19]

The first issue to unwrap is what is meant by using the term "bioregional governance" and how it relates to local ecoregions. Although these two terms share common ground, they differ in their narratives. Ecoregions are the unique biotic subregions within the principal biogeographic regions of the planet. Alfred Russel Wallace, who along with Charles Darwin advanced the theory of the evolution of species, was the first to classify the biogeographic regions of the earth. That process is being further refined and reworked to this day. Wallace described such regions as "those primary divisions of the earth's surface of approximately continental extent, which are characterized by distinct assemblages of animal types."[20] Today, the commonly accepted definition of a biogeographical region is one in which ecosystems share a broadly similar biota, corresponding roughly to a specific continent. The earth's eight biogeographical regions are Australasian, Afrotropic, Nearctic, Oceanian, Antarctic, Indomalayan, Neotropic, and Palearctic.[21]

In turn, the World Wildlife Fund defines ideal ecoregions as "the most distinctive examples of biodiversity for a given major habitat type." They must include species richness; endemism; higher taxonomic uniqueness; extraordinary ecological or evolutionary phenomena; and global rarity of the major habitat type.[22]

These classifications allow scientists, governments, and local communities to assess the biodiversity and health of the regions' ecosystems they inhabit for the dual purpose of adapting the societal realm to the larger natural realm and to better identify weaknesses in the ecoregions that need to be ameliorated.

Bioregional governance, by contrast, represents that part of an ecoregion that is stewarded by government and which provides a sense of affiliation, attachment, and identity, as well as engagement, be it anthropological, psychological, social, economic, or political in nature. The sense of attachment to a bioregion more often than not crosses arbitrary political boundaries to encompass the ecoregion in which a human community dwells. This supra-border ecological identification has become more poignant in recent years as floods, droughts, wildfires, and hurricanes brought on by climate change have affected adjoining political jurisdictions across state lines, forcing a collective response between states that share common ecoregions.

Bioregionalism was first introduced by journalist Peter Berg and the late ecologist Raymond Dasmann, a professor of ecology at the University of California, Santa Cruz. They describe a bioregion in social, psychological, and biological terms by introducing the idea of "Living-in-Place," by which they mean a society that lives in "balance with its region of support through links between human lives, other living things, and the processes of the planet—seasons, weather, water cycles—as revealed by the place itself."[23]

While the term "bioregion" is relatively new, the concept is age-old. The economist Elinor Ostrom, the first woman to receive the Nobel Prize in economics, was as much an anthropologist as an economist. She went back over human history, cataloging how most societies were deeply attached to place and their immediate ecosystem and organized their economy, social life, and governance collectively around comanaging their shared commons, the ecological region in which they dwelled.[24] By doing so, they ensured that their practices would not exceed the carrying capacity of their bioregion, but be regenerative by way of living within the seasonal and annual renewal of the nineteen kilometers of the biosphere that encompassed their governing commons.

Although often lost in the day-to-day flux of national and global politics and economic machinations, the deep-seated affiliation with one's region traditionally held sway in America and elsewhere, at least until the industrial age and mass resettlement in urban communities. Thomas Jefferson was of the opinion that given preference, governance performs best when it's closest to where people dwell. Lest there be any doubt of the staying power of bioregionalism—living in place—as one's primary identity, when the U.S. government established a Natural Resources Committee in 1934 to study the regions of America during the height of the Great Depression, to ascertain how citizens identify their affiliations, they concluded that "regional differentiation may turn out to be the true expression of American life and culture [reflecting] American ideals, needs, and viewpoints far more adequately than does State consciousness and loyalty."[25]

Some of the best-defined bioregions in the United States where there is already active political and cultural engagement include Central Appalachia, the Mississippi Alluvial Plain, the Mississippi River Delta, the Southeastern black belt, the Great Plains, the Laurentian/Great Lakes region, the Southern California coast, the Sonoran Desert, the Mojave Desert, the Central Valley of California, the Central California coast, the Sierra Nevada, the Northern California coast, the Southern Cascade Range, and the Intermountain Desert region.[26]

FIRST MOVERS:
The Cascadian and Great Lakes Bioregions

Several bioregional approaches to governance in the continental United States are far enough along to give a sense of how this emerging political revolution is evolving. The Northwest Pacific Cascadia Bioregion and the Laurentian Great Lakes Bioregion offer grist for understanding the political transformation that is likely to change the nature of governance in America and elsewhere as we venture deeper into the Anthropocene.

The Cascadia Bioregion is the oldest and best known in the world. Its beginnings date back to the early 1970s and the birth of the modern environmental movement. The region crosses the United States–Canada border and contains seventy-five distinct ecoregions that encompass 2,500 miles from the Copper River in Southern Alaska to Cape Mendocino to the south, and east to the Yellowstone Caldera and the Continental Divide.[27] If we include only the center of the Cascadia Bioregion—Washington State, Oregon, and British Columbia—the extended region is home to sixteen million inhabitants, with a landmass that would make it the twentieth-largest country in the world. Cascadia boasts the largest tracks of pristine temperate rain forests anywhere on the planet, and seven of the ten largest carbon-absorbing forests.[28]

The Portland, Seattle, and Vancouver corridor is home to the second-largest tech hub in the world. Many of the leading tech giants, including Amazon, Microsoft, Boeing, and T-Mobile, are headquartered in the Cascadia Bioregion. The Cascadia region, not including California, would rank as the ninth-largest economy in the world. Approximately 30 percent of the land area of Cascadia is given over to agriculture.[29]

In 1991, U.S. states and Canadian provinces and territories came together to create an intracontinental collaborative to steward the greater Cascadia Bioregion under the auspices of the Pacific Northwest Economic Region (PNWER). The governing jurisdictions are Washington, Oregon, British Columbia, Idaho, Montana, Alberta, Saskatchewan, Yukon, the Northwest Territories, and Alaska. In the years since, PNWER broadened its collaborative with the inclusion of the nonprofit sector and private companies. The governing council is made up of the governors of U.S. participating states and the premiers of the Canadian provinces, as well as their legislatures.

PNWER lists among its primary objectives "achiev[ing] economic growth while maintaining the regions' natural environment" and, toward that end, is charged with "communicating provincial and state policies throughout the region."[30] Much of PNWER's work in recent years has turned toward adapting to climate change by initiating a bioregional response to climate disasters and climate resilience and launching collaborative projects to steward the ecoregions within its jurisdiction.

In the last several years, climate impacts and disasters—especially droughts, wildfires, seawater rise, insect outbreaks, and forest die-off across the Cascadia region—have ravaged the environment, threatening the survival of its seventy-five ecoregions. A federal government report projects a grim scenario and a shrinking timeline to address the climatic changes brought on by global warming in the region. Among the concerns, the report warns that:

> Changes in the timing of streamflow related to changing snowmelt are already observed and will continue, reducing the supply of water for many competing demands and causing far-reaching ecological and socioeconomic consequences . . . the effects of sea-level rise, erosion, inundation, threats to infrastructure and habitat, and increasing ocean acidity collectively pose a major threat to the region; the combined impacts of increasing wildfires, insect outbreaks, and tree diseases are already causing widespread tree die-off . . . and long-term transformation of forest landscapes. . . . There remain critical concerns for agriculture with respect to costs of adaptation, development of more climate resilient technologies and management, and availability and timing of water.[31]

While the Cascadia region is far along in establishing a formalized approach to bioregional governance, so too are the governing jurisdictions in the United States and Canada that share the Laurentian Great Lakes. The Great Lakes of the United States and Canada are the largest bodies of fresh water on Earth and hold 20 percent of all the surface fresh water on the planet.[32]

The vast economic potential of the Laurentian Great Lakes ecoregion was apparent from the first time the French explorer Samuel de Champlain laid eyes on these vast inland seas in 1615. Eight U.S. states and two Canadian provinces abut the Great Lakes: Minnesota, Wisconsin, Illinois, Indiana, Michigan, New York, Ohio, Pennsylvania, Ontario, and Quebec.

The Great Lakes region was the cradle of both the First and Second Industrial Revolutions. Many of America's industrial giants sprang up across the Great Lakes region, including International Harvester, U.S. Steel, Standard Oil, Ford, General Motors, Chrysler, and Goodyear. The pulp, paper, and chemical industries also settled across the Great Lakes region. Today, the area is inhabited by 107 million people, supports 51 million jobs, and boasts a GDP of $6 trillion.[33]

Using the Great Lakes region as the hub for the industrial age came with its own entropic bill. That bill came due on June 22, 1969. A single spark flared from a moving train crossing the bridge along the Cuyahoga River in Cleveland around noon, and jumped to the river, igniting industrial debris floating on the surface of the water. The flames quickly spread across the river, reaching more than five stories in the air in some places.[34] The 1969 fire wasn't the first time the Cuyahoga River went up in flames. There had been nine other river fires between 1868 and 1962.[35] Nor was the Cuyahoga River, whose polluted waters empty into Lake Erie, an anomaly. The Chicago River in Illinois, the Buffalo River in New York, and the Rouge River in Michigan, all of which empty into the Great Lakes, also went up in flames during the heyday of the industrial era.

The dumping of oil, solvents, industrial chemicals, and feces into the Great Lakes from its tributary rivers was long regarded as business as usual. Most Americans living along the perimeter of the Great Lakes during the 19th and 20th centuries took the matter of industrial pollution spewing into the Great Lakes in stride as simply the price to be paid for economic progress. The author John Hartig, whose book *Burning Rivers* chronicles the history of the Great Lakes river fires, summed up the popular thinking at the time, noting "industry was King, and dirty rivers were considered a sign of prosperity."[36]

By 1969, public attitudes about the environment were changing. Rachel Carson's *Silent Spring*, chronicling the effects of DDT and other pesticides in the killing off of birds and other wildlife, touched a nerve that alerted the public to the negative impacts of industrial pollution in the early 1960s.[37] It was the Cuyahoga River fire, however, that stirred a full-scale awakening of the negative externalities—the entropy bill—that had built up over 150 years of industrial development. Ten months after the river fire, in April 1970, twenty million Americans took to the streets in U.S. cities in peaceful gatherings calling for fundamental environmental reforms in celebration of the first Earth Day. In December 1970, Congress authorized the creation of the Environmental Protection Agency (EPA) to take on environmental issues and reforms.

It wasn't until 1983 that the governors of Illinois, Indiana, Michigan, Minnesota, Ohio, and Wisconsin created the Council of Great Lakes Governors. In 1989, the governors of New York and Pennsylvania joined the council. Several years later, the provinces of Ontario and Quebec came on board as associate members, and in 2015 the Canadian premiers became full-fledged members, and the organization was rechartered as the Conference of Great Lakes and St. Lawrence Governors and Premiers. The governors and premiers recognize that the stewardship of the Great Lakes and the region's environment is crucial to the economic and social well-being of the citizenry living around the lakes.

The bioregional governance of the Great Lakes also includes the Great Lakes Commission. The commission's board of directors is composed of public officials from each of the member states and provinces and works on developing specific legislative missions to align environmental protection and environmental goals to the task of leveraging "water resources as assets to support strong economies." The objective is to ensure that "water resources are protected from pollution and impacts from climate change."[38]

This alignment of governing jurisdictions—the ecoregion, the economy, and the society—is a tall order that will test this new form of bioregional governance as it begins to make the transition from the traditional metrics of economic success that characterized the First and Second Industrial Revolutions to the new set of metrics that underscore the emerging Third Industrial Revolution and its metamorphosis into the Resilient Revolution. Recalibrating economic performance from efficiency to adaptivity, progress to resilience, productivity to regenerativity, externality to circularity, ownership to access, and GDP to QLI is a heavy load. Balancing the transition will be the overriding task confronting bioregional governance in Cascadia, the Great Lakes, and other bioregions in the United States, Canada, and the world.

In the Great Lakes, time is running out to shift from models and pilots to an immersive infrastructure transition. A comprehensive study and report commissioned by the Environmental Law and Policy Center and the Chicago Council on Global Affairs and prepared by eighteen scientists and researchers from universities in the Great Lake states and Ontario reveal what's in store for the Great Lakes bioregion over the next several decades as climate change barrels down on the ecoregion.

The following are some of the findings in the report, entitled *An Assessment on the Impacts of Climate Change on the Great Lakes*. The human impact over the past two hundred years has resulted in severe habitat loss, the spread of invasive species, and polluted air and water. Petrochemical-intensive agricultural practices have led to soil erosion and nutrient depletion. Industrial-scale animal feedlot operations have wreaked havoc on native wildlife and compromised water quality. More concerning, the Great Lakes basin has warmed by 1.6 degrees Fahrenheit in annual temperature as compared to a 1.2-degree Fahrenheit rise in warming in the rest of the continental United States. A warming of the atmosphere, in turn, has increased both the frequency and intensity of heavy rains and snowfalls. While precipitation across the United States between 1901 and 2015 increased by 4 percent, the Great Lakes region experienced a nearly 10 percent rise in precipitation. The assessment report warns that "these increases in precipitation will likely increase flooding across the Great Lakes region," crippling water treatment infrastructure and leading to sewer overflows and a proliferation of waterborne pathogens flowing into local streams, rivers, and the Great Lakes.[39]

The future is already here. It will require far more strenuous adaptivity initiatives to shore up resilience than are currently underway. Even though the Great Lakes region is far ahead of other governing jurisdictions in establishing a bioregional approach to climate change and creating a more resilient economy and society, it falls far short of the mark. In 2019, Detroit declared a state of emergency as a relentless downpour coming off Lake Erie flooded the city and raced through homes and sewer systems, threatening public health and safety. In Duluth, Minnesota, an unusually strong storm over Lake Superior caused extensive damage to lakefront property and infrastructure. Buffalo, New York, in 2019 experienced record floods because of rising water levels on Lake Erie. And in Chicago, record water levels on Lake Michigan are resulting in increased coastal flooding in the spring and summer months with each passing year. The water depth in the Great Lakes in 2019 ranged from fourteen inches to nearly three feet above the average over the year.[40]

Climate change is no longer just a future to plan for, but a present emergency crisis to contend with and adapt to, requiring not just conventional stewardship of the bioregion's ecosystem but, in addition, disaster management and the implementation of climate-resilient infrastructure across the shared governance of the lakes' ecoregion.

The inherent dilemma facing the Great Lakes bioregional governance and the Cascadia bioregional governance as well as all the incipient efforts in bioregional governance underway or yet to happen is that the moment the decision is made to cogovern a bioregion, the governing jurisdictions are caught between two competing worldviews. Do they follow the conventional wisdom passed down during the whole of the industrial era and embedded in the Gospel of Efficiency by which conservation is viewed strictly in commercial terms? That is, do they see their primary mission as the efficient management of the resources of the Great Lakes Bioregion for the purposes of commercial exploitation into the future? If this traditional thinking gains the upper hand, bioregional governance will continue in its more myopic human-centered relationship to the Great Lakes ecosystem, with an eye to how it can be adapted to the utilitarian requisites of society rather than how society might adapt to the requisites of the ecosystem.

It's an important distinction and an urgent discussion that needs to be had as which agency needs to adapt to the other will largely determine whether management or stewardship of the Great Lakes will be the standard going forward—a tough bridge to cross and a road less traveled until now, but from here forward the path to follow if our species is to survive and flourish.

12

REPRESENTATIVE DEMOCRACY MAKES WAY FOR DISTRIBUTED PEEROCRACY

When disaster strikes, be it climate- or pandemic-related, government alone is too shallow, understaffed, and ill-equipped to govern by itself and oversee the emergency and inevitably calls upon the citizenry to respond and pitch in. With this in mind, a younger generation is just beginning to temper representative democracy, with all of its successes, failed hopes, and shortcomings, with a broader, more inclusive, and lateral form of political engagement that embeds communities within the ecosystems, biomes, and planetary spheres with which we are intimately entwined. This emergent new political identity comes with a more direct activist engagement in governance that extends beyond just voting for a small number of one's cohorts to govern, to each citizen becoming an intimate part of the governing process itself.

Just as citizens are called upon to sit on juries periodically through their lifetime to become active players in applying the laws and administering justice, local governments are beginning to enlist their citizenry in participating in "peer assemblies" working alongside government, providing advice, counsel, and recommendations related to governance of their biosphere. These citizen assemblies are not focus groups or stakeholder groups, but rather, more formal and deeply embedded extensions of governance—like juries—that lateralize decision-making, ensuring that the citizenry actively engages in governance. This lateralization of governance is sprouting up in thousands of regions and deepening the roots of civic engagement. Representative democracy is making room for distributed "peerocracy" just as local governance is making room for bioregional governance, as the citizenry regroups to meet both the challenges and opportunities that come with safeguarding their bioregions.

REFORMATTING FREEDOM:
Autonomy vs. Inclusivity

Peerocracy is not just about bringing citizens to the table to confer, debate, and concur on governing legislation, policies, and protocols. Rather, it represents a fundamental rethinking of the very notion of freedom that has steered political discourse and underwritten the variety of approaches to governance since the Enlightenment and the dawn of the Age of Progress.

The cry of freedom was intimately infused with the rise of the Industrial Revolution and capitalism. From the fall of the Roman Empire to the time the first inklings of an agrarian proto-industrial revolution appeared in the 13th century, Europe was loosely ruled by the Catholic Church and its priesthood and, in descending order, regional kings and their coteries and at the provincial level, princes ruling over local principalities, and at the base of the pyramid, lords residing over their manors and the serfs who came with the land.

In this tightly structured feudal world, serfs literally belonged to the land and could not flee. They were domiciled and lived in servitude. They owed their complete allegiance and security to the lords of the manor to which they belonged. Their loyalty was in the nature of homage—that is, providing services to the lord of the manor in strict obeyance to his commands.

The great enclosure movements that began in earnest in the 15th century in England signaled a fundamental change in the relationship of people to the land. Parliamentary acts in England and later across the European continent allowed local lords to sell off parts of their land, transforming their estates into real estate and reducing the land to a salable commodity while ejecting serfs en masse from their domiciles. There were many reasons for this abrupt change in the relationship of people to the land, but at the top of the list was the commercial prospect of using the land for the more lucrative practice of pasturing sheep for the emerging textile and wool markets that would become the first industries to cross into the agrarian industrial revolution and, soon thereafter, into factory production of textiles, marking the beginning of the modern industrial revolution.

Millions of serfs were removed from the land and told they were free to contract their labor for compensation, ushering in the very beginnings of a proto-industrial workforce. Feudal homage gave way and was replaced by individual freedom. Although it's reasonable to assume that for the masses of serfs whose families' security had for centuries been safeguarded by their attachment to the land that they belonged to, regardless of how miserable their circumstances, this abrupt change—this detachment—was devastating. What did it mean to be free and to learn how to bargain and contract one's labor in a developing marketplace?

With freedom came autonomy—a notion previously restricted to emperors and kings, and to a lesser degree princes and lords. Thereon, freedom and autonomy would ride together into the modern era. To be autonomous was to be free, and to be free was to be autonomous. But this was a unique kind of freedom. This form of freedom that held firm across the Age of Progress was a negative freedom—it was the right to exclusivity, the right to be self-sufficient, to not be beholden to others, to be an island to oneself, and would remain so until recently.

Among the Gen-X, millennial, and Gen-Z generations, this traditional notion of freedom has increasingly come to be regarded as an alien concept. They've grown up in a world that is shifting from ownership to access, from exchange value to share value, from markets to networks, from an obsession with exclusivity to a passion for inclusivity. For a smartly connected global cohort of digital natives, autonomy and exclusivity—being walled off from the world—would be tantamount to a death sentence. Absent cell phones and internet connectivity, digital natives would be lost.

Hundreds of millions, if not already billions, of digitally connected human beings take for granted that freedom is about access and inclusivity rather than autonomy and exclusivity and judge their freedom by the degree of access they have to participate in platforms proliferating across the planet. And the inclusivity they have in mind is laterally directed and expansive, often encompassing gender, race, sexual orientation, and even affiliation with our fellow creatures on an animated planet. To be free for a digital generation is to be able to participate with all of the rich and diverse agencies on Earth to which they are beholden for their life and well-being.

This is the notion of freedom that's emerging in a world that is increasingly being experienced as interconnected and in which everyone's well-being—their freedom, if you will—is bound to the social capital they are able to amass on the global digital commons. Freedom as access and inclusivity is the political foundation of peerocracy.

As the saying goes, "be careful what you wish for." Granted, governments around the world are taking the first tentative steps toward introducing citizen assemblies to provide advice and counsel. At best, these early political forays are well intentioned and, at worst, used as cover for a governing structure increasingly perceived as out of touch with the needs and aspirations of their constituents and often thought of as a self-promoting elite using public office for personal gain. Still, history suggests that we're headed for this fundamental political change toward a greater role for distributed peerocracy in the affairs of governance or, in its absence, a period of increasingly brutal authoritarian rule. Yet, peer assemblies are not meant to be ad hoc appendages of representative democracy but something far more transformational. Distributed peerocracy challenges the very notion of representative democracy as the only way to govern, as well as the particular notion of freedom that rides with it. If allowed to blossom, this newest extension of governance will inevitably change what it means to be a free and active citizen in a resilient society.

Most Americans would be surprised to learn that the term "democracy" is not referenced in the Declaration of Independence, the Constitution, nor the Bill of Rights. An oversight? Hardly! The very word was anathema to the men who founded the country. James Madison, a principal author of the Federalist Papers and the fourth president of the United States, reflected the thinking of his contemporaries on the subject, declaring that "democracies have ever been spectacles of turbulence and contention . . . and have in general been as short in their lives as they have been violent in their deaths."[1] John Adams, America's second president, was equally disparaging. He argued that "democracy never lasts long. It soon wastes, exhausts, and murders itself. There never was a democracy yet that did not commit suicide."[2]

The founders worried that a popular democracy would inevitably pit factions and interest groups against one another, and that popular rule could easily lead to mob rule and the silencing and marginalizing of minorities. For all of these reasons, they favored a republic with built-in safeguards like the Electoral College and the Bill of Rights that would temper the heat of popular passions while allowing elected representatives to manage the affairs of state.

Two centuries later, the film *The Candidate,* starring Robert Redford, was released into theaters. (The screenplay won an Academy Award.) The movie features a young liberal civil rights and environmental activist who runs for a Senate seat in California. While addressing a political gathering, he paused to ruminate out loud, remarking that the "idea of two guys [the senators of California] making decisions for twenty million people is pretty funny." Clearly one of those rare moments of speaking truth to power.[3] Everyone watching the film no doubt got it but quickly tucked the reflection away, lest it further erode their belief in representative democracy and one's loyalty to the republic.

INSIDE THE PEEROCRATIC MIND

Peerocracy is both an extension of and an antidote to the shortcomings of representative democracy. Citizen assemblies take governance to a new level. While national governments and state and local governments are not likely to disappear, they will probably shift over the course of coming decades and centuries from a top-down pyramidical structure to a more lateral and distributed pattern, with decision-making increasingly being exercised at the most intimate level of the bioregion where people live their lives. From there, decision-making will circle out to other layers of government, creating deeper patterns of interconnectivity across multiple bioregions and the continent.

It's worth repeating that bioregional governance, by its very nature and mission, is a commons, and not a marketplace, in which human agency is continually adapting to the many other agencies that make up the ecoregions within which it is embedded. The new notion of freedom as inclusivity rather than exclusivity—connectedness that stretches beyond our species to include our fellow creatures and all of the other agencies of the planet—is the defining dynamic of a future governed by bioregions. This more embedded schema will likely also transform economic activity and social life as well as governance in the years ahead, hopefully providing a new sense of place, affiliation, and political representation in a resilient society where "all politics is bioregional."

At present, the embryonic bioregional governance initiatives, with minor exceptions, are only experimenting around the edges while governance is unraveling. The increasing political alienation in America, which has led to the second impeachment trial of President Donald Trump and the insurrection and violent siege of the U.S. Capitol is telling.

The growing economic divide and increasing marginalization of human populations has deepened political alienation, threatening the very existence of national governments. A 2018 Gallup poll in OECD countries found that "only 45 percent of citizens trust their government."[4] The Edelman Trust Barometer is even more worrisome. Its 2020 survey in twenty-eight countries shows that 66 percent of the citizenry do not have confidence in their current government.[5] The United States is particularly troubling. In 1958, as the Second Industrial Revolution was peaking, 73 percent of Americans in a national election study said they could trust the government.[6] In 2001 only 31 percent of Americans said they could trust the government.[7]

These and other surveys indicate that social cohesion is fraying in countries on every continent while conspiratorial cults and movements are ascendant, in large part aided by the rise of unmonitored and unregulated social media spreading disinformation. Sociologist and political economist William Davies, writing in *The Guardian,* summed up the nature of the crisis:

> The project that was launched over three centuries ago, of trusting elite individuals to know, report, and judge things on our behalf, may not be viable in the long term, at least not in its existing form. It is tempting to indulge the fantasy that we can reverse the forces that have undermined it, or else batter them into retreat with an even bigger arsenal of facts. But this is to ignore the more fundamental ways in which the nature of trust is changing.[8]

If there is a recurring theme heard over and over again in survey after survey and country after country, it's "my voice is not being heard." A 2019 OECD report on the failure of representative democracy as a form of governance cut to the chase, concluding that "current democratic and governance structures are failing to deliver."[9]

PARTICIPATORY BUDGETING:
An Evolution of Governance

Although it's long been assumed by governing elites that the public is not interested in taking an active role in governance and expect their elected representatives and their experts to deliver the appropriate programs and services, that's not true. The match that lit the fire was struck in Porto Alegre, the capital city of the state of Rio Grande do Sul, Brazil, in 1989.[10] The relatively new Workers Party of Brazil came into power in the city. One of its first acts of office was to invert the most essential component of the governing process—the decision-making procedures for selecting and financing government programs and services. They called the political innovation "participatory budgeting."

This new budgeting process is jointly administered by representatives of the government and community organizations in a nearly yearlong political process that includes solicitation of proposals from citizens and community organizations within the region, the selection of delegates, and the holding of citizen assemblies to debate the merits of each proposal from which an agreed-upon set of items is cobbled together. The particulars of the vetting process are meticulous, but in the end the participatory budgeting proposals are given back to the executive and legislative branches of government, which enact the line items recommended by the peer assemblies. Although legally the final budget is the administrative responsibility of the government under the laws of the country and region, the budgets are generally affirmed by the government. To do otherwise would kill the legitimacy of the process and turn the citizenry against the ruling party.

The intent behind participatory budgeting is to give the people a voice, especially those living in disadvantaged neighborhoods and communities. Participatory budgeting in Porto Alegre has been a qualified success. By 1997, the Porto Alegre participatory budgets had resulted in an increase in sewer and water connections from 75 to 98 percent; an expansion in the health and education budgets from 13 to 40 percent; a quadrupling in schools; and a fivefold increase in road construction, mostly in the city's poorest neighborhoods. Equally impressive, peer assembly meetings grew exponentially, from just a thousand citizens in 1990 to nearly forty thousand in 1999.[11]

Today, there are upward of eleven thousand active examples of participatory budgeting in governments around the world, including world-class cities like New York and Paris.[12] Participatory budgeting in New York City is interesting because of the diversity of the population and the fact that the city is composed of five distinct boroughs, each with its own unique history and public footprint. A research team at the Berlin School of Economics and Law and New York University (NYU) assessed the impact of the city's participatory budgeting process from 2009 until 2018. They found that when New York City Council members adopted participatory budgeting, "greater proportions of their discretionary capital budgets were allocated to schools, streets and traffic improvements, and public housing."[13] Erin Godfrey, an associate professor of applied psychology at NYU's Steinhardt School of Culture, Education, and Human Development, summed up the findings of the study, saying, "what is exciting about this research is that it tells us for the first time that PB [participatory budgeting] can shift spending priorities in NYC to better reflect the immediate needs and concerns of community members."[14]

Participatory budgeting continues to grow in popularity across every continent, but it doesn't come without glitches that can undermine its deeper integration as a new form of peer governance. For example, while the model used in the participatory budgeting process has remained intact in Porto Alegre, the fall of the Worker's Party in 2004 and the elevation of centrist and right-wing parties dampened funding availability for big-picture infrastructure projects and weakened the inclusive engagement of the citizenry. Then, in 2017, the center-right Brazilian Socialist Democratic party came into office and suspended the participatory budgeting peer assemblies and

meetings for two years, listing a lack of sufficient resources and the need to institute reforms to the process itself.

Both the process and the scope of participatory budgeting need to be formalized in law by existing governments to ensure that a change in political party with incoming administrations doesn't undermine the fledgling institution, further alienating the citizenry with a precipitous decline in public trust.

Citizen assemblies have since spread into other aspects of governance including education, public health, community oversight of policing, infrastructure planning, climate adaptation, and citizen science, to name just a few of the governing realms getting a makeover. Although the new governance model goes under a number of names, including citizen assemblies, deliberative governance, and participatory governance, it's probably more appropriate to label it peer governance, reflecting the networked orientation of a younger generation of digital natives who are more likely to think of participation in terms of platforms and themselves as peers engaged in a distributed political process.

Peer governance didn't just suddenly appear in Porto Alegre as a revelation. There is a history that led up to its appearance across society. The modern roots of this extension of governance to include the citizenry trace back to the 1960s and the coming of age of the baby boom generation. The civil rights movement, the peace movement, the feminist movement, the environmental movement, the gay rights movement, the new age movement, and the counterculture movement shared a common denominator—a deep alienation from the existing order of governance that largely favored the interests of a mostly white, educated, urban, male, and middle-class cohort at the expense of the marginalization of "the others."

"The others" mobilized their own constituencies and made their demands heard for greater "inclusivity" in governance. In fact, inclusivity became the way a younger generation defined freedom. The movements that emerged spawned thousands of civil society organizations in communities around the world, offering up both a counterforce to the existing capitalist business model and an informal kind of governance that exists alongside conventional governing jurisdictions. Food kitchens, squatter movements, public health clinics, the environmental movement, open universities, and the like popped up everywhere, accompanied by political movements pushing against formal governments tightly controlled by elites.

The birth of peerocracy is both an evolution and a revolution. It represents the coming of age of civil society organizations (CSOs) that blossomed under many banners. Still, even today, when civil society is referenced in the conventional media and within government and business circles, it is described pejoratively as either nongovernmental organizations (NGOs) or nonprofit organizations

(NPOs), as if to characterize it by what it isn't. The inference is that CSOs are of lesser importance. The unwarranted disparagement of civil society organizations by both the government and commercial sector is all the more telling when we look at the numbers. By 2019, the so-called nonprofit organizations were the third-largest employment sector in the United States, behind only retail trade and food services, and on par with manufacturing.[15] Although the prevailing myth is that the nonprofit workforce is made up of lower-paying jobs, it's not so. Nonprofit workforce wages average 30 percent more than the wages paid in retail trade, and 60 percent more than the construction industry.[16]

The other mischaracterization of civil society organizations is they only exist by the goodwill of the market, government, and private charity and are not self-generating entities. Again, not true. Private contributions and government grants make up only 13 percent and 9 percent, respectively, of nonprofit revenue in the United States. By contrast, 50 percent of nonprofit revenue comes from fees for services in the private sector, and 23 percent from fees for government services.[17] In 2019, there were approximately 1.5 million nonprofit organizations registered with the U.S. Internal Revenue Service, and the sector contributed more than $1 trillion to the U.S. economy, amounting to 5.6 percent of the nation's GDP.[18] In addition to paid employment, an estimated 25 percent of American adults volunteered in 2017, contributing more than 8.8 billion hours of their time, and the value of these volunteer hours totaled approximately $195 billion.[19]

The size and scope of the civil society sector in the United States is formidable, and comparable in many other industrialized nations, yet nary a business school in the nation or elsewhere devotes a single study session to the role that civil society organizations play in the economic life of society.

These CSOs are social movements, economic enterprises, and new forms of proto-governance that bring the citizenry into the political arena. They are the forerunners of a new layer of governance—peerocracy—that distributes participation in governance more laterally and in greater depth at the most intimate space to which people are attached, their neighborhoods where they work, play, and thrive.

COMMUNITY CONTROL OF THE SCHOOLS

At the very same time that participatory budgeting was taking off in Porto Alegre, Brazil, a similar peer governance experiment was unfolding in the Chicago school system, the United States' third-largest school district. In

1988, the city enacted the Chicago School Reform Act. A year earlier, William Bennett, the secretary of education in President Ronald Reagan's cabinet, had targeted the Chicago public schools as the worst in the nation.[20] The School Reform Act established local school councils for all of Chicago's public schools. Each school council consists of six parents, two community members, two teachers, the principal and, in high schools, one student representative and one nonteaching staff member. With the exception of teachers, all the members of the school council are elected by residents of the community. Teachers are polled to fill the two teacher and staff positions, but their voting is nonbinding. These positions are appointed by the board of education. Every council member must undergo a training program in preparation for their tenure.

The reform act ended the long-established practice of tenure for school principals. Under the new local governance, principals are selected by the local school council and given four-year contracts, after which they have to reapply. Local school councils exercise considerable control over their schools' use of funds by both shaping and approving school budgets. Finally, curricula changes are also determined by the local school council.[21]

In November 2017, just twenty-nine years after this radical shift in the Chicago school system's approach to public education, giving local communities greater control over their operation, a Stanford University study reported that students, on average, "learn more from third grade through eighth grade than any other moderate or large sized school district in the country."[22] The turnaround in educational achievement is significant given that the Chicago public schools are in some of the poorest and most violent neighborhoods of any American city, giving hope that this new approach to community-centered peer governance might, in the long run, break the cycle of poverty and violence that has rocked this city and other cities across America for generations.

What is particularly noteworthy in ceding some governing power to local school councils in Chicago is that unlike most other peer assemblies, which are still largely advisory in nature but with political clout, in Chicago the city actually ceded authority to the local school councils in the hiring and firing of their school principals, establishing budget priorities, and preparing school improvement agendas. This represents a substantial transfer of governing power.

While an important achievement, peerocracy often suffers from other drawbacks, including maintaining the initial enthusiasm and engagement of the populace. In Chicago, for example, more than three hundred thousand citizens voted to choose representatives on their local school councils at the

inception of the plan. Twenty-five years later, public participation in the local school council elections had waned. That's probably to be expected, and
might be because the citizenry and local school districts were pleased with
the overall reforms that had been instituted and the subsequent improvements in the academic performance of the schools.[23]

PEEROCRACY AND COMMUNITY OVERSIGHT OF POLICING

Some lateral forms of governance are likely to be more contentious than others
when it comes to distributing power to bring governance closer to the communities being served. The current national debate in the United States on
community oversight of policing is a case in point. Recall, our federal republic has long sported a distributed policing authority, with the federal government, the states, the counties, and municipalities all having their own police
forces in which each is best fitted to the scale in which they operate, but all
cooperate across jurisdictions. The policing authority is both distributed and
shared. To the extent that a further stage of distributed governance in policing is in the offing with the current debate sweeping America around community governance of policing should not be shocking but, rather, regarded
as the next rung in distributed governance to secure the entire system.

Still, when it comes to the issue of community oversight of policing, the wag-
ons are drawn. The string of killings of unarmed African Americans by police
officers over the past several years has awakened the public to police brutality,
reopening the discussion on America's long and ugly history of racism. The killings of Eric Garner, Breonna Taylor, and George Floyd have spawned a massive
new civil rights movement under the banner "Black Lives Matter." The recent
outcry comes as police forces have become more professionalized and heavily
armed with the latest in military equipment and attire and equipped with state-
of-the-art surveillance, analytic tools, and new forms of policing that favor prediction and preemption of likely crimes before they occur.

Big-city police budgets tell of a country that's becoming an armed fortress.
The 2021 police budget for the city of Los Angeles topped $1.8 billion.[24] In the
nation's largest city, the New York Police Department's proposed budget in
2020 was $6 billion even as the city debated huge cuts in education and other
programs and services.[25] In Philadelphia, the proposed police and prisons budgets in 2020 exceeded $970 million, or 20 percent of the entire general fund.[26]
Meanwhile, incarceration rates in the United States relative to population are

far and away the highest of any nation. A vast majority of the prisoners are people of color and among the country's poorest citizens. Many are serving long sentences for minor criminal offenses while white-collar crime is generally met with acquittals or short-term imprisonment and early parole.

Racial profiling and arrest and conviction of mostly people of color is often seen as a race issue—which it is. Yet, on a deeper level it is as much an economic issue. It's about a country that, for all of its success in welcoming immigrants and providing opportunity for achieving the American dream, is sullied by the enslavement, indenture, and exploitation of Native American, Black, Hispanic, and Asian labor. From the very beginning of the American experiment, this starker reality has existed side by side with the American success story.

So, when Black Lives Matter became the rallying cry in the wake of murders of African Americans at the hands of police, the newest iteration of the civil rights movement came with the demand to defund the police. Most Americans were sympathetic to Black Lives Matter but largely opposed to defunding the police. A Pew Research Center survey taken in June 2020, shortly after the killing of George Floyd, found that only 25 percent of Americans believed that funding should be decreased, while 42 percent said that funding should stay the same. Twenty percent said that it should be increased a little, and 11 percent said that it should be increased a lot.

However, when asked if the police should be shielded from civilian lawsuits, the majority of Americans agreed that "civilians need to have the power to sue police officers in order to hold them accountable for excessive use of force or misconduct."[27] Clearly, this response suggests a strong latent support for formalized community peer governance assemblages to oversee neighborhood policing.

Lost in all of the polarization around calls by the Black community to defund the police is that the argument put forth by the Black Lives Matter movement favored "partial defunding" accompanied by the re-funding of vitally needed improvements in public education and making available affordable housing, improved public health services, training for jobs, and upgrading public services, including roads and lighting, as well as providing incentives to fund neighborhood commercial districts, et cetera. Given that a disproportionate percentage of public funds in major urban communities is given over to militarizing the police, which only serves to tighten the noose around the city's most disadvantaged communities, the proposal to partially defund the police and re-fund community services and underwrite the creation of economic opportunities in at-risk neighborhoods was not at all unreasonable. How else would it be possible to reverse the cycle of increasing poverty, escalating criminal activity, and greater police surveillance and crackdowns that have spiraled in inner cities?

Once again, Chicago offers a case study of introducing a peer approach to community governance—in this instance over policing and public safety—although with more discouraging results than the moderately successful implementation of the local school councils. Chicago's South Side has become infamous around the world for its street gangs, violence, murders, and police surveillance, making it particularly dicey to even entertain community-based, peer oversight of policing. Still, the attempt was made.

In the late 1980s, the Chicago police force, like other police departments, was harboring doubts about the future of policing and public safety. There was a great deal of internal questioning as to whether preventative patrolling in marked cars and 911 police calls were adequate means to address the mounting crime rate in the city—especially on the South Side. It was at this time that the police department introduced the idea of community policing and working together with neighborhood organizations and the citizenry in a more structured partnership to improve public safety.

The mayor, Richard M. Daley, warmed to the proposal. The result was the establishment of community policing assemblages in five of the city's police districts in 1993, expanding to all twenty-two police districts in 1995. Police "beat" teams were assigned to specific neighborhoods with the intent of integrating them into the community. Community beat team meetings were held in each neighborhood in which officers and residents could assess the safety of their neighborhood, discuss new problems, and make recommendations to enhance public safety. There was, however, no formal governance council in each neighborhood made up of elected citizen representatives nor were there specific protocols governing how recommendations coming from the community were to be processed up the chain of police command and properly addressed. Even so, peer deliberation in this rudimentary form of community oversight of policing followed along similar lines as the local school councils, with brainstorming sessions leading to analysis and agreed-upon consensus around specific recommendations to be taken and strategies to pursue.

Despite the lack of formally binding protocols that would ensure that the recommendations put forth by the peer assemblies would be acted upon, the city did commit funds to hire the Chicago Alliance for Neighborhood Safety—a nonprofit community-based organization—to teach residents and officers their responsibilities and mandates and provide pedagogical tools to ensure successful collaborations. In subsequent years, more than twelve thousand citizens and several hundred police officers were trained in deliberative peer governance procedures and practices.[28]

The initial program, called Chicago Alternative Policing Strategy (CAPS), proved moderately successful, especially in the early stages. A report notes that initially citizen participation was significant in minority communities with high crime rates and in the initial rollout of these proto-peer assemblies, crime dropped in CAPS neighborhoods.[29]

Citizens of the poorest neighborhoods began to feel that, for the first time, they had a voice in the policing of their own neighborhoods and communities. Unfortunately, as often happens with deliberative governance and peer assemblies, a change in leadership at the top—in this case, the succession of three new superintendents of the Chicago Police Department in ensuing years— came with a deprioritization of the CAPS program, including defunding and destaffing. Eventually, the program had so dwindled, according to Skogen, that it had become "a shadow of its former self."[30] The lesson here is that as in so many other instances of peer governance, it is necessary to formalize their existence by law and institutionalize funding commitments over a sufficient period of time to allow the citizen assemblies to grow, stabilize, and mature as ongoing distributed forms of peer governance.

As history would have it, community peer assemblies to oversee policing were fortunately given a second life in Chicago—this time established by law. In July 2021, Lori E. Lightfoot, the mayor of Chicago, and the Chicago City Council passed a historic piece of legislation that established a "first-of-its-kind independent civilian oversight body to oversee the Chicago Police Department, the Civilian Office of Police Accountability (COPA), and the Police Board." The Community Commission for Public Safety and Accountability consists of seven residents of Chicago appointed by the city. The commission will have the authority to "recommend to the Public Safety Inspector General to conduct research or audits on specific topics or issues . . . , appoint the Chief Administrator with the advice and consent of the City Council . . . , [and] recommend changes to the proposed Department budget appropriation," among other powers.[31]

The legislation also establishes neighborhood councils in every police district, to be made up of community residents elected by the citizenry. Unlike earlier community peer assemblies, these elected neighborhood councils will have "the power to make and approve policy for the Chicago Police Department."[32]

Peerocratic governance of community policing is a highly charged issue in many countries and will likely remain so in the near future. Eventually, distributed governance and shared community oversight of policing and public safety is likely inevitable as peer governance takes hold across the other public policy domains, bringing governance ever closer to communities.

DISTINGUISHING DISTRIBUTED VS. DECENTRALIZED GOVERNANCE

It's important to emphasize that distributed peerocracy is not a replacement for representative democracy but a deepening of governance that engages a broader segment of the citizenry more intimately and acutely. While most of these early citizen assembly experiments are characterized in both the academic literature and public discourse as "decentralized forms of governance," this is a misreading of what is occurring. "Decentralized" suggests a severing of traditional representative governance, which is not the case. Rather, deliberative local governance in the form of peer assemblies is a "distributed" phenomenon. For example, when it comes to participatory budgeting, local school councils, and community oversight of policing, some conventional governance in the hands of representative government is distributed to peer networks, while other governing powers remain in the hands of the centralized governing jurisdiction.

This is not unusual. The United States exists as a federal republic, which distributes power between the federal government, the state governments, the counties, and municipalities. None of the governing jurisdictions stand alone and all serve one another. In the EU, the cornerstone of the Treaty of the European Union is the subsidiarity principle, which distributes governing powers among the regions, the member states, and the European Union, with each contributing to the other, depending on the scale needed to ensure the viability of society as a whole.

Archon Fung of Harvard University's Kennedy School and Erik Olin Wright, professor of sociology at the University of Wisconsin, writing on how best to situate the new peer governance model, point out that peerocratic governance in the hands of the citizenry is not a devolution of governance but an evolution in the extension of governance to include the active commitment of every citizen during their lifetime in the governance of their lives and communities. Fung writes:

> First, the current institutional structure is neither centralized nor decentralized. Although local officials and ordinary citizens enjoy much more power and voice than under the previous, more top-down, arrangements, they remain dependent on central offices for various kinds of support and accountable to those offices for both process integrity and performance outcomes. Second, the role of central power shifts fundamentally from that of directing local

units (in the previous, hierarchical system) to that of supporting local units in their own problem-solving endeavors and holding them accountable to the norms of deliberation and achievement of demanding but feasible public outcomes. Third, support and accountability from the center advances the three democratic goals—of participation, deliberation, and empowerment.[33]

While distributive democracy is a new form of democracy that deepens and extends citizen participation in the affairs that govern society, it also introduces a new pedagogy in decision-making. Collaborative governance is the process used in peer assemblages to address timely issues and make decisions and recommendations that can be exercised informally or be enacted into law. Although peer governance shares common ground with practices emphasized in representative governance in policy making, it makes distinctions as well—the primary one being the weight given over to consensus building. Conventional legislative decision-making is generally exercised with consensus building in mind. Yet, decisions are often made more expediently by bargaining and making trade-offs to appease diverse interests and agendas. Deliberative governance seeks higher ground, at least in theory, by establishing a process to get to yes.

Advocates of deliberative democracy would argue that for a truly democratic decision to be regarded as legitimate, the political process should aim for common ground that best conforms to "the public will" and that supports legislation that reflects a consensus. Although majority rule is often the default position, it's viewed more as a failure than a success. In this sense, the process of peer deliberation is often regarded as important as the product. That process requires that all the peers at the table be free to share their opinions and views but also be open to attentively listening to others' perspectives in an effort to find common ground. Or, if not possible, explore wholly new approaches to handling the issue under consideration, and then incorporating their intent in a way that surpasses their initial approaches to the subject.

If this sounds like common sense, although often difficult to exercise in practice, especially in a world of so many divided voices, this is what a jury of one's peers is expected to do when the judge asks them to listen carefully to the evidence and the conflicting perspectives of the prosecution and defense and then retire to deliberate, make a judgment, and deliver a verdict that hopefully reflects a unanimous consensus.

But how do we tackle the more difficult process of finding consensus in a world where millions of people get caught up in thousands of virtual echo chambers on social media sites listening to a single narrative, buttressed and reinforced by millions of others, at the exclusion of listening to other slants on reality? The only way out of this box, it seems, is the coming together of citizens in their neighborhoods where they work, play, live, and interact, sharing common experiences of what's going on around them in the real world. Peer assemblies are very physical, up-front, face-to-face, human engagements of neighbors charged with the task of making sense of their shared daily experiences of reality, and making consensual decisions on how to improve the lot of their communities.

It would be difficult to find anyone opposed to establishing peer assemblies to work alongside representative governance, at least in theory. In practice, however, it's complicated. Peerocracy comes in many shades and degrees, from deep to lite, but at a time in history when our very survival depends on how the body politic coalesces around a new role as stewards of the biosphere, defining the process will be critical to determining the effectiveness of this new extension of governance. Our very lives will depend on it.

TWO APPROACHES TO PEEROCRACY:
The United Kingdom and France Square Off
over Climate Change

In 2019, both the United Kingdom and France established citizen assemblies to deliberate and propose initiatives and programs to address the climate crisis that could become road maps for government action at the national level. The two very different approaches and outcomes are instructive of what to embrace and exclude as regions around the world establish their own citizen assemblies to steward their bioregions. Two researchers, Claire Mellier of the Centre for Climate Change and Social Transformation at Cardiff University, and Rich Wilson of the Osca Agency, did a detailed analysis of the two peer assembly approaches and published their findings in an article entitled "Getting Climate Citizens' Assemblies Right" in the journal *Carnegie Europe*.[34] Here's what they found.

Both peer assemblies were instituted in the wake of escalating public protests around climate change. The French peer assembly came on the heels of the "Yellow Vests" protests across France in response to increasing the gas tax to reduce global warming emissions. The protests, led by truck drivers, shut down vital public arteries across the country and rocked President Emmanuel Macron's government. The British peer assembly came in the aftermath of street protests by Extinction Rebellion, an organization dedicated to raising the issue of climate change, which also shut down road arteries around the UK. The protests led to a parliamentary declaration calling for a climate emergency in the spring of 2019.

Each citizen assembly was selected by random sampling and sortition to represent a cross section of the population. The UK peer assembly totaled 108 participants while the French peer assembly was comprised of 150 peers. Both peer assemblies were divided into working subgroups. The UK citizen assembly topic areas were travel, in the home, what people buy, food, farming, and land use. The French subgroups covered housing, traveling, eating, consuming, and working and manufacturing. Both peer assemblies' final reports and recommendations were far more ambitious in scope than those previously introduced by elected officials to mitigate the climate crisis. But here is where the two citizen assemblies parted ways.

The budget granted to the French peer assembly was far more generous than the British one—nearly ten times that of the UK citizen assembly. More important, the French peer assembly recommendations, from the outset, were meant to be enacted by a national referendum, parliamentary vote, or by direct executive order on the part of President Macron's government. The British peer assembly recommendations were meant to be advisory in nature, even though the initiative was partially funded by six UK parliamentary committees.

Equally informative is how the agenda was established for each citizen assembly. The French left the decision of framing the questions that would steer the discussion up to the citizens who made up the assembly, while the UK Parliament oversaw the framing of the agenda for its citizen assembly without any input from the advisory panel. Moreover, the French peer assembly was encouraged to reach out and discuss ideas in the media and enlist opinions from experts. The British citizen assembly was instructed not to discuss the workings of the group or solicit outside advice.

The results of the two contrasting approaches to citizen deliberation were evident. The French citizen assembly recommended 149 different climate change measures, far and away exceeding the British proposals in both scale and depth. To be generous, the British government's oversight of the citizen assembly was more technically rigorous, with input from experts in the fields, and professional facilitators taking part by managing the table discussions, while the French process was more open-ended, letting the citizen peers steer the discussion and find consensus on the recommendations.

These two very different ways of managing citizen assemblies each incorporate strong and weak approaches to peer governance. The French approach is closer to the mark when it comes to ceding more agency to the citizen assembly and establishing distributed peerocracy as a semiformal extension of governance. However, the British use of experts to provide technical input and share professional expertise made for a more thorough peer experience. Combining the best attributes of both would give peer assemblies the gravitas to hold their own as a lateral extension of formal democratic governance.

JUMP-STARTING A POLITICAL REVOLUTION

Budgets, public education, and policing are among the hard-core nuts and bolts of what governments are all about. Now, after two centuries of representative democracy, citizens around the world are tiring, convinced that their interests, concerns, and aspirations are being ignored, or at best, circumscribed. The political alienation and loss of confidence in representative democracy are taking place at the very moment that our species is confronted with its biggest challenge in human history—how to survive and flourish on a rewilding planet.

Placed within the context of global warming and climate change, all of the aspects of governance fold into a larger political mission and governing mandate. Each local governing jurisdiction will need to prepare for and operationalize a public agenda dedicated to deep stewardship of local bioregions by framing multiple approaches to adapting to disruptive climate events. In the Anthropocene, every sector of governance will need to be reenvisioned within the larger context of an evolving resilient society.

Rethinking governance on this scale will require the active participation of the entire body politic. Neither conventional centralized governance functioning under the rubric of representative democracy nor decentralized local governance operating in silos and going solo will be capable of approaching the enormity of what's before us. Only a distributed peer governance acting as an intermediary between the neighborhood and the bioregion, civil society and representative government, will ensure that the entire weight of the community will be brought to bear in response to the rewilding of the earth.

Until recently, climate emergencies have resulted in a spontaneous outpouring of public assistance, mostly from civil society organizations—neighborhood watch groups, listservs, food pantries, community health centers, and the like. First responders become everyone within sight, rushing to the aid of those in peril. Of late, as climate catastrophes have increased in intensity and frequency, these more spontaneous civic responses have begun to institutionalize, with neighborhood associations creating peer assemblies working alongside local governments, learning together from the experience of past disasters and deliberating on how best to prepare for future emergencies. These peer assemblies will continue to evolve in the years and decades ahead, giving ballast to a lateralization of governance that emanates in local neighborhoods and stretches across a common bioregion.

The struggle to adapt to climate change will likely be won or lost by whether every neighborhood and community can mobilize and deploy a resilient infrastructure that will breathe new life onto the earth and give us a second chance to find our proper niche. The smart Third Industrial Revolution zero-emission infrastructure is the hardware and software by which our species can reprioritize governance by extending it across bioregions and continents. Peer assemblage governance, in turn, brings whole communities into a shared responsibility for their commons, empowering each citizen to be a steward of the bioregion in which they live. Without the distributed resilient infrastructure, bioregional governance will be an impossibility. And, without distributed peer governance, ecoregions cannot be properly stewarded.

Our species has shown itself to be among the most resilient, able to withstand and adapt to extreme climate changes over history, from ice ages to warming periods and back again. Our genetic makeup is unchanged, but our cognitive drive and worldliness have evolved over time, giving us a leg up over our ancient ancestors in understanding the planetary forces to which we need to adapt.

Bringing governance down to the ground on which we stand and where we dwell with our fellow creatures with a keen eye and sensitive ear to stewarding our local bioregions is the only viable way to hold on to our own future as a species while making amends for the violence we have inflicted on the earth. This doesn't mean a simplistic return to a forager-hunter lifestyle. It does mean making a conscious choice to rejoin the community of life, and adapt to our planetary home with a new degree of sophistication using complex adaptive social/ecological systems modeling. This is what is meant by being resilient. Only then will we have the wherewithal to flourish in wholly new ways.

The first step is a species-wide commitment to collectively participate in strong peerocratic governance in our respective bioregions with the mission of nurturing and healing the ecological commons that we and our fellow creatures co-inhabit. That process begins by freeing up our species' most defining attribute wired into our biology—our ability to feel and experience a deep empathic attachment to other beings. Extending the empathic drive to our fellow creatures is the beginning of a new chapter that will bring us back into the fold with our relatives across the natural world.

13

THE RISE OF BIOPHILIA
CONSCIOUSNESS

auretta Bender was the head of the child psychiatric ward at Bellevue
Hospital in New York City in 1941 when she realized something was
terribly wrong. She had begun to notice that children in the ward were
eerily antihuman. She shared her feelings in an article published in the *American Journal of Psychiatry*, writing that the children:

"Have no play pattern, cannot enter into group play, but abuse other children and cling to adults and exhibit a temper tantrum when cooperation is
expected. They are hyperkinetic and distractable; they are completely confused about human relationships and . . . lose themselves in a destructive fantasy life directed both against the world and themselves."[1]

She wondered, was it possible that the antisocial behavior was the result
of parental care deprivation?

COMFORT THE BABY:
Just Good Enough Parenting

The scientific thinking at the time was that babies are born with an inherent
drive to be autonomous, befitting a worldview that promoted the belief that
autonomy and freedom were two sides of the same coin. Hygienic practices
in children's wards and orphanages everywhere reinforced the notion that
the sooner a baby could be weaned to be independent, the better adjusted the
child would be. With that in mind, babies were prop-fed so that attendants
would not need to come into physical contact with them. Picking up and cuddling the infant was forbidden, lest it risk lifelong infantilization.

John B. Watson, one of the pioneers of psychology, argued in the 1920s that coddling babies destroyed their drive to be autonomous and independent. His advice to young mothers was:

> Treat [the babies] as though they were young adults. Dress them, bathe them with care and circumspection. Let your behavior always be objective and kindly firm. Never hug and kiss them, never let them sit in your lap. If you must, kiss them once on the forehead when they say good night. Shake hands with them in the morning. Give them a pat on the head if they have made an extraordinarily good job of a difficult task.[2]

Although well cared for, infants were dying in droves in Bellevue and elsewhere, particularly in orphanages, with death rates skyrocketing in the first two years of infancy. Doctors had no explanation, except to blame it on a known unknown they characterized loosely as "hospitalism."[3] At that time, Harry Bakwin became head of the pediatric unit at Bellevue. He noticed that staff had even devised a box equipped with "inlet and outlet valves and sleeve arrangements for the attendants" in which the infant was placed so that he or she could "be taken care of almost untouched by human hands."[4]

Bakwin reasoned that the infants were deprived of being touched and caressed. What was absent was human affection. He had signs put up throughout the pediatric unit that read: "Do not enter the nursery without picking up a baby."[5] The infection rates and deaths declined immediately, and infants thrived.

It wasn't until the late 1950s that practice led to theory when a British psychiatrist, John Bowlby, published three journal articles in which he described a new theory of child development, which he called "attachment theory." Bowlby reasoned that infants' primary drive was not to seek self-gratification and autonomy but rather to seek affection and attachment.

Bowlby writes that early on, an infant "come[s] quickly to distinguish familiars from strangers but amongst his familiars he chooses one or more favorites. They are greeted with delight; they are followed when they depart; and they are sought when absent. Their loss causes anxiety and distress; their recovery, relief, and a sense of security. On this foundation, it seems, the rest of his emotional life is built—without this foundation, there is risk for his future happiness and health."[6]

But there is a snag. While an infant seeks emotional attachment with adult figures, that same infant is also interested in exploring the world—knowing that he or she can always return to the safe haven offered by a primary caregiver. Bowlby wrote: "Children and other young creatures are notoriously curious and inquiring, which commonly leads them to move away from their attachment figure. In this sense exploratory behavior is antithetical to attachment behavior. In healthy individuals the two kinds of behavior normally alternate."[7]

Bowlby connects the dots, concluding that a parent has to be "just good enough." They must exhibit:

> an intuitive and sympathetic understanding of the child's attachment behaviour and a willingness to meet it and thereby terminate it, and, second, recognition that one of the commonest sources of a child's anger is the frustration of his desire for love and care, and that his anxiety commonly reflects uncertainty whether parents will continue to be available. Complementary in importance to a parent's respect for a child's attachment desires is respect for his desire to explore and gradually to extend his relationships both with peers and with other adults.[8]

If the parent can maintain a secure attachment while simultaneously allowing the child to explore and become independent, he or she will acquire the emotional security to develop relationships. If the parent is too smothering or too absent, the child will grow up with an arrested sense of selfhood and be unable to develop mature emotional relationships with others.

Worse still, if parents reject their child or physically abuse the child, the infant or toddler is likely to grow up living in a constant state of anxiety: becoming aggressive, manifesting neurotic and phobic tendencies, and even psychotic and sociopathic behavior; or as the youngster approaches adulthood, acting out by attempting to be completely autonomous, by isolating himself or herself from any emotional attachment altogether.

EMPATHY AND ATTACHMENT:
It's What Makes Us Human

Since Bowlby's original insight into the role attachment behavior plays in a child's development, cognitive scientists, psychologists, and sociologists, among others, have peered into the biology of our species with particular attention to understanding the workings of the empathic impulse deeply woven into our neurocircuitry. What they have discovered is that at the core of our being—and what makes our species so special—is the innate biological drive to empathize with "the other."

We know, for example, that when a baby cries in a nursery, all of the other babies begin to cry, although they have no awareness of why they are doing so. Nonetheless, they are feeling the suffering of another as if it's their own.

While the empathic impulse exists in our neurocircuitry, whether it evolves or is suppressed is dependent on the nurturing environment of primary caregivers to whom the babies are attached and, in later interactions, with brothers and sisters, relatives, teachers, and others to whom they are similarly attached.

The attachment of an infant to a caregiver is the first act in the life drama of a newborn. If the caregiver is unable to empathize with the infant's suffering or feel their joy and express their compassion by nurture and by actively assisting the infant in becoming human—that is, an empathic socially evolved being—that child's development is likely to be arrested for the rest of their life. He or she will be unable to fully flourish as a social animal in solidarity with his or her fellow human beings and fellow creatures.

The maturing of the empathic response is deeply related to a child's growing awareness of mortality and death. Most children come to fully understand the concept of death between the ages of five and seven years. They realize that one day the people they love and care about will pass away and the same fate will one day befall them as well. It's at this point in a child's development that they come to emotionally and cognitively understand the most important aspect of being alive—that it's temporary and fleeting. It's this realization that allows empathy to flourish.

When we experience others' pain and suffering—and even joy—as if it were our own, the empathic impulse that emanates from deep inside our neurocircuitry is an emotional and cognitive recognition of the other person's vulnerability and their struggle to flourish in their one and only life. Our emotional solidarity is the deepest expression of our support as a kindred spirit who, too, carries this ultimate burden and blessing of mortality with us at every moment of our existence. Our compassion is our way of reaching out and saying we are fellow travelers who are each here for a moment of time for one another in the indescribable journey we call existence.

Interestingly, there would be no empathy in heaven or paradise, or in imagined utopias because there is no mortality, no suffering, no struggle to flourish and be. In these other realms, everything is perfect and without blemish or hardship, or even momentary joy and sorrow. Immortality brooks no role for empathy.

Bowlby understood the connection between "just good enough" caregiving and the nurturing of the empathic drive in infants, toddlers, and children, and the consequences that would result for the rest of their lives. Many studies since then have borne out Bowlby's intuition. Writing in the *Journal of Personality and Social Psychology* on "Attachment Theory and Reactions to Others' Needs," researchers found that "the activation of the sense of attachment security promotes empathic responses."[9] The report examined a number of studies over the years that found that children who are denied proper nurturing and grow up exhibiting attachment avoidance for fear that closeness to others will not be reciprocated, as well as those who suffer from attachment anxiety from fear of being rejected or abandoned, will in both instances lack the emotional reserves to empathize with others because they are so tangled up in their own sense of rejection or abandonment.

While Bowlby focused mostly on mothers as critical caregivers during a child's earliest stages, studies since of different cultures around the world and changing demographics suggest that primary caretakers often include fathers, older brothers and sisters, and close relatives. In the study of forager-hunter societies, which is the archetype for nurturing their young and preparing them to be adaptive and resilient to the natural world around them, nurturant caretaking of the very young is often a shared responsibility of extended families. The modern-day kibbutz in Israel offers a contemporary validation of the practice of sharing parental and familial caretaking of the very young.

If just good enough adult caretaking of infants and toddlers is the key to preparing successive generations to be adaptive to adversity and become the torchbearers of the Age of Resilience, a troubling reality presents itself. A study prepared by the London-based Sutton Trust and a team of researchers from Princeton University, Columbia University, the London School of Economics, and the University of Bristol on parental attachment of infants and toddlers in the United States is not comforting. What they found is that children with insecure attachment are at greatest risk of behavioral problems, poor literacy, and dropping out of school at an early age. They also found that children growing up without strong bonds of parental attachment are more likely to be aggressive, defiant, and hyperactive as adults.[10]

A strong correlation also exists between growing up in a poverty-ridden environment where parents are living day-to-day with a constant sense of hopelessness and despair, not even knowing if the family will have food to eat or a place to live, and poor attachment behavior. It's difficult to imagine in these circumstances how parents would have the emotional reserves to be steady nurturing caregivers to their young. Susan Campbell, a professor of psychology at the University of Pittsburgh, sums up the reality of poverty's effects on parental nurturing and child attachment. She explains, "When caregivers are overwhelmed because of their own difficulties, infants are more likely to learn that the world is not a safe place—leading them to become needy, frustrated, withdrawn, or disorganized."[11]

Researchers found that 60 percent of children in the United States in a representative survey of fourteen thousand children born in 2001 "developed strong attachments to their parents." But what was really troubling is that 40 percent of all the children surveyed grew up in houses with poor parental attachment and suffered the psychological consequences that would follow them for the rest of their lives.[12]

Bowlby and Mary Ainsworth, his colleague who took his insights and followed up with a rigorous scientific approach to examining behavior across an individual's and family's lifetime, concentrated for the most part on the period of infancy and early childhood where the secure attachment or its absence makes its primary mark. Other researchers across a range of disciplines began exploring the role other attachment figures play in different stages of one's life. Spouses, close friends, teachers, mentors, therapists, employers, and others often take on the role as attachment figures, either reinforcing or modifying earlier patterns of attachment, affecting a person's sense of secure attachment and empathic drive.

The empathic impulse, however, is not only about child-rearing practices and a succession of attachment figures over one's lifetime. Empathy also evolves over history and is deeply intertwined with the evolution of society and the rise and fall of civilizations—a social terrain little explored by social scientists.

It's when a new infrastructure is being erected and deployed across society that empathy evolves and expands. Each civilization's infrastructure brings with it a unique economic paradigm, a new social order, a new form of governance, and an ecological footprint along with an accompanying narrative worldview to which its population can give its allegiance. In each instance, the new infrastructure enables a more expansive empathic bond that can encompass and emotionally unite the diverse populations living, working, and attending to the new infrastructure. The non-blood-related population comes to define itself as a social organism that acts as a fictional family in which the members empathize with one another as kin.

Recall, forager-hunters lived in small isolated bands with populations of twenty to one hundred or so, while occasionally interacting in slightly larger kinship groups. Their beliefs and rituals were largely absent of gods. They mostly venerated their ancestors in the afterworld, and their worldview was steeped in animist consciousness. Their attachment figures and empathic impulse were strong but localized to their small band of blood-related families and slightly larger kinship groups.

The shift to agriculture and sedentary life some ten thousand years ago brought with it secure attachment to local gods who resided in the mountains, the soil, and the rivers and streams whose nurturance or wrath were a constant concern. The empathic drive rarely extended beyond the fringe of small farming communities in valleys and fishing communities nestled along coastlines.

The great leap forward in empathic extension came with the rise of the massive hydraulic agricultural civilizations in the Middle East along the Tigris, Euphrates, and Nile Rivers, the Indus River in what is now known as Pakistan, and the Yellow and Yangtze Rivers in China between 4000 and 1700 BCE. Populations were seized from across a wide geographic terrain and put to work designing, deploying, and operating massive hydraulic infrastructures to sustain large-scale agricultural production.

Hydraulic technologies were invented and employed to tame the great seasonal floods, capture and store the waters, and distribute them over the planting season, creating sufficient food for the moment and massive surpluses for storage and later dissemination. These hydraulic civilizations were an engineering feat made up of canals, dikes, irrigation systems, royal granaries, and royal roads and overseen by centralized bureaucracies made up of skilled technicians supervising mass indentured labor forces.

In the centuries before Christ, the great axial religions of Judaism, Buddhism, Hinduism, and Daoism matured, and later Christianity and Islam emerged, and each of these religions became the new attachment figures. This marked the turning point from animist consciousness as a dominant narrative to religious consciousness. These great axial religions succeeded in converting hundreds of thousands of unrelated individuals to a new common attachment figure, allowing them to identify themselves as part of an extended fictional family to whom they owed their loyalty and allegiance, and with whom they empathized.

Try to imagine what it must have been like for tens of thousands of migrants in isolated and remote farm villages who picked up their meager belongings and trekked across hundreds of miles of Roman roads to settle in the capital city of Rome and its outskirts. Alone in a city of several million people, many of them recent wayfarers uprooted from their ancestral lands and local gods, the migrants found their new attachment figure in Jesus Christ and Christianity, a cult that would become the official religion of the Roman Empire by edict of Emperor Constantine in 313 CE.

For the early Christian converts in the first century CE, Christ became a father figure who looked over his flock from heaven as family and provided nurture and love to each and every true believer. Christians who greeted one another would kiss each other on the cheek, calling each other brother or sister, whose loving parent was Jesus Christ. Empathy expanded to encompass this newest fictional family.

If the Paleolithic era, characterized by a forager-hunter society, gave rise to animist consciousness and the rise of the great hydraulic agricultural empires ushered in religious consciousness, the emergence of the industrial revolution gave birth to ideological consciousness. The new era was rooted in the belief that science, technology, the Industrial Revolution, and the capitalist economy would bring forth a materialist utopia and a facsimile of human immortality on Earth. These materialist utopias would come to be attached to various iterations of ideological consciousness under the banners of representative democracies, socialism, fascism, and communism.

But ideological consciousness also needed a governing narrative that could bundle large numbers of diverse populations together as a social organism. As mentioned previously, the deployment of fossil fuel–based industrial infrastructures in the late 18th century in Europe and America, and the shift from regional to national markets, spawned nation-state governance. However, by and large, these states were not comprised of a single ethnic group, but rather were composed of a hodgepodge of ethnicities and races with their own languages, dialects, cultural heritages, prevailing myths, and attachment figures. With this in mind, newly minted nation-states embarked on massive social indoctrination programs designed to turn a disparate lot of ethnicities into citizens, converts to ideological consciousness, and defenders of the nation.

As noted in chapter four, each state established a vernacular language. They then introduced public school systems with curricula that glorified the state and established holidays commemorating past historical events—some of which were more fictional than factual—to create a common fraternal bond. It didn't take more than a few generations to create Italian, German, Spanish, French cultures, et cetera, in which the state became the principal attachment figure. In the name of the "motherland" or "fatherland," the masses were drilled in patriotic rituals and asked to give allegiance to the state.

What emerged through it all is generation upon generation of citizens, each attached to their nation-state as a secure mother or father figure. Every citizen came to regard all others as extended family with whom they empathized, even to the extent of being willing to make the ultimate sacrifice of fighting and dying for their fellow countrymen. Wars were fought, blood was spilled, and millions of people died across Europe in the succeeding two centuries to protect their extended fictional families and show their allegiance to their motherland and fatherland—their overarching attachment figure.

Nelli Ferenczi, professor of philosophy at Brunel University, and Tara Marshall, professor of philosophy at McMaster University, were among the first researchers to study attachment to one's nation. Their study, "Exploring Attachment to the 'Homeland' and Its Association with Heritage Culture Identification," found similar results to Bowlby's and Ainsworth's writings on attachment to primary caregivers, penned a half century earlier. The researchers enlisted 232 participants between the ages of sixteen and sixty-five, 126 females, 105 males, and one whose gender was not stated. Thirty-five percent of participants reported living in a country different from their birth country, and 65 percent reported living in the country of their birth.[13] What Ferenczi and Marshall found is that attachment to country correlated along similar psychological lines as the attachment that infants and toddlers have with primary caregivers.

The subjects in the study separated along three lines. Those who were successfully integrated into society, whether it be their country of origin or adopted country, identified with its narrative and felt protected and cared for. They saw themselves as part of an extended fictional family who shared a common identity and exhibited all the trademarks of attachment. Others felt their attachment figure—the state—was either absent from their lives or rejecting. They exhibited the classic Bowlby-Ainsworth reaction of feeling either fearful and anxious, or abandoned and dismissed and on their own. Typical responses in the study were "I worry about being abandoned by my country" or "It's very important for me to feel independent from my country."[14]

Animist consciousness, religious consciousness, and ideological consciousness represent the great narrative frames—the historical watersheds—by which our species has come to make sense of our existence: our understanding of birth, life, death, and the afterworld, our spirit and drives, our obligations and relations. And each represented a new and different approach to how humanity organized its economic life, governance, and relationship to the natural world.

Historians and anthropologists are drawn to the prime technological infrastructures that brought legions of human beings together—beyond simple blood ties—in complex relationships made up of diverse roles and responsibilities in order to expropriate ever more expansive tracts of the natural wealth of the planet. Less noticed is that the infrastructure revolutions that took us to hydraulic civilizations, the proto-agricultural industrial revolution, and the fully matured industrial revolution expanded our species' empathic reach from blood ties to religious affiliations, and then to ideological identification. Unfortunately, the new infrastructures and accompanying empathic attachments also came with new boundaries, separating the true believers from the others—the infidels and anarchists—often with monstrous and terrifying consequences: wars and bloodbaths, and new kinds of discrimination.

Still, it's true that each of these empathic expansions led to the furthering of the empathic evolution of our species, with greater religious tolerance, the elimination of slavery and servitude, the outlawing of torture, the criminalization of genocide, the advancement of democratic governance and human rights and, more recently, the recognition of equality based on gender and sexual orientation. These breakthroughs were made possible by the increasing interconnectivity of our species across time and space enabled by the new more integrative infrastructures that have brought the human race ever closer, along with the accompanying empathic attachments that bound more diverse populations together as extended "fictional" families.

None of this is to suggest that lapses and throwbacks to earlier times won't continue to plague our species. Every new infrastructure leap forward, bringing greater numbers of people together in the guise of more expansive fictional families and greater empathic identification is, at the same time, a threat to waning collectivities—be they tribal, religious, or now ideological. These former cohorts don't entirely disappear, but continue to exist even if on an ever-narrowing temporal plane. If there is a hook, it's that those past cultural attachments, although seemingly retired to history, remain alive as remnants ready to rear up at a moment's notice and do battle.

So, while our species' attachment figures and empathic nature have evolved in sprints and leaps and, on occasion, collapsed altogether, taking our kind into extended periods of darkness, the basic wiring of our neurocircuitry keeps the empathic spirit alive, and there is no doubt that it is now taking humanity into the next stage of our empathic evolution—this time, hopefully in time to save our species and our fellow creatures.

A younger generation is beginning to break ranks from religious and ideological attachments, and stepping into a new more inclusive biological family. Biophilia consciousness is just now emerging and is likely to be the defining narrative of the Age of Resilience as our species begins to empathize with our fellow creatures.

REAFFILIATING WITH NATURE

First, the setting. Biophilia consciousness—the empathic embrace of our fellow creatures—is not just a recommendation or wish. Absent this next empathic extension—this time with our "real" extended family of relatives that cohabit the planet and sojourn with us—it's a sure thing that climate change will take both them and us into a tortuous endgame on Earth. Only by deeply and empathically identifying with our fellow creatures' struggle to flourish can we hope to secure our own future.

Biophilia doesn't come alone. It's part of a package. The new resilient digital infrastructure and accompanying interconnectivity gives our species the distributed reach we will need to facilitate a more hands-on adaptive governance across bioregions and ecosystems. The extension of government to bioregional governance brings the citizenry into a more intimate relationship with its nineteen kilometers of the biosphere where people and our fellow creatures live out their lives. This is vital because the power of the empathic embrace lies, in part, with the closeness of the experience. Bioregional governance, coupled with more intimate peerocratic stewardship of local ecosystems, puts our species directly in touch, in an embodied way, with our fellow creatures, allowing the power of empathy to flourish.

Lest anyone think that a more intimate relationship between citizenry and the ecosystems within which we live is unlikely or even romantic drivel, that intimacy has already been forced on the whole of humanity everywhere. The devastating toll climate disasters and the rewilding of the earth are having on people's everyday lives, if not intimate, is without doubt personally felt up front and close, and is quickly becoming an ever-present force affecting everything we do—the way we work, play, live out our lives, and imagine our futures. How then do we prepare our children to be adaptive and resilient on a rewilding planet?

In 2019, researchers in Europe from the field of psychology published a detailed meta report of experiments and studies on the relationship between childhood attachment and adaptivity and resilience. What they found is that whether a child grows up with a capacity to successfully adapt to a world swirling with disruptions and eruptions and be resilient is largely determined by his or her parental and family caretaker's nurturance during infancy and childhood. The researchers discovered "a consistency in the literature to suggest that resilience is predicated on two core concepts: adversity and positive adaptation," and concluded that "secure attachment may then be the prerequisite for positive adaptation."[15]

Turning the existential threat of climate change from trepidation to adaptation is the door to our future. The empathic extension—the biophilia connection—with our fellow creatures is the single most powerful force by which to animate the Age of Resilience. All of which circles us back to attachment, in this instance "attachment to place."

Although attachment theory has been studied across a range of sociological phenomena including religious and ideological affiliations, less attention has been given to "place attachment" even though place is the first dimension of exploration and attachment beyond parental caregiving—an infant's early sense of attachment is to his or her surroundings. It's by exploring the world—its physicality and presence and "goings-on"—that infants and toddlers create their embodied relationship to the environment.

Nowhere is place attachment more critical to a child's development and sense of belonging than the natural world, as evidenced by the fascination toddlers have with every creature that crawls, walks, flies, or swims. Whether a child is encouraged to explore his or her natural environment or warned by caretakers of its dangers and restrained can affect the child's sense of place attachment, or lack thereof, for the rest of their life. Then too, in an increasingly urbanized culture, lived mostly inside and more recently in virtual worlds, the natural environment can be experienced as alien and menacing, or even worse, of no interest. Richard Louv, the author of *Last Child in the Woods*, recounts a conversation he had with a fourth grader who expressed the feelings of many of today's youngsters. When asked why he didn't play outdoors, he replied, "I like to play indoors, because that's where the electrical outlets are."

If we tend to take attachment to place for granted, it's probably because it's so familiar and commonplace to how we define our existence in time and space that we forget how it has shaped our presence in the world. Even the development of language relies on our earliest explorations of place. The activity and interactivity that we notice and experience provides us with a rich store of spatial and temporal metaphors by which we construct language, understand relationships, and create our identities.

To the extent that a toddler or child grows up largely bereft of experience of the outside environment and the comings and goings of life, his or her experience of place is significantly narrowed, leaving the child with less secure attachment to the larger environment within which he or she will have to cope later in life. Unfortunately, in the rush to urbanization in the industrial era, little notice was given to the loss of environmental connection so crucial to establishing attachment to the natural world. Infant and toddler child care, and later on school attendance, makes little room for experiencing the natural world. Even recess in schools, which allows children unstructured time outdoors, has been significantly reduced or even eliminated altogether, replaced by virtual worlds where children are passive voyeurs simply manipulating pixels on a flat screen.

Attachment to place, like attachment to caregivers, depends on the type of exposure and experience. If the experience of nature is secure—that is, steady, alluring, reaffirming, and comforting—the positive attachment will generally stay with the child for a lifetime. Studies of place attachment fall roughly along the same curve as parental caregiving attachment, religious attachment, and attachment to one's country. If one's experience is perceived as harsh and uncaring or nonexistent, a child's behavior can run the gamut from anxious to avoidant. If, however, one's exposure and experience is nurturing and generative, the attachment to place becomes a meaningful part of one's identity in the world.

Secure attachment to one's natural environment doesn't always equate with adapting to its requisites or stewarding its regenerativity. For example, individuals with strong attachment to their natural environment are often reluctant after repeated climate disasters to hear arguments backed up by scientists that global warming in their region is only going to lead to ever more dangerous climate disasters. Nor do they want to hear that the better course might be to relocate and let the region rewild with the appropriate environmental stewardship. Instead, they resist and remain committed to rebuilding over and over again in the same place and in the same way as before, because that is what they have always known. It does reflect their secure sense of deep attachment to place, but can be detrimental to their future well-being and the ecosystems that they inhabit.

This inability to let go of one's attachment to place and environment often shows up in an unwillingness to learn new skills or find work elsewhere, even if the natural environment has been depleted and no longer offers opportunities to make a living or if the nature of the work is destructive to the environment—for example, strip-mining of coal, logging, and the like.

Other situations are even more complicated. Individuals with similar secure and close attachments to their environment and who even share a love of nature might disagree on whether wind turbines should be placed offshore or utility-scale solar farms be erected on adjacent land. Those opposed voice their concern that the installations will despoil the natural beauty of the region and compromise the environment. Those in favor argue that the shift from fossil fuels to renewable energy is the only way to slow global warming and climate change and regenerate a more resilient ecosystem. In these instances where both parties exhibit secure attachment to their natural environment but disagree on how best to protect it, they often do find common ground.[16]

A number of studies on place attachment have found that a joint commitment to stewarding the environment often motivates civic activism and engagement as neighbors band together to find an acceptable and agreed to adaptive approach to a more resilient future for their families and descendants. This bodes well for the extension of distributed peerocracy and citizen assemblies working alongside conventional governance in stewarding local bioregions.

While one's secure attachment to place and, particularly, the natural environment, provides a safe haven and a lifeworld by which to place oneself, it turns out it also performs two other equally vital functions. A secure attachment to the natural environment is the way to achieve personal happiness as well as the path forward in the evolution of empathic extension to include nature writ large.

RETHINKING HAPPINESS

Jeremy Bentham's ideas about what constitutes happiness have gone largely unquestioned for most of the industrial era. Bentham is the 19th-century philosopher best known for his utilitarian theory that all human behavior is driven by the desire to experience pleasure and avoid pain. He argued that we are each hedonists and utilitarian by nature and spend a lifetime in pursuit of satisfying our insatiable desires. The advertising community took Bentham's catechism at face value and used it to entice generations of our species to consume the earth's treasures in the form of endless new products and services. As far back as the 1950s, economist Victor Lebow wrote in the *Journal of Retailing* on the benefits of consumer culture, remarking that:

> Our enormously productive economy demands that we make consumption our way of life, that we convert the buying and use of goods into rituals, that we seek our spiritual satisfaction and our ego satisfaction in consumption. We need things consumed, burned up, worn out, replaced and discarded, at an ever-increasing rate.[17]

Although no one would argue that pauperization makes people happy, on the other end of the scale, is too much consumerism a bad thing?

Just as the consumer culture was peaking and driving entire populations into debt from which they would never recover, studies began to appear on the one-to-one correlation of consumerism and unhappiness. Psychologists, sociologists, and anthropologists did the research and ran the numbers, and the almost unanimous conclusion is that consumerism is an addiction like drugs, and the more one partakes, the more miserable one becomes. In a like manner, the more we possess, the more our possessions end up possessing us.

As might also be expected, the more we are surrounded by our possessions, the more we are locked into artificial worlds and detached from the natural world. This reality is all the more dispiriting given that scientists in recent years have concluded that exposure to nature is not just an aesthetic experience or a leisure activity but something of far greater import. Our most intimate bodily functions, down to the workings of every cell, as well as our cognitive functions, are cued to the rhythms and flows of the natural world from which we evolved and to which we are still entwined. This realization takes us right back to biophilia: the idea that the very sinew of our being is

alert to both the succor of nature and the dangers—characterized by our biophilic instincts and our biophobias.

Living in urban enclaves, we are often unaware of how our moods, behavior, and bodily functions are unconsciously affected by our physiological relationship to the environment, especially our mental and physical well-being.
Consider, for example, a simple walk through a forest versus a walk in an urban
setting. The forest walk lowers, on average, the salivary cortisol, which is a measurement of stress, by 13.4 percent upon viewing the forest and 15.8 percent
after the walk, and pulse rate by 3.9 percent upon viewing to 6 percent after
walking while also lowering systolic blood pressure. Parasympathetic nervous
activity—the feeling of relaxation—increases by 102 percent after walking and
sympathetic activity—the feeling of stress—decreases by 19.4 percent. All of
these changes occurring in our own body are just the result of taking a simple
walk in the woods.[18]

The nature–health connection became part of a national debate in Japan
in the 1980s. The working population was experiencing burnout from a highly
stressed and compressed urban existence bound up in relentless work. Japan
earned the dubious distinction of being the first 24/7 society. While the Japanese public's hedonistic desires were being well fed, their restorative needs
were going unmet. Around that time, a new cultural phenomenon caught on
across the country called *shinrin-yoku*, which in English translates to "forest bathing"—a walk in the woods—a therapeutic exercise to restore one's
physical well-being. The testaments came flooding in. People felt renewed
and scientists coined the term "restorative health."

To make sure it wasn't just all in people's heads, researchers tested their
glucose levels as they took a leisurely three-to-six-kilometer walk in the forest and found that blood glucose levels dropped by 39.7 percent, compared
to other similar forms of exercise on treadmills and in swimming pools,
which reduced blood glucose levels by only 21.2 percent.[19] Clearly the milieu made a difference. The difference, ecologists would argue, was the biophilia connection.

A report published in the *Annual Review of Environment and Resources* a
few years ago entitled "Humans and Nature: How Knowing and Experiencing
Nature Affect Well-Being" assessed studies in ten categories that cover the
dimensions of well-being to see how they correlated overall with experiences
in nature. The researchers reported that "the balance of evidence indicates
conclusively that knowing and experiencing nature makes us generally hap-
pier, healthier people."[20] When the researchers dove deeper and looked at the
impact that nature had on each of the ten dimensions of human well-being,

it became apparent that the relationship was strongly correlated. Among the findings of the studies is that greater immersion in nature improved physical health, reduced stress, increased self-discipline, restored mental health, fostered greater spirituality, extended attention span, improved learning capability, inspired imagination, deepened one's sense of identity, and spurred greater connectedness and a sense of belonging.[21]

The humanist psychologist Erich Fromm coined the term *biophilia* to describe the feeling of being attracted to all phenomena that are alive. But it was E. O. Wilson who grounded the concept deep in the biological tissue of all that is human. He makes the point that biophilia is an innate characteristic deeply woven into our DNA: a primal sense that we are of the family of life, and that our individual and collective well-being, in some felt way, is dependent on our deep relationship to everything that is alive. Our common bond is the drive we share with all of our fellow creatures to flourish to the full extent of our being.

That does not mean to diminish the dark and foreboding side of living reality. While we feel in our very biological being the kinship with life, also written into our genetic makeup is our fear of certain species whose own drive to flourish might threaten our own. Like other mammals, most of us either curl up or back off in the presence of snakes, spiders, and other creatures. Our genetic makeup contains a distinct memory of the harm they might cause. So, while our physiological and cognitive being is biophilia driven, it is also biophobia cautious. Both biophilia and biophobia are with us from the very beginning to the end of our lives.

In simple terms, E. O. Wilson defines biophilia as the "innate tendency to focus on life and life-like processes."[22] For Wilson, the biophilia connection partially rewrites the human story from a species perspective. The idea of "survival of the fittest," a phrase coined by the English philosopher Herbert Spencer and picked up by Darwin and inserted in the fifth edition of *On the Origin of Species* in 1869, has partially sullied Darwin's thesis ever since. The phrase suggested that nature is a struggle pitting the stronger over the weaker—a theory used to justify the argument that nature is "red in tooth and claw." Darwin, it should be noted, never intended that meaning to prevail.

E. O. Wilson takes the evolution of life to a better place, suggesting that our species' innate drive, like every other species, is to flourish rather than dominate, and that biophilia reflects our inherent inclination to empathize with our fellow creatures and the natural world. With a single stroke, he takes our species away from the struggle to master nature and to an innate genetic predisposition to affiliate with nature and by doing so, our species flourishes.

NATURE'S CLASSROOM

Nurturing biophilia begins at an early age. Italian researchers Giuseppe Barbiero and Chiara Marconato argue that exposing toddlers and young children
to nature ought to follow the same principles of engagement that make for
effective attachment in society. Since biophilia is about emotional connection
with nature, the parent, older sibling, or teacher needs to provide a safe place
that allows the child to wander about and experience nature in short intervals,
knowing that he or she can scamper back to the primary caretaker. Further explorations over longer time intervals and secure returns expand the child's safe
place, broadening the feeling of home to include the natural environment itself.

This caring temporal/spatial dynamic helps the child expand his or her
relationship beyond the primary caregivers to other life that abounds. This
is the way to move beyond "socializing" a child to "naturalizing" a child, and
erasing the artificial boundaries civilization has established between our species and the rest of our evolutionary kin. In this way, the biophilic connection
becomes the most radical transformation of human consciousness, virtually
eliminating the last remaining "other." That is, we come to experience our
fellow creatures—our evolutionary family—as our living relatives and nature
as our extended place and home.[23]

Nor is this just wishful thinking. A new educational phenomenon is sweeping the world—largely unnoticed in the media and public discourse—that is
shifting the worldview from socialization to naturalization. It goes by different names—Forest Schools, Environ Schools, Bush Kindergartens, Nature-
Havens—and they are popping up in Germany, Italy, Denmark, Sweden, the
United Kingdom, the United States, Canada, Australia, New Zealand, China,
and Japan. They are taking the next generation of toddlers and youngsters
along the path to biophilic consciousness with the hope of reconciling humanity's relationship with the rest of its evolutionary family.

Lest the skeptic think that these nature schools are fringe experiments,
there are already over two thousand forest schools operating in Germany. In the
United States, there were nearly six hundred nature-based preschools by 2020.[24]

Children of four to six years of age in small cohorts are taken out into nature with adult guides specially trained in biophilic pedagogy. The teachers
and children come to resemble more of a pack than a class. The outdoor class-
rooms remain open all year round, rain or shine, warm or cold, and the pack is
expected to show up every day. Often, the only abode is a small shack for storing provisions. There are no toilets and the children are taught how to distance

themselves for short moments to relieve themselves, but to stay within sight of the teacher. With rules in place not to wander beyond the range of the adult caregiver, the children are let loose to explore the open classroom of nature, freed to experience the flora and fauna, interact with the natural environment, tell of their experiences, ask questions of the guides, and share thoughts.

If there was any good news coming out of the coronavirus pandemic and the closure of schools and preschools around the world in 2020, it was the sudden interest in forest schools or nature schools. Educators and parents took notice of a possible antidote to remote learning and to exposure to the virus at the same time. With preschool and K–12 students isolated from any real-time socialization with their friends, and tempers boiling over in households with restless children isolated from their peers, families began to look to forest schools as a pragmatic remedy. Like her colleagues, pediatric occupational therapist Angela Hanscom noted that "more and more people are turning to the outdoors as a way to cope with the challenges of COVID." She cited the obvious that "it's much safer to be outdoors because the rates of transmission are far lower outside," adding that "children just aren't born to sit still for most of the day [in front of a screen]. It's basic neuroscience. They need to move."[25]

Traci Moren of Berkeley, California, the mother of two sons, ages five and ten, said that "forest school has been a game changer. . . . I don't think our family would survive all of this without forest school . . . now they get their enjoyment, are calmed being out in nature and the learning comes when you are moving around. . . . They are happy when they come home." Liana Chavarín, the founder of the Berkeley Forest School, which operates in scenic César Chávez Park overlooking San Francisco Bay, says that the benefit of nature schooling is that it "helps build resilience . . . children feel the land is their own."[26]

Forest school teachers say that nature as a classroom learning experience introduces children to the complex relationships in the natural world, and especially the ever-evolving and adapting interactivity going on in a system that is alive and pulsing with novel experiences at every moment. Joanna Ferraro, the founder of Oakland's Early Ecology Preschool, which operates in various parks in San Francisco's East Bay, observes that "nature is your co-teacher. You may have a plan, but then a cluster of ladybugs starts flying through the air and suddenly that's your new curriculum." Or we might change, if our interest is piqued, and "stop and watch a spider as long as we want."[27]

The natural environment as classroom experience is so utterly different from sitting alone in front of a sterile screen, interacting in virtual worlds. Chavarín says that being in nature's classroom, so packed with the drama of interactive life unfolding in new ways at every turn, provides a treasure trove of experiences, each worthy of inquiry. She notes that "anything children stumble upon in nature can become a springboard to learning. A dead bird can spark a discussion about the circle of life. The fog kissing one's face can turn into a lesson on the water cycle. A muddy stream can become the source of a clay-based art project. We harvest the creek for mud to make ceramics. Then we learn how to fire the clay."[28]

The biophilic instinct is strongest among toddlers and preschool children and diminishes as they move through the traditional educational system. In Australia, Tony Loughland and colleagues at the School of Education of the University of New South Wales conducted a study on "factors influencing young people's conceptions of environment." A total of 2,249 students between the ages of nine and seventeen in seventy schools were asked to ponder "what I think the word/term environment means." The short answer, according to researchers, is that the limiting conceptions were associated with the idea that the environment is some sort of object, while the more integrated conceptions were associated with an idea that there is some sort of relation between people and the environment.[29]

The most interesting finding was that younger students were likely to have a more relational focus, while older students tended to think of the environment more as an object, suggesting that a child is born with an innate biophilic orientation wired into his or her genetic makeup, only to be extinguished rather than nurtured by how he or she is taught to think and act on the environment through the traditional learning process. Toddlers and young children instinctively bond with other animals, converse with them, and emotionally identify with them as extended family—again, it's woven into our biological being.

Studies show that when children under the age of six dream, upward of 80 percent of their dreams are about animals.[30] Other studies show that young children are extremely curious about animals and express their curiosity openly, especially toward baby animals.[31] The biophilic connection has been observed in children even younger than two years of age.[32]

As to whether exposing children to nature as their classroom sets these youngsters behind their peers, the evidence in studies conducted over the past four decades suggests quite the opposite. Their verbal skills, attention span, mindfulness, critical thinking skills, and emotional maturation have generally been shown to exceed their peers'.

Why spend so much ink on how young children perceive nature as their primordial community and a nurturing place to which they are intrinsically attached only to have that instinctual biophilic sense erased, or at least suppressed, as their school experience increasingly teaches them that nature is a mere resource to expropriate and use to quench their hedonistic impulse to

consume? Again, we get back to two different ways to describe freedom. Very young children, in their descriptions of their experiences with nature, repeatedly describe their feeling of freedom, and that freedom is always expressed in terms of inclusivity, the feeling of intimate belonging to a familial lifeworld. As they grow up, their schooling increasingly centers on describing the world in objective terms while preparing students to think of freedom as being an autonomous agent and a self-contained island to oneself: to wit, freedom as exclusivity. The idea of freedom as autonomy and exclusivity was the perfect fit for the Age of Progress, with its underlying theme that everyone has an unalienable, God-given right to life, liberty, and property, with property being synonymous with happiness. That narrative has run its course and is now deadly on a rewilding Earth where resilience, not progress, is the only clear path to reconnecting with our natural community.

To reset the human story to fit the Age of Resilience, we will need to rethink the pedagogy by which we educate our children—to let the natural biophilic impulse embedded in a child's genetic makeup be expressed and flourish in preschool and continue to mature throughout the schooling experience, and later in careers and occupations. What's promising is a growing number of K–12 public school systems across the United States have formalized environmental courses across curriculum focusing on sustainability to introduce students to the natural world and, in the process, tweak their biophilic sensibilities. By 2016, eight of the twelve largest school districts in the United States, with 3.6 million children attending 5,726 schools, had embedded courses on the ecological sciences into the curriculum. Students are learning about climate change and engaging in fieldwork—often as part of their service-learning requirement—tracking wildlife, monitoring rainfall changes and drought and soil conditions, cleaning watersheds, measuring carbon footprint, and rejuvenating local ecosystems.[33]

Researchers at Stanford University analyzed more than one hundred peer-reviewed studies over a twenty-year period on the impact of introducing environmental studies into the K–12 curriculum. They found that aside from learning about the environment in the classroom and engaging in hands-on environmental research and stewardship in the community, students experience positive impacts such as "enhancing critical thinking skills to developing personal growth and life-building skills" including "confidence and leadership."[34] The studies also showed that environmental education, both in the classroom and the community, increased student civic engagement and personal environmental behavior.[35]

Nor does the environmental curriculum stop after K–12. Hundreds of universities in America offer environmental courses, often taught across disciplines, to introduce students to complex adaptive social/ecological systems approaches to studying and understanding the natural world.

Here is the point. The study of ecology was, at best, a tiny add-on in standard biology courses, worthy of perhaps a single classroom lecture fifty years ago. Today, in America and other countries, biology and the rest of the academic disciplines and accompanied curricula are increasingly being rethought and retaught from an ecological perspective.

School systems and universities are ramping up a paradigm shift in pedagogy that will prepare a younger generation to think and act as a species—a reframing of identity that they can take with them both in their work life, which will increasingly revolve around stewardship of the biosphere, and their civic life, where they will be called upon to serve in peer assemblies and help shape the governance of local bioregions.

A new extension of science is blooming. It's called "citizen science." Millions of people around the world volunteer their time as citizen scientists in over five hundred thousand local groups in civil society where they are monitoring wildlife, surveying biodiversity, taking measurements on air pollution and carbon footprint, checking water tables, restoring local watersheds, reforesting land, rehabilitating injured wildlife, studying the nutrient health of local soils, preparing climate disaster recovery plans, and participating in a host of other initiatives.[36]

Citizen science assemblages equip citizens with deeper field experience in the practices of ecology, dramatically democratizing scientific knowledge and expertise across bioregions. This fieldwork prepares present and future generations to engage more fully in the stewardship and governance of their regional ecosystems armed with the technical and practical expertise needed to provide counsel and make recommendations for legislative action and administrative review in their citizen peer assemblies.

The dramatic shift in pedagogy toward an ecological understanding of selfhood and our species' embeddedness in the natural world is exposing a younger generation to biophilia consciousness. That exposure unexpectedly took on wings in the midst of the COVID pandemic. As the pandemic stretched on, entrenchment indoors in an artificial environment soured into a feeling of despair. The virtual world was no longer as entertaining and comforting and was even becoming anathema. For millennials and Gen-Zs, whose virtual worlds have been much of their reality, the creeping feeling of being trapped in cyberspace, which offered up only simulations of reality, seemed too meager an existence. Rather unexpectedly and spontaneously, a growing number of millennials and Gen-Zs partially let go of their algorithmic existence and broke away to the outside—to feel the wind on their faces, gaze at the clouds crossing the sun, listen to the sounds of nature, and breathe in the life force of the earth, experiencing a liberation of sorts. All in all, a surprise and welcomed tonic.

The first year of COVID—2020—saw seven million more Americans, mostly younger people, visit the country's national parks. *The New York Times* opinion columnist Timothy Egan made note of the unanticipated rediscovery of nature, remarking that "the outdoors are crowded with refugees from the stifled indoors." Egan reflected on the turnaround, opining: "Building a fearsome lobby for the planet often starts with getting religion—that moment when the grays of the human-built environment give way to the technicolor of the world not of our making . . . it's not unlike falling in love."[37]

He wondered whether the new love affair might signal a "transition moment" in our species' reawakening of our primal home—the natural world.

It was Taylor Swift who spoke to the new hunger welling up inside her and her generation with the surprise release of two albums of songs she had composed during the COVID lockdown: *Folklore* and *Evermore*. The albums focused on her deep connection with nature growing up. And now her early biophilia consciousness as a child had been reawakened in the midst of the COVID crisis. *Folklore* received a Grammy Award for best album in 2021. But of far greater significance, she spoke for a younger generation suddenly rediscovering or discovering for the first time nature's breadth, perhaps signaling the beginnings of a disenchantment with the meager offerings of a virtual world and an awakening to the natural one.[38]

Taylor Swift's albums embracing nature seemed to come out of the blue. A 2017 scientific paper published in the *Journal of the Association of Psychological Sciences* documented that references to nature had all but disappeared in books, movie scripts, and, most of all, songs from the 1950s to the present as each succeeding generation increasingly grew up in virtual environments—first in front of the television screen, and later the computer screen. The researchers "scanned the lyrics of six thousand songs [since 1950] and found that the frequency of nature-themed words had declined by 63 percent."[39] Researchers concluded that as each generation retreated indoors interacting increasingly in virtual realities, nature became distant and even absent from their everyday experience.

Swift's rejoinder is a quiet call to her generation to feel the wind at their back and experience the sweetness of choosing to participate in the life force of nature. Her songs are a gentle ode to finding her generation's way back into a deep embrace of an animated Earth.

SOLVING THE EMPATHY PARADOX

E. O. Wilson, writing on the subject of "The Biological Basis of Morality" in *The Atlantic* magazine, specifically references the terms "empathy" and "attachment." Wilson pondered whether biophilia is imprinted into our species' genetic makeup. He suggested that "among traits with documented inheritability, those closest to moral aptitude are 'empathy' with the distress of others and certain processes of 'attachment' between infants and their caregivers."[40] But Wilson leaves the insight hanging.

Other scientists, however, have begun to explore the intimate relationship between empathy and attachment behavior in describing the biophilia connection human beings have with other animals, if not nature at large, but with a qualification. Human empathy, in this instance, is truncated or "asymmetric empathy," because unlike human-to-human empathy, which is a shared emotion, asymmetric empathy toward another creature cannot be a shared experience, even if that creature is able to cue into the emotional state of the human being.[41] Even when other animals—particularly dogs—are able to perceive human emotions, their experience of them is different. Nevertheless, it doesn't take away our species' ability to empathize, to feel the suffering and struggle of our fellow creatures to flourish as if it were our own struggle, and to show our compassion by acts of care.

The video of a polar bear and her cub being stranded on a small sliver of ice in the Arctic Ocean, victims of a changing climate, touched the heartstrings of millions of people around the world. They felt the bears' plight as their own. More recently, the dramatic rescue in Australia of a baby koala burned and singed by a wildfire brought on by climate change and caught on video was emotionally felt by millions of people. Most everyone has similar stories to tell, whether it's empathizing with an abused dog or comforting an injured bird. Biophilia is the next evolution of empathic consciousness.

While empathic extension is at the heart of biophilia consciousness, there is a paradox that lies deeply embedded in the evolution of empathy that, to my knowledge, has gone unexplored by historians, anthropologists, and philosophers over the years. I first came across the paradox in a seven-year period between 2003 and 2010 when I turned my attention to the role empathy has played in the historical development of our species. I had written about empathy in several previous books over a thirty-year period, but never in depth. This time, I decided to explore the evolution of empathy in greater detail—its anthropology and history, and its effect on the most salient aspects of society—our family and social life, our economy, modes of governance, and worldviews. Somewhere far along into the study, I became aware of the paradox and admit it shook me. Here's what I found and wrote in *The Empathic Civilization:*

> At the very core of the human story is the paradoxical relationship between empathy and entropy. Throughout history, ever more sophisticated infrastructure revolutions have brought together more expansive forms of communication, more intensive sources of energy, and more swift modes of mobility and logistics, creating ever more complex societies. More technologically advanced civilizations, in turn, have brought diverse people together, heightened empathic sensitivity, and expanded human consciousness. But these increasingly more complicated milieus require expropriating ever more swaths of nature's bounty, further depleting the earth's resources. The irony is that our growing empathic awareness has been made possible by an ever-greater consumption of the earth's energy and other resources, resulting in a dramatic deterioration of the health of the planet. We now face the haunting prospect of approaching global empathy in a highly energy-intensive, interconnected world, riding on the back of an escalating entropy bill that now threatens catastrophic climate change and our very existence. Resolving the empathy/entropy paradox will likely be the critical test of our species' ability to survive and flourish on Earth in the future. This will necessitate a fundamental rethinking of our philosophical, economic, and social models.[42]

We need not despair. Ideological consciousness that went in lockstep with the Age of Progress and the fossil fuel–based industrial infrastructure has exhausted its once dominant appeal. Biophilic consciousness is ascending, especially among the younger generation, with its promise of expanding the empathic drive to embrace the whole of the natural world. But a shift in consciousness of this magnitude will not come without backlash. Already, the remnants of older forms of consciousness are rising up, sensing a threat to whatever slight hold they still have on the human story. The birth of biophilic consciousness and the extension of the empathic impulse to our fellow creatures goes beyond economic and political considerations to the very core of how humanity perceives its essence.

I PARTICIPATE, THEREFORE I EXIST

If animist consciousness was anchored in blood ties, ancestor worship, and eternal return, religious consciousness around salvation in heaven, and ideological consciousness around material progress and technological immortality on Earth, what then is the foundational bedrock of biophilia consciousness? The universalization of biophilia takes the human narrative from a fixation with autonomy to an attachment to relationality. René Descartes's classic utterance, "I think, therefore I am," is already passé as a younger generation growing up in virtual and physical worlds conditioned by layers of laterally embedded interconnectivity are more disposed to the maxim, "I participate, therefore I exist." In this new era of ceaseless adaptivity among multiple interactive agencies, the concept of autonomy gives way to the principle of relationality. If the earth we inhabit is one of interlapping patterns rather than hard forces butting up against one another, the very idea that each of us is an autonomous agent seeking hard ground with which to protect our sovereignty in a world of competing agencies is all but dead and buried—so too our long-held ideas formed in the Age of Progress about the nature of equality.

In the Age of Progress, equality only bears weight as a derivative of autonomy. One can't champion equality without first believing in autonomy. To the extent that one believes himself or herself to be an autonomous agent, he or she will demand equality. It goes with the territory. If every individual's basic nature is to seek autonomy, the urge to be treated as an equal will inevitably follow as a vigilant shadow companion, always on guard to ensure that one's autonomy is secured.

Ideological consciousness is so tightly tethered to autonomy as to be inseparable. The whole of the Age of Progress rides atop this foundation. Thus, "human rights" becomes the marker by which autonomy is sought and secured. Every individual asserts the unalienable right to be autonomous in body, mind, and spirit. Human rights, then, if played out on a grand scale, would envision nearly eight billion autonomous human agents left undeterred and free to pursue their existence as they see fit with the proviso that they don't do harm to others' rights to autonomy.

But what if none of us are autonomous agents, either in the political sense or, deeper still, in the marrow of our biological being? What we have learned in the preceding chapters is that while each of us and every living creature is unique, not a single one of us is autonomous, at least not from a biological perspective. We are, every one of us, an embodiment of all the relationships within which we have been immersed over a lifetime from the emergence of the embryo to death's door and even beyond.

The interactive approach to understanding the nature of nature and human nature forces a basic rethink of the philosophical and political narrative that ran afoot the Age of Progress. If reality is a deeply participatory experience at every moment and throughout our lifetime, then one's experience of self can only be in relationship to the other. It follows naturally that the more rich, varied, and immersive the relationships, the deeper we become embedded in what we call "existence."

Biophilic consciousness is the deepest expression of equality—not equality born of autonomy, but of inclusivity. The purest expression of equality comes not from recognition afforded in legal charters and declarations but by the simplest acts of empathy. Deeply feeling another's struggle to flourish as if it were one's own creates the most intimate bond—the feeling of oneness on life's journey. The philosopher Martin Buber put it best. In such moments, there is no "mine and thine," but only "I and thou."[43] The empathic embrace is the ultimate political leveler. It casts aside every differentiation, leaving only bonded companions.

The evolution of empathy over history is characterized by the increasing elimination of "the other" until there is only "one for all and all for one." Within this context, the evolution of empathy and the evolution of equality are inseparable. We, "the body politic," become immersed in one another's lives at the most basic political level—the communities to which we are attached. Our empathic engagement—that is, our biophilia consciousness—becomes the sensibility by which we steward rather than merely manage the life force of that small part of the earth's biosphere where we live out our existence.

In the Age of Progress, we came to regard individual sovereignty as the basis of democracy, although they are not a comfortable fit. If everyone is truly sovereign and an island to themselves, and not beholden to others, in what regard would they hold democracy? Why bend to any other sovereign's will? It's the ability to recognize oneself in the other that animates democracy. Empathy is the binding element of democracy. If empathy is the deepest expression of equality, then it follows that it is also the emotional spark of democracy.

The empathic reach has traveled alongside the evolution of democracy at every stage of its development. The more empathic the culture, the more democratic its values and governing protocols. The less empathic the culture, the more totalitarian its values and governing institutions. All of this seems obvious, which makes it all the more inexplicable how little attention is given over to the relationship between empathy and democratic processes in the governing of society. The extension from representative democracy to distributed peerocracy and from sovereign governance to extended bioregional governance will likely succeed to the extent that the body politic embraces an empathic biophilia consciousness.

The idea of resilience, from an empathic perspective, is also quite different from how we have been accustomed to thinking of the term in the past. It's worth reemphasizing that being resilient traditionally has meant having the moral character to bounce back from misfortune and personal tragedy and recover one's autonomy. Translated, that means having the physical, mental, and emotional stamina to restore one's selfhood, rather than being beholden to others or life's circumstances or simply cast adrift. Resilience means not being vulnerable to destabilizing external circumstances, whatever their origins—but rather, being strong.

For the relational self, resilience comes from being open and vulnerable to "the other" rather than being self-contained and autonomous. It's openness to sharing life-affirming experiences that creates a rich web of relationships that strengthens one's own resilience. Biophilia consciousness extends one's deep participation to the whole of nature, letting its life-affirming force shore us up and take us along with the flow of life's passage.

This notion of resilience is not a recent revelation. Two centuries before E. O. Wilson introduced the concept of biophilia consciousness, the great German philosopher and scientist Johann Wolfgang von Goethe offered up biophilia consciousness as a counternarrative to Newton's sterile vision of a dead, rational, and mechanistic universe. Goethe believed that one's selfhood and resilience is a composite of the relationships one experiences that weave him or her into the fabric of life. He wrote, "We are surrounded and embraced by her [nature]—incapable of stepping out of her, incapable of penetrating deeper into her."[44]

Goethe was awed by the simple fact that every creature is unique yet connected in a single unity, noting that "each one of her [nature] creations has its own character . . . that all together make one." Goethe experienced nature as ever changing, continually in flux, always evolving, and creating ever new realities. Unlike the rational scientists of the period, Goethe's nature was not fixed and unchanging but, rather, pulsing with novelty and replete with surprises and synergies. In short, brimming with aliveness. He observed that:

"For permanence she [nature] has no use, and puts her curse on all that stands still. . . . She spits forth her creatures out of the Nothing and does not tell them whence they come and whither they go. Let them run; she knows the course."[45]

Goethe felt the empathic experience centuries before the feeling had a name. He wrote, "To find my way into the condition of others, to sense the specific mode of any human existence and to partake of it with pleasure" is to affirm the oneness of life.[46] Reflecting on his own life and times, he concluded that the "beautiful feeling that only mankind together is the true man, and that the single individual can be joyful and happy only when it has the courage to feel itself as part of one."[47]

For Goethe, "being one" didn't stop at the edge of our species, but rather, extended to all of nature. Goethe gave us the earliest read on what today we call biophilia—empathizing with all of life. Our individual resilience draws from our biophilia embeddedness. It's the realization of that indestructible bond that makes us resilient to the misfortunes that come our way.

Bear in mind that empathy is not just an emotive feeling but a cognitive experience that organizes one's thinking about the very nature of existence and one's relationship to it. We've each come to know about our existence by experiencing the other. If there were no others, there would be no reference by which to make comparisons or even understand that one is alive and truly exists. Our very existence is only validated by the other.

Our empathic neurocircuitry is continuously prodding us to transcend ourselves, to experience life, and to use that experience to make connections and adjust to the world around us. We know the importance of empathy, because were it absent in our neurocircuitry we would not be able to feel the fragility of another person's life and their drive to flourish. It's at these moments that we come to understand the awe of existence. And without awe we would have no way to wonder. And without wonder, we would be absent imagination. And without imagination, we would not be able to experience transcendence. And without the ability to transcend ourselves, we would not be able to empathize with another. This is the great interactive ensemble by which we know our existence. This ensemble is not experienced linearly, but rather, as a whole. Awe, wonder, imagination, and transcendence, brought on by the triggering of the empathic drive, allow each of us to continuously reach beyond ourselves in search of the meaning of existence. These are the fundamental qualities bound up in the empathic impulse. They are what makes each of us human.

In a sense, the search for meaning is with us at every moment of our lives, whether consciously thought about in that way or not. To the extent that the empathic impulse is nurtured, one's life is experienced and lived more thoroughly. We know this to be true because when we look back on our lives at the end, the most vivid experiences that come to mind, at least the ones that give our lives meaning, are the moments of empathic embrace—they are the markers of our search for personal meaning.

Think of the great philosophers of the Enlightenment and modern era who viewed bodily experience as inconsequential at best and corrupting at worst, preferring to cast their lot with mathematical certainty and pure reason rather than empathic transcendence as the alpha and omega of human existence. This misguided view of the essence of our humanity has done untold damage to our collective psyche and even greater damage to the natural world and the prospects of our fellow creatures.

Thankfully, these perverse ideas about the nature of human nature are fast losing currency because we are now waking up to where they have led civilization—a sure sign that our thinking about how our species navigates its journey has begun to turn around. We can see it in the soul-searching rethinking currently going on in the scientific community about how best to approach the deepest questions about the meaning of existence and how our species fits in. In a way, the new approach to scientific exploration and explanation that comes under the rubric of complex adaptive social-ecological systems is a testimonial to the way we are reconditioning our thinking about cognition. Recent studies of how systems thinkers think find that they "express an elevated capacity for the allocentric components of cognitive and affective empathy."[48]

In the Age of Resilience, we will need to deepen our empathic drive and reach out to the next stage of empathic extension—a biophilia consciousness that brings our species back into the family of life. The litmus test will be how we nurture and prepare our children and they their children to let the sense of awe awaken, even to the terrifying ways the earth is convulsing. That renewed sense of awe, although frightening, is also potentially liberating. If met head-on, it can trigger a new and more enveloping sense of wonder, spark our collective imagination, ready us to explore new paths toward adapting to nature's calling, and become resilient—to not just survive but to flourish in unexpected ways with our extended evolutionary family.

COMING HOME

We are the great wanderers of history, cast off on a thousand and one journeys over continents and oceans, braving treacherous climactic disturbances and perils of every kind, in a restless search of our place, our attachment in the world. Our outsized brain atop a bipedal body has been both our bane and our blessing. If any species on Earth deserves to be thought of as an anomaly, it most certainly is us. No other species, to our knowledge, is consumed with the question of the "why of things," although all our species' relatives are well equipped to manage the "how of things." Why the empathic impulse deeply embedded in our neurocircuitry? Why, of all the creatures, do we alone experience awe and wonderment and know of our own mortality?

We've come to believe that beyond ourselves is simply inchoate matter—resources—whose existence takes on import only in relation to our hedonist drives and gratifications. Still, the empathic pulse beats relentlessly in our neurocircuitry, surfacing repeatedly during our individual lifetimes and expanding outward in historical periods to embrace ever larger numbers of our species, only to fall back again, taking us into darkness.

What keeps us going if it's not to find our place of secure attachment in this world? What does it mean to be burdened by such angst? If alien beings were to look in on us and witness our plight, they might likely observe that our most unusual trait is our search for universal intimacy, a term that might seem like a contradiction. How can one experience both universality and deep intimacy at the same time? Yet, that appears to be our cross to bear or, to turn it around, perhaps a transcendent gift of incalculable weight.

The journey has been long, exhilarating, and tortuous at times, and now, at the very moment where we sense the end of our earthly existence, we are beginning to find our way home. We are awakening as a species to biophilia consciousness, the feeling and experience of universal intimacy, of being one with the life force of the earth.

Owen Barfield, a British philosopher in the 20th century, captured the essence and drama of the human saga, cutting it into three decisive stages, each marked by a foundational change in human consciousness along with the adoption of a new worldview.

Our forager-hunter ancestors felt little differentiation from their fellow species. They lived their lives in deep participation with the natural world, continually adapting to the immediacy of the earth's rhythms, seasons, and cycles. They lived communally, organizing their social life in cohorts rather than hierarchies. They saw the world with animist eyes. They experienced their fellow creatures as related spirits whose existence was little differentiated from their own and even deeply intertwined. Animist consciousness brooked no place for what later generations would come to see as "history," being content with the eternal return of annual and seasonal cycles.

As there was little differentiation in roles, with communal life shared and with no surpluses to dispose of that might give rise to distinctions and hierarchies, selfhood remained largely undeveloped. They lived as a communal "we" rather than a collection of individualized selves in what psychologists today might call an "undifferentiated, oceanic oneness." Their consciousness was lived out in a duality of biophilia and biophobia commensurate with their deep participation in nature.

The journey since has taken our species into the Neolithic era of primitive agriculture and pastoralization and, later, the great hydraulic agricultural civilizations and more recently the Industrial Age, ultimately separating our species from nature, which came to be thought of as a passive reserve of resources of little value until expropriated and transformed into useful goods by our hands. Today, our species lives in ever more integrative societies made up of more differentiated skills and division of labor embedded in more extensive infrastructures, servicing billions of human beings, all living side by side, increasingly walled off from the rest of the world. Currently, the average American spends 90 percent of their day indoors—often in artificially cooled and warmed temperatures with electric lighting—far removed from the natural world our ancestors, living as hunter-gatherers, called home for upward of 95 percent of our species' existence on Earth.[49]

The sense of security living in a second artificially contrived environment of our own making, and now even in virtual worlds and the metaverse, was always an illusion. We alienated ourselves from our ancestral abode, and deceived ourselves into believing we had secured an autonomous existence, only to experience the price of our folly—the entropy bill brought on by global warming emissions and the sixth extinction of life in Earth's history. Still, there is a lesson here.

Climate change and increasing global pandemics have taught us that everything we do in this world intimately affects everything else and vice versa. We have become aware that no human being is an island to themselves, an autonomous agent acting on the world but, rather, dependent, one way or another, on every other living agency and the dynamic of the earth's spheres for our existence. This nonnegotiable reality has been a driving force in the furthering of biophilic consciousness—the feeling of deep empathic resonance with life—doubly so now that our very future is in question.

Barfield believed that our species is on the cusp of a third great stage of human consciousness—a reassertion of our kinship with the natural world. But this time around, the biophilic empathic leap is a self-aware choice to re-participate wholly and unreservedly with the rest of life on the planet . . . to experience universal intimacy. This comes not out of blind superstition but, rather, out of a deep empathic, mindful, and cognitive understanding of our abiding attachment to life. It is a long journey of epic proportions that is bringing our species back home once again, grounded and hopefully renewed and ready for the great struggle before us of reanimating the breath of life. The earth beckons.

ACKNOWLEDGMENTS

I began researching the critical themes in *The Age of Resilience* in 2013 and have spent the better part of eight years immersed in the research. Books are always a collaborative adventure. In this regard, I'd like to especially acknowledge the editorial assistance of Claudia Salvador, who serves as chief of staff of our various endeavors. Claudia's contribution has been immeasurable, from researching, categorizing, and aligning literally thousands of journal articles, studies, and reports, to overseeing the voluminous endnoting process. Claudia's wise and insightful editorial suggestions appear throughout the book and have helped refine the final work.

Thanks to Daniel Christensen, our office's former chief of staff, for his contributions in the early research stages that went into the book, as well as to Joey Bilyk for his assistance in the final stages. I'd also like to extend my appreciation to Jon Cox for his deep dive into the mechanics of the manuscript and his editorial suggestions for streamlining the book.

I'd like to thank my domestic literary agent, Meg Thompson, for her support and wise counsel throughout the process, and for keeping the book on track. Also, I'd like to thank my foreign literary agent, Sandy Hodgman, for liaising with our foreign publishers and ensuring a wide global audience for the book.

Many thanks, also, to Kevin Reilly for shepherding the manuscript through the various editing stages leading up to publication, eliminating roadblocks, making suggestions along the way, and keeping the book on track. Also, thanks to Rima Weinberg for her astute editing in the final stages.

I'd also like to acknowledge my editor, Tim Bartlett at St. Martin's Press, for his enthusiastic support of the project and his personal commitment to bring the critical themes of the book to the reading public. Having an editor who cares deeply about the existential crises facing humanity at this seminal point in our species' history has been a source of great encouragement.

Finally, as always, I'd like to thank my wife, Carol Grunewald, above all, for her input to the story lines and content and the numerous conversations we've shared over the years, which helped shape my own thinking in approaching this project.

NOTES

INTRODUCTION

1. Vivek V. Venkataraman, Thomas S. Kraft, and Nathaniel J. Dominy, "Hunter-Gatherer Residential Mobility and the Marginal Value of Rainforest Patches," *Proceedings of the National Academy of Sciences* 114, no. 12 (March 6, 2017): 3097, https://doi.org/10.1073/pnas.1617542114.

2. Marie-Jean-Antoine-Nicolas Caritat, Marquis de Condorcet, *Outlines of an Historical View of the Progress of the Human Mind* (Philadelphia: M. Carey, 1796), https://oll.libertyfund.org/titles/1669%20 (accessed May 11, 2019).

3. *The Bible: Authorized King James Version with Apocrypha* (Oxford: Oxford University Press Oxford World Classics, 2008), 2.

4. Nicholas Wade, "Your Body Is Younger Than You Think," *New York Times*, August 2, 2005, https://www.nytimes.com/2005/08/02/science/your-body-is-younger-than-you-think.html; Ron Milo and Robert B. Phillips, *Cell Biology by the Numbers* (New York: Garland Science, 2015), 279.

5. Wade, "Your Body Is Younger Than You Think."

6. Helmut Haberl, Karl-Heinz Erb, Fridolin Krausmann, Veronika Gaube, Alberte Bondeau, Christoph Plutzar, Simone Gingrich, Wolfgang Lucht, and Marina Fischer-Kowalski, "Quantifying and Mapping the Human Appropriation of Net Primary Production in Earth's Terrestrial Ecosystems," *Proceedings of the National Academy of Sciences* 104, no. 31 (2007): 12942–12947, https://www.pnas.org/doi/pdf/10.1073/pnas.0704243104; Fridolin Krausmann et al., "Global Human Appropriation of Net Primary Production Doubled in the 20th Century," *Proceedings of the National Academy of Sciences* 110, no. 25 (June 2013): 10324–10329, https://doi.org/10.1073/pnas.1211349110.

7. Krausmann et al., "Global Human Appropriation of Net Primary Production Doubled in the 20th Century."

CHAPTER 1: MASKS, VENTILATORS, AND TOILET PAPER

1. Adam Smith, *An Inquiry into the Nature and Causes of the Wealth of Nations* (Oxford: Oxford University Press, 1976) (original work published 1776), 454.

2. Alex T. Williams, "Your Car, Toaster, Even Washing Machine, Can't Work Without Them. And There's a Global Shortage," *New York Times*, May 14, 2021, https://www

.nytimes.com/2021/05/14/opinion/semicondctor-shortage-biden-ford.html?referringSource
=articleShare.

3. "Enhanced Execution, Fresh Portfolio of Exciting Vehicles Drive Ford's Strong Q1 Profitability, As Trust in Company Rises," Ford Motor Company, April 28, 2021, https://s23.q4cdn.com/799033206/files/doc_financials/2021/q1/Ford-1Q2021-Earnings -Press-Release.pdf.

4. Williams, "Your Car, Toaster, Even Washing Machine, Can't Work Without Them."

5. William Galston, "Efficiency Isn't the Only Economic Virtue," *Wall Street Journal*, March 10, 2020.

6. Ibid.

7. Marco Rubio, "We Need a More Resilient American Economy," *New York Times*, April 20, 2020.

8. Ibid.

9. "Rethinking Efficiency," *Harvard Business Review*, 2019, https://hbr.org/2019/01 /rethinking-efficiency.

10. Roger Martin, "The High Price of Efficiency," *Harvard Business Review* (January– February 2019), 42–55.

11. Ibid.

12. Annette McGivney, "'Like Sending Bees to War': The Deadly Truth Behind Your Almond Milk Obsession," *The Guardian*, January 8, 2020, https://www.theguardian .com/environment/2020/jan/07/honeybees-deaths-almonds-hives-aoe; Selina Bruckner, Nathalie Steinhauer, S. Dan Aurell, Dewey Caron, James Ellis, et al., "Loss Management Survey 2018–2019 Honey Bee Colony Losses in the United States: Preliminary Results," Bee Informed Partnership, https://beeinformed.org/wp-content/uploads/2019 /11/2018_2019-Abstract.pdf (accessed June 23, 2021).

13. Tom Philpott and Julia Lurie, "Here's the Real Problem with Almonds," *Mother Jones*, April 15, 2015, https://www.motherjones.com/environment/2015/04/real-problem-almonds/; Almond Board of California, About Almonds and Water, n.d., https://www.almonds.com/sites /default/files/content/attachments/about_almonds_and_water_-_september_2015_1.pdf.

14. Almond Board of California, California Almond Industry Facts, 2016, https:// www.almonds.com/sites/default/files/2016_almond_industry_factsheet.pdf.

15. Hannah Devlin and Ian Sample, "Yoshinori Ohsumi Wins Nobel Prize in Medicine for Work on Autophagy," *The Guardian*, October 3, 2016, https://www.theguardian .com/science/2016/oct/03/yoshinori-ohsumi-wins-nobel-prize-in-medicine.

16. "The Nobel Prize in Physiology or Medicine 2016," Nobel Assembly at Karolinska Institutet, 2016, https://www.nobelprize.org/uploads/2018/06/press-34.pdf.

17. Pat Lee Shipman, "The Bright Side of the Black Death," *American Scientist* 102, no. 6 (2014): 410, https://doi.org/10.1511/2014.111.410.

CHAPTER 2: TAYLORISM AND THE LAWS OF THERMODYNAMICS

1. Charlie Chaplin, *Modern Times* (United Artists, 1936).

2. Samuel Haber, *Efficiency and Uplift: Scientific Management in the Progressive Era, 1890–1920* (Chicago: University of Chicago Press, 1965), 62; Martha Bensley Bruère and Robert W. Bruère, *Increasing Home Efficiency* (New York: Macmillan, 1912), 291.

3. Christine Frederick, "The New Housekeeping: How It Helps the Woman Who Does Her Own Work," *Ladies' Home Journal*, September–December 1912, 13, 23.

4. Christine Frederick, *The New Housekeeping: Efficiency Studies in Home Management* (Doubleday, Page, 1913), 30.

5. Mary Pattison, *The Business of Home Management: The Principles of Domestic Engineering* (New York: R. M. McBride, 1918); Haber, *Efficiency and Uplift,* 62.

6. Haber, *Efficiency and Uplift,* 62.

7. William Hughes Mearns, "Our Medieval High Schools: Shall We Educate Children for the Twelfth or the Twentieth Century?" *Saturday Evening Post*, March 12, 1912; Raymond E. Callahan, *Education and the Cult of Efficiency: A Study of the Social Forces That Have Shaped the Administration* (Chicago: University of Chicago Press, 1964), 50.

8. Maude Radford Warren, "Medieval Methods for Modern Children," *Saturday Evening Post*, March 12, 1912; Callahan, *Education and the Cult of Efficiency,* 50.

9. Wayne Au, "Teaching Under the New Taylorism: High-Stakes Testing and the Standardization of the 21st Century Curriculum," *Journal of Curriculum Studies* 43, no. 1 (2011): 25–45, https://doi.org/10.1080/00220272.2010.521261.

10. Samuel P. Hays, *Conservation and the Gospel of Efficiency: The Progressive Conservation Movement, 1890–1920* (Pittsburgh: University of Pittsburgh Press, 1999), 127.

11. "Open for Business and Not Much Else: Analysis Shows Oil and Gas Leasing Out of Whack on BLM Lands." Wilderness Society, n.d., https://www.wilderness.org/articles/article/open-business-and-not-much-else-analysis-shows-oil-and-gas-leasing-out-whack-blm-lands.

12. "In the Dark: The Hidden Climate Impacts of Energy Development on Public Lands," Wilderness Society, n.d., https://www.wilderness.org/sites/default/files/media/file/In%20the%20Dark%20Report_FINAL_Feb_2018.pdf (accessed April 16, 2021); Matthew D. Merrill, Benjamin M. Sleeter, Philip A. Freeman, Jinxun Liu, Peter D. Warwick, and Bradley C. Reed, "Federal Lands Greenhouse Gas Emissions and Sequestration in the United States: Estimates for 2005–14. Scientific Investigations Report 2018–5131," U.S. Geological Survey, U.S. Department of the Interior, 2018.

13. Chris Arsenault, "Only 60 Years of Farming Left If Soil Degradation Continues," *Scientific American*, December 5, 2014, https://www.scientificamerican.com/article/only-60-years-of-farming-left-if-soil-degradation-continues/.

14. "Fact Sheet: What on Earth Is Soil?" Natural Resources Conservation Service, 2003, https://www.nrcs.usda.gov/Internet/FSE_DOCUMENTS/nrcs144p2_002430.pdf.

15. Robin McKie, "Biologists Think 50 Percent of Species Will Be Facing Extinction by the End of the Century," *The Guardian*, February 25, 2017, https://www.theguardian.com/environment/2017/feb/25/half-all-species-extinct-end-century-vatican-conference (accessed August 22, 2020).

16. Yadigar Sekerci and Sergei Petrovskii, "Global Warming Can Lead to Depletion of Oxygen by Disrupting Phytoplankton Photosynthesis: A Mathematical Modelling Approach," *Geosciences* 8, no. 6 (June 2018): 201, https://doi.org/10.3390/geosciences8060201; "Research Shows Global Warming Disaster Could Suffocate Life on Planet Earth," University of Leicester, December 1, 2015, https://www2.le.ac.uk/offices/press/press-releases/2015/december/global-warming-disaster-could-suffocate-life-on-planet-earth-research-shows.

17. Abrahm Lustgarten, "The Great Climate Migration," *New York Times Magazine*,

July 23, 2020, https://www.nytimes.com/interactive/2020/07/23/magazine/climate
-migration.html (accessed August 22, 2020).

18. James E. M. Watson et al., "Protect the Last of the Wild," *Nature* 563 (2018): 27–40, http://dx.doi.org/10.1038/d41586-018-07183-6.

19. John Herman Randall, *The Making of the Modern Mind* (Cambridge: Houghton Mifflin, 1940), 241; quotation by René Descartes in René Descartes, *Rules for the Direction of the Mind* (1684).

20. Ibid., 241–242.

21. René Descartes, *Treatise of Man*, translated by Thomas Steele Hall (Cambridge, MA: Harvard University Press, 1972).

22. Daniel Everett, "Beyond Words: The Selves of Other Animals," *New Scientist*, July 8, 2015, https://www.newscientist.com/article/dn27858-beyond-words-the-selves -of-other-animals/ (accessed July 31, 2020).

23. Gillian Brockwell, "During a Pandemic, Isaac Newton Had to Work from Home, Too. He Used the Time Wisely," *Washington Post*, March 12, 2020, https://www.washingtonpost .com/history/2020/03/12/during-pandemic-isaac-newton-had-work-home-too-he-used -time-wisely/ (accessed July 20, 2020).

24. "Philosophiæ Naturalis Principia Mathematica (MS/69)" (University of Cambridge Digital Library, n.d.), https://cudl.lib.cam.ac.uk/view/MS-ROYALSOCIETY-00069/7.

25. National Aeronautics and Space Administration, "More on Newton's Law of Universal Gravitation," *High Energy Astrophysics Science Archive Research Center*, May 5, 2016, https://imagine.gsfc.nasa.gov/features/yba/CygX1_mass/gravity/more.html (accessed July 20, 2020).

26. Isaac Newton, *Newton's Principia: The Mathematical Principles of Natural Philosophy* (New York: Daniel Adee, 1846).

27. Norriss S. Hetherington, "Isaac Newton's Influence on Smith's Natural Laws in Economics," *Journal of the History of Ideas* 44, no. 3 (1983): 497–505, http://www .jstor.com/stable/2709178.

28. Martin J. Klein, "Thermodynamics in Einstein's Thought: Thermodynamics Played a Special Role in Einstein's Early Search for a Unified Foundation of Physics," *Science* 157, no. 3788 (August 4, 1967): 509–513, https://doi.org/10.1126/science.157.3788.509.

29. Mark Crawford, "Rudolf Julius Emanuel Clausius," ASME, April 11, 2012, https:// www.asme.org/topics-resources/content/rudolf-julius-emanuel-clausius.

30. National Aeronautics and Space Administration, "Meteors & Meteorites," *NASA Science*, December 19, 2019, https://solarsystem.nasa.gov/asteroids-comets-and-meteors /meteors-and-meteorites/in-depth/ (accessed August 23, 2020).

31. Brian Greene, "That Famous Equation and You," *New York Times*, September 30, 2005.

32. Nahid Aslanbeigui, "Pigou, Arthur Cecil (1877–1959)," in *The New Palgrave Dictionary of Economics*, edited by Steven N. Durlauf and Lawrence E. Blume (London: Palgrave Macmillan, 2008).

33. Erwin Schrödinger, *What Is Life?* (New York: Macmillan, 1947), 72–75.

34. G. Tyler Miller, *Energetics, Kinetics and Life: An Ecological Approach* (Belmont: Wadsworth, 1971), 293.

35. Ibid., 291.

36. Elias Canetti, *Crowds and Power* (London: Gollancz, 1962), 448.

37. "James Watt," *Encyclopedia Britannica*, https://www.britannica.com/biography/James-Watt (accessed August 23, 2020).

38. Margaret Schabas, "Alfred Marshall, W. Stanley Jevons, and the Mathematization of Economics," *Isis, A Journal of the History of Science Society* 80, no. 1 (March 1989): 60–72, http://www.jstor.com/stable/234344.

39. William Stanley Jevons, *The Progress of the Mathematical Theory of Political Economy* (J Roberts, 1875), https://babel.hathitrust.org/cgi/pt?id=ien.35556020803433&view=1up&seq=22&skin=2021 (accessed July 25, 2022).

40. William Stanley Jevons, *The Theory of Political Economy*, 3rd ed. (London: Macmillan, 1888).

41. Ibid., vii.

42. Frederick Soddy, *Matter and Energy* (New York: H. Holt, 1911), 10–11.

43. Ilya Prigogine, "Only an Illusion," *Tanner Lectures on Human Values*, December 18, 1982, https://tannerlectures.utah.edu/_resources/documents/a-to-z/p/Prigogine84.pdf (accessed August 23, 2020).

44. Ibid., 46.

45. Ibid., 50.

46. Ibid.

CHAPTER 3: THE REAL WORLD

1. "Historical Estimates of World Population," U.S. Census Bureau, July 5, 2018, https://www.census.gov/data/tables/time-series/demo/international-programs/historical-est-worldpop.html (accessed August 24, 2020).

2. Helmut Haberl, Karl-Heinz Erb, Fridolin Krausmann, Veronika Gaube, Alberte Bondeau, Christoph Plutzar, Simone Gingrich, Wolfgang Lucht, and Marina Fischer-Kowalski, "Quantifying and Mapping the Human Appropriation of Net Primary Production in Earth's Terrestrial Ecosystems," *Proceedings of the National Academy of Sciences* 104, no. 31 (2007), https://www.pnas.org/doi/pdf/10.1073/pnas.0704243104.

3. Fridolin Krausmann, Karl-Heinz Erb, Simone Gingrich, Helmut Haberl, Alberte Bondeau, Veronika Gaube, Christian Lauk, Christoph Plutzar, and Timothy D. Searchinger, "Global Human Appropriation of Net Primary Production Doubled in the 20th Century," *Proceedings of the National Academy of Sciences* 110, no. 25 (June 13, 2013), https://doi.org/10.1073/pnas.1211349110.

4. "What on Earth Is Soil?" United States Department of Agriculture Natural Resources Conservation Service, n.d., https://www.nrcs.usda.gov/wps/PA_NRCSConsumption/download?cid=nrcseprd994617&ext=pdf (accessed August 25, 2020).

5. Prabhu L. Pingali and Mark W. Rosegrant, "Confronting the Environmental Consequences of the Green Revolution in Asia," International Food Policy Research Institute, August 1994, http://citeseerx.ist.psu.edu/viewdoc/download?doi=10.1.1.80.3270&rep=rep1&type=pdf (accessed August 25, 2020).

6. Anju Bala, "Green Revolution and Environmental Degradation," *National Journal of Multidisciplinary Research and Development* 3, no. 1 (January 2018), http://www.nationaljournals.com/archives/2018/vol3/issue1/2-3-247.

7. "The Hidden Costs of Industrial Agriculture," Union of Concerned Scientists,

August 24, 2008, https://www.ucsusa.org/resources/hidden-costs-industrial-agriculture (accessed August 25, 2020).

8. Ibid.

9. Boyd A. Swinburn et al., "The Global Syndemic of Obesity, Undernutrition, and Climate Change: *The Lancet* Commission Report," *The Lancet* 393 (2019): 791–846, https://doi.org/10.1016/S0140-6736(18)32822-8.

10. Ibid.

11. Ibid.

12. Ibid.

13. Ibid.

14. Kevin E. Trenberth, "Changes in Precipitation with Climate Change," *Climate Research* 47 (March 2011): 123, https://doi.org/10.3354/cr00953.

15. Kim Cohen et al., "The ICS International Chronostratigraphic Chart," *Episodes* 36, no. 3 (September 1, 2013): 200–201, https://doi.org/10.18814/epiiugs/2013/v36i3/002.

16. "Healthy Soils Are the Basis for Healthy Food Production," Food and Agriculture Organization of the United Nations, March 26, 2015, http://www.fao.org/3/a-i4405e.pdf (accessed August 25, 2020).

17. David Wallinga, "Today's Food System: How Healthy Is It?" *Journal of Hunger and Environmental Nutrition* 4, no. 3–4 (December 2009): 251–281, https://doi.org/10.1080/19320240903336977.

18. Ibid.

19. Peter Dolton and Mimi Xiao, "The Intergenerational Transmission of Body Mass Index Across Countries," *Economics and Human Biology* 24 (February 2017): 140–152, https://doi.org/10.1016/j.ehb.2016.11.005.

20. Michelle J. Saksena et al., "America's Eating Habits: Food Away from Home," U.S. Department of Agriculture, September 2018, https://www.ers.usda.gov/webdocs/publications/90228/eib-196_ch8.pdf?v=3344.

21. Ibid.

22. "Antibiotic Resistance Threats in the United States, 2019," Centers for Disease Control and Prevention (2019), 18, http://dx.doi.org/10.15620/cdc:82532.

23. Ibid., vii.

24. Susan Brink, "Why Antibiotic Resistance Is More Worrisome Than Ever," NPR, May 14, 2020, https://www.npr.org/sections/goatsandsoda/2020/05/14/853984869/antibiotic-resistance-is-still-a-top-health-worry-its-a-pandemic-worry-too (accessed August 25, 2020).

25. "Drug-Resistant Infections: A Threat to Our Economic Future," World Bank, March 2017, viii, http://documents1.worldbank.org/curated/en/323311493396993758/pdf/final-report.pdf.

26. Ibid., 18.

27. Ibid.

28. "Bacterial Pneumonia Caused Most Deaths in 1918 Influenza Pandemic," U.S. National Institutes of Health, August 19, 2008, https://www.nih.gov/news-events/news-releases/bacterial-pneumonia-caused-most-deaths-1918-influenza-pandemic#:~:text=Bacterial%20Pneumonia%20Caused%20Most%20Deaths%20in%201918%20Influenza%20Pandemic,-Implications%20for%20Future&text=The%20majority%20of%20

deaths%20during,the%20National%20Institutes%20of%20Health (accessed August 25, 2020).

29. Morgan McFall-Johnsen, "These Facts Show How Unsustainable the Fashion Industry Is," World Economic Forum, January 31, 2020, https://www.weforum.org /agenda/2020/01/fashion-industry-carbon-unsustainable-environment-pollution/ (accessed August 31, 2020).

30. Kirsi Niinimäki et al., "The Environmental Price of Fast Fashion," *Nature Reviews* 1 (April 2020): 189–200, https://doi.org/10.1038/s43017-020-0039-9.

31. Ibid., 190.

32. "How Much Do Our Wardrobes Cost to the Environment?" World Bank, September 23, 2019, https://www.worldbank.org/en/news/feature/2019/09/23/costo-moda -medio-ambiente (accessed September 1, 2020); Rep. *Pulse of the Fashion Industry 2017.* Global Fashion Agenda & The Boston Consulting Group, 2017.

33. Niinimäki et al., "The Environmental Price of Fast Fashion."

34. Ibid., 191–193; "Chemicals in Textiles—Risks to Human Health and the Environment," Report from a Government Assignment, KEMI Swedish Chemicals Agency, 2014, https://www.kemi.se/download/18.6df1d3df171c243fb23a98f3/1591454110491 /rapport-6-14-chemicals-in-textiles.pdf.

35. Ibid., 195; Ellen MacArthur Foundation and Circular Fibres Initiative, "A New Textiles Economy: Redesigning Fashion's Future" (2017), https://emf.thirdlight.com /link/2axvc7eob8zx-za4ule/@/preview/1?o.

CHAPTER 4: THE GREAT DISRUPTION

1. "What Hath God Wrought?" Library of Congress, May 24, 2020, https://www .loc.gov/item/today-in-history/may-24 (accessed September 1, 2020).

2. Sebastian de Grazia, *Of Time, Work, and Leisure* (New York: Century Foundation, 1962), 41.

3. Ibid.

4. Reinhard Bendix, *Max Weber: An Intellectual Portrait* (Garden City: Anchor-Doubleday, 1962), 318.

5. Lewis Mumford, *Technics and Civilization* (New York: Harbinger, 1947), 13–14.

6. Daniel J. Boorstin, *The Discoverers* (New York: Random House, 1983), 38.

7. Mary Bellis, "The Development of Clocks and Watches over Time," *ThoughtCo.*, February 6, 2019, https://www.thoughtco.com/clock-and-calendar-history-1991475.

8. Jonathan Swift, *Gulliver's Travels: The Voyages to Lilliput and Brobdingnag* (Ann Arbor: University of Michigan Press, 1896) (original work published 1726), 48.

9. Alfred W. Crosby, *The Measure of Reality: Quantification in Western Europe, 1250–1600* (Cambridge: Cambridge University Press, 1996), 171.

10. Encyclopedia Britannica, "Linear Perspective," https://www.britannica.com/art /linear-perspective (accessed April 30, 2021).

11. Galileo Galilei, "The Assayer," in *Discoveries and Opinions of Galileo* (New York: Anchor Books, 1957) (original work published 1623).

12. Philipp H. Lepenies, *Art, Politics, and Development* (Philadelphia: Temple University Press, 2013), 48–50.

13. Walter J. Ong, *Orality and Literacy* (London: Routledge, 1982), 117.

14. Eric J. Hobsbawm, *Nations and Nationalism Since 1780: Programme, Myth, Reality* (Cambridge: Cambridge University Press, 1990), 60.

15. Tullio De Mauro, *Storia Linguistica Dell'Italia Unita* (Rome: Laterza, 1963).

16. Charles Killinger, *The History of Italy* (Westport, CT: Greenwood Press, 2002), 1; Massimo D'Azeglio, *I Miei Ricordi* (1891), 5.

17. Bob Barton, "The History of Steam Trains and Railways," Historic UK, n.d., https://www.historic-uk.com/HistoryUK/HistoryofBritain/Steam-trains-railways/ (accessed September 1, 2020).

18. Eric J. Hobsbawm, *The Age of Revolution, 1789–1848* (New York: Vintage Books, 1996), 298.

19. Warren D. TenHouten, *Time and Society* (Albany: State University of New York Press, 2015), 62.

CHAPTER 5: THE ULTIMATE HEIST

1. John Locke, *Two Treatises on Civil Government* (London: George Routledge and Sons, 1884) (original work published 1689), 207.

2. Ibid.

3. "The Critical Zone: National Critical Zone Observatory," The Critical Zone | National Critical Zone Observatory, https://czo-archive.criticalzone.org/national/research/the-critical-zone-1national/ (accessed April 30, 2021).

4. Renee Cho, Joan Angus, Sarah Fecht, and Shaylee Packer, "Why Soil Matters," State of the Planet, May 1, 2012, https://news.climate.columbia.edu/2012/04/12/why-soil-matters/.

5. Ibid.

6. Food and Agriculture Organization of the United Nations, *Livestock and Landscapes*, 2012, http://www.fao.org/3/ar591e/ar591e.pdf (accessed March 23, 2019), 1.

7. Ibid.

8. Geoff Watts, "The Cows That Could Help Fight Climate Change," BBC Future, August 6, 2019, https://www.bbc.com/future/article/20190806-how-vaccines-could-fix-our-problem-with-cow-emissions (accessed July 12, 2021).

9. Nicholas LePan, "This Is What the Human Impact on the Earth's Surface Looks Like," World Economic Forum, December 4, 2020, https://www.weforum.org/agenda/2020/12/visualizing-the-human-impact-on-the-earth-s-surface/ (accessed April 30, 2021).

10. "What's Driving Deforestation?" Union of Concerned Scientists, February 2016, https://www.ucsusa.org/resources/whats-driving-deforestation.

11. *USDA Coexistence Fact Sheets: Soybeans.* U.S. Department of Agriculture, 2015.

12. Wannes Hubau et al., "Asynchronous Carbon Sink Saturation in African and Amazonian Tropical Forests," *Nature* 579 (March 2020): 80–87.

13. Ibid.

14. Ibid.

15. Ibid.

16. Research and Markets, *World—Beef (Cattle Meat)—Market Analysis, Forecast, Size, Trends and Insights*, 2021.

17. Reportlinker, *Forestry and Logging Global Market Report 2021: COVID-19 Impact and Recovery to 2030*, 2020.

18. IMARC Group, *Soy Food Market: Global Industry Trends, Share, Size, Growth, Opportunity and Forecast 2021–2026*, 2021; Reportlinker, *Palm Oil Market Size, Share & Trends Analysis Report by Origin (Organic, Conventional), by Product (Crude, RBD, Palm Kernel Oil, Fractionated), by End Use, by Region, and Segment Forecasts, 2020–2027*, 2020.

19. M. Garside, "Topic: Mining," Statista, https://www.statista.com/topics/1143 /mining/ (accessed April 30, 2021).

20. Marvin S. Soroos, "The International Commons: A Historical Perspective," *Environmental Review* 12, no. 1 (Spring 1988): 1–22, https://www.jstor.org/stable/3984374.

21. Sir Walter Raleigh, "A Discourse of the Invention of Ships, Anchors, Compass, &c.," in *Oxford Essential Quotations*, edited by Susan Racliffe (2017), https://www .oxfordreference.com/view/10.1093/acref/9780191843730.001.0001/q-oro-ed5-00008718.

22. "The United Nations Convention on the Law of the Sea (A historical perspective)," United Nations, 1998, https://www.un.org/depts/los/convention_agreements/convention _historical_perspective.htm.

23. R. R. Churchill and A. V. Lowe, *The Law of the Sea*, vol. 1 (Oxford: Oxford University Press, 1983), 130; U.S. maritime limits & amp; Boundaries, https://nauticalcharts .noaa.gov/data/us-maritime-limits-and-boundaries.html#general-information (accessed August 21, 2021). Continental Shelf (Tunis. v. Libya) (International Court of Justice February 24, 1982). http://www.worldcourts.com/icj/eng/decisions/1982.02.24_conti nental_shelf.htm (accessed July 25, 2022).

24. Clive Schofield and Victor Prescott, *The Maritime Political Boundaries of the World* (Leiden: Martinus Nijhoff, 2004), 36; Food and Agriculture Organization of the United Nations, "The State of World Fisheries and Aquaculture 2020. Sustainability in Action," 2020, 94; "United Nations Convention on the Law of the Sea (UNCLOS)," Encyclopedia.com, https://www.encyclopedia.com/environment/energy-government-and -defense-magazines/united-nations-convention-law-sea-unclos (acessed May 20, 2021).

25. "Ocean Governance: Who Owns the Ocean?" *Heinrich Böll Stiftung: Brussels*, June 2, 2017, https://eu.boell.org/en/2017/06/02/ocean-governance-who-owns-ocean.

26. Enric Sala et al., "The Economics of Fishing the High Seas," *Science Advances* 4, no. 6 (June 2018); David Tickler, Jessica J. Meeuwig, Maria-Lourdes Palomares, Daniel Pauly, and Dirk Zeller, "Far from Home: Distance Patterns of Global Fishing Fleets," *Science Advances* 4, no. 8 (August 2018), https://doi.org/10.1126/sciadv.aar3279.

27. "Trawling Takes a Toll," *American Museum of Natural History*, n.d., https:// www.amnh.org/explore/videos/biodiversity/will-the-fish-return/trawling-takes-a-toll (accessed September 4, 2020).

28. Ibid. Andy Sharpless and Suzannah Evans, "Net Loss: How We Continually Forget What the Oceans Really Used to Be Like [Excerpt]," *Scientific American*, May 24, 2013, https://www.scientificamerican.com/article/shifting-baselines-in-ocean-fish -excerpt/ (accessed July 25, 2022).

29. Hilal Elver. "The Emerging Global Freshwater Crisis and the Privatization of Global Leadership." Essay. In *Global Crises and the Crisis of Global Leadership*, edited by Stephen Gill (Cambridge: Cambridge University Press, 2011).

30. Ibid.

31. Maude Barlow, *Whose Water Is It, Anyway?* (Toronto: ECW Press, 2019), 18.

32. "1 in 3 People Globally Do Not Have Access to Safe Drinking Water—UNICEF, WHO," World Health Organization, June 18, 2019, https://www.who.int/news/item /18–06–2019-1-in-3-people-globally-do-not-have-access-to-safe-drinking-water-unicef -who (accessed September 3, 2020).

33. "Water Privatization: Facts and Figures," Food and Water Watch, August 31, 2015, https://www.foodandwaterwatch.org/print/insight/water-privatization-facts-and -figures (accessed September 3, 2020).

34. Ibid.

35. Diamond v. Chakrabarty, 447 U.S. 3030 (1980).

36. Ibid.

37. Ibid.

38. "Genentech Goes Public." Genentech: Breakthrough Science, April 28, 2016, https://www.gene.com/stories/genentech-goes-public.

39. Keith Schneider, "Harvard Gets Mouse Patent, A World First," *New York Times*, April 13, 1988, A1.

40. Association for Molecular Pathology et al. v. Myriad Genetics, US 12–398 (2013).

41. Kelly Servick, "No Patent for Dolly the Cloned Sheep, Court Rules, Adding to Industry Jitters," *Science*, May 14, 2014, https://www.sciencemag.org/news/2014/05/no -patent-dolly-cloned-sheep-court-rules-adding-industry-jitters.

42. "Monsanto v. U.S. Farmers," a report by the Center for Food Safety (2005), 11, https://www.centerforfoodsafety.org/files/cfsmonsantovsfarmerreport11305.pdf.

43. Sheldon Krimsky, James Ennis, and Robert Weissman, "Academic-Corporate Ties in Biotechnology: A Quantitative Study," *Science, Technology, & Human Values* 16, no. 3 (July 1991).

44. Association for Molecular Pathology et al. v. Myriad Genetics.

45. Sergio Sismondo, "Epistemic Corruption, the Pharmaceutical Industry, and the Body of Medical Science," *Frontiers in Research Metrics and Analytics* 6 (2021), https://doi.org/10.3389/frma.2021.614013; Bernard Lo and Marilyn J. Field, *Conflict of Interest in Medical Research, Education, and Practice* (Washington, D.C.: National Academies Press, 2009), 84; Sharon Lerner, "The Department of Yes: How Pesticide Companies Corrupted the EPA and Poisoned America," *The Intercept*, June 30, 2021, https://theintercept.com/2021/06/30/epa-pesticides-exposure-opp/; Jack T. Pronk, S. Lee, J. Lievense, et al., "How to Set Up Collaborations Between Academia and In-dustrial Biotech Companies," *Nature Biotechnology* 33 (2015): 237–240, https://doi .org/10.1038/nbt.3171.

46. Carolyn Brokowski and Mazhar Adli, "CRISPR Ethics: Moral Consideration for Applications of a Powerful Tool," *Journal of Molecular Biology* 431, no. 1 (January 2019), https://www.ncbi.nlm.nih.gov/pmc/articles/PMC6286228/pdf/nihms973582.pdf.

47. Jon Cohen, "CRISPR, the Revolutionary Genetic 'Scissors,' Honored by Chemis-try Nobel," *Science*, October 7, 2020, https://www.sciencemag.org/news/2020/10/crispr -revolutionary-genetic-scissors-honored-chemistry-nobel#:~:text=This%20year's%20 Nobel%20Prize%20in,wheat%20to%20mosquitoes%20to%20humans (accessed Oc-tober 12, 2020); Martin Jinek, Krzysztof Chylinski, Ines Fonfara, Jennifer A. Doudna,

and Emmanuelle Charpentier, "A Programmable Dual-RNA–Guided DNA Endonuclease in Adaptive Bacterial Immunity," *Science* 337, no. 6096 (2012): 816–821, https://doi.org/10.1126/science.1225829.

48. Cohen, "CRISPR, the Revolutionary Genetic 'Scissors' Honored by Chemistry Nobel."

49. Dennis Normille, "Chinese Scientist Who Produced Genetically Altered Babies Sentenced to 3 Years in Jail," *ScienceMag*, December 30, 2019, https://www.sciencemag.org/news/2019/12/chinese-scientist-who-produced-genetically-altered-babies-sentenced-3-years-jail.

50. Katelyn Brinegar, Ali K. Yetisen, Sun Choi, Emily Vallillo, Guillermo U. Ruiz-Esparza, Anand M. Prabhakar, Ali Khademhosseini, and Seok-Hyun Yun, "The Commercialization of Genome-Editing Technologies," *Critical Reviews in Biotechnology* 37, no. 7 (2017): 924–932.

51. Brokowski and Adli, "CRISPR Ethics: Moral Considerations."

52. Mauro Salvemini, "Global Positioning System," in *International Encyclopedia of the Social & Behavioral Sciences*, 2nd ed., edited by James D. Wright (Amsterdam: Elsevier, 2015), 174–177.

53. Greg Milner, *Pinpoint: How GPS Is Changing Technology, Culture, and Our Minds* (New York: W. W. Norton, 2016).

54. Ibid.

55. Thomas Alsop, "Global Navigation Satellite System (GNSS) Device Installed Base Worldwide in 2019 and 2029," Statista, 2020, https://www.statista.com/statistics/1174544/gnss-device-installed-base-worldwide/#statisticContainer.

56. "Global Navigation Satellite System (GNSS) Market Size," Fortune Business Insights, 2020, https://www.fortunebusinessinsights.com/global-navigation-satellite-system-gnss-market-103433.

57. Ashik Siddique, "Getting Lost: What Happens When the Brain's 'GPS' Mapping Malfunctions," *Medical Daily*, May 1, 2013, https://www.medicaldaily.com/getting-lost-what-happens-when-brains-gps-mapping-malfunctions-245400 (accessed November 1, 2020).

58. Ibid.

59. Milner, *Pinpoint*.

60. Patricia Greenfield et al., "Technology and Informal Education: What Is Taught, What Is Learned," *Science* 323, no. 69 (2009).

61. Stuart Wolpert, "Is Technology Producing a Decline in Critical Thinking and Analysis?" *UCLA Newsroom*, January 27, 2009, https://newsroom.ucla.edu/releases/is-technology-producing-a-decline-79127.

62. Ibid.

63. Joseph Firth, John Torous, Brendon Stubbs, Josh A. Firth, Genevieve Z. Steiner, Lee Smith, Mario Alvarez-Jimenez, John Gleeson, Davy Vancampfort, Christopher J. Armitage, and Jerome Sarris, "The Online Brain: How the Internet May Be Changing Our Cognition," *World Psychiatry* 18 (2019): 119–129.

64. Ibid., 119.

65. Ibid., 121.

66. Ibid.

67. Firth et al., "The Online Brain," 123; N. Barr, G. Pennycook, J. A. Stolz, et al., "The Brain in Your Pocket: Evidence That Smartphones Are Used to Supplant Thinking," *Computers in Human Behavior* 48 (2015): 473–480.

68. Donald Rumsfeld, "Press Conference by U.S. Secretary of Defense, Donald Rumsfeld," NATO HQ, June 6, 2002, https://www.nato.int/docu/speech/2002/s020606g.htm.

69. John Cheney-Lippold, "A New Algorithmic Identity: Soft Biopolitics and the Modulation of Control," *Theory, Culture and Society* 28, no. 6 (2011): 164–181.

70. Lee Rainie and Janna Anderson, "Code-Dependent: Pros and Cons of the Algorithm Age," Pew Research Center, February 8, 2017.

71. Ibid., 9.

72. Ibid.

73. Ibid., 12.

74. George W. Bush, "President Bush Delivers Graduation Speech at West Point," The White House, June 1, 2002, https://georgewbush-whitehouse.archives.gov/news/releases/2002/06/20020601-3.html.

75. Svati Kirsten Narula, "The Real Problem with a Service Called Ghetto Tracker," *The Atlantic*, September 6, 2013, https://www.theatlantic.com/technology/archive/2013/09/the-real-problem-with-a-service-called-ghetto-tracker/279403/.

76. Ian Kerr and Jessica Earle, "Prediction, Preemption, Presumption: How Big Data Threatens Big Picture Privacy," *Stanford Law Review*, Symposium 2013—Privacy and Big Data, https://www.stanfordlawreview.org/online/privacy-and-big-data-prediction-preemption-presumption/.

CHAPTER 6: THE CATCH-22 OF CAPITALISM

1. Bennett Harrison and Barry Bluestone, *The Great U-Turn: Corporate Restructuring and the Polarizing of America* (New York: HarperCollins, 1990), 38.

2. Isadore Lubin, "The Absorption of the Unemployed by American Industry," In *Brookings Institution Pamphlet Series* 1, no. 3 (Washington, D.C.: Brookings Institution, 1929); Isadore Lubin, "Measuring the Labor Absorbing Power of American Industry," *Journal of the American Statistical Association* 24, no. 165 (1929): 27–32, https://www.jstor.org/stable/2277004.

3. Henry Ford, *My Life and Work* (London: William Heinemann, 1923), 72.

4. Charles Kettering, "Keep the Consumer Dissatisfied," *Nation's Business* 17, no. 1 (January 1929): 30–31.

5. Committee on Recent Economic Change, "Report of the Committee on Recent Economic Changes of the President's Conference on Unemployment," in *Recent Economic Changes in the United States*, Volumes 1 and 2 (Cambridge, MA: National Bureau of Economic Research, 1929), xviii.

6. Will Slayter, *The Debt Delusion: Evolution and Management of Financial Risk* (Boca Raton: Universal Publishers, 2008), 29.

7. Christopher Lasch, *The Culture of Narcissism: American Life in an Age of Diminishing Expectations* (New York: W. W. Norton, 1979).

8. Frederick C. Mills, *Employment Opportunities in Manufacturing Industries in the United States* (Cambridge, MA: National Bureau of Economic Research, 1938), 10–15.

9. Benjamin Kline Hunnicutt, "Kellogg's Six-Hour Day: A Capitalist Vision of Liberation Through Managed Work Reduction," *Business History Review* 66, no. 3 (Autumn 1992): 475, https://www.jstor.org/stable/3116979.

10. Robert Higgs, "The Two-Price System: U.S. Rationing During World War II Price Controls and Rationing Led to Law-Breaking and Black Markets," *Foundation for Economic Education*, April 24, 2009, https://fee.org/articles/the-two-price-system-us-rationing-during-world-war-ii/ (accessed August 21, 2020).

11. Louis Hyman, *Debtor Nation: The History of America in Red Ink* (Princeton, NJ: Princeton University Press, 2011), 136.

12. "Number of TV Households in America: 1950–1978," *American Century*, November 15, 2014, https://americancentury.omeka.wlu.edu/items/show/136 (accessed August 21, 2020).

13. "Television and Health," California State University Northridge Internet Resources, https://www.csun.edu/science/health/docs/tv&health.html (accessed June 24, 2021).

14. Hyman, *Debtor Nation*, 156–70.

15. Ibid., 270; Michael A. Turner, Patrick Walker, and Katrina Dusek, "New to Credit from Alternative Data," *PERC*, March 2009, https://www.perc.net/wp-content/uploads/2013/09/New_to_Credit_from_Alternative_Data_0.pdf.

16. Norbert Wiener, *The Human Use of Human Beings: Cybernetics and Human Beings* (New York: Avon Books, 1954), 278.

17. Ibid., 162.

18. Betty W. Su, "The Economy to 2010: Domestic Growth with Continued High Productivity, Low Unemployment Rates, and Strong Foreign Markets Characterize the Expected Outlook for the Coming Decade (Employment Outlook: 2000–10)," *Monthly Labor Review* 124, no. 11 (November 2001): 4, https://www.bls.gov/opub/mlr/2001/11/art1full.pdf.

19. Michael Simkovic, "Competition and Crisis in Mortgage Securitization," *Indiana Law Journal* 88, no. 213 (2013): 227, https://dx.doi.org/10.2139/ssrn.1924831.

20. Stefania Albanesi et al., "Credit Growth and the Financial Crisis: A New Narrative," National Bureau of Economic Research Working Paper 23740 (2017), 2, http://www.nber.org/papers/w23740.

21. "Median Sales Price for New Houses Sold in the United States," U.S. Census Bureau, July 1, 2020, https://fred.stlouisfed.org/series/MSPNHSUS (accessed September 17, 2020).

22. Susanna Kim, "2010 Had Record 2.9 Million Foreclosures," ABC News, January 12, 2011, https://abcnews.go.com/Business/2010-record-29-million-foreclosures/story?id=12602271 (accessed August 21, 2020).

23. Meta Brown et al., "The Financial Crisis at the Kitchen Table: Trends in Household Debt and Credit," *Federal Reserve Bank of New York Current Issues in Economics and Finance* 19, no. 2 (2013), https://www.newyorkfed.org/medialibrary/media/research/current_issues/ci19–2.pdf.

24. "GDP-United States," n.d. World Bank National Accounts Data, and OECD National Accounts Data Files, https://data.worldbank.org/indicator/NY.GDP.MKTP.CD?locations=US (accessed August 23, 2021).

25. Felix Richter, "Pre-Pandemic Household Debt at Record High," Statista, July 22, 2020, https://www.statista.com/chart/19955/household-debt-balance-in-the-united

-states/ (accessed August 21, 2020); Jeff Cox, "Consumer Debt Hits New Record of $14.3 Trillion," *CNBC*, May 5, 2020, https://www.cnbc.com/2020/05/05/consumer-debt-hits -new-record-of-14point3-trillion.html.

26. James Womack et al., *The Machine That Changed the World: The Story of Lean Production—Toyota's Secret Weapon in the Global Car Wars That Is Now Revolution- izing World Industry* (New York: Harper Perennial, 1991), 11.

27. Charles House and Raymond Price, "The Return Map: Tracking Product Teams," *Harvard Business Review* (January–February 1991), https://hbr.org/1991/01/the-return -map-tracking-product-teams#.

28. Christopher Huxley, "Three Decades of Lean Production: Practice, Ideology, and Resistance," *International Journal of Sociology* 45, no. 2 (August 2015): 140, https://doi .org/10.1080/00207659.2015.1061859; Satoshi Kamata, Ronald Philip Dore, and Tatsuru Akimoto, *Japan in the Passing Lane: An Insider's Account of Life in a Japanese Auto Factory* (New York: Pantheon Books, 1982); Mike Parker and Jane Slaughter, *Choosing Sides: Unions and the Team Concept* (Boston: South End Press, 1988).

29. Ibid., 140.

30. Ibid.

31. Hayley Peterson, "Amazon's Delivery Business Reveals Staggering Growth as It's on Track to Deliver 3.5 Billion Packages Globally This Year," *Business Insider*, De- cember 19, 2019, https://www.businessinsider.com/amazon-package-delivery-business -growth-2019-12#:~ (accessed August 20, 2020).

32. "Forbes 400: #1 Jeff Bezos," *Forbes* (September 2020), https://www.forbes.com /profile/jeff-bezos/?sh=1d26aa0a1b23; "The World's Real-Time Billionaires," *Forbes*, 2022, https://www.forbes.com/real-time-billionaires/#3bfb2bde3d78 (accessed March 8, 2022).

33. Áine Cain and Hayley Peterson, "Two Charts Show Amazon's Explosive Growth as the Tech Giant Prepares to Add 133,000 Workers Amid Record Online Sales," *Business Insider*, September 15, 2020, https://markets.businessinsider.com/news/stocks/amazon -number-of-employees-workforce-workers-2020-9-1029591975 (accessed August 20, 2020).

34. Jodi Kantor and David Streitfeld, "Inside Amazon: Wrestling Big Ideas in a Bruis- ing Workplace," *New York Times*, August 15, 2015.

35. Ibid.

36. Jay Greene and Chris Alcantara, "Amazon Warehouse Workers Suffer Serious Injuries at Higher Rates Than Other Firms," *Washington Post*, June 1, 2021, https:// www.washingtonpost.com/technology/2021/06/01/amazon-osha-injury-rate/.

37. Emily Guendelsberger, *On the Clock: What Low-Wage Work Did to Me and How It Drives America Insane* (Boston: Little, Brown, 2019).

38. Esther Kaplan, "The Spy Who Fired Me: The Human Costs of Workplace Moni- toring," *Harper's Magazine*, March 2015, https://harpers.org/archive/2015/03/the-spy -who-fired-me/ (accessed August 21, 2020).

39. Johan Huizinga, "Homo Ludens: A Study of the Play-Element in Culture" (Bos- ton: Beacon Press, 1950), 46.

40. Jennifer deWinter et al., "Taylorism 2.0: Gamification, Scientific Management and the Capitalist Appropriation of Play," *Journal of Gaming & Virtual Worlds* 6, no. 2 (June 2014): 109–127, http://dx.doi.org/10.1386/jgvw.6.2.109_1.

41. Ibid., 113.

42. "Stone City: Learn the Relationship Portion Sizes and Profitability in an Ice Cream Franchise," Cold Stone Creamery Inc., http://persuasivegames.com/game/coldstone.

43. Anna Blake and James Moseley, "Frederick Winslow Taylor: One Hundred Years of Managerial Insight," *International Journal of Management* 28, no. 4 (December 2011): 346–353, https://www.researchgate.net/profile/Anne_Blake/publication/286930119_Frederick_Winslow_Taylor_One_Hundred_Years_of_Managerial_Insight/links/5670846c08aececfd5532970/Frederick-Winslow-Taylor-One-Hundred-Years-of-Managerial-Insight.pdf.

44. Jill Lepore, "Not So Fast: Scientific Management Started as a Way to Work. How Did It Become a Way of Life?" *New Yorker*, October 5, 2009, https://www.newyorker.com/magazine/2009/10/12/not-so-fast (accessed August 21, 2020).

45. Edward Cone and James Lambert, "How Robots Change the World: What Automation Really Means for Jobs and Productivity," *Oxford Economics*, June 26, 2019, https://www.oxfordeconomics.com/recent-releases/how-robots-change-the-world; Susan Lund, Anu Madgavkar, James Manyika, Sven Smit, Kweilin Ellingrud, and Olivia Robinson, "The Future of Work After COVID-19," McKinsey and Company, 2019, https://www.mckinsey.com/featured-insights/future-of-work/the-future-of-work-after-covid-19; John Hawksworth, Richard Berriman, and Saloni Noel, "Will Robots Really Steal Our Jobs? An International Analysis of the Potential Long-Term Impact of Automation," PricewaterhouseCoopers, 2018, https://www.pwc.co.uk/economic-services/assets/international-impact-of-automation-feb-2018.pdf.

46. Henry Blodget, "CEO of Apple Partner Foxconn: 'Managing One Million Animals Gives Me a Headache,'" *Business Insider*, January 12, 2012, https://www.businessinsider.com/foxconn-animals-2012-1 (accessed August 21, 2020).

47. Cone and Lambert, "How Robots Change the World."

CHAPTER 7: THE ECOLOGICAL SELF

1. Erich Kahler, *Man the Measure: A New Approach to History* (Cleveland: Meridian Books, 1967).

2. Lewis Mumford, *Technics and Human Development* (New York: Harcourt Brace Jovanovich/Harvest Books, 1966), 101.

3. Mircea Eliade, *The Myth of the Eternal Return* (Princeton, NJ: Princeton Classics, 2019), originally published in English in 1954.

4. Jeremy Rifkin, "The Risks of Too Much City," *Washington Post*, December 17, 2006, https://www.washingtonpost.com/archive/opinions/2006/12/17/the-risks-of-too-much-city/db5c3e65-4daf-465f-8e58-31b47ba359f8/.

5. Ludwig von Bertalanffy, *Problems of Life* (New York: Harper and Brothers, 1952), 134.

6. Norbert Wiener, *The Human Use of Human Beings: Cybernetics and Society* (New York: Da Capo Press, 1988), 96.

7. Alfred North Whitehead, *Science and the Modern World* (Cambridge: Cambridge University Press, 1926), 22.

8. Ronald Desmet and Andrew David Irvine, "Alfred North Whitehead," *Stan-

ford Encyclopedia of Philosophy, September 4, 2018, https://plato.stanford.edu/entries
/whitehead/.

9. Alfred North Whitehead, *Science and the Modern World: Lowell Lectures 1925*
(Cambridge London: Cambridge University Press, 1929), 61; Alfred North Whitehead,
Nature and Life (Chicago: Chicago University Press, 1934) and reprinted (Cambridge:
Cambridge University Press, 2011).

10. Whitehead, *Nature and Life*, 65.

11. Robin G. Collingwood, *The Idea of Nature* (Oxford: Oxford University Press,
1945), 146.

12. Ibid.

13. Fritjof Capra, *The Tao of Physics: An Exploration of the Parallels Between Modern Physics and Eastern Mysticism* (Berkeley: Shambhala Publications, 1975), 138.

14. Whitehead, *Nature and Life*, 45–48.

15. Ernst Haeckel, *The Wonders of Life: A Popular Study of Biological Philosophy*
(London: Watts, 1904), 80.

16. Whitehead, *Nature and Life*, 61.

17. Water Science School, "The Water in You: Water and the Human Body," U.S.
Geological Survey, May 22, 2019, https://www.usgs.gov/special-topic/water-science
-school/science/water-you-water-and-human-body?qt-science_center_objects=0#qt
-science_center_objects.

18. H. H. Mitchell, T. S. Hamilton, F. R. Steggerda, and H. W. Bean, "The Chemical
Composition of the Adult Human Body and Its Bearing on the Biochemistry of Growth,"
Journal of Biological Chemistry 158, no. 3 (May 1, 1945): 625–637, https://doi.org/10
.1016/S0021-9258(19)51339-4.

19. "What Does Blood Do?" Institute for Quality and Efficiency in Health Care,
InformedHealth.org, U.S. National Library of Medicine, August 29, 2019, https://www
.ncbi.nlm.nih.gov/books/NBK279392/.

20. Water Science School, "The Water in You."

21. Alison Abbott, "Scientists Bust Myth That Our Bodies Have More Bacteria Than
Human Cells," *Nature*, January 8, 2016, https://doi.org/10.1038/nature.2016.19136; Ron
Sender, Shai Fuchs, and Ron Milo, "Revised Estimates for the Number of Human and
Bacteria Cells in the Body," *PLOS Biology*, August 19, 2016, https://doi.org/10.1371
/journal.pbio.1002533.

22. Kirsty L. Spalding, Ratan D. Bhardwaj, Bruce A. Buchholz, Henrik Druid, and
Jonas Frisén, "Retrospective Birth Dating of Cells in Humans," *Cell* 122, no. 1 (July
15, 2005): 133–143, https://doi.org/10.1016/j.cell.2005.04.028.

23. Nicholas Wade, "Your Body Is Younger Than You Think," *New York Times*, August 2, 2005, https://www.nytimes.com/2005/08/02/science/your-body-is-younger-than
-you-think.html.

24. Ibid.

25. Ibid.; Spalding et al., "Retrospective Birth Dating of Cells in Humans"; Stavros
Manolagas, "Birth and Death of Bone Cells: Basic Regulatory Mechanisms and Implications for the Pathogenesis and Treatment of Osteoporosis," *Endocrine Reviews* 21,
no. 2 (April 1, 2000): 116, https://doi.org/10.1210/edrv.21.2.0395; Ron Milo and Robert
B. Phillips, *Cell Biology by the Numbers* (New York: Garland Science, 2015), 279.

26. Curt Stager, *Your Atomic Self; The Invisible Elements That Connect You to Everything Else in the Universe* (New York: Thomas Dunne Books, 2014), 212; Bente Langdahl, Serge Ferrari, and David W. Dempster, "Bone Modeling and Remodeling: Potential as Therapeutic Targets for the Treatment of Osteoporosis," *Therapeutic Advances in Musculoskeletal Disease* 8, no. 6 (October 5, 2016), https://dx.doi.org/10.1177%2F1759720X16670154; Elia Beniash et al., "The Hidden Structure of Human Enamel," *Nature Communications* 10, no. 4383 (2019), https://www.nature.com/articles/s41467-019-12185-7.

27. Brian Clegg, "20 Amazing Facts About the Human Body," *The Guardian*, January 26, 2013, https://www.theguardian.com/science/2013/jan/27/20-human-body-facts-science.

28. J. Gordon Betts et al., *Anatomy and Physiology* (Houston: Rice University, 2013), 43; Curt Stager, *Your Atomic Self*, 197.

29. Ethan Siegel, "How Many Atoms Do We Have in Common with One Another?" *Forbes*, April 30, 2020, https://www.forbes.com/sites/startswithabang/2020/04/30/how-many-atoms-do-we-have-in-common-with-one-another/?sh=75adfe6a1b38 (accessed November 1, 2020).

30. Ibid.

31. Amit Shraga, "The Body's Elements," Davidson Institute of Science Education, April 1, 2020, https://davidson.weizmann.ac.il/en/online/orderoutofchaos/body%E2%80%99s-elements; Davey Reginald, "What Chemical Elements Are Found in the Human Body?" *News Medical Life Sciences*, May 19, 2021, https://www.news-medical.net/life-sciences/What-Chemical-Elements-are-Found-in-the-Human-Body.aspx#:~:text=The%20human%20body%20is%20approximately,carbon%2C%20calcium%2C%20and%20phosphorus. Body.aspx#:~:text=The%20human%20body%20is%20approximately,carbon%2C%20calcium%2C%20and%20phosphorus.

32. Elizabeth Pennisi, "Plants Outweigh All Other Life on Earth," *Science*, May 21, 2018, https://doi.org/10.1126/science.aau2463; Yinon M. Bar-On, Rob Phillips, and Ron Milo, "The Biomass Distribution on Earth," *Proceedings of the National Academy of Sciences* 115, no. 25 (May 21, 2018), https://doi.org/10.1073/pnas.1711842115.

33. Sender, Fuchs, and Milo, "Revised Estimates for the Number of Human and Bacteria Cells in the Body."

34. Anne E. Maczulak, *Allies and Enemies: How the World Depends on Bacteria* (FT Press, 2010); Molika Ashford, "Could Humans Live Without Bacteria?" *Live Science*, August 12, 2010, https://www.livescience.com/32761-good-bacteria-boost-immune-system.html.

35. Anil Kumar and Nikita Chordia, "Role of Microbes in Human Health," *Applied Microbiology: Open Access* 3, no. 2 (April 2017): 131, https://www.longdom.org/open-access/role-of-microbes-in-human-health-2471-9315-1000131.pdf; Ana Maldonado-Contreras, "A Healthy Microbiome Builds a Strong Immune System That Could Help Defeat COVID-19," University of Massachusetts Medical School, January 25, 2021, https://www.umassmed.edu/news/news-archives/2021/01/a-healthy-microbiome-builds-a-strong-immune-system-that-could-help-defeat-covid-19/.

36. Patrick C. Seed, "The Human Mycobiome," *Cold Spring Harbor Perspectives in Medicine* 5, no. 5 (2015), https://dx.doi.org/10.1101%2Fcshperspect.a019810.

37. Gary B. Huffnagle and Mairi C. Noverr, "The Emerging World of the Fungal

Microbiome," *Trends in Microbiology* 21, no. 7 (2013): 334–341, https://doi.org/10.1016 /j.tim.2013.04.002.

38. Mahmoud A. Ghannoum, Richard J. Jurevic, Pranab K. Mukherjee, Fan Cui, Masoumeh Sikaroodi, Ammar Naqvi, and Patrick M. Gillevet, "Characterization of the Oral Fungal Microbiome (Mycobiome) in Healthy Individuals," *PLOS Pathogens*, January 8, 2010, https://doi.org/10.1371/journal.ppat.1000713; Bret Stetka, "The Human Body's Complicated Relationship with Fungi," MPR News, April 16, 2016, https:// www.mprnews.org/story/2016/04/16/npr-the-human-bodys-complicated-relationship -with-fungi.

39. Kaisa Koskinen, Manuela R. Pausan, Alexandra K. Perras, Michael Beck, Corinna Bang, Maximillian Mora, Anke Schilhabel, Ruth Schmitz, and Christine Moissl-Eichinger, "First Insights into the Diverse Human Archaeome: Specific Detection of Archaea in the Gastrointestinal Tract, Lung, and Nose and on Skin," *mBio* 8, no. 6 (November 14, 2017), http://dx.doi.org/10.1128/mBio.00824-17.

40. Mor N. Lurie-Weinberger and Uri Gophna, "Archaea in and on the Human Body: Health Implications and Future Directions," *PLOS Pathogens* 11, no. 6 (2015), https://doi.org/10.1371/journal.ppat.1004833.

41. Graham P. Harris, *Phytoplankton Ecology: Structure, Function and Fluctuation* (London: Chapman and Hall, 1986); Yadigar Sekerci and Sergei Petrovskii, "Global Warming Can Lead to Depletion of Oxygen by Disrupting Phytoplankton Photosynthesis: A Mathematical Modelling Approach," *Geosciences* 8, no. 6 (June 3, 2018), doi:10.3390/ geosciences8060201.

42. John Corliss, "Biodiversity and Biocomplexity of the Protists and an Overview of Their Significant Roles in Maintenance of Our Biosphere," *Acta Protozoologica* 41 (2002): 212.

43. Karin Mölling, "Viruses More Friends Than Foes," *Electroanalysis* 32, no. 4 (November 26, 2019): 669–673, https://doi.org/10.1002/elan.201900604.

44. David Pride, "Viruses Can Help Us as Well as Harm Us," *Scientific American*, December 1, 2020, https://www.scientificamerican.com/article/viruses-can-help-us-as -well-as-harm-us/#.

45. David Pride and Chandrabali Ghose, "Meet the Trillions of Viruses That Make Up Your Virome," *The Conversation*, October 9, 2018, https://theconversation.com /meet-the-trillions-of-viruses-that-make-up-your-virome-104105#:~:text=It%20has%20 been%20estimated%20that,infections%20like%20Ebola%20or%20dengue (accessed November 1, 2020).

46. James Gallagher, "More Than Half Your Body Is Not Human," BBC News, April 10, 2018, https://www.bbc.com/news/health-43674270 (accessed November 1, 2020).

47. Ibid.

48. Prabarna Ganguly, "Microbes in Us and Their Role in Human Health and Disease," National Human Genome Research Institute, May 29, 2019, https://www.genome .gov/news/news-release/Microbes-in-us-and-their-role-in-human-health-and-disease.

49. "Biome," *Lexico: Powered by Oxford*, https://www.lexico.com/en/definition/biome (accessed November 20, 2021).

50. "Ecosystem," *Lexico: Powered by Oxford*, https://www.lexico.com/en/definition /ecosystem (accessed November 20, 2021).

51. Peter Turnbaugh, Ruth Ley, Micah Hamady, Claire M. Fraser-Liggett, Rob Knight, and Jeffrey Gordon, "The Human Microbiome Project," *Nature* 449 (October 2007): 804, https://www.nature.com/articles/nature06244.pdf.

52. Gallagher, "More Than Half Your Body Is Not Human."

53. Ibid.

54. Bertalanffy, *Problems of Life*, 134.

55. Dominique Frizon de Lamotte, Brendan Fourdan, Sophie Leleu, François Leparmentier, and Philippe de Clarens, "Style of Rifting and the Stages of Pangea Breakup," *Tectonics* 34, no. 5 (2015): 1009–1029, https://doi.org/10.1002/2014tc003760.

56. Stager, *Your Atomic Self*, 193–194.

CHAPTER 8: A NEW ORIGIN STORY

1. James D. Watson, *The Double Helix: A Personal Account of the Discovery of the Structure of DNA* (New York: Simon & Schuster, 1968).

2. Patricia J. Sollars and Gary E. Pickard, "The Neurobiology of Circadian Rhythms," *Psychiatric Clinics of North America* 38, no. 4 (2015): 645–65, https://doi.org/10.1016/j.psc.2015.07.003.

3. Joseph Zubin and Howard F. Hunt, *Comparative Psychopathology: Animal and Human* (New York: Grune & Stratton, 1967), https://www.gwern.net/docs/psychology/1967-zubin-comparativepsychopathology.pdf.

4. Ueli Schibler, "The Mammalian Circadian Timekeeping System," in *Ultradian Rhythms from Molecules to Mind: A New Vision of Life*, edited by David Lloyd and Ernest Rossi (Heidelberg: Springer Netherlands, 2008), 261–279.

5. J. O'Neill and A. Reddy, "Circadian Clocks in Human Red Blood Cells," *Nature* 469 (January 26, 2011): 498–503.

6. Michelle Donahue, "80 Percent of Americans Can't See the Milky Way Anymore," *National Geographic*, June 10, 2016, https://www.nationalgeographic.com/science/article/milky-way-space-science.

7. Abraham Haim and Boris A. Portnov, *Light Pollution as a New Risk Factor for Human Breast and Prostate Cancers* (New York: Springer Nature, 2013).

8. A. L. Baird, A. N. Coogan, A. Siddiqui, R. M. Donev, and J. Thome, "Adult Attention Deficit Hyperactivity Disorder Is Associated with Alterations in Circadian Rhythms at the Behavioural, Endocrine and Molecular Levels," *Molecular Psychiatry* 17, no. 10 (2012): 988–995.

9. Elaine Waddington Lamont, Daniel L. Coutu, Nicolas Cermakian, and Diane B. Bolvin, "Circadian Rhythms and Clock Genes in Psychotic Disorders," *Israel Journal of Psychiatry and Related Sciences* 47, no. 1 (2010), 27–35.

10. Russell Foster, "Waking Up to the Link Between a Faulty Body Block and Mental Illness," *The Guardian*, July 22, 2013.

11. G. J. Whitrow, *The Natural Philosophy of Time* (Oxford: Oxford University Press, 1980), 146.

12. E. T. Pengelley and K. C. Fisher, "The Effect of Temperature and Photoperiod on the Yearly Hibernating Behavior of Captive Golden-Mantled Ground Squirrels," *Canadian Journal of Zoology* 41 (1963): 1103–1120.

13. David Lloyd, "Biological Timekeeping: The Business of a Blind Watchmaker," *Science Progress* 99, no. 2 (2016): 113–132.

14. Ibid., 124.

15. Grace H. Goh, Shane K. Maloney, Peter J. Mark, and Dominique Blache, "Episodic Ultradian Events—Ultradian Rhythms," *Biology* 8, no. 1 (March 2019): 12.

16. Ibid.

17. B. P. Tu, A. Kudlicki, M. Rowicka, and S. L. McKnight, "Logic of the Yeast Metabolic Cycle: Temporal Compartmentalization of Cellular Processes," *Science* 310, no. 5751 (November 2005), and B. P. Tu and S. L. McKnight, "Metabolic Cycles as an Underlying Basis of Biological Oscillations," *Nature Reviews Molecular Cell Biology* 7, no. 9 (2006).

18. Maximilian Moser, Matthias Frühwirth, Reiner Penter, and Robert Winker, "Why Life Oscillates—From a Topographical Towards a Functional Chronobiology," *Cancer Causes & Control* 17, no. 4 (June 2006): 591–599.

19. Thomas A. Wehr, "Photoperiodism in Humans and Other Primates: Evidence and Implications," *Journal of Biological Rhythms* 16, no. 4 (August 2001): 348–364.

20. Ibid., 349.

21. Nicola Davis and Ian Sample, "Nobel Prize for Medicine Awarded for Insights into Internal Biological Clock," *The Guardian*, October 2, 2017, https://www.theguardian.com/science/2017/oct/02/nobel-prize-for-medicine-awarded-for-insights-into-internal-biological-clock.

22. Ian Sample, "Nobel Prizes 2017: Everything You Need to Know About Circadian Rhythms," *The Guardian*, October 2, 2017.

23. Gina Kolata, "2017 Nobel Prize in Medicine Goes to 3 Americans for Body Clock Studies," *New York Times*, October 2, 2017.

24. Michael A. Persinger and Rütger Wever, "ELF-Effects on Human Circadian Rhythms," Essay, in *ELF and VLF Electromagnetic Field Effects* (New York: Plenum Press, 1974), 101–144.

25. R. A. Wever, "Basic Principles of Human Circadian Rhythm," *Temporal Variations of the Cardiovascular System* (1992).

26. Richard H. W. Funk, Thomas Monsees, and Nurdan Ozkucur, "Electromagnetic Effects—From Cell Biology to Medicine," *Progress in Histochemistry and Cytochemistry* 43, no. 4 (2009): 177–264; R. Wever, "Effects of Electric Fields on Circadian Rhythmicity in Men," *Life Sciences in Space Research* 8 (1970): 177–187.

27. James Clerk Maxwell, "Inaugural Lecture at King's College London" (1860), http://www.michaelbeeson.com/interests/GreatMoments/MaxwellDiscoversLightIsElectromagnetic.pdf.

28. "Earth's Magnetic Field and Its Changes in Time," NASA, n.d., https://image.gsfc.nasa.gov/poetry/tour/AAmag.html#:~:text=The%20magnetic%20field%20of%20earth%20actually%20changes%20its%20polarity%20over,years%20according%20to%20geological%20evidence.

29. Karen Fox, "Earth's Magnetosphere," NASA, January 28, 2021, https://www.nasa.gov/magnetosphere; "Magnetospheres," NASA Science, https://science.nasa.gov/heliophysics/focus-areas/magnetosphere-ionosphere (accessed August 26, 2021).

30. Ronald Desmet, "Alfred North Whitehead," *Stanford Encyclopedia of Philosophy*.

31. Alfred North Whitehead, *Nature and Life* (London: Cambridge University Press, 1934), 15.

32. Ibid., 86.

33. "Morphogenesis," Encyclopædia Britannica, https://www.britannica.com/science/morphogenesis (accessed April 16, 2021).

34. A. G. Gurwitsch, *A Biological Field Theory* (Moscow: Sovetskaya Nauka, 1944); Daniel Fels, Michal Cifra, and Felix Scholkmann, *Fields of the Cell* (Kerala: Research Signpost, 2015), 274.

35. Paul A. Weiss, *The Science of Life: The Living System—A System for Living* (Mount Kisco, NY: Futura, 1973), 19.

36. Ibid., 45.

37. Ibid., 47.

38. Harold Saxton Burr, *Blueprint for Immortality* (London: Neville Spearman, 1972), 30.

39. Ibid., 107.

40. Ibid.

41. Mats-Olof Mattsson and Myrtill Simkó, "Emerging Medical Applications Based on Non-Ionizing Electromagnetic Fields from 0 Hz to 10 THz," *Dovepress* (September 12, 2019), 347–368, https://doi.org/10.2147/MDER.S214152.

42. Daniel Fels, "The Double-Aspect of Life," *Biology (Basel)* 7, no. 2 (May 2018): 28

43. "The Face of a Frog: Time-Lapse Video Reveals Never-Before-Seen Bioelectric Pattern," *Tufts Now*, July 18, 2011, https://now.tufts.edu/news-releases/face-frog-time-lapse-video-reveals-never-seen#:~:text=%2D%2DFor%20the%20first%20time,where%20eyes%2C%20nose%2C%20mouth%2C.

44. Ibid.

45. Ibid.

46. Denis Noble, Eva Jablonka, Michael J. Joyner, Gerd B. Müller, and Stig W. Omholt, "Evolution Evolves: Physiology Returns to Centre Stage," *Journal of Physiology* 592 (Pt. 11) (June 2014): 2237–2234.

47. Charles Darwin, "Difficulties of Theory—The Eye," in *On the Origin of Species*, https://www.theguardian.com/science/2008/feb/09/darwin.eye.

48. Patrick Collins, "Researchers Discover That Changes in Bioelectric Signals Trigger Formation of New Organs," *Tufts Now* December 8, 2011, https://now.tufts.edu/news-releases/researchers-discover-changes-bioelectric-sign.

49. Ibid.

50. Ibid.

51. Vaibhav P. Pai, Sherry Aw, Tal Shomrat, Joan M. Lemire, and Michael Levin, "Transmembrane Voltage Potential Controls Embryotic Eye Patterning in *Xenopus laevis*," *Development* 139, no. 2 (January 2012): 313–323; Collins, "Researchers Discover That Changes in Bioelectric Signals Trigger Formation of New Organs."

CHAPTER 9: BEYOND THE SCIENTIFIC METHOD

1. Francis Bacon, as quoted in John Randall Herman Jr., *The Making of the Modern Mind* (Cambridge, MA: Houghton Mifflin, 1940), 223.

2. Francis Bacon, *The New Atlantis: A Work Unfinished* (London: Printed by Tho. Newcomb, 1983).

3. Donald Worster, *Nature's Economy* (Cambridge: Cambridge University Press, 1977), 30.

4. James Spedding, Robert Leslie Ellis, and Douglas Denon Heath, eds., *The Works of Francis Bacon*, vol. 3, *Philosophical Works* (Cambridge: Cambridge University Press, 2011), doi:10.1017/CBO9781139149563.

5. Francis Bacon, "Novum Organum," in *The Works of Francis Bacon*, vol. 4 (London: W. Pickering, 1850), 114.

6. "Pioneering the Science of Surprise," Stockholm Resilience Centre, https://www .stockholmresilience.org/research/research-news/2019-08-23-pioneering-the-science -of-surprise-.html (accessed April 4, 2021).

7. "Case," *Merriam-Webster*, n.d., https://www.merriam-webster.com/dictionary /cases?utm_campaign=sd&utm_medium=serp&utm_source=jsonld.

8. C. S. Holling, "Resilience and Stability of Ecological Systems," *Annual Review of Ecology and Systematics* 4 (November 1973): 1–23

9. Ibid., 17–21.

10. Lance H. Gunderson, "Ecological Resilience—In Theory and Application," *Annual Review of Ecology and Systematics* 31 (November 2000): 425–439

11. Fiona Miller et al., "Resilience and Vulnerability: Complementary or Conflicting Concepts?" *Ecology and Society* 15, no. 3 (2010).

12. Hanne Andersen and Brian Hepburn, "Scientific Method," in *The Stanford Encyclopedia of Philosophy* (Winter 2020), edited by Edward Zalta, https://plato.stanford .edu/archives/win2020/entries/scientific-method/

13. Cynthia Larson, "Evidence of Shared Aspects of Complexity Science and Quantum Phenomena," *Cosmos and History: The Journal of Natural and Social Philosophy* 12, no. 2 (2016).

14. Rika Preiser, Reinette Biggs, Alta De Vos, and Carl Folke, "Social-Ecological Systems as Complex Adaptive Systems: Organizing Principles for Advancing Research Methods and Approaches," *Ecology and Society* 23, no. 4 (December 2018): 46.

15. "Where Is Frozen Ground?" National Snow and Ice Data Center, https://nsidc .org/cryosphere/frozenground/whereis_fg.html (accessed July 25, 2021).

16. Richard Field, "John Dewey (1859–1952)," *Internet Encyclopedia of Philosophy*, n.d., https://iep.utm.edu/john-dewey/.

17. "Adaptation and Survival," *National Geographic Magazine*, April 23, 2020.

18. Martin Reeves and Mike Deimler, "Adaptability: The New Competitive Advantage," *Harvard Business Review* (July–August 2011).

19. Ibid.

20. J. H. Barkow, L. Cosmides, and J. Tooby, *The Adapted Mind: Evolutionary Psychology and the Generation of Culture* (Oxford: Oxford University Press, 1992), 5.

21. Susan C. Anton, Richard Potts, and Leslie C. Aiello, "Evolution of Early *Homo*: An Integrated Biological Perspective," *Science* 345, no. 6192 (July 4, 2014).

22. Ibid.

23. Ibid.

24. Mohi Kumar, "Ability to Adapt Gave Early Humans the Edge over Other Homi-

nins," *Smithsonian Magazine* (July 4, 2014), https://www.smithsonianmag.com/science
-nature/ability-to-adapt-gave-early-humans-edge-hominin-180951959/.

25. "Quaternary Period," *National Geographic*, https://www.nationalgeographic.com
/science/prehistoric-world/quaternary/#close.

26. Nathaniel Massey, "Humans May Be the Most Adaptive Species," *Scientific American* (September 25, 2013), https://www.scientificamerican.com/article/humans-may
-be-most-adaptive-species/#:~:text=In%20the%205%20million%20years,climate%20
has%20grown%20increasingly%20erratic.

27. Ibid.

28. World Bank Group, *Piecing Together the Poverty Puzzle* (Washington, D.C.:
World Bank, 2018), 7.

29. Deborah Hardoon, "An Economy for the 99%," Oxfam International Briefing
Paper, January 2017, https://www-cdn.oxfam.org/s3fs-public /file_attachments/bp
-economy-for-99-percent-160117-en.pdf (accessed March 12, 2019), 1.

30. Indu Gupta, "Sustainable Development: Gandhi Approach," *OIDA International
Journal of Sustainable Development* 8, no. 7 (2015).

CHAPTER 10: THE RESILIENT REVOLUTION INFRASTRUCTURE

1. "Global 500," *Fortune* (August–September 2020), https://fortune.com/global500/;
Brian O'Keefe and Nicolas Rapp, "These 18 Big Companies Made More Than $250,000 in
Profit Per Employee Last Year," *Fortune*, August 10, 2020, https://fortune.com/longform
/global-500-companies-profits-employees/.

2. "Number of Smartphone Subscriptions Worldwide from 2016 to 2027," Statista,
February 23, 2022, https://www.statista.com/statistics/330695/number-of-smartphone
-users-worldwide/; David R. Scott, "Would Your Mobile Phone Be Powerful Enough
to Get You to the Moon?" *The Conversation*, July 1, 2019, https://theconversation.com
/would-your-mobile-phone-be-powerful-enough-to-get-you-to-the-moon-115933.

3. Mark Muro et al., "Advancing Inclusion Through Clean Energy Jobs," Brookings Institution, 2019, https://www.brookings.edu/wp-content/uploads/2019/04/2019
.04_metro_Clean-Energy-Jobs_Report_Muro-Tomer-Shivaran-Kane.pdf.

4. TIR Consulting Group, "America 3.0: The Resilient Society: A Smart Third Industrial Revolution Infrastructure and the Recovery of the American Economy," Office of Jeremy Rifkin, July 28, 2021, https://www.foet.org/about/tir-consulting-group/.

5. Harriet Festing et al., "The Case for Fixing the Leaks: Protecting People and
Saving Water While Supporting Economic Growth in the Great Lakes Region," Center for Neighborhood Technology, 2013, https://cnt.org/sites/default/files/publications/
CNT_CaseforFixingtheLeaks.pdf.

CHAPTER 11: THE ASCENDANCE OF BIOREGIONAL GOVERNANCE

1. Karla Schuster, "Biden Widens Lead, But Voter Mistrust of Process Runs Deep:
Kalikow School Poll," Hofstra College of Liberal Arts and Sciences, September 29, 2020,
https://news.hofstra.edu/2020/09/29/biden-widens-lead-but-voter-mistrust-of-process
-runs-deep-kalikow-school-poll/.

2. Christopher Keating, "Quinnipiac Poll: 77% of Republicans Believe There Was Widespread Fraud in the Presidential Election; 60% Overall Consider Joe Biden's Victory Legitimate," *Hartford Courant*, December 10, 2020, https://www.courant.com/politics/hc -pol-q-poll-republicans-believe-fraud-20201210-pcie3uqqvrhyvnt7geohhsyepe-story.html.

3. Mario Carpo, "Republics of Makers," e-flux, https://www.e-flux.com/architecture /positions/175265/republics-of-makers/ (accessed January 20, 2021).

4. Frank Newport, "Americans Big on Idea of Living in the Country," Gallup, December 7, 2018, https://news.gallup.com/poll/245249/americans-big-idea-living-country.aspx.

5. Robert Bonnie, Emily Pechar Diamond, and Elizabeth Rowe, "Understanding Rural Attitudes Toward the Environment and Conservation in America," Nicholas Institute for Environmental Policy Solutions, February 2020.

6. "Ford to Lead America's Shift to Electric Vehicles with New Mega Campus in Tennessee and Twin Battery Plants in Kentucky; $11.4B Investment to Create 11,000 Jobs and Power New Lineup of Advanced EVS," Ford Media Center, September 27, 2021, https://media.ford.com/content/fordmedia/fna/us/en/news/2021/09/27/ford-to -lead-americas-shift-to-electric-vehicles.html.

7. Kyle Johnson, "Ford F-Series Made $42 Billion in Revenue in 2019," *News Wheel*, June 25, 2020, https://thenewswheel.com/ford-f-series-42-billion-revenue-2019/.

8. "Ford to Lead America's Shift to Electric Vehicles with New Mega Campus in Tennessee and Twin Battery Plants in Kentucky."

9. Bill Howard, "Vehicles and Voting: What Your Car Might Say About How You'll Vote," *Forbes*, October 1, 2020, https://www.forbes.com/wheels/news/what-your-car -might-say-about-how-you-vote/.

10. Craig Mauger, "Whitmer: Michigan Lacked 'Real Opportunity' to Compete for Ford Plants," *Detroit News*, September 29, 2021, https://www.detroitnews.com/story /news/politics/2021/09/29/whitmer-michigan-lacked-real-opportunity-compete-ford -plants/5917610001/.

11. E. Dinerstein et al., "A Global Deal for Nature: Guiding Principles, Milestones, and Targets," *Science Advances* 5 (2019): 1.

12. Ibid.

13. Ibid.

14. Sarah Gibbens, "The U.S. Commits to Tripling Its Protected Lands. Here's How It Could Be Done," *National Geographic*, January 27, 2021, https://www.nationalgeographic .com/environment/article/biden-commits-to-30-by-2030-conservation-executive-orders; "Fact Sheet: President Biden Takes Executive Actions to Tackle the Climate Crisis at Home and Abroad, Create Jobs, and Restore Scientific Integrity Across Federal Government," The White House, January 27, 2021, https://www.whitehouse.gov/briefing-room /statements-releases/2021/01/27/fact-sheet-president-biden-takes-executive-actions-to -tackle-the-climate-crisis-at-home-and-abroad-create-jobs-and-restore-scientific-integrity -across-federal-government/.

15. Matt Lee-Ashley, "How Much Nature Should America Keep?" Center for American Progress, August 6, 2019, https://www.americanprogress.org/issues/green/reports /2019/08/06/473242/much-nature-america-keep/.

16. Sandra Diaz, Josef Settele, and Eduardo Brondizio, "Summary for Policymakers of the Global Assessment Report on Biodiversity and Ecosystem Services of the

Intergovernmental Science-Policy Platform on Biodiversity and Ecosystem Services," *Intergovernmental Science-Policy Platform on Biodiversity and Ecosystem Services* (2019), https://www.ipbes.net/sites/default/files/downloads/spm_unedited_advance_for _posting_htn.pdf

17. Lee-Ashley, "How Much Nature Should America Keep?"

18. "Federal Land Ownership: Overview and Data," Congressional Research Center, February 21, 2020, https://sgp.fas.org/crs/misc/R42346.pdf; Lee-Ashley, "How Much Nature Should America Keep?"; Robert H. Nelson, "State-Owned Lands in the Eastern United States: Lessons from State Land Management Practice," Property and Environment Research Center, March 2018, https://www.perc.org/2018/03/13/state-owned-lands -in-the-eastern-united-states/; Ryan Richards and Matt Lee-Ashley, "The Race for Nature," Center for American Progress, June 23, 2020, https://www.americanprogress .org/article/the-race-for-nature/.

19. "Forests Programs," U.S. Department of Agriculture, National Institute of Food and Agriculture, https://www.nifa.usda.gov/grants/programs/forests-programs.

20. A. R. Wallace, "What Are Zoological Regions?" *Nature* 49 (April 26, 1894): 610–613.

21. Karl Burkart, "Bioregions 2020," *One Earth*, n.d., https://www.oneearth.org /bioregions-2020/.

22. "Ecoregions," World Wildlife Fund, n.d., https://www.worldwildlife.org/biomes.

23. Peter Berg and Raymond Dasmann, "Reinhabiting California," *The Ecologist* 7, no. 10 (1977); Cheryll Glotfelty and Eve Quesnel, *The Biosphere and the Bioregion: Essential Writings of Peter Berg* (London: Routledge, 2015), 35.

24. David Bollier, "Elinor Ostrom and the Digital Commons," *Forbes*, October 13, 2009.

25. Kirkpatrick Sale, "Mother of All: An Introduction to Bioregionalism," in *Third Annual E. F. Schumacher Lectures,* edited by Hildegarde Hannum (October 1983); Regional Factors in National Planning and Development, 1935.

26. "Bioregions of the Pacific U.S.," USGS, https://www.usgs.gov/centers/werc/science /bioregions-pacific-us?qt-science_center_objects=0#qt-science_center_objects (accessed June 30, 2021).

27. "Ecoregions and Watersheds," Cascadia Department of Bioregion, n.d., https:// cascadiabioregion.org/ecoregions-and-watersheds/.

28. "The Cascadia Bioregion: Facts & Figures," Cascadia Department of Bioregion, n.d., https://cascadiabioregion.org/facts-and-figures.

29. Ibid.

30. "About PNWER," Pacific Northwest Economic Region, n.d., http://www.pnwer .org/about-us.html.

31. P. Mote, A. K. Snover, S. Capalbo, S. D. Eigenbrode, P. Glick, J. Littell, R. Ray-mondi, and S. Reeder, "Northwest," in *Climate Change Impacts in the United States: The Third National Climate Assessment,* edited by J. M. Melillo, Terese Richmond, and G. W. Yohe for the U.S. Global Change Research Program (2014), 487–513, 488.

32. Alan Steinman, Bradley Cardinale, Wayne Munns Jr., et al., "Ecosystem Services in the Great Lakes," *Journal of Great Lakes Research* 43, no. 3 (June 2017): 161–68, https:// www.ncbi.nlm.nih.gov/pmc/articles/PMC6052456/pdf/nihms976653.pdf.

33. Jeff Desjardins, "The Great Lakes Economy: The Growth Engine of North

America," *Visual Capitalist*, August 16, 2017, https://www.visualcapitalist.com/great -lakes-economy/.

34. Tim Folger, "The Cuyahoga River Caught Fire 50 Years Ago. It Inspired a Movement," *National Geographic*, June 21, 2019, https://www.nationalgeographic.com/environment /article/the-cuyahoga-river-caught-fire-it-inspired-a-movement.

35. Erin Blakemore, "The Shocking River Fire That Fueled the Creation of the EPA," *History Channel*, April 22, 2019, edited December 1, 2020, https://www.history.com /news/epa-earth-day-cleveland-cuyahoga-river-fire-clean-water-act.

36. "When Our Rivers Caught Fire," Michigan Environmental Council, July 11, 2011, https://www.environmentalcouncil.org/when_our_rivers_caught_fire; John H. Hartig, *Burning Rivers: Revival of Four Urban Industrial Rivers That Caught on Fire* (Burling- ton, Ontario: Aquatic Ecosystem Health and Management Society, 2010).

37. Rachel Carson, *Silent Spring* (Boston: Houghton Mifflin, 1962).

38. *Strategic Plan for the Great Lakes Commission 2017–2022*, Great Lakes Com- mission.

39. "An Assessment of the Impacts of Climate Change on the Great Lakes," *Environ- mental Law & Policy Center*, n.d., https://elpc.org/wp-content/uploads/2020/04/2019 -ELPCPublication-Great-Lakes-Climate-Change-Report.pdf.

40. Tom Perkins, "'Bigger Picture, It's Climate Change': Great Lakes Flood Ravages Homes and Roads," *The Guardian*, September 3, 2019.

CHAPTER 12: REPRESENTATIVE DEMOCRACY MAKES WAY
FOR DISTRIBUTED PEEROCRACY

1. James Madison, "Federalist No. 10: The Same Subject Continued: The Union as a Safeguard Against Domestic Faction and Insurrection," Library of Congress from the *New York Packet*, November 23, 1787.

2. John Adams to John Taylor, No. 18, December 17, 1814, National Archives, https:// founders.archives.gov/documents/Adams/99-02-02-6371.

3. *The Candidate*, Redford-Ritchie Productions and Wildwood Enterprises, 1972.

4. Claudia Chwalisz, *Innovative Citizen Participation and New Democratic In- stitutions: Catching the Deliberative Wave*, Organisation for Economic Co-operation and Development, June 10, 2020.

5. "Edelman Trust Barometer 2020," Daniel J. Edelman, https://www.edelman.com /sites/g/files/aatuss191/files/2020–01/2020%20Edelman%20Trust%20Barometer%20 Executive%20Summary_Single%20Spread%20without%20Crops.pdf.

6. "Beyond Distrust: How Americans View Their Government," Pew Research Center, November 23, 2015, https://www.pewresearch.org/politics/2015/11/23/1-trust -in-government-1958-2015/.

7. Ibid.

8. William Davies, "Why We Stopped Trusting Elites," *The Guardian*, November 29, 2018, https://www.theguardian.com/news/2018/nov/29/why-we-stopped-trusting -elites-the-new-populism.

9. Chwalisz, *Innovative Citizen Participation and New Democratic Institutions*.

10. "Case Study: Porto Alegre, Brazil," Local Government Association, December

12, 2016, https://www.local.gov.uk/case-studies/case-study-porto-alegre-brazil; Valeria Lvovna Gelman and Daniely Votto, "What if Citizens Set City Budgets? An Experiment That Captivated the World—Participatory Budgeting—Might Be Abandoned in Its Birthplace," *World Resources Institute*, June 13, 2018, https://www.wri.org/blog/2018/06/what-if-citizens-set-city-budgets-experiment-captivated-world-participatory-budgeting.

11. William W. Goldsmith, "Participatory Budgeting in Brazil," Planners Network, 1999, http://www.plannersnetwork.org/wp-content/uploads/2012/07/brazil_goldsmith.pdf.

12. Peter Yeung, "How Paris's Participatory Budget Is Reinvigorating Democracy," *City Monitor*, January 8, 2021, https://citymonitor.ai/government/civic-engagement/how-paris-participatory-budget-is-reinvigorating-democracy; "World," Participatory Budgeting World Atlas, https://www.pbatlas.net/world.html (accessed February 4, 2022).

13. "New Research on Participatory Budgeting Highlights Community Priorities in Public Spending," New York University, July 22, 2020, https://www.nyu.edu/about/news-publications/news/2020/july/new-research-on-participatory-budgeting-highlights-community-pri.html; Carolin Hagelskamp, Rebecca Silliman, Erin B. Godfrey, and David Schleifer, "Shifting Priorities: Participatory Budgeting in New York City Is Associated with Increased Investments in Schools, Street and Traffic Improvements, and Public Housing," *New Political Science* 42, no. 2 (2020): 171–196, https://doi.org/10.1080/07393148.2020.1773689.

14. New York University, "New Research on Participatory Budgeting Highlights Community Priorities in Public Spending."

15. Lester M. Salamon and Chelsea L. Newhouse, "2020 Nonprofit Employment Report," Johns Hopkins Center for Civil Society Studies, http://ccss.jhu.edu/wp-content/uploads/downloads/2020/06/2020-Nonprofit-Employment-Report_FINAL_6.2020.pdf.

16. Lester M. Salamon, Chelsea L. Newhouse, and S. Wojciech Sokolowski, "The 2019 Nonprofit Employment Report," Johns Hopkins Center for Civil Society Studies, 2019, https://philanthropydelaware.org/resources/Documents/The%202019%20Nonprofit%20Employment%20Report%20-%20Nonprofit%20Economic%20Data%20Bulletin%20-%20John%20Hopkins%20Center%20for%20Civil%20Society%20Studies%20_1.8.2019.pdf.

17. Brice S. McKeever and Sarah L. Pettijohn, "The Nonprofit Sector in Brief 2014," Urban Institute, October 2014, https://www.urban.org/sites/default/files/publication/33711/413277-The-Nonprofit-Sector-in-Brief—.PDF.

18. "The Nonprofit Sector in Brief 2019," Urban Institute, 2020, https://nccs.urban.org/publication/nonprofit-sector-brief-2019#the-nonprofit-sector-in-brief-2019; "Table 1.3.5., Gross Value Added by Sector at 'National Income and Product Accounts: National Data: Section 1-Domestic Product and Income,'" Bureau of Economic Analysis, n.d.

19. NCCS Team, "The Nonprofit Sector in Brief 2019."

20. Karin Chenoweth and Catherine Brown, "A Few Unique Facts About Chicago Public Schools," Center for American Progress, 2018, https://www.americanprogress.org/article/unique-things-chicago-public-schools/.

21. Dorothy Shipps, Joseph Kahne, and Mark Smylie, "The Politics of Urban School Reform: Legitimacy, City Growth, and School Improvement in Chicago," *Educational Policy* 13, no. 4 (1999): 518–545, https://doi.org/10.1177/0895904899013004003.

22. Chenoweth and Brown, "A Few Unique Facts About Chicago Public Schools"; Sean F. Reardon and Rebecca Hinze-Pifer, "Test Score Growth Among Chicago Public School Students, 2009–2014," Center for Education Policy Analysis, November 2, 2017, https://cepa.stanford.edu/content/test-score-growth-among-chicago-public-school-students-2009-2014.

23. Denisa R. Superville, "Chicago's Local School Councils 'Experiment' Endures 25 Years of Change," *Education Week*, October 7, 2021, https://www.edweek.org/leadership/chicagos-local-school-councils-experiment-endures-25-years-of-change/2014/10.

24. "City of Los Angeles Open Budget," City of Los Angeles, http://openbudget.lacity.org/#!/year/2021/operating/0/source_fund_name/General+Fund/0/department_name/Police/0/program_name.

25. Abby Narishkin et al., "The Real Cost of the Police, and Why the NYPD's Actual Price Tag Is $10 Billion a Year," *Business Insider*, August 12, 2020, https://www.businessinsider.com/the-real-cost-of-police-nypd-actually-10-billion-year-2020-8#:~:text=In%202020%2C%20the%20NYPD%20had,billion%20dollars%20off%20of%20that.

26. Juliana Feliciano Reyes, "Philly Plans to Increase Police Funding While Cutting City Services. Critics Say That's a Mistake," *Philadelphia Inquirer*, June 2, 2020.

27. Scott Neuman, "Police Viewed Less Favorably, But Few Want to 'Defund' Them, Survey Finds," National Public Radio, July 9, 2020, https://www.npr.org/sections/live-updates-protests-for-racial-justice/2020/07/09/889618702/police-viewed-less-favorably-but-few-want-to-defund-them-survey-finds; "Majority of Public Favors Giving Civilians the Power to Sue Police Officers for Misconduct," Pew Research Center, July 2020.

28. Archon Fung and Erik Olin Wright, *Deepening Democracy: Institutional Innovations in Empowered Participatory Governance* (London: Verso, 2003), 120.

29. "Recommendations for Reform: Restoring Trust between the Chicago Police and the Communities They Serve," Police Accountability Task Force, 2016.

30. "Can Chicago Restore Public Trust in Police?" Institute for Policy Research, April 26, 2016, https://www.ipr.northwestern.edu/news/2016/skogan-chicago-police-task-force-accountability.html.

31. City of Chicago, Office of the Mayor, "Mayor Lori E. Lightfoot and Empowering Communities for Public Safety Pass Proposal for Civilian Oversight of Chicago's Police Department and Accountability Agencies," July 21, 2021, https://www.chicago.gov/content/dam/city/depts/mayor/Press%20Room/Press%20Releases/2021/July/CivilianOversightChicagoPoliceDepartmentAccountabilityAgencies.pdf.

32. Janelle Griffith, "Is Chicago's New Layer of Police Oversight as 'Unique' as Sponsors Say?" NBC News, July 30, 2021, https://www.nbcnews.com/news/us-news/chicago-s-new-layer-police-oversight-unique-sponsors-say-n1275414.

33. Fung and Wright, *Deepening Democracy*, 137.

34. Claire Mellier and Rich Wilson, "Getting Climate Citizens' Assemblies Right," Carnegie Europe, November 5, 2020, https://carnegieeurope.eu/2020/11/05/getting-climate-citizens-assemblies-right-pub-83133 (accessed August 20, 2021).

CHAPTER 13: THE RISE OF BIOPHILIA CONSCIOUSNESS

1. Lauretta Bender, "An Observation Nursery: A Study of 250 Children on the Psychiatric Division of Bellevue Hospital," *American Journal of Psychiatry* (1941).

2. John Broadus Watson, *Psychological Care of Infant and Child* (New York: W. W. Norton, 1928).

3. Robert Karen, *Becoming Attached; First Relationships and How They Shape Our Capacity to Love* (New York: Oxford University Press, 1988), 19.

4. Harry Bakwin, "Loneliness in Infants," *American Journal of Diseases of Children* 63 (1942): 31.

5. Karen, *Becoming Attached,* 20.

6. John Bowlby, foreword in M. D. S. Ainsworth, Infancy in Uganda: *Infant Care and the Growth of Love* (Baltimore: Johns Hopkins University Press, 1967), v.

7. John Bowlby, *The Making and Breaking of Affectional Bonds* (London: Routledge, 2015), 133.

8. Ibid., 136.

9. M Mikulincer, O. Gillath, V. Halevy, N. Avihou, S. Avidan, and N. Eshkoli, "Attachment Theory and Reactions to Others' Needs: Evidence That Activation of the Senses of Attachment Security Promotes Empathetic Responses," *Journal of Personality and Social Psychology* 81, no. 6 (2001).

10. Sophie Moullin, Jane Waldfogel, and Elizabeth Washbrok, "Baby Bonds: Parenting, Attachment and a Secure Base for Children," Sutton Trust, March 2014.

11. Huber, B. Rose. "Four in 10 Infants Lack Strong Parental Attachments." Princeton University, March 27, 2014. https://www.princeton.edu/news/2014/03/27/four-10-infants-lack-strong-parental-attachments#:~:text=March%2027%2C%202014%2C%201%3A,according%20to%20a%20new%20report.

12. Ibid.

13. Nelli Ferenczi and Tara Marshall, "Exploring Attachment to the 'Homeland' and Its Association with Heritage Culture Identification," *PLOS One* (January 2013).

14. Ibid.

15. Pernille Darling Rasmussen, Ole Jakob Storebø, Trine Løkkeholt, Line Gaunø Voss, Yael Shmueli-Goetz, Anders Bo Bojesen, Erik Simonsen, and Niels Bilenberg, "Attachment as a Core Feature of Resilience: A Systematic Review and Meta-Analysis," *Psychological Reports* 122, no. 4 (August 2019).

16. Giuseppe Carrus, Massimiliano Scopelliti, Ferdinando Fornara, Mirilia Bonnes, and Marino Bonaiuto, "Place Attachment, Community Identification, and Pro-Environment Engagement," in *Advances in Theory, Methods and Application*, edited by Lynne C. Manzo and Patrick Devine-Wright (London: Routledge, 2014).

17. Victor Lebow, "Price Competition," *Journal of Retailing* (Spring 1955).

18. Bum Jin Park, Yuko Tsunetsugu, Tamami Kasetani, Takahide Kagawa, and Yoshifumi Miyazaki, "The Physiological Effects of *Shinrin-yoku* (Taking in the Forest of Forest Bathing): Evidence from Field Experiments in 24 Forests Across Japan," *Environmental Health and Preventative Medicine* 15, no. 1 (2010): 21.

19. Yoshinori Ohtsuka, Noriyuki Yabunaka, and Shigeru Takayama, "Shinrin-yoku

(Forest-Air Bathing and Walking) Effectively Decreases Blood Glucose Levels in Diabetic Patients," *International Journal of Biometeorolgy* 41, no. 3 (February 1998).

20. Roly Russell, Anne D. Guerry, Patricia Balvanera, Rachelle K. Gould, Xavier Basurto, Kai M. A. Chan, Sarah Klain, Jordan Levine, and Jordan Tam, "Humans and Nature: How Knowing and Experiencing Nature Affect Well-Being," *Annual Review of Environmental Resources* 38 (2013): 43.

21. Ibid.

22. Edward O. Wilson, *Biophilia* (Cambridge, MA: Harvard University Press, 1984).

23. Giuseppe Barbiero and Chiara Marconato, "Biophilia as Emotion," *Visions for Sustainability* 6 (2016).

24. Karen D'Souza, "Outdoor Classes and 'Forest Schools" Gain New Prominence amid Distance Learning Struggles," *EdSource*, October 1, 2020, https://edsource.org /2020/outdoor-classes-and-forest-schools-gain-new-prominence-amid-distance-learning -struggles/640853; Tina Deines, "Outdoor Preschools Grow in Popularity but Most Serve Middle Class White Kids," Hechinger Report, February 26, 2021, https://hechingerreport .org/outdoor-preschools-grow-in-popularity-but-most-serve-middle-class-white-kids/.

25. Ibid.

26. Ibid.

27. Ibid.

28. Ibid.

29. Tony Loughland, Anna Reid, Kim Walker, and Peter Petocz, "Factors Influencing Young People's Conception of Environment," *Environmental Education Research* 9 (February 2003).

30. Daniel Acuff, *What Kids Buy and Why: The Psychology of Marketing to Kids* (New York: Simon & Schuster, 2010).

31. David Sobel, *Beyond Ecophobia: Reclaiming the Heart in Nature Education* (Great Barrington, MA: Orion Society, 1999); Mary Renck Jalongo, *The World's Children and Their Companion Animals: Developmental and Educational Significance of the Child/Pet Bond* (Association for Childhood Education International, 2014).

32. Robin C. Moore and Clare Cooper Marcus, "Healthy Planet, Healthy Children: Designing Nature into Childhood," in *Biophilic Design: The Theory, Science, and Practice of Bringing Buildings to Life,* edited by Stephen R. Kellert, Judith Heerwagen, and Martin L. Mador (Hoboken, NJ: John Wiley, 2008), 163.

33. Veronique Pittman, "Large School Districts Come Together to Prioritize Sustainability," *Huffington Post*, February 22, 2016, https://www.huffpost.com/entry/large -school-districts-co_b_9279314.

34. "Stanford Analysis Reveals Wide Array of Benefits from Environmental Education," North American Association for Environmental Education, n.d., https://cdn.naaee .org/sites/default/files/eeworks/files/k-12_student_key_findings.pdf.

35. Nicole Ardoin, Alison Bowers, Noelle Wyman Roth, and Nicole Holthuis, "Environmental Education and K–12 Student Outcomes: A Review and Analysis of Research," *Journal of Environmental Education* 49, no. 1 (2018).

36. Cathy Conrad and Krista Hilchey, "A Review of Citizen Science and Community-Based Environmental Monitoring Issues and Opportunities," *Environmental Monitoring and Assessment* 176 (2011).

37. "2021 Outdoor Participation Trends Report," Outdoor Foundation, 2021, https://ip0o6y1ji424m0641msgjlfy-wpengine.netdna-ssl.com/wp-content/uploads/2015/03/2021-Outdoor-Participation-Trends-Report.pdf.

38. Jeff Opperman, "Taylor Swift Is Singing Us Back to Nature," *New York Times*, March 12, 2021.

39. Opperman, "Taylor Swift Is Singing Us Back to Nature"; Selin Kesebir and Pelin Kesebir, "A Growing Disconnection from Nature Is Evident in Cultural Products," *Perspectives on Psychological Science* 12, no. 2 (March 27, 2017): 258–269, https://doi.org/10.1177/1745691616662473.

40. Edward O. Wilson, "The Biological Basis of Morality," *The Atlantic*, April 1998, https://www.theatlantic.com/magazine/archive/1998/04/the-biological-basis-of-morality/377087/.

41. Giuseppe Barbiero, "Biophilia and Gaia: Two Hypotheses for an Affective Ecology," *Journal of Biourbanism* 1 (2011).

42. Jeremy Rifkin, *The Empathic Civilization* (New York: TarcherPerigee, 2009), 2.

43. Martin Buber, *I and Thou,* (1923).

44. Johann Wolfgang von Goethe, *Werke, Briefe und Gespräche. Gedenkausgabe.* 24 vols. *Naturwissneschaftliche Schriften*, Vols. 16–17, edited by Ernst Beutler (Zurich: Artemis, 1948–53), 921–923.

45. Ibid.

46. Goethe, *Werke, Briefe und Gespräche. Dichtung und Wahrheit,* vol. 10, 168.

47. Ibid., 425.

48. Adam C. Davis et al., "Systems Thinkers Express an Elevated Capacity for the Allocentric Components of Cognitive and Affective Empathy," *Systems Research and Behavioral Science* 35, no. 2 (July 19, 2017): 216–229.

49. U.S. Environmental Protection Agency, Report to Congress on indoor air quality: Volume 2, EPA/400/1–89/001C, Washington, D.C., 1989; Kim R. Hill et al., "Co-Residence Patterns in Hunter-Gatherer Societies Show Unique Human Social Structure," *Science* 331, no. 6022 (March 11, 2011): 1286–1289.

INDEX